2003 SUPPLEMENT

CASES AND MATERIALS

CONSTITUTIONAL LAW

ELEVENTH EDITION

by

WILLIAM COHEN
C. Wendell and Edith M. Carlsmith
Professor Emeritus, Stanford Law School

JONATHAN D. VARAT
Dean and Professor of Law
University of California, Los Angeles

FOUNDATION PRESS
NEW YORK, NEW YORK
2003

COPYRIGHT © 2001, 2002 FOUNDATION PRESS
COPYRIGHT © 2003 By FOUNDATION PRESS
      395 Hudson Street
      New York, NY 10014
      Phone Toll Free 1–877–888–1330
      Fax (212) 367–6799
      fdpress.com
Printed in the United States of America

ISBN 1–58778–533–1

TEXT IS PRINTED ON 10% POST
CONSUMER RECYCLED PAPER

TABLE OF CONTENTS
(**Bold** Indicates Principal Cases)

CHAPTER 14 RESTRICTIONS ON TIME, PLACE, OR MANNER OF EXPRESSION

CHAPTER 15 PROTECTION OF PENUMBRAL FIRST AMENDMENT RIGHTS

TABLE OF CASES

Principal cases are in bold type. Non-principal cases are in roman type. References are to Pages.

2003 SUPPLEMENT

CONSTITUTIONAL LAW

(1)   (MT)   : All T's are M's and all M's are T's

(2)   (T)(M)   : No T's are M's

(3)   (M T)   : All T's are M's but some M's are not T's

(4)   (T M)   : All M's are T's but some T's are not M's

(5)   (T ( ) M)   : Some T's are M's; some T's are not M's; and some M's are not T's

One of these five relationships holds in fact in any case of legislative classification, and we will consider each from the point of view of its "reasonableness."

"The first two situations represent respectively the ideal limits of reasonableness and unreasonableness. . . .

"Classification of the third type may be called "under-inclusive.' All who are included in the class are tainted with the mischief, but there are others also tainted whom the classification does not include. Since the classification does not include all who are similarly situated with respect to the purpose of the law, there is a prima facie violation of the equal protection requirement of reasonable classification.

"But the Court has recognized the very real difficulties under which legislatures operate...difficulties arising out of both the nature of the legislative process and of the society which legislation attempts perennially to reshape...and it has refused to strike down indiscriminately all legislation embodying the classificatory inequality here under consideration.

"In justifying this refusal, the Court has defended under-inclusive classifications on such grounds as: the legislature may attack a general problem in a piecemeal fashion; "some play must be allowed for the joints of the machine'; "a statute aimed at what is deemed an evil, and hitting it presumably where experience shows it to be most felt, is not to be upset. . . .'; "the law does all that is needed when it does all that it can. . . .;' and—perhaps with some impatience—the equal protection clause is not "a pedagogic requirement of the impracticable.'

"These generalities, while expressive of judicial tolerance, are not, however, very helpful. They do not constitute a clear statement of the circumstances and conditions which justify such tolerance—which justify a departure from the strict requirements of the principle of equality. . . . .

"The fourth type of classification imposes a burden upon a wider range of individuals than are included in the class of those tainted with the mischieft which the law aims. It can thus be called "over-inclusive.' Herod, ordering the death of all male children born on a particular day because one of them woud some day bring about his downfall, employed such a classification. It is exemplified by the quarantine and the dragnet. The wartime treatment of American citizens of Japanese ancestry is a striking recent instance of the imposition of burdens upon a large class of individuals because some of them were believed to be disloyal.

PART II

Allocation of Governmental Powers: The Nation and the States; The President, The Congress, and the Courts

CHAPTER 4

The Scope of National Power

SECTION 2. Sources of National Power: Early Developments

A. The Marshall Court's View

Page 145. Add at end of Note, "McCulloch and State Power to Control the Selection of Members of Congress":

Following similar reasoning, the Court later invalidated another state attempt to influence congressional elections in favor of candidates who supported congressional term limits. Cook v. Gralike, 531 U.S. 510 (2001). A state constitutional amendment adopted by Missouri voters attempted to "instruct" the members of Missouri's congressional delegation, and nonincumbent congressional candidates who might win election, to support a particular form of Congressional Term Limits Amendment to the United States Constitution. Incumbents who did not comply were to have "DISREGARDED VOTERS' INSTRUCTION ON TERM LIMITS" placed next to their name on all primary and general ballots; nonincumbents who refused to pledge support were to have "DECLINED TO PLEDGE TO SUPPORT TERM LIMITS" placed next to their names on all such ballots.

Justice Stevens' majority opinion first found insufficient evidence "that either the people or the States had a right to give legally binding, *i.e.*, nonadvisory, instructions to their representatives that the Tenth Amendment reserved, much less that such a right would apply to federal representatives." Moreover, "even assuming the existence of the reserved right ..., the question remains whether the State may use ballots for congressional elections as a means of giving its instructions binding force." As to that question, he wrote:

> "The federal offices at stake 'aris[e] from the Constitution itself.' U.S. Term Limits, Inc. v. Thornton.... Because any state authority to regulate election to those offices could not precede their very creation by the Constitution, such power 'had to be delegated to, rather than reserved by, the States.' Id., ... Through the Elections Clause, the Constitution delegated to the States the power to regulate the 'Times, Places and Manner of holding Elections for Senators and Representatives,' subject to a grant of authority to Congress to 'make or alter such Regulations.' Art. I, § 4, cl. 1.... No other constitutional provision gives the States authority over congressional elections, and no such authority could be reserved under the Tenth Amendment. By process of elimination, the States may regulate the incidents of such elections, including balloting, only within the exclusive delegation of power under the Elections Clause."

Because the adverse ballot designations were intended to "handicap candidates for the United States Congress" just at the crucial time when votes were cast, they constituted attempts to "dictate electoral outcomes" rather than regulations of "the procedural mechanisms of elections," however, and thus the state law did not fall within the power delegated to the State by the Elections Clause.

In a concurring opinion, Justice Kennedy wrote:

> "A State is not permitted to interpose itself between the people and their National Government as it seeks to do here. Whether a State's concern is with the proposed enactment of a constitutional amendment or an ordinary federal statute it simply lacks the power to impose any conditions on the election of Senators and Representatives, save neutral provisions as to the time, place, and manner of elections pursuant to Article I, § 4....

> "The dispositive principle in this case is fundamental to the Constitution, to the idea of federalism, and to the theory of representative government. The principle is that Senators and Representatives in the National Government are responsible to the people who elect them, not to the States in which they reside. The Constitution was ratified by Conventions in the

several States, not by the States themselves, U.S. Const., Art. VII, a historical fact and a constitutional imperative which underscore the proposition that the Constitution was ordained and established by the people of the United States. U.S. Const., preamble. The idea of federalism is that a National Legislature enacts laws which bind the people as individuals, not as citizens of a State; and, it follows, freedom is most secure if the people themselves, not the States as intermediaries, hold their federal legislators to account for the conduct of their office. If state enactments were allowed to condition or control certain actions of federal legislators, accountability would be blurred, with the legislators having the excuse of saying that they did not act in the exercise of their best judgment but simply in conformance with a state mandate. . . . Neither the design of the Constitution nor sound principles of representative government are consistent with the right or power of a State to interfere with the direct line of accountability between the National Legislature and the people who elect it. . . ."

Justice Thomas continued to "disagree with the Court's premise, derived from *U.S. Term Limits*, that the States have no authority to regulate congressional elections except for the authority that the Constitution expressly delegates to them[,]" but he concurred because the parties had conceded its validity. Chief Justice Rehnquist, joined by Justice O'Connor, concurred in the judgment on the ground that the State had violated the First Amendment by "discriminat[ing] on the basis of viewpoint because only those candidates who fail to conform to the State's position receive derogatory labels."

SECTION 3. THE SCOPE OF NATIONAL POWER TODAY

A. THE COMMERCE POWER

Page 190. Add before Reno v. Condon:

PIERCE COUNTY v. GUILLEN, 537 U.S. 129 (2003). To receive funding to improve dangerous public road conditions under the federal Hazard Elimination Program, states and localities must identify hazardous locations, 23 U.S.C. § 152. To overcome state fears that doing so without the protection of confidentiality would subject them to increased liability risks at hazardous locations before improvements could be made, Congress provided state and local agencies with a federal privilege to decline to disclose information compiled or collected for purposes of the Program only, 23 U.S.C. § 409. In a suit to extract such information brought under a state public disclosure law, the Court unanimously rejected a challenge to the commerce power of Congress to provide the federal privilege, saying: ". . . Congress could reasonably believe that adopting a measure eliminating an unforeseen side effect of the information-gathering requirement of § 152 would result in more diligent efforts to collect the relevant information, more candid discussions of hazardous locations, better informed decisionmaking, and, ultimately, greater safety on our Nation's roads. Consequently, [§ 409 and its 1995 amendment] can be viewed as legislation aimed at improving safety in the channels of commerce and increasing protection for the instrumentalities of interstate commerce. As such, they fall within Congress' Commerce Clause power."

Page 191.   Add at end of subsection:

SOLID WASTE AGENCY v. UNITED STATES ARMY CORPS OF ENGINEERS, 531 U.S. 159 (2001). Pursuant to § 404(a) of the Clean Water Act of 1972 (CWA), which regulates the discharge of dredged or fill material into "navigable waters"—defined under the Act as "the waters of the United States"—the Corps of Engineers asserted jurisdiction over non-navigable intrastate waters, "the use, degradation or destruction of which could affect interstate or foreign commerce," and specifically over intrastate waters used as habitat by migratory birds that crossed state lines. When the Corps denied a permit to a consortium of municipalities (the Solid Waste Agency) to dispose of baled nonhazardous solid waste in long abandoned gravel mining pits that had become permanent and seasonal ponds used as habitat by a variety of species of migratory birds, the Agency challenged the Corps' jurisdiction. The Court held, 5–4, that the Corps had exceeded its authority under § 404(a), obviating the need to reach the Agency's further claim that Congress lacked power under the Commerce Clause to authorize such jurisdiction. Nonetheless, in the course of rejecting the Corps' argument that at best "Congress did not address the precise question of § 404(a)'s scope with regard to nonnavigable, isolated, intrastate waters" and thus the Court should defer to its "Migratory Bird Rule," the majority opinion by Chief Justice Rehnquist said:

"Where an administrative interpretation of a statute invokes the outer limits of Congress' power, we expect a clear indication that Congress intended that result.... This concern is heightened where the administrative interpretation alters the federal-state framework by permitting federal encroachment upon a traditional state power....

"Twice in the past six years we have reaffirmed the proposition that the grant of authority to Congress under the Commerce Clause, though broad, is not unlimited. See United States v. Morrison, 529 U.S. 598 (2000); United States v. Lopez, 514 U.S. 549 (1995). Respondents argue that the 'Migratory Bird Rule' falls within Congress' power to regulate intrastate activities that 'substantially affect' interstate commerce. They note that the protection of migratory birds is a 'national interest of very nearly the first magnitude,' Missouri v. Holland, 252 U.S. 416, 435 (1920), and that, as the Court of Appeals found, millions of people spend over a billion dollars annually on recreational pursuits relating to migratory birds. These arguments raise significant constitutional questions. For example, we would have to evaluate the precise object or activity that, in the aggregate, substantially affects interstate commerce. This is not clear, for although the Corps has claimed jurisdiction over petitioner's land because it contains water areas used as habitat by migratory birds, respondents now, *post litem motam*, focus upon the fact that the regulated activity is petitioner's municipal landfill, which is 'plainly of a commercial nature.' ... But this is a far cry, indeed, from the 'navigable waters' and 'waters of the United States' to which the statute by its terms extends.

"These are significant constitutional questions ... and yet we find nothing approaching a clear statement from Congress that it intended § 404(a) to reach [such] an abandoned sand and gravel pit.... Permitting respondents to claim federal jurisdiction over ponds and mudflats falling within the 'Migratory Bird Rule' would result in a significant impingement of the States' traditional and primary power over land and water use.... We thus read the statute as written to avoid the significant constitutional and federalism questions raised by respondents' interpretation, and therefore reject the request for administrative deference...."

Justice Stevens, joined by Justices Souter, Ginsburg and Breyer, dissented. Based, among other reasons, on the expansive statutory definition of "navigable waters," and in light of Congress's mid–20th century shift in federal water regulation "away from an exclusive focus on protecting navigability and toward a concern for preventing environmental degradation," Justice Stevens concluded "that the term 'navigable waters' operates in the statute as a shorthand for 'waters over which federal authority may properly be asserted.' " He also urged that administrative deference to the Corps was warranted, responding to the majority in part:

"Contrary to the Court's suggestion, the Corps' interpretation of the statute does not 'encroac[h]' upon 'traditional state power' over land use. 'Land use planning in essence chooses particular uses for the land; environmental regulation, at its core, does not mandate particular uses of the land but requires only that, however the land is used, damage to the environment is kept within prescribed limits.' ... The CWA is not a land-use code; it is a paradigm of environmental regulation. Such regulation is an accepted exercise of federal power. Hodel v. Virginia Surface Mining & Reclamation Assn., Inc., 452 U.S. 264, 282 (1981)."

More directly, the dissent found "no merit in petitioner's constitutional argument":

"... The Corps' exercise of its § 404 permitting power over 'isolated' waters that serve as habitat for migratory birds falls well within the boundaries set by this Court's Commerce Clause jurisprudence.

"... In order to constitute a proper exercise of Congress' power over intrastate activities that 'substantially affect' interstate commerce, it is not necessary that each individual instance of the activity substantially affect commerce; it is enough that, taken in the aggregate, the *class of activities* in question has such an effect. Perez v. United States, 402 U.S. 146 (1971)....

"The activity being regulated in this case (and by the Corps' § 404 regulations in general) is the discharge of fill material into water. The Corps did not assert jurisdiction over petitioner's land simply because the waters were 'used as habitat by migratory birds.' It asserted jurisdiction because petitioner planned to *discharge fill* into waters 'used as habitat by migratory birds.' Had petitioner intended to engage in some other activity besides discharging fill (*i.e.*, had there been no activity to regulate), or, conversely, had the waters not been habitat for migratory birds (i.e., had there been no basis for federal jurisdiction), the Corps would never have become involved in petitioner's use of its land. There can be no doubt that, unlike the class of activities Congress was attempting to regulate in United States v. Morrison, ... (2000) ('[g]ender-motivated crimes'), and Lopez, ... (possession of guns near school property), the discharge of fill material into the Nation's waters is almost always undertaken for economic reasons...."

"Moreover, no one disputes that the discharge of fill into 'isolated' waters that serve as migratory bird habitat will, in the aggregate, adversely affect migratory bird populations.... Nor does petitioner dispute that the particular waters it seeks to fill are home to many important species of migratory birds, including the second-largest breeding colony of Great Blue Herons in northeastern Illinois ... and several species of waterfowl protected by international treaty and Illinois endangered species laws....

"In addition to the intrinsic value of migratory birds, ... it is undisputed that literally millions of people regularly participate in birdwatching and hunting and that those activities generate a host of commercial activities of great value. The causal connection between the filling of wetlands and the decline of commercial activities associated with migratory birds is not 'attenuated,' Morrison ...; it is direct and concrete.

"Finally, the migratory bird rule does not blur the 'distinction between what is truly national and what is truly local.' Morrison.... Justice Holmes cogently observed in *Missouri v. Holland* that the protection of migratory birds is a textbook example of a *national* problem.... The destruction of aquatic migratory bird habitat, like so many other environmental problems, is an action in which the benefits (e.g., a new landfill) are disproportionately local, while many of the costs (e.g., fewer migratory birds) are widely dispersed and often borne by citizens living in other States. In such situations, described by economists as involving 'externalities,' federal regulation is both appropriate and necessary.... Identifying the Corps' jurisdiction by reference to waters that serve as habitat for birds that migrate over state lines also satisfies this Court's expressed desire for some 'jurisdictional element' that limits federal activity to its proper scope. Morrison....

"The power to regulate commerce among the several States necessarily and properly includes the power to preserve the natural resources that generate such commerce.... Migratory birds, and the waters on which they rely, are such resources. Moreover, the protection of migratory birds is a well-established federal responsibility. As Justice Holmes noted in *Missouri v. Holland*, the federal interest in protecting these birds is of 'the first magnitude.' ... Because of their transitory nature, they 'can be protected only by national action.' ...

"... If, as it does, the Commerce Clause empowers Congress to regulate particular 'activities causing air or water pollution, or other environmental hazards that may have effects in more than one State,' Hodel ..., it also empowers Congress to control individual actions that, in the aggregate, would have the same effect. Perez ...; Wickard...."

F.   OTHER FEDERAL POWERS

Page 216.   Add at end of Chapter a new subsection:

5.   THE COPYRIGHT AND PATENT POWERS

ELDRED v. ASHCROFT, 537 U.S. 186 (2003). Under the 1998 Copyright Term Extension Act (CTEA), Congress increased by 20 years the general duration of copyright protection—for both existing and future copyrights—over that contained in the 1976 Copyright Act, from a term measured from the work's creation until 50 years after the author's death to a term measured from the work's creation until 70 years after the author's death. The Court upheld the CTEA over the objection that Congress, by extending the duration of *existing* copyrights, had exceeded its power under Art. I, § 8, cl. 8, to bestow copyright protection only "for limited Times."[a] Justice Ginsburg's majority opinion said, in part:

"Petitioners' argument essentially reads into the text of the Copyright Clause the command that a time prescription, once set, becomes forever 'fixed' or 'inalterable.' The word 'limited,' however, does not convey a meaning so constricted. At the time of the Framing, that word meant what it means today: 'confine[d] within certain bounds,' 'restrain[ed],' or 'circumscribe[d].'

"... History reveals an unbroken congressional practice of granting to authors of works with existing copyrights the benefit of term extensions so that all under copyright protection will be governed evenhandedly under the same regime. [T]he First Congress accorded the protections of the Nation's first federal copyright statute to existing and future works alike. 1790 Act § 1. Since then, Congress has regularly applied duration extensions to both existing and future copyrights. 1831 Act . . .; 1909 Act . . .; 1976 Act . . .[6]

"Because the Clause empowering Congress to confer copyrights also authorizes patents, congressional practice with respect to patents informs our inquiry. We count it significant that early Congresses extended the duration of numerous individual patents as well as copyrights. . . . The courts saw no 'limited Times' impediment to such extensions; renewed or extended terms were upheld in the early days, for example, by Chief Justice Marshall and Justice Story sitting as circuit justices. . . .

"Further, although prior to the instant case this Court did not have occasion to decide whether extending the duration of existing copyrights complies with the 'limited Times' prescription, the Court has found no constitutional barrier to the legislative expansion of existing patents. *McClurg v. Kingsland*, 1 How. 202 (1843). . . .

"... Guided by text, history, and precedent, we cannot agree with petitioners' submission that extending the duration of existing copyrights is categorically beyond Congress' authority under the Copyright Clause.

"Satisfied that the CTEA complies with the 'limited Times' prescription, we turn now to whether it is a rational exercise of the legislative authority conferred by the Copyright Clause. On that point, we defer substantially to Congress. . . .

"The CTEA reflects judgments of a kind Congress typically makes, judgments we cannot dismiss as outside the Legislature's domain. . . . [A] key factor in the CTEA's passage was a 1993 European Union (EU) directive instructing EU members to establish a copyright term of life plus 70 years. . . . Consistent with the Berne Convention, the EU directed its members to deny this longer

---

a. The Court also rejected a First Amendment challenge to the CTEA, which is discussed infra, p. 280.

6. Moreover, the precise duration of a federal copyright has never been fixed at the time of the initial grant. . . .

term to the works of any non-EU country whose laws did not secure the same extended term.... By extending the baseline United States copyright term to life plus 70 years, Congress sought to ensure that American authors would receive the same copyright protection in Europe as their European counterparts. The CTEA may also provide greater incentive for American and other authors to create and disseminate their work in the United States....

"In addition to international concerns, Congress passed the CTEA in light of demographic, economic, and technological changes ... and rationally credited projections that longer terms would encourage copyright holders to invest in the restoration and public distribution of their works....

"In sum, we find that the CTEA is a rational enactment; we are not at liberty to second-guess congressional determinations and policy judgments of this order, however debatable or arguably unwise they may be. Accordingly, we cannot conclude that the CTEA—which continues the unbroken congressional practice of treating future and existing copyrights in parity for term extension purposes—is an impermissible exercise of Congress' power under the Copyright Clause."

The Court also rejected "several novel readings of the Clause." The period of creation to author's death plus 70 years "did not create perpetual copyrights[,]" as the challengers urged. To the argument that the "CTEA's extension of existing copyrights categorically fails to 'promote the Progress of Science,' ... because it does not stimulate the creation of new works but merely adds value to works already created[,]" the Court "stressed ... that it is generally for Congress, not the courts, to decide how best to pursue the Copyright Clause's objectives" and the "justifications we earlier set out for Congress' enactment of the CTEA ... provide a rational basis for the conclusion that the CTEA 'promote[s] the Progress of Science.' " As for the claim that "Congress' power to confer copyright protection ... is ... contingent upon an exchange [whereby t]he author of an original work receives an 'exclusive Right' for a 'limited Tim[e]' in exchange for a dedication to the public thereafter [and that e]xtending an existing copyright without demanding additional consideration ... bestows an unpaid-for benefit on copyright holders and their heirs, in violation of the *quid pro quo* requirement[,]" the Court responded that, given the history it had described, "the author of a work created in the last 170 years would reasonably comprehend [that] the 'this' offered her [was] a copyright not only for the time in place when protection is gained, but also for any renewal or extension legislated during that time. Congress could rationally seek to 'promote ... Progress' by including in every copyright statute an express guarantee that authors would receive the benefit of any later legislative extension of the copyright term." Finally, the Court responded as follows to the request "to apply the 'congruence and proportionality' standard described in cases evaluating exercises of Congress' power under § 5 of the Fourteenth Amendment. See, *e.g., City of Boerne v. Flores,* 521 U.S. 507 (1997)":

> "But we have never applied that standard outside the § 5 context; it does not hold sway for judicial review of legislation enacted, as copyright laws are, pursuant to Article I authorization.
>
> "Section 5 authorizes Congress to *enforce* commands contained in and incorporated into the Fourteenth Amendment.... The Copyright Clause, in contrast, empowers Congress to *define* the scope of the substantive

right. . . . Judicial deference to such congressional definition is 'but a corollary to the grant to Congress of any Article I power.' . . . It would be no more appropriate for us to subject the CTEA to 'congruence and proportionality' review under the Copyright Clause than it would be for us to hold the Act unconstitutional *per se*."

A lengthy dissent by Justice Stevens contained the following passages:

"[The] twin purposes of encouraging new works and adding to the public domain apply to copyrights as well as patents. . . . *Ex post facto* extensions of copyrights result in a gratuitous transfer of wealth from the public to authors, publishers, and their successors in interest. Such retroactive extensions do not even arguably serve either of the purposes of the Copyright/Patent Clause.

. . .

"The express grant of a perpetual copyright would unquestionably violate the textual requirement that the authors' exclusive rights be only 'for limited Times.' Whether the extraordinary length of the grants authorized by the 1998 Act are invalid because they are the functional equivalent of perpetual copyrights is a question that need not be answered in this case because the question presented by the certiorari petition merely challenges Congress' power to extend retroactively the terms of existing copyrights. . . . It is important to note, however, that a categorical rule prohibiting retroactive extensions would effectively preclude perpetual copyrights. More importantly, . . . unless the Clause is construed to embody such a categorical rule, Congress may extend existing monopoly privileges *ad infinitum* under the majority's analysis.

"By failing to protect the public interest in free access to the products of inventive and artistic genius—indeed, by virtually ignoring the central purpose of the Copyright/Patent Clause—the Court has quitclaimed to Congress its principal responsibility in this area of the law. Fairly read, the Court has stated that Congress' actions under the Copyright/Patent Clause are, for all intents and purposes, judicially unreviewable. That result cannot be squared with the basic tenets of our constitutional structure. . . ."

A separate lengthy dissent by Justice Breyer found "that the statute lacks the constitutionally necessary rational support [in that] (1) . . . the significant benefits that it bestows are private, not public; (2) . . . it threatens seriously to undermine the expressive values that the Copyright Clause embodies; and (3) . . . it cannot find justification in any significant Clause-related objective." He concluded "that the statute cannot be understood rationally to advance a constitutionally legitimate interest[; it] falls outside the scope of legislative power that the Copyright Clause, read in light of the First Amendment, grants to Congress."

CHAPTER 5

STATE SOVEREIGNTY AND FEDERAL REGULATION

SECTION 2. ENFORCEMENT OF FEDERAL RIGHTS IN SUITS AGAINST STATE OFFICERS: THE ELEVENTH AMENDMENT

Page 264. Add before last two sentences in note, "Congressional Power to Authorize Suits Against States in Federal Court":

Board of Trustees of the University of Alabama v. Garrett, 531 U.S. 356 (2001), held that Congress could not authorize damage suits against State agencies for failure to comply with the provisions of Title I of the Americans with Disabilities Act of 1990.

Page 264. Add at end of note, "Congressional Power to Authorize Suits Against States in Federal Court":

Nevada Department of Human Resources v. Hibbs, ___ U.S. ___, 123 S.Ct. 1972 (2003), however, upheld a damages action against the State in the 1993 Federal Family and Medical Leave Act. The decision in *Garrett* appears infra on page 130. The decision in *Hibbs* appears infra on p. 139.

Page 264. Add at end of chapter:

Federal Maritime Commission v. South Carolina State Ports Authority

535 U.S. 743, 122 S.Ct. 1864, 152 L.Ed.2d 962 (2002).

Justice Thomas delivered the opinion of the Court.

This case presents the question whether state sovereign immunity precludes petitioner Federal Maritime Commission (FMC or Commission) from adjudicating a private party's complaint that a state-run port has violated the Shipping Act of 1984.... We hold that state sovereign immunity bars such an adjudicative proceeding.

I

... South Carolina Maritime Services, Inc. (Maritime Services), asked respondent South Carolina State Ports Authority (SCSPA) for permission to berth a cruise ship, the M/V *Tropic Sea,* at the SCSPA's port facilities in Charleston, South Carolina. ...

10

The SCSPA repeatedly denied Maritime Services' requests, contending that it had an established policy of denying berths in the Port of Charleston to vessels whose primary purpose was gambling. As a result, Maritime Services filed a complaint with the FMC, contending that the SCSPA's refusal to provide berthing space to the M/V *Tropic Sea* violated the Shipping Act.

To remedy its injuries, Maritime Services prayed that the FMC: (1) seek a temporary restraining order and preliminary injunction in the United States District Court for the District of South Carolina "enjoining [the SCSPA] from utilizing its discriminatory practice to refuse to provide berthing space and passenger services to Maritime Services;" (2) direct the SCSPA to pay reparations to Maritime Services as well as interest and reasonable attorneys' fees; (3) issue an order commanding, among other things, the SCSPA to cease and desist from violating the Shipping Act; and (4) award Maritime Services "such other and further relief as is just and proper."

... Maritime Services' complaint was referred to an administrative law judge (ALJ) [who dismissed the complaint].

. . .

While Maritime Services did not appeal the ALJ's dismissal of its complaint, the FMC on its own motion decided to review the ALJ's ruling to consider whether state sovereign immunity from private suits extends to proceedings before the Commission. ... [T]he FMC held that sovereign immunity did not bar the Commission from adjudicating private complaints against state-run ports and reversed the ALJ's decision dismissing Maritime Services' complaint.

The SCSPA filed a petition for review, and the United States Court of Appeals for the Fourth Circuit reversed ... and remanded the case with instructions that it be dismissed.

We ... affirm.

II

Dual sovereignty is a defining feature of our Nation's constitutional blueprint.... States, upon ratification of the Constitution, did not consent to become mere appendages of the Federal Government. Rather, they entered the Union "with their sovereignty intact." ...

States, in ratifying the Constitution, did surrender a portion of their inherent immunity by consenting to suits brought by sister States or by the Federal Government. ... Nevertheless, the Convention did not disturb States' immunity from private suits, thus firmly enshrining this principle in our constitutional framework.

. . .

... [T]he Eleventh Amendment does not define the scope of the States' sovereign immunity; it is but one particular exemplification of that immunity.

III

We now consider whether the sovereign immunity enjoyed by States as part of our constitutional framework applies to adjudications conducted by the

FMC. Petitioner FMC and respondent United States initially maintain that the Court of Appeals erred because sovereign immunity only shields States from exercises of "judicial power" and FMC adjudications are not judicial proceedings. . . .

For purposes of this case, we will assume, *arguendo,* that in adjudicating complaints filed by private parties under the Shipping Act, the FMC does not exercise the judicial power of the United States. Such an assumption, however, does not end our inquiry as this Court has repeatedly held that the sovereign immunity enjoyed by the States extends beyond the literal text of the Eleventh Amendment. . . .

A

"[L]ook[ing] first to evidence of the original understanding of the Constitution," . . . as well as early congressional practice, . . . we find a relatively barren historical record, from which the parties draw radically different conclusions. . . .

In truth, the relevant history does not provide direct guidance for our inquiry. The Framers, who envisioned a limited Federal Government, could not have anticipated the vast growth of the administrative state. . . . Because formalized administrative adjudications were all but unheard of in the late 18th century and early 19th century, the dearth of specific evidence indicating whether the Framers believed that the States' sovereign immunity would apply in such proceedings is unsurprising.

This Court, however, has applied a presumption—first explicitly stated in *Hans v. Louisiana, supra*—that the Constitution was not intended to "rais[e] up" any proceedings against the States that were "anomalous and unheard of when the Constitution was adopted." . . . We therefore attribute great significance to the fact that States were not subject to private suits in administrative adjudications at the time of the founding or for many years thereafter. . . .

B

To decide whether the *Hans* presumption applies here, however, we must examine FMC adjudications to determine whether they are the type of proceedings from which the Framers would have thought the States possessed immunity when they agreed to enter the Union.

. . .

. . . [N]either the Commission nor the United States disputes the Court of Appeals' characterization below that such a proceeding "walks, talks, and squawks very much like a lawsuit." . . .

A review of the FMC's Rules of Practice and Procedure confirms that FMC administrative proceedings bear a remarkably strong resemblance to civil litigation in federal courts. . . .

. . .

C

The preeminent purpose of state sovereign immunity is to accord States the dignity that is consistent with their status as sovereign entities. . . .

Given both this interest in protecting States' dignity and the strong similarities between FMC proceedings and civil litigation, we hold that state sovereign immunity bars the FMC from adjudicating complaints filed by a private party against a nonconsenting State. Simply put, if the Framers thought it an impermissible affront to a State's dignity to be required to answer the complaints of private parties in federal courts, we cannot imagine that they would have found it acceptable to compel a State to do exactly the same thing before the administrative tribunal of an agency, such as the FMC. ... The affront to a State's dignity does not lessen when an adjudication takes place in an administrative tribunal as opposed to an Article III court. In both instances, a State is required to defend itself in an adversarial proceeding against a private party before an impartial federal officer. Moreover, it would be quite strange to prohibit Congress from exercising its Article I powers to abrogate state sovereign immunity in Article III judicial proceedings, ... but permit the use of those same Article I powers to create court-like administrative tribunals where sovereign immunity does not apply.

D

The United States suggests two reasons why we should distinguish FMC administrative adjudications from judicial proceedings for purposes of state sovereign immunity. Both of these arguments are unavailing

1

The United States first contends that sovereign immunity should not apply to FMC adjudications because the Commission's orders are not self-executing. Whereas a court may enforce a judgment through the exercise of its contempt power, the FMC cannot enforce its own orders. Rather, the Commission's orders can only be enforced by a federal district court. ...

The United States presents a valid distinction between the authority possessed by the FMC and that of a court. For purposes of this case, however, it is a distinction without a meaningful difference. To the extent that the United States highlights this fact in order to suggest that a party alleged to have violated the Shipping Act is not coerced to participate in FMC proceedings, it is mistaken. The relevant statutory scheme makes it quite clear that, absent sovereign immunity, States would effectively be required to defend themselves against private parties in front of the FMC.

A State seeking to contest the merits of a complaint filed against it by a private party must defend itself in front of the FMC or substantially compromise its ability to defend itself at all. ...

. . .

2

The United States next suggests that sovereign immunity should not apply to FMC proceedings because they do not present the same threat to the financial integrity of States as do private judicial suits. ...

This argument, however, reflects a fundamental misunderstanding of the purposes of sovereign immunity. ...

Sovereign immunity does not merely constitute a defense to monetary liability or even to all types of liability. Rather, it provides an immunity from suit. The statutory scheme, as interpreted by the United States, is thus no more permissible than if Congress had allowed private parties to sue States in federal court for violations of the Shipping Act but precluded a court from awarding them any relief.

. . .

* * *

While some might complain that our system of dual sovereignty is not a model of administrative convenience, . . . that is not its purpose. . . . By guarding against encroachments by the Federal Government on fundamental aspects of state sovereignty, such as sovereign immunity, we strive to maintain the balance of power embodied in our Constitution . . . Although the Framers likely did not envision the intrusion on state sovereignty at issue in today's case, we are nonetheless confident that it is contrary to their constitutional design, and therefore affirm the judgment of the Court of Appeals.

. . .

Justice Stevens, dissenting.

. . . I join [Justice Breyer's] opinion without reservation, but add these words . . .

. . .

. . . [T]he Eleventh Amendment is best understood as having overruled *Chisholm*'s subject-matter jurisdiction holding, thereby restricting the federal courts' diversity jurisdiction. However, the Amendment left intact *Chisholm*'s personal jurisdiction holding: that the Constitution does not immunize States from a federal court's process. . . .

. . .

Justice Breyer, with whom Justice Stevens, Justice Souter, and Justice Ginsburg join, dissenting.

The Court holds that a private person cannot bring a complaint against a State to a federal administrative agency where the agency (1) will use an internal adjudicative process to decide if the complaint is well founded, and (2) if so, proceed to court to enforce the law. Where does the Constitution contain the principle of law that the Court enunciates? I cannot find the answer to this question in any text, in any tradition, or in any relevant purpose. . . .

I

At the outset one must understand the constitutional nature of the legal proceeding before us. . . .

The Court long ago laid to rest any constitutional doubts about whether the Constitution permitted Congress to delegate rulemaking and adjudicative powers to agencies. . . . [I]n exercising those powers, the agency is engaging in an Article II, Executive Branch activity. And the powers it is exercising are powers that the Executive Branch of Government must possess if it is to enforce modern law through administration.

. . .

... [T]his case involves a typical Executive Branch agency exercising typical Executive Branch powers seeking to determine whether a particular person has violated federal law. ... [T]he Constitution created a Federal Government empowered to enact laws that would bind the States and it empowered that Federal Government to enforce those laws against the States. ... It also left private individuals perfectly free to complain to the Federal Government about unlawful state activity, and it left the Federal Government free to take subsequent legal action. Where then can the Court find its constitutional principle—the principle that the Constitution forbids an Executive Branch agency to determine through ordinary adjudicative processes whether such a private complaint is justified? As I have said, I cannot find that principle anywhere in the Constitution.

II

The Court's principle lacks any firm anchor in the Constitution's text. The Eleventh Amendment cannot help. . . .

. . .

Considered purely as constitutional text, these words—"constitutional design," "system of federalism," and "plan of the convention"—suffer several defects. Their language is highly abstract, making them difficult to apply. They invite differing interpretations at least as much as do the Constitution's own broad liberty-protecting phrases, such as "due process of law" or the word "liberty" itself. And compared to these latter phrases, they suffer the additional disadvantage that they do not actually appear anywhere in the Constitution.
. . .

III

Conceding that its conception of sovereign immunity is ungrounded in the Constitution's text, the Court attempts to support its holding with history. But this effort is similarly destined to fail . . .

... [T]otal 18th-century silence about state immunity in Article I proceedings would argue against, not in favor of, immunity.

In any event, the 18th-century was not totally silent. The Framers enunciated in the "plan of the convention," the principle that the Federal Government may sue a State without its consent. ... They also described in the First Amendment the right of a citizen to petition the Federal Government for a redress of grievances. ... The first principle applies here because only the Federal Government, not the private party, can—in light of this Court's recent sovereign immunity jurisprudence—bring the ultimate court action necessary legally to force a State to comply with the relevant federal law. The second principle applies here because a private citizen has asked the Federal Government to determine whether the State has complied with federal law and, if not, to take appropriate legal action in court. Of course these two principles apply only through analogy. . . .

. . .

This is not to say that the analogy (with a citizen petitioning for federal intervention) is, historically speaking, a perfect one. As the Court points out, the Framers may not have "anticipated the vast growth of the administrative state," and the history of their debates "does not provide direct guidance." . . . But the Court is wrong to ignore the relevance and importance of what the Framers did say. And it is doubly wrong to attach "great" legal "significance" to the absence of 18th-and 19th-century administrative agency experience. Even if those alive in the 18th century did not "anticipat[e] the vast growth of the administrative state," they did write a Constitution designed to provide a framework for Government across the centuries, a framework that is flexible enough to meet modern needs. And we cannot read their silence about particular means as if it were an instruction to forbid their use.

. . .

V

The Court cannot justify today's decision in terms of its practical consequences. The decision, while permitting an agency to bring enforcement actions against States, forbids it to use agency adjudication in order to help decide whether to do so. Consequently the agency must rely more heavily upon its own informal staff investigations in order to decide whether a citizen's complaint has merit. The natural result is less agency flexibility, a larger federal bureaucracy, less fair procedure, and potentially less effective law enforcement. . . .

These consequences are not purely theoretical. The Court's decision may undermine enforcement against state employers of many laws designed to protect worker health and safety. . . . And it may inhibit the development of federal fair, rapid, and efficient, informal non-judicial responses to complaints, for example, of improper medical care (involving state hospitals). . . .

* * *

The Court's decision threatens to deny the Executive and Legislative Branches of Government the structural flexibility that the Constitution permits and which modern government demands. . . . An overly restrictive judicial interpretation of the Constitution's structural constraints (unlike its protections of certain basic liberties) will undermine the Constitution's own efforts to achieve its far more basic structural aim, the creation of a representative form of government capable of translating the people's will into effective public action.

This understanding, underlying constitutional interpretation since the New Deal, reflects the Constitution's demands for structural flexibility sufficient to adapt substantive laws and institutions to rapidly changing social, economic, and technological conditions. . . . This understanding led the New Deal Court to reject overly restrictive formalistic interpretations of the Constitution's structural provisions, thereby permitting Congress to enact social and economic legislation that circumstances had led the public to demand. And it led that Court to find in the Constitution authorization for new forms of administration, including independent administrative agencies, with the legal authority flexibly to implement, *i.e.,* to "execute," through adjudication, through rule-making, and in other ways, the legislation that Congress subsequently enacted. . . .

. . . These decisions set loose an interpretive principle that restricts far too severely the authority of the Federal Government to regulate innumerable relationships between State and citizen. Just as this principle has no logical starting place, I fear that neither does it have any logical stopping point.

Today's decision reaffirms the need for continued dissent—unless the consequences of the Court's approach prove anodyne, as I hope, rather than randomly destructive, as I fear.

CHAPTER 6

THE SCOPE OF STATE POWER

SECTION 4. IMPLIED RESTRICTIONS OF THE COMMERCE CLAUSE—PRODUCTION AND TRADE

A. RESTRICTING IMPORTATION AND INSULATING IN-STATE BUSINESS FROM OUT-OF-STATE COMPETITION

Page 310. Add at end of subsection:

PHARMACEUTICAL RESEARCH AND MANUFACTURERS OF AMERICA v. WALSH, ___ U.S. ___, 123 S.Ct. 1855 (2003). In part on dormant commerce clause grounds, an association of nonresident drug manufacturers challenged a Maine law, establishing the "Maine Rx Program," that required drug manufacturers selling prescription drugs in the state through any publicly supported financial assistance program to agree to provide rebates on those sales. The rebates were to go to a state-administered fund for distribution to participating pharmacies from which needy residents could purchase the prescription drugs at discounted prices. The Court rejected the contention "that the rebate requirement constitutes impermissible extraterritorial regulation," because the law " 'does not regulate the price of any out-of-state transaction, either by its express terms or by its inevitable effect.' " The Court also rejected the argument that the law "discriminates against interstate commerce in order to subsidize in-state retail sales[,]" saying:

> "Petitioner argues that Maine's Rx fund is similar [to the Massachusetts milk pricing order invalidated in West Lynn Creamery, Inc. v. Healy, *supra*,] because it would be created entirely from rebates paid by out-of-state manufacturers and would be used to subsidize sales by local pharmacists to local consumers. Unlike the situation in *West Lynn*, however, the Maine Rx Program will not impose a disparate burden on any competitors. A manufacturer could not avoid its rebate obligation by opening production facilities in Maine and would receive no benefit from the rebates even if it did so; the payments to the local pharmacists provide no special benefit to competitors of rebate-paying manufacturers. The rule that was applied in *West Lynn* is thus not applicable to this case."

18

SECTION 5. EFFECT OF OTHER CONSTITUTIONAL PROVISIONS ON STATE REGULATORY POWER

Page 384. Add new subsection:

C. THE FOREIGN AFFAIRS POWER

American Insurance Association v. Garamendi

___ U.S. ___, 123 S.Ct. 2374, ___ L.Ed.2d ___ (2003).

Justice Souter delivered the opinion of the Court.

California's Holocaust Victim Insurance Relief Act of 1999 (HVIRA or Act), Cal. Ins.Code Ann. §§ 13800–13807 (West Cum.Supp.2003), requires any insurer doing business in that State to disclose information about all policies sold in Europe between 1920 and 1945 by the company itself or any one "related" to it. The issue here is whether HVIRA interferes with the National Government's conduct of foreign relations. We hold that it does, with the consequence that the state statute is preempted.

I

A

[Before and during World War II, the Nazi Government in Germany seized the value or proceeds of many insurance policies issued to Jews. Even after the War, "a policy that had escaped confiscation was likely to be dishonored, whether because insurers denied its existence or claimed it had lapsed from unpaid premiums during the persecution, or because the government would not provide heirs with documentation of the policyholder's death." Post-war allied diplomacy initially sought to address these "confiscations and frustrations of claims," but that effort was "intentionally deferred ... when the western allies moved to end their occupation and reestablish a sovereign Germany as a buffer against Soviet expansion," leaving "the obligation to provide restitution ... [with] the new West German Government" in a way that would not "cripple [it] economically." The 1953 London Debt Agreement implementing that approach was "construed by German courts as postponing resolution of foreign claims against both the German Government and German industry, to await the terms of an ultimate postwar treaty."]

... West Germany enacted its own restitution laws in 1953 and 1956 ... and signed agreements with 16 countries for the compensation of their nationals.... Despite a payout of more than 100 billion deutsch marks as of 2000, ... these measures left out many claimants and certain types of claims, and when the [1990] agreement reunifying East and West Germany ... was read by the German courts as lifting the London Debt Agreement's moratorium on Holocaust claims by foreign nationals, class-action lawsuits for restitution poured into United States courts against companies doing business in Germany during the Nazi era....

These suits generated much protest by the defendant companies and their governments, to the point that the Government of the United States took action. . . . From the beginning, the Government's position, represented principally by Under Secretary of State (later Deputy Treasury Secretary) Stuart Eizenstat, stressed mediated settlement "as an alternative to endless litigation" promising little relief to aging Holocaust survivors. . . . Ensuing negotiations at the national level produced the German Foundation Agreement, signed by President Clinton and German Chancellor Schroeder in July 2000, in which Germany agreed to enact legislation establishing a foundation funded with 10 billion deutsch marks contributed equally by the German Government and German companies, to be used to compensate all those "who suffered at the hands of German companies during the National Socialist era." . . .

The willingness of the Germans to create a voluntary compensation fund was conditioned on some expectation of security from lawsuits in United States courts, and after extended dickering President Clinton put his weight behind two specific measures toward that end. . . . First, the Government agreed that whenever a German company was sued on a Holocaust-era claim in an American court, the Government of the United States would submit a statement that "it would be in the foreign policy interests of the United States for the Foundation to be the exclusive forum and remedy for the resolution of all asserted claims against German companies arising from their involvement in the National Socialist era and World War II." . . . Though unwilling to guarantee that its foreign policy interests would "in themselves provide an independent legal basis for dismissal," that being an issue for the courts, the Government agreed to tell courts "that U.S. policy interests favor dismissal on any valid legal ground." Also, the Government promised to use its "best efforts, in a manner it considers appropriate," to get state and local governments to respect the foundation as the exclusive mechanism. . . .

As for insurance claims specifically, both countries agreed that the German Foundation would work with the International Commission on Holocaust Era Insurance Claims (ICHEIC), a voluntary organization formed in 1998 by several European insurance companies, the State of Israel, Jewish and Holocaust survivor associations, and the National Association of Insurance Commissioners, the organization of American state insurance commissioners. The job of the ICHEIC, chaired by former Secretary of State Eagleburger, includes negotiation with European insurers to provide information about unpaid insurance policies issued to Holocaust victims and settlement of claims brought under them. It has thus set up procedures for handling demands against participating insurers, including "a reasonable review . . . of the participating companies' files" for production of unpaid policies, "an investigatory process to determine the current status" of insurance policies for which claims are filed, and a "claims and valuation process to settle and pay individual claims," employing "relaxed standards of proof." . . .

In the pact with the United States, Germany stipulated that "insurance claims that come within the scope of the current claims handling procedures adopted by the [ICHEIC] and are made against German insurance companies shall be processed by the companies and the German Insurance Association on the basis of such procedures and on the basis of additional claims handling procedures that may be agreed among the Foundation, ICHEIC, and the

German Insurance Association." ... And ... in October 2002, the German Foundation agreed to set aside 200 million deutsch marks, to be used for insurance claims approved by the ICHEIC and a portion of the ICHEIC's operating expenses, with another 100 million in reserve if the initial fund should run out.... The foundation also bound itself to contribute 350 million deutsch marks to a "humanitarian fund" administered by the ICHEIC, ... and it agreed to work with the German Insurance Association and the German insurers who had joined the ICHEIC, "with a view to publishing as comprehensive a list as possible of holders of insurance policies issued by German companies who may have been Holocaust victims,".... Those efforts, which control release of information in ways that respect German privacy laws limiting publication of business records, have resulted in the recent release of the names of over 360,000 Holocaust victims owning life insurance policies issued by German insurers....

The German Foundation pact has served as a model for similar agreements with Austria and France, and the United States Government continues to pursue comparable agreements with other countries....

B

While these international efforts were underway, California's Department of Insurance began its own enquiry into the issue of unpaid claims under Nazi-era insurance policies, prompting state legislation designed to force payment by defaulting insurers. In 1998, the state legislature made it an unfair business practice for any insurer operating in the State to "fai[l] to pay any valid claim from Holocaust survivors." ... The legislature placed "an affirmative duty" on the Department of Insurance "to play an independent role in representing the interests of Holocaust survivors," including an obligation to "gather, review, and analyze the archives of insurers ... to provide for research and investigation" into unpaid insurance claims....

[In 1999, the California legislature enacted a law] to allow state residents to sue in state court on insurance claims based on acts perpetrated in the Holocaust[and to] extend[] the governing statute of limitations to December 31, 2010.... The section ... codified as HVIRA ... requires "[a]ny insurer currently doing business in the state" to disclose the details of "life, property, liability, health, annuities, dowry, educational, or casualty insurance policies" issued "to persons in Europe, which were in effect between 1920 and 1945." ... The duty is to make disclosure not only about policies the particular insurer sold, but also about those sold by any "related company," ... whether or not the companies were related during the time when the policies subject to disclosure were sold.... Nor is the obligation restricted to policies sold to "Holocaust victims" as defined in the Act ...; it covers policies sold to anyone during that time.... The insurer must report the current status of each policy, the city of origin, domicile, or address of each policyholder, and the names of the beneficiaries, ... all of which is to be put in a central registry open to the public.... The mandatory penalty for default is suspension of the company's license to do business in the State, ... and there are misdemeanor criminal sanctions for falsehood in certain required representations about whether and to whom the proceeds of each policy have been distributed....

HVIRA was meant to enhance enforcement of both the unfair business practice provision ... and the provision for suit on the policies in question ... by "ensur[ing] that any involvement [that licensed California insurers] or their related companies may have had with insurance policies of Holocaust victims are [sic] disclosed to the state." ... While the legislature acknowledged that "[t]he international Jewish community is in active negotiations with responsible insurance companies through the [ICHEIC] to resolve all outstanding insurance claims issues," it still thought the Act "necessary to protect the claims and interests of California residents, as well as to encourage the development of a resolution to these issues through the international process or through direct action by the State of California, as necessary." ...

After HVIRA was enacted, administrative subpoenas were issued against several subsidiaries of European insurance companies participating in the ICHEIC.... Immediately, in November 1999, Deputy Secretary Eizenstat wrote to the insurance commissioner of California that although HVIRA "reflects a genuine commitment to justice for Holocaust victims and their families, it has the unfortunate effect of damaging the one effective means now at hand to process quickly and completely unpaid insurance claims from the Holocaust period, the [ICHEIC]." ... The Deputy Secretary said that "actions by California, pursuant to this law, have already threatened to damage the cooperative spirit which the [ICHEIC] requires to resolve the important issue for Holocaust survivors," and he also noted that ICHEIC Chairman Eagleburger had expressed his opposition to "sanctions and other pressures brought by California on companies with whom he is obtaining real cooperation." ... The same day, Deputy Secretary Eizenstat also wrote to California's Governor making the same points, and stressing that HVIRA would possibly derail the German Foundation Agreement: "Clearly, for this deal to work ... German industry and the German government need to be assured that they will get 'legal peace,' not just from class-action lawsuits, but from the kind of legislation represented by the California Victim Insurance Relief Act." ... These expressions of the National Government's concern proved to be of no consequence, for the state commissioner announced at an investigatory hearing in December 1999 that he would enforce HVIRA to its fullest, requiring the affected insurers to make the disclosures, leave the State voluntarily, or lose their licenses....

II

After this ultimatum, the petitioners here, several American and European insurance companies and the American Insurance Association [sued,] challenging the constitutionality of HVIRA. [The District Court ruled for petitioners but the Ninth Circuit reversed,] ruling that the Act violated neither the foreign affairs nor the foreign commerce powers.... [W]e granted certiorari ... and now reverse.

III

The principal argument for preemption made by petitioners and the United States as *amicus curiae* is that HVIRA interferes with foreign policy of the Executive Branch, as expressed principally in the executive agreements with Germany, Austria, and France. The major premises of the argument, at least, are beyond dispute. There is, of course, no question that at some point an exercise of state power that touches on foreign relations must yield to the

National Government's policy, given the "concern for uniformity in this country's dealings with foreign nations" that animated the Constitution's allocation of the foreign relations power to the National Government in the first place....

Nor is there any question generally that there is executive authority to decide what that policy should be.... While Congress holds express authority to regulate public and private dealings with other nations in its war and foreign commerce powers, in foreign affairs the President has a degree of independent authority to act....

[T]he President has authority to make "executive agreements" with other countries, requiring no ratification by the Senate or approval by Congress, this power having been exercised since the early years of the Republic.... Making executive agreements to settle claims of American nationals against foreign governments is a particularly longstanding practice, the first example being as early as 1799.... Given the fact that the practice goes back over 200 years to the first Presidential administration, and has received congressional acquiescence throughout its history, the conclusion "[t]hat the President's control of foreign relations includes the settlement of claims is indisputable." ...

The executive agreements at issue here do differ ... insofar as they address claims associated with formerly belligerent states, but against corporations, not the foreign governments. But the distinction does not matter. Historically, wartime claims against even nominally private entities have become issues in international diplomacy, and three of the postwar settlements dealing with reparations implicating private parties were made by the Executive alone. Acceptance of this historical practice is supported by a good pragmatic reason for depending on executive agreements to settle claims against foreign corporations associated with wartime experience. [U]ntangling government policy from private initiative during war time is often so hard that diplomatic action settling claims against private parties may well be just as essential in the aftermath of hostilities as diplomacy to settle claims against foreign governments. While a sharp line between public and private acts works for many purposes in the domestic law, insisting on the same line in defining the legitimate scope of the Executive's international negotiations would hamstring the President in settling international controversies....

Generally, then, valid executive agreements are fit to preempt state law, just as treaties are, and if the agreements here had expressly preempted laws like HVIRA, the issue would be straightforward.... But petitioners and the United States as *amicus curiae* both have to acknowledge that the agreements include no preemption clause, and so leave their claim of preemption to rest on asserted interference with the foreign policy those agreements embody. Reliance is placed on our decision in *Zschernig v. Miller,* 389 U.S. 429 (1968).

Zschernig dealt with an Oregon probate statute prohibiting inheritance by a nonresident alien, absent showings that the foreign heir would take the property "without confiscation" by his home country and that American citizens would enjoy reciprocal rights of inheritance there.... Two decades earlier, *Clark v. Allen,* 331 U.S. 503 (1947), had held that a similar California reciprocity law "did not on its face intrude on the federal domain," ... but by the time Zschernig (an East German resident) brought his challenge, it was clear that the Oregon law in practice had invited "minute inquiries concerning the actual administration of foreign law," ... and so was providing occasions for state judges to disparage certain foreign regimes, employing the language of the anti-Communism prevalent here at the height of the Cold War.... Although the Solicitor General, speaking for the State Department, denied that the state statute "unduly interfere[d] with the United States' conduct of foreign relations," ... the Court was not deterred from exercising its own judgment to invalidate the law as an "intrusion by the State into the field of foreign affairs which the Constitution entrusts to the President and the Congress,"....

The *Zschernig* majority relied on statements in a number of previous cases open to the reading that state action with more than incidental effect on foreign affairs is preempted, even absent any affirmative federal activity in the subject area of the state law, and hence without any showing of conflict....

Justice Harlan, joined substantially by Justice White, disagreed with the *Zschernig* majority on this point, arguing that its implication of preemption of the entire field of foreign affairs was at odds with some other cases suggesting that in the absence of positive federal action "the States may legislate in areas of their traditional competence even though their statutes may have an incidental effect on foreign relations." ... Thus, for Justice Harlan it was crucial that the challenge to the Oregon statute presented no evidence of a "specific interest of the Federal Government which might be interfered with" by the law.... He would, however, have found preemption in a case of "conflicting federal policy," ... and on this point the majority and Justices Harlan and White basically agreed: state laws "must give way if they impair the effective exercise of the Nation's foreign policy,"....

It is a fair question whether respect for the executive foreign relations power requires a categorical choice between the contrasting theories of field and conflict preemption evident in the *Zschernig* opinions,[11] but the question requires no answer here. For even on Justice Harlan's view, the likelihood that state legislation will produce something more than incidental effect in conflict with express foreign policy of the National Government would require preemption of the state law. And since on his view it is legislation within "areas of ... traditional competence" that gives a State any claim to prevail, ... it would be reasonable to consider the strength of the state interest, judged by standards of traditional practice, when deciding how serious a conflict must be shown before declaring the state law preempted. Cf. *Southern Pacific Co. v. Arizona ex rel. Sullivan*, 325 U.S. 761, 768–769 (1945) (under negative Commerce Clause, "reconciliation of the conflicting claims of state and national power is to be attained only by some appraisal and accommodation of the competing demands of the state and national interests involved"); Henkin, Foreign Affairs and the

---

11. The two positions can be seen as complementary. If a State were simply to take a position on a matter of foreign policy with no serious claim to be addressing a traditional state responsibility, field preemption might be the appropriate doctrine, whether the National Government had acted and, if it had, without reference to the degree of any conflict, the principle having been established that the Constitution entrusts foreign policy exclusively to the National Government.... Where, however, a State has acted within what Justice Harlan called its "traditional competence," ... but in a way that affects foreign relations, it might make good sense to require a conflict, of a clarity or substantiality that would vary with the strength or the traditional importance of the state concern asserted. Whether the strength of the federal foreign policy interest should itself be weighed is, of course, a further question....

United States Constitution, at 164 (suggesting a test that "balance[s] the state's interest in a regulation against the impact on U.S. foreign relations").... Judged by these standards, we think petitioners and the Government have demonstrated a sufficiently clear conflict to require finding preemption here.

IV

A

To begin with, resolving Holocaust-era insurance claims that may be held by residents of this country is a matter well within the Executive's responsibility for foreign affairs.... The issue of restitution for Nazi crimes has in fact been addressed in Executive Branch diplomacy and formalized in treaties and executive agreements over the last half century, and although resolution of private claims was postponed by the Cold War, securing private interests is an express object of diplomacy today, just as it was addressed in agreements soon after the Second World War. Vindicating victims injured by acts and omissions of enemy corporations in wartime is thus within the traditional subject matter of foreign policy in which national, not state, interests are overriding, and which the National Government has addressed.

The exercise of the federal executive authority means that state law must give way where, as here, there is evidence of clear conflict between the policies adopted by the two.... [T]he consistent Presidential foreign policy has been to encourage European governments and companies to volunteer settlement funds in preference to litigation or coercive sanctions.... As for insurance claims in particular, the national position, expressed unmistakably in the executive agreements signed by the President with Germany and Austria, has been to encourage European insurers to work with the ICHEIC to develop acceptable claim procedures, including procedures governing disclosure of policy information.... This position ... has also been consistently supported in the high levels of the Executive Branch.... The approach taken serves to resolve the several competing matters of national concern apparent in the German Foundation Agreement: the national interest in maintaining amicable relationships with current European allies; survivors' interests in a "fair and prompt" but nonadversarial resolution of their claims so as to "bring some measure of justice ... in their lifetimes"; and the companies' interest in securing "legal peace" when they settle claims in this fashion.... As a way for dealing with insurance claims, moreover, the voluntary scheme protects the companies' ability to abide by their own countries' domestic privacy laws limiting disclosure of policy information....[13]

---

13. The dissent would discount the executive agreements as evidence of the Government's foreign policy governing disclosure, saying they "do not refer to state disclosure laws specifically, or even to information disclosure generally." But this assertion gives short shrift to the agreements' express endorsement of the ICHEIC's voluntary mechanism, which encompasses production of policy information, not just actual payment of unpaid claims.... The dissent would also dismiss the other Executive Branch expressions of the Government's policy, ... insisting on nothing short of a formal statement by the President himself.... But there is no suggestion that these high-level executive officials were not faithfully representing the President's chosen policy, and there is no apparent reason for adopting the dissent's "nondelegation" rule to apply within the Executive Branch.

California has taken a different tack of providing regulatory sanctions to compel disclosure and payment, supplemented by a new cause of action for Holocaust survivors if the other sanctions should fail. The situation created by the California legislation calls to mind the impact of the Massachusetts Burma law on the effective exercise of the President's power, as recounted in the statutory preemption case, *Crosby v. National Foreign Trade Council*, 530 U.S. 363 (2000). HVIRA's economic compulsion to make public disclosure, of far more information about far more policies than ICHEIC rules require, employs "a different, state system of economic pressure," and in doing so undercuts the President's diplomatic discretion and the choice he has made exercising it.... Whereas the President's authority to provide for settling claims in winding up international hostilities requires flexibility in wielding "the coercive power of the national economy" as a tool of diplomacy, ... HVIRA denies this, by making exclusion from a large sector of the American insurance market the automatic sanction for noncompliance with the State's own policies on disclosure. "Quite simply, if the [California] law is enforceable the President has less to offer and less economic and diplomatic leverage as a consequence." ... The law thus "compromise[s] the very capacity of the President to speak for the Nation with one voice in dealing with other governments" to resolve claims against European companies arising out of World War II....[14]

[Also,] HVIRA threatens to frustrate the operation of the particular mechanism the President has chosen. The letters from Deputy Secretary Eizenstat to California officials show well enough how the portent of further litigation and sanctions has in fact placed the Government at a disadvantage in obtaining practical results from persuading "foreign governments and foreign companies to participate voluntarily in organizations such as ICHEIC." ... In addition to thwarting the Government's policy of repose for companies that pay through the ICHEIC, California's indiscriminate disclosure provisions place a handicap on the ICHEIC's effectiveness (and raise a further irritant to the European allies) by undercutting European privacy protections.... [T]rue, ... the disclosure requirement's object of obtaining compensation for Holocaust victims is a goal espoused by the National Government as well. But "[t]he fact of a common end hardly neutralizes conflicting means," *Crosby* ..., and here HVIRA is an obstacle to the success of the National Government's chosen "calibration of force" in dealing with the Europeans using a voluntary approach....

B

The express federal policy and the clear conflict raised by the state statute are alone enough to require state law to yield. If any doubt about the clarity of the conflict remained, however, it would have to be resolved in the National Government's favor, given the weakness of the State's interest, against the backdrop of traditional state legislative subject matter, in regulating disclosure of European Holocaust-era insurance policies in the manner of HVIRA.

---

14. It is true that the President in this case is acting without express congressional authority, and thus does not have the "plenitude of Executive authority" that "controll[ed] the issue of preemption" in *Crosby*.... But in *Crosby* we were careful to note that the President possesses considerable independent constitutional authority to act on behalf of the United States on international issues, ... and conflict with the exercise of that authority is a comparably good reason to find preemption of state law.

The commissioner would justify HVIRA's ambitious disclosure requirement as protecting "legitimate consumer protection interests" in knowing which insurers have failed to pay insurance claims.... But, quite unlike a generally applicable "blue sky" law, HVIRA effectively singles out only policies issued by European companies, in Europe, to European residents, at least 55 years ago.... Limiting the public disclosure requirement to these policies raises great doubt that the purpose of the California law is an evaluation of corporate reliability in contemporary insuring in the State.

Indeed, there is no serious doubt that the state interest actually underlying HVIRA is concern for the several thousand Holocaust survivors said to be living in the State....

But ... the very same objective dignifies the interest of the National Government in devising its chosen mechanism for voluntary settlements, there being about 100,000 survivors in the country, only a small fraction of them in California.... As against the responsibility of the United States ..., the humanity underlying the state statute could not give the State the benefit of any doubt in resolving the conflict with national policy.

C

The basic fact is that California seeks to use an iron fist where the President has consistently chosen kid gloves. We have heard powerful arguments that the iron fist would work better, and it may be that if the matter of compensation were considered in isolation from all other issues involving the European allies, the iron fist would be the preferable policy. But our thoughts on the efficacy of the one approach versus the other are beside the point, since our business is not to judge the wisdom of the National Government's policy; dissatisfaction should be addressed to the President or, perhaps, Congress. The question relevant to preemption in this case is conflict, and the evidence here is "more than sufficient to demonstrate that the state Act stands in the way of [the President's] diplomatic objectives." ...

V

The State's remaining submission is that ... Congress authorized state law of this sort in the McCarran–Ferguson Act ... and the ... U.S. Holocaust Assets Commission Act of 1998.... There is, however, no need to consider the possible significance for preemption doctrine of tension between an Act of Congress and Presidential foreign policy, ... for neither statute does the job....

[With respect to] the McCarran–Ferguson Act ..., a federal statute directed to implied preemption by domestic commerce legislation cannot sensibly be construed to address preemption by executive conduct in foreign affairs.

Nor does the Holocaust Commission Act authorize HVIRA....

... Congress has done nothing to express disapproval of the President's policy. Legislation along the lines of HVIRA has been introduced in Congress repeatedly, but none of the bills has come close to making it into law....

In sum, Congress has not acted on the matter addressed here. Given the President's independent authority "in the areas of foreign policy and national security, ... congressional silence is not to be equated with congressional disapproval." ...

. . .

The judgment ... is reversed.

Justice Ginsburg, with whom Justice Stevens, Justice Scalia, and Justice Thomas join, dissenting.

... Although the federal approach differs from California's, no executive agreement or other formal expression of foreign policy disapproves state disclosure laws like the HVIRA. Absent a clear statement aimed at disclosure requirements by the "one voice" to which courts properly defer in matters of foreign affairs, I would leave intact California's enactment.

I

. . .

... At least until very recently, ... ICHEIC's progress has been slow and insecure.... Initially, ICHEIC's insurance company members represented little more than one-third of the Holocaust-era insurance market.... Petitioners note that participation in ICHEIC has expanded in the past year, ... but it remains unclear whether ICHEIC does now or will ever encompass all relevant insurers.

Moreover, ICHEIC has thus far settled only a tiny proportion of the claims it has received.... Evidence submitted in a series of class actions filed against Italian insurer Generali indicated that by November 2001, ICHEIC had resolved only 797 of 77,000 claims. ...

Finally, although ICHEIC has directed its members to publish lists of unpaid Holocaust-era policies, that non-binding directive had not yielded significant compliance at the time this case reached the Court.... Shortly after oral argument, ICHEIC-participating German insurers made more substantial disclosures.... But other insurers have been less forthcoming. For a prime example, Generali—which may have sold more life insurance and annuity policies in Eastern Europe during the Holocaust than any other company, ... reportedly maintains a 340,000—name list of persons to whom it sold insurance between 1918 and 1945, but has refused to disclose the bulk of the information on the list. ...

II

A

. . .

... Information published in the HVIRA's registry could ... reveal to a Holocaust survivor residing in California the existence of a viable claim, which she could then present to ICHEIC for resolution.[1]

---

1. In addition, California may deem an insurer's or its affiliate's continuing failure to resolve Holocaust-era claims relevant mar-ketplace information for California consumers.... The Court discounts the HVIRA's pursuit of this objective, stressing that the

... The HVIRA imposes no duty to pay any claim, nor does it authorize litigation on any claim. It mandates only information *disclosure,* and our assessment of the HVIRA is properly confined to that requirement alone.

B

The Federal Government, after prolonged inaction, has responded to the Holocaust-era insurance issue by diplomatic means. . . .

The German Foundation Agreement . . . makes clear, however, that "[t]he United States does not suggest that its policy interests concerning the Foundation in themselves provide an independent legal basis for dismissal." . . .

III

A

. . .

... [E]xecutive agreements directed at claims settlement may sometimes preempt state law. The Court states that if the executive "agreements here had expressly preempted laws like HVIRA, the issue would be straightforward." One can safely demur to that statement, for, as the Court acknowledges, no executive agreement before us expressly preempts the HVIRA. Indeed, no agreement so much as mentions the HVIRA's sole concern: public disclosure.

B

Despite the absence of express preemption, the Court holds that the HVIRA interferes with foreign policy objectives implicit in the executive agreements. I would not venture down that path.

The Court's analysis draws substantially on *Zschernig v. Miller,* 389 U.S. 429 (1968). . . .

We have not relied on *Zschernig* since it was decided, and I would not resurrect that decision here. The notion of "dormant foreign affairs preemption" with which *Zschernig* is associated resonates most audibly when a state action "reflect[s] a state policy critical of foreign governments and involve[s] 'sitting in judgment' on them." . . . The HVIRA entails no such state action or policy. It takes no position on any contemporary foreign government and requires no assessment of any existing foreign regime. It is directed solely at private insurers doing business in California, and it requires them solely to disclose information in their or their affiliates' possession or control. I would not extend *Zschernig* into this dissimilar domain.[4]

HVIRA covers only certain policies issued in Europe more than 50 years ago. But States have broad authority to regulate the insurance industry, ... and a State does not exceed that authority by assigning special significance to an insurer's treatment of claims arising out of an era in which government and industry collaborated to rob countless Holocaust victims of their property.

4. The Court also places considerable weight on *Crosby v. National Foreign Trade Council,* 530 U.S. 363 (2000). As the Court acknowledges, however, *Crosby* was a statutory preemption case. The state law there at issue posed "an obstacle to the accomplishment of Congress's full objectives under the [relevant] federal Act." ... That statutory decision provides little support for preempting a state law by inferring preclusive foreign policy objectives from precatory language in executive agreements.

Neither would I stretch ... to support implied preemption by executive agreement.... [N]one of the executive agreements extinguish any underlying claim for relief.... It remains uncertain ... whether even *litigation* on Holocaust-era insurance claims must be abated in deference to the German Foundation Agreement or the parallel agreements with Austria and France. Indeed, ambiguity on this point appears to have been the studied aim of the American negotiating team....

If it is uncertain whether insurance *litigation* may continue given the executive agreements on which the Court relies, it should be abundantly clear that those agreements leave *disclosure* laws like the HVIRA untouched.... [T]he Court invalidates a state disclosure law on grounds of conflict with foreign policy "embod[ied]" in certain executive agreements, although those agreements do not refer to state disclosure laws specifically, or even to information disclosure generally.[5] It therefore is surely an exaggeration to assert that the "HVIRA threatens to frustrate the operation of the particular mechanism the President has chosen" to resolve Holocaust-era claims. If that were so, one might expect to find some reference to laws like the HVIRA in the later-in-time executive agreements. There is none.

To fill the agreements' silences, the Court points to statements by individual members of the Executive Branch.... We should not do so here lest we place the considerable power of foreign affairs preemption in the hands of individual sub-Cabinet members of the Executive Branch. [N]o authoritative text accords such officials the power to invalidate state law simply by conveying the Executive's views on matters of federal policy. The displacement of state law by preemption properly requires a considerably more formal and binding federal instrument.

Sustaining the HVIRA would not compromise the President's ability to speak with one voice for the Nation. To the contrary, by declining to invalidate the HVIRA in this case, we would reserve foreign affairs preemption for circumstances where the President, acting under statutory or constitutional authority, has spoken clearly to the issue at hand.... And judges should not be the expositors of the Nation's foreign policy, which is the role they play by acting when the President himself has not taken a clear stand. As I see it, courts step out of their proper role when they rely on no legislative or even executive text, but only on inference and implication, to preempt state laws on foreign affairs grounds.

In sum, assuming, *arguendo,* that an executive agreement or similarly formal foreign policy statement targeting disclosure could override the HVIRA, there is no such declaration here. Accordingly, I would leave California's enactment in place, and affirm the judgment of the Court of Appeals.

5. The Court apparently finds in the executive agreements' "express endorsement of ICHEIC's voluntary mechanism" a federal purpose to preempt any information disclosure mechanism not controlled by ICHEIC itself. But nothing in the executive agreements suggests that the Federal Government supports the resolution of Holocaust era insurance claims only to the extent they are based upon information disclosed by ICHEIC. The executive agreements do not, for example, prohibit recourse to ICHEIC to resolve claims based upon information disclosed through laws like the HVIRA.

PART III

GOVERNMENT AND THE INDIVIDUAL: THE PROTECTION OF LIBERTY AND PROPERTY UNDER THE DUE PROCESS AND EQUAL PROTECTION CLAUSES

CHAPTER 8

THE BILL OF RIGHTS, THE CIVIL WAR AMENDMENTS AND THEIR INTER-RELATIONSHIP

SECTION 3.   APPLICATION OF THE BILL OF RIGHTS TO THE STATES

Page 495.   In Note, "Due Process as a Limitation on Procedures Not Forbidden by the Bill of Rights," add to end of footnote b:

For a discussion of the substantive due process limitations the Court has applied to the review of punitive damages awards, see Note, "Due Process Limitations on State Punitive Damages Awards," infra p. 33.

CHAPTER 9

THE DUE PROCESS, CONTRACT, AND JUST COMPENSATION CLAUSES AND THE REVIEW OF THE REASONABLENESS OF LEGISLATION

SECTION 1. ECONOMIC REGULATORY LEGISLATION

A. THE RISE AND FALL OF DUE PROCESS

Page 520. Add at end of subsection:

DUE PROCESS LIMITATIONS ON STATE PUNITIVE DAMAGES AWARDS

In contrast to its highly deferential approach to due process review of the reasonableness of economic legislation, the Court in the 1990's began to define substantive due process limits to assure the reasonableness of punitive damages awards imposed in civil trials, based on the perception that "[p]unitive damages pose an acute danger of arbitrary deprivation of property[,]" Honda Motor Co. v. Oberg, 512 U.S. 415, 432 (1994). In State Farm Mutual Automobile Insurance Co. v. Campbell, ___ U.S. ___, 123 S.Ct. 1513 (2003), the Court affirmed that the "Due Process Clause of the Fourteenth Amendment prohibits the imposition of grossly excessive or arbitrary punishments on a tortfeasor" and overturned as "neither reasonable nor proportionate to the wrong committed, and . . . an irrational deprivation of the property of the defendant" a punitive damages award of $145 million, where full compensatory damages were $1 million. Justice Kennedy's majority opinion applied "three guideposts" the Court had adopted in BMW of North America, Inc. v. Gore, 517 U.S. 559 (1996), as instructions for courts reviewing punitive damages to consider: "(1) the degree of reprehensibility of the defendant's misconduct; (2) the disparity between the actual or potential harm suffered by the plaintiff and the punitive damages award; and (3) the difference between the punitive damages awarded by the jury and the civil penalties authorized or imposed in comparable cases." The majority also declared more generally:

"We decline . . . to impose a bright-line ratio which a punitive damages award cannot exceed. Our jurisprudence and the principles it has now established demonstrate, however, that, in practice, few awards exceeding a single-digit ratio between punitive and compensatory damages, to a significant degree, will satisfy due process. In [Pacific Mutual Life Insurance Co. v. Haslip, 499 U.S. 1, 23–24 (1991)], in upholding a punitive damages award, we concluded that an award of more than four times the amount of compensatory damages might be close to the line of constitutional impropriety.... We cited that 4-to-1 ratio again in *Gore*.... The Court further referenced a long legislative history, dating back over 700 years and going forward to today, providing for sanctions of double, treble, or quadruple damages to deter and punish.... While these ratios are not binding, they are instructive. They demonstrate what should be obvious: Single-digit multipliers are more likely to comport with due process, while still achieving the State's goals of deterrence and retribution, than awards with ratios in range of 500 to 1, or, in this case, of 145 to 1.

"Nonetheless, because there are no rigid benchmarks that a punitive damages award may not surpass, ratios greater than those we have previously upheld may comport with due process where 'a particularly egregious act has resulted in only a small amount of economic damages.' ... The converse is also true, however. When compensatory damages are substantial, then a lesser ratio, perhaps only equal to compensatory damages, can reach the outermost limit of the due process guarantee. The precise award in any case, of course, must be based upon the facts and circumstances of the defendant's conduct and the harm to the plaintiff.

"In sum, courts must ensure that the measure of punishment is both reasonable and proportionate to the amount of harm to the plaintiff and to the general damages recovered."

Three Justices dissented. Justice Scalia "adhere[d] to the view expressed in my dissenting opinion in ... *Gore* ... that the Due Process Clause provides no substantive protections against 'excessive' or 'unreasonable' awards of punitive damages." He added "that the punitive damages jurisprudence which has sprung forth from *BMW v. Gore* is insusceptible of principled application...." Justice Thomas " 'continue[d] to believe that the Constitution does not constrain the size of punitive damages awards.' *Cooper Industries, Inc. v. Leatherman Tool Group, Inc.,* 532 U.S. 424, 443 (2001)." Finally, Justice Ginsburg opined that although "[t]he large size of the award upheld by the Utah Supreme Court in this case indicates why damage-capping legislation may be altogether fitting and proper[, n]either the amount of the award nor the trial record ... justifies this Court's substitution of its judgment for that of Utah's competent decisionmakers." She also wrote: "In a legislative scheme or a state high court's design to cap punitive damages, the handiwork in setting single-digit and 1-to-1 benchmarks could hardly be questioned; in a judicial decree imposed on the States by this Court under the banner of substantive due process, the numerical controls today's decision installs seem to me boldly out of order." She concluded her opinion as follows: "I remain of the view that this Court has no warrant to reform state law governing awards of punitive damages. *Gore,* 517 U.S., at 607 (Ginsburg, J., dissenting). Even if I were prepared to accept the flexible guides prescribed in *Gore,* I would not join the Court's swift conversion of those guides into instructions that begin to resemble marching orders."

C. THE JUST COMPENSATION CLAUSE OF THE FIFTH AMENDMENT—WHAT DOES IT ADD TO DUE PROCESS?

Page 537. Add at end of Note, "Introduction":

In Brown v. Legal Foundation of Washington, ___ U.S. ___, 123 S.Ct. 1406 (2003), the Court determined that paying for legal services for the needy using interest earned on pooled client funds that lawyers hold in trust accounts "unquestionably satisfied" the "public use" requirement:

"If the State had imposed a special tax, or perhaps a system of user fees, to generate the funds to finance the legal services supported by the Foundation, there would be no question as to the legitimacy of the use of the public's money. The fact that public funds might pay the legal fees of a lawyer representing a tenant in a dispute with a landlord who was compelled to contribute to the program would not undermine the public character of the 'use' of the funds. Provided that she receives just compensation for the taking of her property, a conscientious pacifist has no standing to object to the government's decision to use the property she formerly owned for the production of munitions. Even if there may be occasional misuses of IOLTA [Interest On Lawyer Trust Account] funds, the overall, dramatic success of these programs in serving the compelling interest in providing legal services to literally millions of needy Americans certainly qualifies the Foundation's distribution of these funds as a 'public use' within the meaning of the Fifth Amendment."

A footnote in Justice Scalia's dissenting opinion for four Justices objected to the Court having "announce[d] a new criterion for 'public use' ... [that] reduces the ... requirement to a negligible impediment indeed, since I am unaware of *any* use to which state taxes cannot constitutionally be devoted. The money thus derived may be given to the poor, or to the rich, or (insofar as the Federal Constitution is concerned) to the girl-friend of the retiring governor. Taxes and user fees, since they are not 'takings,' see *United States v. Sperry Corp.,* 493 U.S. 52 (1989), are simply not subject to the 'public use' requirement, and so their constitutional legitimacy is entirely irrelevant to the existence *vel non* of a public use."

1. RESTRICTIONS ON PROPERTY USE

Page 549. Add at end of subsection:

Tahoe–Sierra Preservation Council, Inc. v. Tahoe Regional Planning Agency

535 U.S. 302, 122 S.Ct. 1465, 152 L.Ed.2d 517 (2002).

Justice Stevens delivered the opinion of the Court.

The question presented is whether a moratorium on development imposed during the process of devising a comprehensive land-use plan constitutes a *per se* taking of property requiring compensation under the Takings Clause of the United States Constitution. This case actually involves two moratoria ordered by respondent Tahoe Regional Planning Agency (TRPA) to maintain the status quo while studying the impact of development on Lake Tahoe and designing a strategy for environmentally sound growth. The first, Ordinance 81–5, was effective from August 24, 1981, until August 26, 1983, whereas the second more restrictive Resolution 83–21 was in effect from August 27, 1983, until April 25, 1984. As a result of these two directives, virtually all development on a substantial portion of the property subject to TRPA's jurisdiction was prohibited for a period of 32 months. . . .

I

[By increasing impervious coverage of land, development in the area surrounding Lake Tahoe increases runoff that carries nutrients which nourish algae growth and thereby degrade the clarity of the lake's unusually transparent water, especially when the development occurs in steeper-sloped high hazard areas and in Stream Environment Zone (SEZ) areas that normally serve as wetland filters for runoff debris. Dissatisfaction with unsuccessful conservation efforts in the 1960's and 1970's led California and Nevada, with congressional approval, to adopt an amended Tahoe Regional Planning Compact in 1980. The Compact directed TRPA to develop regional "environmental threshold carrying capacities" within 18 months, and within a year thereafter to adopt an amended regional plan achieving and maintaining those carrying capacities. The Compact also contained a finding by the Legislatures of California and Nevada "that in order to make effective the regional plan as revised by [TRPA], it is necessary to halt temporarily works of development in the region which might otherwise absorb the entire capability of the region for further development or direct it out of harmony with the ultimate plan." Accordingly, for the period before adoption of the final plan, the Compact itself prohibited the development of new subdivisions, condominiums, and apartment buildings, and also prohibited each city and county in the 500 square mile Basin from granting any more permits in 1981, 1982, or 1983 than had been granted in 1978.

[Recognizing that it could not meet the deadlines in the Compact, TRPA first enacted the Ordinance for two years and then the Resolution for an additional eight months. In combination, they "effectively prohibited all construction on sensitive lands in California and on all SEZ lands in the entire Basin for 32 months, and on sensitive lands in Nevada (other than SEZ lands) for eight months." When the 1984 plan finally was adopted, California immediately secured an injunction against its implementation on the ground that it failed to establish land-use controls sufficiently stringent to protect the Basin. The injunction] remained in effect until a completely revised plan was adopted in 1987. Both the 1984 injunction and the 1987 plan contained provisions that prohibited new construction on sensitive lands in the Basin. As the case comes to us, however, we have no occasion to consider the validity of those provisions.

II

[Shortly after the adoption of the 1984 Plan, the Tahoe Sierra Preservation Council, a nonprofit membership corporation representing about 2,000 owners of both improved and unimproved parcels of real estate in the Lake Tahoe Basin, and a class of some 400 individual owners of vacant lots located either on SEZ lands or high hazard lands who purchased their properties before the effective date of the 1980 Compact, primarily for the purpose of constructing "at a time of their choosing" a single-family home "to serve as a permanent, retirement or vacation residence," sued TRPA in federal court claiming, *inter alia*, that] Ordinance 81–5, Resolution 83–21, and the 1984 regional plan ... constituted takings of petitioners' property without just compensation. [T]he challenge to the 1984 plan is not before us because both the District Court and the Court of Appeals held that it was the federal injunction against implementing that plan, rather than the plan itself, that caused the post–1984 injuries that petitioners allegedly suffered, and those rulings are not encompassed within our limited grant of certiorari.

. . .

[Applying the analysis adopted in Penn Central Transp. Co. v. New York City, 438 U.S. 104 (1978), and e]mphasizing the temporary nature of the regulations, the testimony that the "average holding time of a lot in the Tahoe area between lot purchase and home construction is twenty-five years," and the failure of petitioners to offer specific evidence of harm, the District Court concluded that "consideration of the *Penn Central* factors clearly leads to the conclusion that there was no taking." In the absence of evidence regarding any of the individual plaintiffs, the court evaluated the "average" purchasers' intent and found that such purchasers "did not have reasonable, investment-backed expectations that they would be able to build single-family homes on their land within the six-year period involved in this lawsuit."[11]

[However, t]he District Court[, a]lthough ... satisfied that petitioners' property did retain some value during the moratoria, ... found that they had been temporarily deprived of "all economically viable use of their land ..." [and thus had suffered] "categorical" takings under our decision in Lucas v. South Carolina Coastal Council, 505 U.S. 1003 (1992)....

... [On appeal,] the Ninth Circuit noted that petitioners had expressly disavowed an argument "that the regulations constitute a taking under the ad hoc balancing approach described in *Penn Central*".... Accordingly, the only question before the court was "whether the rule set forth in *Lucas* applies— that is, whether a categorical taking occurred because Ordinance 81–5 and Resolution 83–21 denied the plaintiffs' 'all economically beneficial or productive use of land.' " ...

Contrary to the District Court, the Court of Appeals held that because the regulations had only a temporary impact on petitioners' fee interest in the properties, no categorical taking had occurred. It reasoned:

"Property interests may have many different dimensions. For example, the dimensions of a property interest may include a physical dimension (which describes the size and shape of the property in question), a functional dimension (which describes the extent to which an owner may use or dispose of the property in question), and a temporal dimension (which describes the duration of the property interest). At base, the plaintiffs' argument is that we should conceptually sever each plaintiff's fee interest into discrete segments in at least one of these dimensions—the temporal

---

11. ... The court stated that petitioners "had plenty of time to build before the restrictions went into effect—and almost everyone in the Tahoe Basin knew in the late 1970s that a crackdown on development was in the works." ...

one—and treat each of those segments as separate and distinct property interests for purposes of takings analysis. Under this theory, they argue that there was a categorical taking of one of those temporal segments." . . .

Putting to one side "cases of physical invasion or occupation," . . . the court read our cases involving regulatory taking claims to focus on the impact of a regulation on the parcel as a whole. In its view a "planning regulation that prevents the development of a parcel for a temporary period of time is conceptually no different than a land-use restriction that permanently denies all use on a discrete portion of property, or that permanently restricts a type of use across all of the parcel." . . . In each situation, a regulation that affects only a portion of the parcel—whether limited by time, use, or space—does not deprive the owner of all economically beneficial use.

The Court of Appeals distinguished *Lucas* as applying to the " 'relatively rare' " case in which a regulation denies all productive use of an entire parcel, whereas the moratoria involve only a "temporal 'slice' " of the fee interest and a form of regulation that is widespread and well established. It also rejected petitioners' argument that our decision in [First English Evangelical Lutheran Church v. County of Los Angeles, 482 U.S. 304 (1987)] was controlling[, as that ruling] concerned the question whether compensation is an appropriate remedy for a temporary taking and not whether or when such a taking has occurred. . . . [T]he court held that *Penn Central* was the appropriate framework for analysis. . . .

Over the dissent of five judges, the Ninth Circuit denied a petition for rehearing en banc. . . . [W]e granted certiorari limited to the question stated at the beginning of this opinion. . . . We now affirm.

III

Petitioners make only a facial attack on Ordinance 81–5 and Resolution 83–21. They contend that the mere enactment of a temporary regulation that, while in effect, denies a property owner all viable economic use of her property gives rise to an unqualified constitutional obligation to compensate her for the value of its use during that period. . . . Under their proposed rule, there is no need to evaluate the landowners' investment-backed expectations, the actual impact of the regulation on any individual, the importance of the public interest served by the regulation, or the reasons for imposing the temporary restriction. For petitioners, it is enough that a regulation imposes a temporary deprivation—no matter how brief—of all economically viable use to trigger a *per se* rule that a taking has occurred. Petitioners assert that our opinions in *First English* and *Lucas* have already endorsed their view, and that it is a logical application of the principle that the Takings Clause was "designed to bar Government from forcing some people alone to bear burdens which, in all fairness and justice, should be borne by the public as a whole." *Armstrong v. United States, 364 U.S. 40, 49 (1960).*

We shall first explain why our cases do not support their proposed categorical rule—indeed, fairly read, they implicitly reject it. Next, we shall explain why the *Armstrong* principle requires rejection of that rule as well as the less extreme position advanced by petitioners at oral argument. In our view the answer to the abstract question whether a temporary moratorium effects a taking is neither "yes, always" nor "no, never"; the answer depends upon the particular circumstances of the case.[16] ... [W]e conclude that the circumstances in this case are best analyzed within the *Penn Central* framework.

IV

... Our jurisprudence involving condemnations and physical takings is as old as the Republic and, for the most part, involves the straightforward application of *per se* rules. Our regulatory takings jurisprudence, in contrast, is of more recent vintage and is characterized by "essentially ad hoc, factual inquiries," ... designed to allow "careful examination and weighing of all the relevant circumstances." ...

When the government physically takes possession of an interest in property for some public purpose, it has a categorical duty to compensate the former owner, United States v. Pewee Coal Co., 341 U.S. 114, 115 (1951), regardless of whether the interest that is taken constitutes an entire parcel or merely a part thereof. Thus, compensation is mandated when a leasehold is taken and the government occupies the property for its own purposes, even though that use is temporary.... Similarly, when the government appropriates part of a rooftop in order to provide cable TV access for apartment tenants, Loretto v. Teleprompter Manhattan CATV Corp., 458 U.S. 419 (1982); or when its planes use private airspace to approach a government airport, United States v. Causby, 328 U.S. 256 (1946), it is required to pay for that share no matter how small. But a government regulation that merely prohibits landlords from evicting tenants unwilling to pay a higher rent, Block v. Hirsh, 256 U.S. 135 (1921); that bans certain private uses of a portion of an owner's property, Village of Euclid v. Ambler Realty Co., 272 U.S. 365 (1926); Keystone Bituminous Coal Assn. v. DeBenedictis, 480 U.S. 470 (1987); or that forbids the private use of certain airspace, *Penn Central* ..., does not constitute a categorical taking....

This longstanding distinction between acquisitions of property for public use, on the one hand, and regulations prohibiting private uses, on the other, makes it inappropriate to treat cases involving physical takings as controlling precedents for the evaluation of a claim that there has been a "regulatory taking," and vice versa. For the same reason that we do not ask whether a physical appropriation advances a substantial government interest or whether it deprives the owner of all economically valuable use, we do not apply our precedent from the physical takings context to regulatory takings claims. Land-use regulations are ubiquitous and most of them impact property values in some tangential way—often in completely unanticipated ways. Treating them all as *per se* takings would transform government regulation into a luxury few governments could afford. By contrast, physical appropriations are relatively rare, easily identified, and usually represent a greater affront to individual property rights.[19] ...

   . . .

---

16. Despite our clear refusal to hold that a moratorium never effects a taking, The Chief Justice accuses us of "allow[ing] the government to ... take private property without paying for it." It may be true that under a *Penn Central* analysis petitioners' land was taken and compensation would be due. But petitioners failed to challenge the District Court's conclusion that there was no taking under *Penn Central*.

19. According to The Chief Justice's dissent, even a temporary, use-prohibiting regulation should be governed by our physical takings cases because, under *Lucas* ...,

... [Our precedents indicate that we generally] resist the temptation to adopt *per se* rules in our cases involving partial regulatory takings, preferring to examine "a number of factors" rather than a simple "mathematically precise" formula. Justice Brennan's opinion for the Court in *Penn Central* did, however, make it clear that even though multiple factors are relevant in the analysis of regulatory takings claims, in such cases we must focus on "the parcel as a whole":

> " 'Taking' jurisprudence does not divide a single parcel into discrete segments and attempt to determine whether rights in a particular segment have been entirely abrogated. In deciding whether a particular governmental action has effected a taking, this Court focuses rather both on the character of the action and on the nature and extent of the interference with rights in the parcel as a whole—here, the city tax block designated as the 'landmark site.' " ...

This requirement that "the aggregate must be viewed in its entirety" explains why, for example, a regulation that prohibited commercial transactions in eagle feathers, but did not bar other uses or impose any physical invasion or restraint upon them, was not a taking. Andrus v. Allard, 444 U.S. 51, 66 (1979). It also clarifies why restrictions on the use of only limited portions of the parcel, such as set-back ordinances, Gorieb v. Fox, 274 U.S. 603 (1927), or a requirement that coal pillars be left in place to prevent mine subsidence, *Keystone Bituminous Coal* ..., were not considered regulatory takings. In each of these cases, we affirmed that "where an owner possesses a full 'bundle' of property rights, the destruction of one 'strand' of the bundle is not a taking." ...

While the foregoing cases considered whether particular regulations had "gone too far" and were therefore invalid, none of them addressed the separate remedial question of how compensation is measured once a regulatory taking is established. In his dissenting opinion in San Diego Gas & Elec. Co. v. San Diego, 450 U.S. 621, 636 (1981), Justice Brennan identified that question and explained how he would answer it:

> "The constitutional rule I propose requires that, once a court finds that a police power regulation has effected a 'taking,' the government entity must pay just compensation for the period commencing on the date the regula-

"from the landowner's point of view," the moratorium is the functional equivalent of a forced leasehold. Of course, from both the landowner's and the government's standpoint there are critical differences between a leasehold and a moratorium. Condemnation of a leasehold gives the government possession of the property, the right to admit and exclude others, and the right to use it for a public purpose. A regulatory taking, by contrast, does not give the government any right to use the property, nor does it dispossess the owner or affect her right to exclude others.

The Chief Justice stretches *Lucas'* "equivalence" language too far. For even a regulation that constitutes only a minor infringement on property may, from the landowner's perspective, be the functional equiva-lent of an appropriation. *Lucas* carved out a narrow exception to the rules governing regulatory takings for the "extraordinary circumstance" of a permanent deprivation of all beneficial use. The exception was only partially justified based on the "equivalence" theory cited by his dissent. It was also justified on the theory that, in the "relatively rare situations where the government has deprived a landowner of all economically beneficial uses," it is less realistic to assume that the regulation will secure an "average reciprocity of advantage," or that government could not go on if required to pay for every such restriction.... But as we explain, these assumptions hold true in the context of a moratorium.

tion first effected the 'taking,' and ending on the date the government entity chooses to rescind or otherwise amend the regulation." ...

Justice Brennan's proposed rule was subsequently endorsed by the Court in *First English*.... *First English* was certainly a significant decision, and nothing that we say today qualifies its holding. Nonetheless, it is important to recognize that we did not address in that case the quite different and logically prior question whether the temporary regulation at issue had in fact constituted a taking.

... [Our] holding was ... unambiguous: "We merely hold that where the government's activities *have already worked a taking* of all use of property, no subsequent action by the government can relieve it of the duty to provide compensation for the period during which the taking was effective." ... (emphasis added). In fact, *First English* expressly disavowed any ruling on the merits of the takings issue because the California courts had decided the remedial question on the assumption that a taking had been alleged.... After our remand, the California courts concluded that there had not been a taking, and we declined review....

To the extent that the Court in *First English* referenced the antecedent takings question, we identified two reasons why a regulation temporarily denying an owner all use of her property might not constitute a taking. First, we recognized that "the county might avoid the conclusion that a compensable taking had occurred by establishing that the denial of all use was insulated as a part of the State's authority to enact safety regulations." ... Second, we limited our holding "to the facts presented" and recognized "the quite different questions that would arise in the case of normal delays in obtaining building permits, changes in zoning ordinances, variances, and the like which [were] not before us." ... Thus, our decision in *First English* surely did not approve, and implicitly rejected, the categorical submission that petitioners are now advocating.

Similarly, our decision in *Lucas* is not dispositive of the question presented. Although *Lucas* endorsed and applied a categorical rule, it was not the one that petitioners propose....

The categorical rule that we applied in *Lucas* states that compensation is required when a regulation deprives an owner of "*all* economically beneficial uses" of his land.... Anything less than a "complete elimination of value," or a "total loss," the Court acknowledged, would require the kind of analysis applied in *Penn Central*....

Certainly, our holding that the permanent "obliteration of the value" of a fee simple estate constitutes a categorical taking does not answer the question whether a regulation prohibiting any economic use of land for a 32–month period has the same legal effect. Petitioners seek to bring this case under the rule announced in *Lucas* by arguing that we can effectively sever a 32–month segment from the remainder of each landowner's fee simple estate, and then ask whether that segment has been taken in its entirety by the moratoria. Of course, defining the property interest taken in terms of the very regulation being challenged is circular. With property so divided, every delay would become a total ban; the moratorium and the normal permit process alike would constitute categorical takings. Petitioners' "conceptual severance" argument is unavailing because it ignores *Penn Central's* admonition that in regulatory takings cases we must focus on "the parcel as a whole." ... We have consistently rejected such an approach to the "denominator" question.... Thus, the District Court erred when it disaggregated petitioners' property into temporal segments corresponding to the regulations at issue and then analyzed whether petitioners were deprived of all economically viable use during each period.... The starting point for the court's analysis should have been to ask whether there was a total taking of the entire parcel; if not, then *Penn Central* was the proper framework.[26]

An interest in real property is defined by the metes and bounds that describe its geographic dimensions and the term of years that describes the temporal aspect of the owner's interest. See *Restatement of Property* §§ 7–9 (1936). Both dimensions must be considered if the interest is to be viewed in its entirety. Hence, a permanent deprivation of the owner's use of the entire area is a taking of "the parcel as a whole," whereas a temporary restriction that merely causes a diminution in value is not. Logically, a fee simple estate cannot be rendered valueless by a temporary prohibition on economic use, because the property will recover value as soon as the prohibition is lifted....

Neither *Lucas,* nor *First English,* nor any of our other regulatory takings cases compels us to accept petitioners' categorical submission. In fact, these cases make clear that the categorical rule in *Lucas* was carved out for the "extraordinary case" in which a regulation permanently deprives property of all value; the default rule remains that, in the regulatory taking context, we require a more fact specific inquiry. Nevertheless, we will consider whether the interest in protecting individual property owners from bearing public burdens "which, in all fairness and justice, should be borne by the public as a whole," *Armstrong* ..., justifies creating a new rule for these circumstances....

V

Considerations of "fairness and justice" arguably could support the conclusion that TRPA's moratoria were takings of petitioners' property based on any of seven different theories. First, even though we have not previously done so, we might now announce a categorical rule that, in the interest of fairness and justice, compensation is required whenever government temporarily deprives an owner of all economically viable use of her property. Second, we could craft a narrower rule that would cover all temporary land-use restrictions except those "normal delays in obtaining building permits, changes in zoning ordinances, variances, and the like" which were put to one side in our opinion in *First English* .... Third, we could adopt a rule like the one suggested by an *amicus* supporting petitioners that would "allow a short fixed period for deliberations to take place without compensation—say maximum one year—after which the just compensation requirements" would "kick in." Fourth, with the benefit of hindsight, we might characterize the successive actions of TRPA as a "series of rolling moratoria" that were the functional equivalent of a permanent taking.... Fifth, were it not for the findings of the District Court that TRPA acted diligently and in good faith, we might have concluded that the agency was

---

26. The Chief Justice's dissent makes the same mistake by carving out a 6–year interest in the property, rather than considering the parcel as a whole, and treating the regulations covering that segment as analogous to a total taking under *Lucas.*

stalling in order to avoid promulgating the environmental threshold carrying capacities and regional plan mandated by the 1980 Compact.... Sixth, apart from the District Court's finding that TRPA's actions represented a proportional response to a serious risk of harm to the lake, petitioners might have argued that the moratoria did not substantially advance a legitimate state interest.... Finally, if petitioners had challenged the application of the moratoria to their individual parcels, instead of making a facial challenge, some of them might have prevailed under a *Penn Central* analysis.

As the case comes to us, however, none of the last four theories is available. The "rolling moratoria" theory was presented in the petition for certiorari, but our order granting review did not encompass that issue ...; the case was tried in the District Court and reviewed in the Court of Appeals on the theory that each of the two moratoria was a separate taking, one for a 2–year period and the other for an 8–month period.... And, as we have already noted, recovery on either a bad faith theory or a theory that the state interests were insubstantial is foreclosed by the District Court's unchallenged findings of fact. Recovery under a *Penn Central* analysis is also foreclosed both because petitioners expressly disavowed that theory, and because they did not appeal from the District Court's conclusion that the evidence would not support it. Nonetheless, each of the three *per se* theories is fairly encompassed within the question that we decided to answer.

With respect to these theories, the ultimate constitutional question is whether the concepts of "fairness and justice" that underlie the Takings Clause will be better served by one of these categorical rules or by a *Penn Central* inquiry into all of the relevant circumstances in particular cases. From that perspective, the extreme categorical rule that any deprivation of all economic use, no matter how brief, constitutes a compensable taking surely cannot be sustained. Petitioners' broad submission would apply to numerous "normal delays in obtaining building permits, changes in zoning ordinances, variances, and the like," ... as well as to orders temporarily prohibiting access to crime scenes, businesses that violate health codes, fire-damaged buildings, or other areas that we cannot now foresee. Such a rule would undoubtedly require changes in numerous practices that have long been considered permissible exercises of the police power.... A rule that required compensation for every delay in the use of property would render routine government processes prohibitively expensive or encourage hasty decisionmaking. Such an important change in the law should be the product of legislative rulemaking rather than adjudication.

More importantly, ... we are persuaded that the better approach to claims that a regulation has effected a temporary taking "requires careful examination and weighing of all the relevant circumstances." ... In rejecting petitioners' *per se* rule, we do not hold that the temporary nature of a land-use restriction precludes finding that it effects a taking; we simply recognize that it should not be given exclusive significance one way or the other.

A narrower rule that excluded the normal delays associated with processing permits, or that covered only delays of more than a year, would certainly have a less severe impact on prevailing practices, but it would still impose serious financial constraints on the planning process. Unlike the "extraordinary circumstance" in which the government deprives a property owner of all economic use, *Lucas* ..., moratoria like Ordinance 81–5 and Resolution 83–21 are used widely among land-use planners to preserve the status quo while formulating a more permanent development strategy. In fact, the consensus in the planning community appears to be that moratoria, or "interim development controls" as they are often called, are an essential tool of successful development. Yet even the weak version of petitioners' categorical rule would treat these interim measures as takings regardless of the good faith of the planners, the reasonable expectations of the landowners, or the actual impact of the moratorium on property values.[34]

The interest in facilitating informed decisionmaking by regulatory agencies counsels against adopting a *per se* rule that would impose such severe costs on their deliberations. Otherwise, the financial constraints of compensating property owners during a moratorium may force officials to rush through the planning process or to abandon the practice altogether. To the extent that communities are forced to abandon using moratoria, landowners will have incentives to develop their property quickly before a comprehensive plan can be enacted, thereby fostering inefficient and ill-conceived growth....

As Justice Kennedy explained in his opinion for the Court in [Palazzolo v. Rhode Island,[a] 533 U.S. 606, 620–21 (2001),] it is the interest in informed decisionmaking that underlies our decisions imposing a strict ripeness requirement on landowners asserting regulatory takings claims:

> "These cases stand for the important principle that a landowner may not establish a taking before a land-use authority has the opportunity, using its own reasonable procedures, to decide and explain the reach of a challenged regulation. Under our ripeness rules a takings claim based on a law or regulation which is alleged to go too far in burdening property depends upon the landowner's first having followed reasonable and necessary steps to allow regulatory agencies to exercise their full discretion in considering development plans for the property, including the opportunity to grant any variances or waivers allowed by law. As a general rule, until these ordinary

---

34. The Chief Justice offers another alternative, suggesting that delays of six years or more should be treated as *per se* takings. However his dissent offers no explanation for why 6 years should be the cut-off point rather than 10 days, 10 months, or 10 years. It is worth emphasizing that we do not reject a categorical rule in this case because a 32-month moratorium is just not that harsh. Instead, we reject a categorical rule because we conclude that the *Penn Central* framework adequately directs the inquiry to the proper considerations—only one of which is the length of the delay.

a. *Palazzolo* involved a claim by the owner of waterfront land that the application of state coastal wetland regulations to his property constituted a taking. The Court found his claim ripe because it had become clear that he would *not* be allowed to develop the protected wetland portion of his property

and that he *would* be allowed to build a residence on the upland portion. The Court also held that a takings claim is not automatically barred by the fact that the owner acquires the property after the restrictive regulation is enacted: "The Takings Clause ... in certain circumstances allows a landowner to assert that a particular exercise of the State's regulatory power is so unreasonable or onerous as to compel compensation" and that it "do[es] not become less so through passage of time or title." Because the upland portion of the property retained $200,000 in development value under the wetland regulations, the Court rejected Palozzolo's categorical *Lucas* claim for "fail[ure] to establish a deprivation of all economic value," but the Court remanded for further consideration of whether there had been a taking under *Penn Central* analysis.

processes have been followed the extent of the restriction on property is not known and a regulatory taking has not yet been established...." ...

We would create a perverse system of incentives were we to hold that landowners must wait for a taking claim to ripen so that planners can make well-reasoned decisions while, at the same time, holding that those planners must compensate landowners for the delay.

Indeed, the interest in protecting the decisional process is even stronger when an agency is developing a regional plan than when it is considering a permit for a single parcel. In the proceedings involving the Lake Tahoe Basin, for example, the moratoria enabled TRPA to obtain the benefit of comments and criticisms from interested parties, such as the petitioners, during its deliberations. Since a categorical rule tied to the length of deliberations would likely create added pressure on decisionmakers to reach a quick resolution of land-use questions, it would only serve to disadvantage those landowners and interest groups who are not as organized or familiar with the planning process. Moreover, with a temporary ban on development there is a lesser risk that individual landowners will be "singled out" to bear a special burden that should be shared by the public as a whole.... At least with a moratorium there is a clear "reciprocity of advantage," ... because it protects the interests of all affected landowners against immediate construction that might be inconsistent with the provisions of the plan that is ultimately adopted.... In fact, there is reason to believe property values often will continue to increase despite a moratorium.... Such an increase makes sense in this context because property values throughout the Basin can be expected to reflect the added assurance that Lake Tahoe will remain in its pristine state. Since in some cases a 1–year moratorium may not impose a burden at all, we should not adopt a rule that assumes moratoria always force individuals to bear a special burden that should be shared by the public as a whole.

It may well be true that any moratorium that lasts for more than one year should be viewed with special skepticism. But given the fact that the District Court found that the 32 months required by TRPA to formulate the 1984 Regional Plan was not unreasonable, we could not possibly conclude that every delay of over one year is constitutionally unacceptable. Formulating a general rule of this kind is a suitable task for state legislatures.[37] In our view, the duration of the restriction is one of the important factors that a court must consider in the appraisal of a regulatory takings claim, but with respect to that factor as with respect to other factors, the "temptation to adopt what amount to *per se* rules in either direction must be resisted." *Palazzolo* ... (O'Connor, J., concurring). There may be moratoria that last longer than one year which interfere with reasonable investment-backed expectations, but ... petitioners' proposed rule is simply "too blunt an instrument," for identifying those cases.... We conclude, therefore, that the interest in "fairness and justice" will be best served by relying on the familiar *Penn Central* approach when deciding cases like this, rather than by attempting to craft a new categorical rule.

37. Several States already have statutes authorizing interim zoning ordinances with specific time limits....

Accordingly, the judgment of the Court of Appeals is affirmed.

Chief Justice Rehnquist, with whom Justice Scalia and Justice Thomas join, dissenting.

... Because the Takings Clause requires the government to pay compensation when it deprives owners of all economically viable use of their land, ... and because a ban on all development lasting almost six years does not resemble any traditional land-use planning device, I dissent.

I

... [T]he Court ignores much of the impact of respondent's conduct on petitioners.... After the adoption of the 1984 Plan, petitioners still could make no use of their land.

... The Court of Appeals is correct that the 1984 Plan did not cause petitioners' injury. But that is the right answer to the wrong question.... [T]he question is whether respondent caused petitioners' injury.

... The injunction in this case issued because the 1984 Plan did not comply with the 1980 Tahoe Regional Planning Compact (Compact) and regulations issued pursuant to the Compact. And, of course, respondent is responsible for the Compact and its regulations.

. . .

... [R]espondent was the "moving force" behind petitioners' inability to develop its land from April 1984 through the enactment of the 1987 plan. Without the environmental thresholds established by the Compact and Resolution 82–11, the 1984 Plan would have gone into effect and petitioners would have been able to build single-family residences. And it was certainly foreseeable that development projects exceeding the environmental thresholds would be prohibited; indeed, that was the very purpose of enacting the thresholds.

Because respondent caused petitioners' inability to use their land from 1981 through 1987, that is the appropriate period of time from which to consider their takings claim.

II

I now turn to determining whether a ban on all economic development lasting almost six years is a taking.... The Court does not dispute that petitioners were forced to leave their land economically idle during this period.... But the Court refuses to apply *Lucas* on the ground that the deprivation was "temporary."

Neither the Takings Clause nor our case law supports such a distinction. For one thing, a distinction between "temporary" and "permanent" prohibitions is tenuous. The "temporary" prohibition in this case that the Court finds is not a taking lasted almost six years. The "permanent" prohibition that the Court held to be a taking in *Lucas* lasted less than two years.... The "permanent" prohibition in *Lucas* lasted less than two years because the law, as it often does, changed.... Land-use regulations are not irrevocable. And the government can even abandon condemned land.... Under the Court's decision today, the takings question turns entirely on the initial label given a regulation

.... There is every incentive for government to simply label any prohibition on development "temporary," or to fix a set number of years. As in this case, this initial designation does not preclude the government from repeatedly extending the "temporary" prohibition into a long-term ban on all development. The Court now holds that such a designation by the government is conclusive even though in fact the moratorium greatly exceeds the time initially specified. Apparently, the Court would not view even a 10–year moratorium as a taking under *Lucas* because the moratorium is not "permanent."

Our opinion in [*First English*] rejects any distinction between temporary and permanent takings when a landowner is deprived of all economically beneficial use of his land.... *First English* stated that "temporary takings which, as here, deny a landowner all use of his property, are not different in kind from permanent takings, for which the Constitution clearly requires compensation." ...

More fundamentally, even if a practical distinction between temporary and permanent deprivations were plausible, to treat the two differently in terms of takings law would be at odds with the justification for the *Lucas* rule. The *Lucas* rule is derived from the fact that a "total deprivation of use is, from the landowner's point of view, the equivalent of a physical appropriation." ... The regulation in *Lucas* was the "practical equivalence" of a long-term physical appropriation, *i.e.,* a condemnation, so the Fifth Amendment required compensation. The "practical equivalence," from the landowner's point of view, of a "temporary" ban on all economic use is a forced leasehold....

... From petitioners' standpoint, what happened in this case is no different than if the government had taken a 6–year lease of their property....

Instead of acknowledging the "practical equivalence" of this case and a condemned leasehold, the Court analogizes to other areas of takings law in which we have distinguished between regulations and physical appropriations. But whatever basis there is for such distinctions in those contexts does not apply when a regulation deprives a landowner of all economically beneficial use of his land... [A] regulation denying all productive use of land does not implicate the traditional justification for differentiating between regulations and physical appropriations. In "the extraordinary circumstance when *no* productive or economically beneficial use of land is permitted," it is less likely that "the legislature is simply 'adjusting the benefits and burdens of economic life' in a manner that secures an 'average reciprocity of advantage' to everyone concerned," ... and more likely that the property "is being pressed into some form of public service under the guise of mitigating serious public harm," *Lucas* ....

The Court also reads *Lucas* as being fundamentally concerned with value, rather than with the denial of "all economically beneficial or productive use of land," .... But *Lucas* repeatedly discusses its holding as applying where "*no* productive or economically beneficial use of land is permitted." ... Moreover, the Court's position that value is the *sine qua non* of the *Lucas* rule proves too much. Surely, the land at issue in *Lucas* retained some market value based on the contingency, which soon came to fruition, that the development ban would be amended.

... The District Court found, and the Court agrees, that the moratorium "temporarily" deprived petitioners of " 'all economically viable use of their land.' " Because the rationale for the *Lucas* rule applies just as strongly in this case, the "temporary" denial of all viable use of land for six years is a taking.

III

The Court worries that applying *Lucas* here compels finding that an array of traditional, short-term, land-use planning devices are takings. But since the beginning of our regulatory takings jurisprudence, we have recognized that property rights "are enjoyed under an implied limitation." ...

When a regulation merely delays a final land use decision, we have recognized that there are other background principles of state property law that prevent the delay from being deemed a taking.... Thus, the short-term delays attendant to zoning and permit regimes are a longstanding feature of state property law and part of a landowner's reasonable investment-backed expectations....

But a moratorium prohibiting all economic use for a period of six years is not one of the longstanding, implied limitations of state property law.[4] ... Typical moratoria ... prohibit only certain categories of development, such as fast-food restaurants ..., or adult businesses ..., or all commercial development .... Such moratoria do not implicate *Lucas* because they do not deprive landowners of all economically beneficial use of their land. As for moratoria that prohibit all development, these do not have the lineage of permit and zoning requirements and thus it is less certain that property is acquired under the "implied limitation" of a moratorium prohibiting all development. Moreover, unlike a permit system in which it is expected that a project will be approved so long as certain conditions are satisfied, a moratorium that prohibits all uses is by definition contemplating a new land-use plan that would prohibit all uses.

But this case does not require us to decide as a categorical matter whether moratoria prohibiting all economic use are an implied limitation of state property law, because the duration of this "moratorium" far exceeds that of ordinary moratoria....

. . .

Because the prohibition on development of nearly six years in this case cannot be said to resemble any "implied limitation" of state property law, it is a taking that requires compensation.

. . .

4. Six years is not a "cut-off point"; it is the length involved in this case. And the "explanation" for the conclusion that there is a taking in this case is the fact that a 6-year moratorium far exceeds any moratorium authorized under background principles of state property law. This case does not require us to undertake a more exacting study of state property law and discern exactly how long a moratorium must last before it no longer can be considered an implied limitation of property ownership (assuming, that is, that a moratorium on all development is a background principle of state property law).

Justice Thomas, with whom Justice Scalia joins, dissenting.

... I write separately to address the majority's conclusion that the temporary moratorium at issue here was not a taking because it was not a "taking of 'the parcel as a whole.' "While this questionable rule has been applied to various alleged regulatory takings, it was, in my view, rejected in the context of *temporal* deprivations of property by [*First English*], which held that temporary and permanent takings "are not different in kind" when a landowner is deprived of all beneficial use of his land.... Consequently, a regulation effecting a total deprivation of the use of a so-called "temporal slice" of property is compensable under the Takings Clause unless background principles of state property law prevent it from being deemed a taking; "total deprivation of use is, from the landowner's point of view, the equivalent of a physical appropriation." *Lucas* ....

. . .

I would hold that regulations prohibiting all productive uses of property are subject to *Lucas' per se* rule, regardless of whether the property so burdened retains theoretical useful life and value if, and when, the "temporary" moratorium is lifted. To my mind, such potential future value bears on the amount of compensation due and has nothing to do with the question whether there was a taking in the first place....

3. REMEDIES FOR TAKINGS

Page 563. Add to end of Note, "Just Compensation":

One peculiar difficulty in determining the proper measure of just compensation arises when the measuring stick of the owner's loss, and the measuring stick of the fair market value of the property taken, arguably lead to different results. In Brown v. Legal Foundation of Washington, __ U.S. __, 123 S.Ct. 1406 (2003), the Court addressed a just compensation claim directed at the uniform state practice that developed rapidly after 1980 (when Congress permitted federally insured banks to begin paying interest on certain checking accounts) of requiring lawyers to place in interest-bearing trust accounts client funds they are required to hold for short periods of time, and to transfer the interest the trust accounts earn to charitable entities providing legal services for the poor. In the aggregate the interest earned on IOLTA's (Interest on Lawyer Trust Accounts) exceeded $200 million nationwide in 2001, but for each individual client the cost of distributing the interest in most cases would exceed the interest earned on the client's funds. The Court previously had ruled that the interest on a client's funds are the "property" of the client, see Phillips v. Washington Legal Foundation, discussed supra at p. 550 n.1, and this case involved whether the property had been "taken," and, if so, what compensation was due. The Court majority assumed the interest had been taken by the transfer, but it held that just compensation in this case was zero. Justice Stevens relied on the rule that "the 'just compensation' required by the Fifth Amendment is measured by the property owner's loss rather than the government's gain." He concluded that because, under the rules adopted by the Washington Supreme Court governing Washington's IOLTA program, client funds must be deposited "in non-IOLTA accounts whenever those funds could generate net earnings for the client[,]" the "owner's pecuniary loss ... is zero whenever the Washington law is obeyed...." Any "mistakes" in placing client funds in IOLTA accounts when they could have generated net income for the client would be "the consequence of the [lawyers'] incorrect private decisions rather than any state action" that "would provide ... support for a claim for compensation from the State...."

Justice Scalia, joined by Chief Justice Rehnquist and Justices Kennedy and Thomas, concluded, by contrast, that "petitioners are entitled to the fair market value of the interest generated by their funds held in interest on lawyers' trust accounts...." He relied on precedents articulating the just compensation requirement as "the amount of the market value of the property on the date it is appropriated" and emphasized that "*after* the interest has been generated in the pooled accounts ... it is at *that* point that just compensation for the taking must be assessed." (Emphasis in original). He found indefensible any reliance by the majority on the notion "that petitioners could not have earned money on their funds absent IOLTA's mandatory pooling arrangements," fearing that the Court had concluded that "the State ... may seize private property, without paying compensation, on the ground that the former owners suffered no 'net loss' because their confiscated property was created by the beneficence of a state regulatory program." (For its part the majority commented in a footnote that its "conclusion does not depend on the fact that interest 'was created by the beneficence of a state regulatory program[,' but] instead on the fact that just compensation for a net loss of zero is zero.") As for the transaction costs that would reduce the interest earned that could be returned to the client to zero or less, Justice Scalia found no precedent for the Court's "net value" approach instead of the actual interest earned, which was both what the client lost and the government gained: "[W]e have repeatedly held that just compensation is the 'market value' of the confiscated property, rather than the 'net loss' to the owner. 'Market value' is not reduced by what the owner would have lost in taxes or other exactions." In his view, the majority may have been resting "on the unfounded assumption that the State must return the interest directly to petitioners[, whereas t]he State could satisfy its obligation to pay just compensation by simply returning petitioners' money to the IOLTA account from which it was seized, leaving others to incur the accounting costs in the event petitioners seek to extract their interest from the account."

SECTION 2.   PROTECTION OF PERSONAL LIBERTIES

C.   PERSONAL AUTONOMY

Pages 644–55.   Replace Note, "Restrictions on Private Consensual Sexual Behavior"; Bowers v. Hardwick; and Romer v. Evans:

Lawrence v. Texas

___ U.S. ___, 123 S.Ct. 2472, ___ L.Ed.2d ___ (2003).

Justice Kennedy delivered the opinion of the Court.

Liberty protects the person from unwarranted government intrusions into a dwelling or other private places. In our tradition the State is not omnipresent in the home. And there are other spheres of our lives and existence, outside the home, where the State should not be a dominant presence. Freedom extends beyond spatial bounds. Liberty presumes an autonomy of self that includes freedom of thought, belief, expression, and certain intimate conduct. The instant case involves liberty of the person both in its spatial and more transcendent dimensions.

I

The question before the Court is the validity of a Texas statute making it a crime for two persons of the same sex to engage in certain intimate sexual conduct.

In Houston, Texas, officers ... respon[ding] to a reported weapons disturbance ... entered an apartment where ... Lawrence ... resided [and] observed Lawrence and another man, Tyron Garner, engaging in a sexual act. The two petitioners were arrested ... and [later] convicted ....

The complaints described their crime as "deviate sexual intercourse, namely anal sex, with a member of the same sex (man)." ... The applicable state law is Tex. Penal Code Ann. § 21.06(a) (2003). It provides: "A person commits an offense if he engages in deviate sexual intercourse with another individual of the same sex." The statute defines "[d]eviate sexual intercourse" as follows:

"(A) any contact between any part of the genitals of one person and the mouth or anus of another person; or

"(B) the penetration of the genitals or the anus of another person with an object." § 21.01(1).

... The petitioners ... were each fined $200 and assessed court costs of $141.25....

The Court of Appeals for the Texas Fourteenth District ... en banc ..., in a divided opinion, ... affirmed the convictions[,] consider[ing] our decision in *Bowers v. Hardwick,* 478 U.S. 186 (1986), to be controlling on the federal due process aspect of the case....

We granted certiorari....

. . .

II

We conclude the case should be resolved by determining whether the petitioners were free as adults to engage in the private conduct in the exercise of their liberty under the Due Process Clause of the Fourteenth Amendment to the Constitution. For this inquiry we deem it necessary to reconsider the Court's holding in *Bowers.*

. . .

The facts in *Bowers* had some similarities to the instant case.... One difference between the two cases is that the Georgia statute prohibited the conduct whether or not the participants were of the same sex, while the Texas statute ... applies only to participants of the same sex.... [In *Bowers,* t]he Court, in an opinion by Justice White, sustained the Georgia law. Chief Justice Burger and Justice Powell joined the opinion of the Court and filed separate, concurring opinions. Four Justices dissented. 478 U.S., at 199 (opinion of Blackmun, J., joined by Brennan, Marshall, and Stevens, JJ.); *id.*, at 214 (opinion of Stevens, J., joined by Brennan and Marshall, JJ.).

The Court began its substantive discussion in *Bowers* as follows: "The issue presented is whether the Federal Constitution confers a fundamental right upon homosexuals to engage in sodomy and hence invalidates the laws of the many States that still make such conduct illegal and have done so for a very long time." That statement, we now conclude, discloses the Court's own failure to appreciate the extent of the liberty at stake. To say that the issue in *Bowers* was simply the right to engage in certain sexual conduct demeans the claim the individual put forward, just as it would demean a married couple were it to be said marriage is simply about the right to have sexual intercourse. The laws involved in *Bowers* and here are, to be sure, statutes that purport to do no more than prohibit a particular sexual act. Their penalties and purposes, though, have more far-reaching consequences, touching upon the most private human conduct, sexual behavior, and in the most private of places, the home. The statutes do seek to control a personal relationship that, whether or not entitled to formal recognition in the law, is within the liberty of persons to choose without being punished as criminals.

Marriage

This, as a general rule, should counsel against attempts by the State, or a court, to define the meaning of the relationship or to set its boundaries absent injury to a person or abuse of an institution the law protects. It suffices for us to acknowledge that adults may choose to enter upon this relationship in the confines of their homes and their own private lives and still retain their dignity as free persons. When sexuality finds overt expression in intimate conduct with another person, the conduct can be but one element in a personal bond that is more enduring. The liberty protected by the Constitution allows homosexual persons the right to make this choice.

Having misapprehended the claim of liberty there presented to it, and thus stating the claim to be whether there is a fundamental right to engage in consensual sodomy, the *Bowers* Court said: "Proscriptions against that conduct have ancient roots." ... In academic writings, and in many of the scholarly *amicus* briefs filed to assist the Court in this case, there are fundamental criticisms of the historical premises relied upon by the majority and concurring opinions in *Bowers*. Brief for Cato Institute as *Amicus Curiae* 16–17; Brief for American Civil Liberties Union et al. as *Amici Curiae* 15–21; Brief for Professors of History et al. as *Amici Curiae* 3–10. We need not enter this debate in the attempt to reach a definitive historical judgment, but the following considerations counsel against adopting the definitive conclusions upon which *Bowers* placed such reliance.

[T]here is no longstanding history in this country of laws directed at homosexual conduct as a distinct matter. Beginning in colonial times there were prohibitions of sodomy derived from the English criminal laws passed in the first instance by the Reformation Parliament of 1533. The English prohibition was understood to include relations between men and women as well as relations between men and men. See, *e.g., King v. Wiseman*, 92 Eng. Rep. 774, 775 (K. B. 1718) (interpreting "mankind" in Act of 1533 as including women and girls). Nineteenth-century commentators similarly read American sodomy, buggery, and crime-against-nature statutes as criminalizing certain relations between men and women and between men and men. See, *e.g.,* 2 J. Bishop, Criminal Law § 1028 (1858); 2 J. Chitty, Criminal Law 47–50 (5th Am. ed. 1847); R. Desty, A Compendium of American Criminal Law 143 (1882); J. May, The Law of Crimes § 203 (2d ed. 1893). The absence of legal prohibitions focusing on homosexual conduct may be explained in part by noting that according to some scholars the concept of the homosexual as a distinct category of person did not emerge until the late 19th century. See, *e.g.,* J. Katz, The Invention of Heterosexuality 10 (1995); J. D'Emilio & E. Freedman, Intimate Matters: A History of Sexuality in America 121 (2d ed. 1997) ("The modern terms *homosexuality* and *heterosexuality* do not apply to an era that had not yet articulated these distinctions"). Thus early American sodomy laws were not directed at homosexuals as such but instead sought to prohibit nonprocreative sexual activity more generally. This does not suggest approval of homosexual conduct. It does tend to show that this particular form of conduct was not thought of as a separate category from like conduct between heterosexual persons.

Laws prohibiting sodomy do not seem to have been enforced against consenting adults acting in private. A substantial number of sodomy prosecutions and convictions for which there are surviving records were for predatory acts against those who could not or did not consent, as in the case of a minor or the victim of an assault. As to these, one purpose for the prohibitions was to ensure there would be no lack of coverage if a predator committed a sexual assault that did not constitute rape as defined by the criminal law. Thus the model sodomy indictments presented in a 19th-century treatise, see 2 Chitty, *supra,* at 49, addressed the predatory acts of an adult man against a minor girl or minor boy. Instead of targeting relations between consenting adults in private, 19th-century sodomy prosecutions typically involved relations between men and minor girls or minor boys, relations between adults involving force, relations between adults implicating disparity in status, or relations between men and animals.

. . . [T]he infrequency of [sodomy] prosecutions . . . makes it difficult to say that society approved of a rigorous and systematic punishment of the consensual acts committed in private and by adults. The longstanding criminal prohibition of homosexual sodomy upon which the *Bowers* decision placed such reliance is as consistent with a general condemnation of nonprocreative sex as it is with an established tradition of prosecuting acts because of their homosexual character.

. . . [F]ar from possessing 'ancient roots,' *Bowers*. . . ., American laws targeting same-sex couples did not develop until the last third of the 20th century. The reported decisions concerning the prosecution of consensual, homosexual sodomy between adults for the years 1880–1995 are not always clear in the details, but a significant number involved conduct in a public place. . . .

It was not until the 1970's that any State singled out same-sex relations for criminal prosecution, and only nine States have done so. . . . Post-*Bowers* even some of these States did not adhere to the policy of suppressing homosexual conduct. Over the course of the last decades, States with same-sex prohibitions have moved toward abolishing them. . . .

In summary, the historical grounds relied upon in *Bowers* are more complex than the majority opinion and the concurring opinion by Chief Justice Burger indicate. Their historical premises are not without doubt and, at the very least, are overstated.

It must be acknowledged, of course, that the Court in *Bowers* was making the broader point that for centuries there have been powerful voices to condemn homosexual conduct as immoral. The condemnation has been shaped by religious beliefs, conceptions of right and acceptable behavior, and respect for the traditional family. For many persons these are not trivial concerns but profound and deep convictions accepted as ethical and moral principles to which they aspire and which thus determine the course of their lives. These considerations do not answer the question before us, however. The issue is whether the majority may use the power of the State to enforce these views on the whole society through operation of the criminal law. "Our obligation is to define the liberty of all, not to mandate our own moral code." *Planned Parenthood of Southeastern Pa. v. Casey*, 505 U.S. 833, 850 (1992).

Chief Justice Burger joined the opinion for the Court in *Bowers* and further explained his views as follows: "Decisions of individuals relating to homosexual conduct have been subject to state intervention throughout the history of Western civilization. Condemnation of those practices is firmly rooted in Judeao–Christian moral and ethical standards." . . . As with Justice White's assumptions about history, scholarship casts some doubt on the sweeping nature of the statement by Chief Justice Burger as it pertains to private homosexual conduct between consenting adults. . . . In all events we think that our laws and traditions in the past half century are of most relevance here. These references show an emerging awareness that liberty gives substantial protection to adult persons in deciding how to conduct their private lives in matters pertaining to sex. "[H]istory and tradition are the starting point but not in all cases the ending point of the substantive due process inquiry." *County of Sacramento v. Lewis*, 523 U.S. 833, 857 (1998) (Kennedy, J., concurring).

This emerging recognition should have been apparent when *Bowers* was decided. In 1955 the American Law Institute promulgated the Model Penal Code and made clear that it did not recommend or provide for "criminal penalties for consensual sexual relations conducted in private." ALI, Model Penal Code § 213.2, Comment 2, p. 372 (1980). It justified its decision on three grounds: (1) The prohibitions undermined respect for the law by penalizing conduct many people engaged in; (2) the statutes regulated private conduct not harmful to others; and (3) the laws were arbitrarily enforced and thus invited the danger of blackmail. ALI, Model Penal Code, Commentary 277–280 (Tent. Draft No. 4, 1955). In 1961 Illinois changed its laws to conform to the Model Penal Code. Other States soon followed. . . .

In *Bowers* the Court referred to the fact that before 1961 all 50 States had outlawed sodomy, and that at the time of the Court's decision 24 States and the District of Columbia had sodomy laws. . . . Justice Powell pointed out that these prohibitions often were being ignored, however. Georgia, for instance, had not sought to enforce its law for decades. . . .

The sweeping references by Chief Justice Burger to the history of Western civilization and to Judeo–Christian moral and ethical standards did not take account of other authorities pointing in an opposite direction. A committee advising the British Parliament recommended in 1957 repeal of laws punishing homosexual conduct.... Parliament enacted the substance of those recommendations 10 years later....

Of even more importance, almost five years before *Bowers* was decided the European Court of Human Rights considered a case with parallels to *Bowers* and to today's case. An adult male resident in Northern Ireland alleged he was a practicing homosexual who desired to engage in consensual homosexual conduct. The laws of Northern Ireland forbade him that right. He alleged that he had been questioned, his home had been searched, and he feared criminal prosecution. The court held that the laws proscribing the conduct were invalid under the European Convention on Human Rights. *Dudgeon v. United Kingdom*, 45 Eur. Ct. H. R. (1981) & para ;52. Authoritative in all countries that are members of the Council of Europe (21 nations then, 45 nations now), the decision is at odds with the premise in *Bowers* that the claim put forward was insubstantial in our Western civilization.

In our own constitutional system the deficiencies in *Bowers* became even more apparent in the years following its announcement. The 25 States with laws prohibiting the relevant conduct referenced in the *Bowers* decision are reduced now to 13, of which 4 enforce their laws only against homosexual conduct. In those States where sodomy is still proscribed, whether for same-sex or heterosexual conduct, there is a pattern of nonenforcement with respect to consenting adults acting in private. The State of Texas admitted in 1994 that as of that date it had not prosecuted anyone under those circumstances. *State v. Morales*, 869 S. W. 2d 941, 943.

Two principal cases decided after *Bowers* cast its holding into even more doubt. In *Planned Parenthood of Southeastern Pa. v. Casey*, 505 U.S. 833 (1992), the Court reaffirmed ... that our laws and tradition afford constitutional protection to personal decisions relating to marriage, procreation, contraception, family relationships, child rearing, and education.... [W]e stated as follows:

"These matters, involving the most intimate and personal choices a person may make in a lifetime, choices central to personal dignity and autonomy, are central to the liberty protected by the Fourteenth Amendment. At the heart of liberty is the right to define one's own concept of existence, of meaning, of the universe, and of the mystery of human life. Beliefs about these matters could not define the attributes of personhood were they formed under compulsion of the State."

Persons in a homosexual relationship may seek autonomy for these purposes, just as heterosexual persons do. The decision in *Bowers* would deny them this right.

The second post-*Bowers* case of principal relevance is *Romer v. Evans*, 517 U.S. 620 (1996). There the Court struck down class-based legislation directed at homosexuals as a violation of the Equal Protection Clause. *Romer* invalidated an amendment to Colorado's constitution which named as a solitary class persons who were homosexuals, lesbians, or bisexual either by "orientation, conduct, practices or relationships," ..., and deprived them of protection under state antidiscrimination laws. We concluded that the provision was "born of animosity toward the class of persons affected" and further that it had no rational relation to a legitimate governmental purpose. . . .

As an alternative argument in this case, counsel for the petitioners and some *amici* contend that *Romer* provides the basis for declaring the Texas statute invalid under the Equal Protection Clause. That is a tenable argument, but we conclude the instant case requires us to address whether *Bowers* itself has continuing validity. Were we to hold the statute invalid under the Equal Protection Clause some might question whether a prohibition would be valid if drawn differently, say, to prohibit the conduct both between same-sex and different-sex participants.

Equality of treatment and the due process right to demand respect for conduct protected by the substantive guarantee of liberty are linked in important respects, and a decision on the latter point advances both interests. If protected conduct is made criminal and the law which does so remains unexamined for its substantive validity, its stigma might remain even if it were not enforceable as drawn for equal protection reasons. When homosexual conduct is made criminal by the law of the State, that declaration in and of itself is an invitation to subject homosexual persons to discrimination both in the public and in the private spheres. The central holding of *Bowers* has been brought in question by this case, and it should be addressed. Its continuance as precedent demeans the lives of homosexual persons.

The stigma this criminal statute imposes, moreover, is not trivial. The offense, to be sure, is but a class C misdemeanor, a minor offense in the Texas legal system. Still, it remains a criminal offense with all that imports for the dignity of the persons charged[—a] record[, . . . possible] registration [as] sex offenders . . . [in] at least four States [and] the other collateral consequences always following a conviction, such as notations on job application forms. . . .

The foundations of *Bowers* have sustained serious erosion from our recent decisions in *Casey* and *Romer*. When our precedent has been thus weakened, criticism from other sources is of greater significance. In the United States criticism of *Bowers* has been substantial and continuing, disapproving of its reasoning in all respects, not just as to its historical assumptions. See, *e.g.,* C. Fried, Order and Law: Arguing the Reagan Revolution—A Firsthand Account 81–84 (1991); R. Posner, Sex and Reason 341–350 (1992). The courts of five different States have declined to follow it in interpreting provisions in their own state constitutions parallel to the Due Process Clause of the Fourteenth Amendment. . . .

To the extent *Bowers* relied on values we share with a wider civilization, it should be noted that the reasoning and holding in *Bowers* have been rejected elsewhere. The European Court of Human Rights has followed not *Bowers* but its own decision in *Dudgeon v. United Kingdom*. . . . Other nations, too, have taken action consistent with an affirmation of the protected right of homosexual adults to engage in intimate, consensual conduct. . . . The right the petitioners seek in this case has been accepted as an integral part of human freedom in many other countries. There has been no showing that in this country the governmental interest in circumscribing personal choice is somehow more legitimate or urgent.

The doctrine of *stare decisis* is essential to the respect accorded to the judgments of the Court and to the stability of the law. It is not, however, an inexorable command.... In *Casey* we noted that when a Court is asked to overrule a precedent recognizing a constitutional liberty interest, individual or societal reliance on the existence of that liberty cautions with particular strength against reversing course.... The holding in *Bowers*, however, has not induced detrimental reliance comparable to some instances where recognized individual rights are involved. Indeed, there has been no individual or societal reliance on *Bowers* of the sort that could counsel against overturning its holding once there are compelling reasons to do so. *Bowers* itself causes uncertainty, for the precedents before and after its issuance contradict its central holding.

[margin note: ✱ no reliance]

The rationale of *Bowers* does not withstand careful analysis. In his dissenting opinion in *Bowers* Justice Stevens came to these conclusions:

"Our prior cases make two propositions abundantly clear. First, the fact that the governing majority in a State has traditionally viewed a particular practice as immoral is not a sufficient reason for upholding a law prohibiting the practice; neither history nor tradition could save a law prohibiting miscegenation from constitutional attack. Second, individual decisions by married persons, concerning the intimacies of their physical relationship, even when not intended to produce offspring, are a form of 'liberty' protected by the Due Process Clause of the Fourteenth Amendment. Moreover, this protection extends to intimate choices by unmarried as well as married persons." ...

Justice Stevens' analysis, in our view, should have been controlling in *Bowers* and should control here.

Bowers was not correct when it was decided, and it is not correct today. It ought not to remain binding precedent. *Bowers v. Hardwick* should be and now is overruled.

The present case does not involve minors. It does not involve persons who might be injured or coerced or who are situated in relationships where consent might not easily be refused. It does not involve public conduct or prostitution. It does not involve whether the government must give formal recognition to any relationship that homosexual persons seek to enter. The case does involve two adults who, with full and mutual consent from each other, engaged in sexual practices common to a homosexual lifestyle. The petitioners are entitled to respect for their private lives. The State cannot demean their existence or control their destiny by making their private sexual conduct a crime. Their right to liberty under the Due Process Clause gives them the full right to engage in their conduct without intervention of the government. "It is a promise of the Constitution that there is a realm of personal liberty which the government may not enter." *Casey*,.... The Texas statute furthers no legitimate state interest which can justify its intrusion into the personal and private life of the individual.

[margin note: no victims]

[margin note: no state interest]

Had those who drew and ratified the Due Process Clauses of the Fifth Amendment or the Fourteenth Amendment known the components of liberty in its manifold possibilities, they might have been more specific. They did not presume to have this insight. They knew times can blind us to certain truths

[margin note: 14th adapt w/ times]

and later generations can see that laws once thought necessary and proper in fact serve only to oppress. As the Constitution endures, ~~persons in every generation can invoke its principles in their own search for greater freedom.~~

[R]eversed ... and ... remanded for further proceedings not inconsistent with this opinion.

Justice O'Connor, concurring in the judgment.

... I joined *Bowers*, and do not join the Court in overruling it. Nevertheless, I agree ... that Texas' statute banning same-sex sodomy is unconstitutional. ... Rather than relying on the substantive component of the Fourteenth Amendment's Due Process Clause, as the Court does, I base my conclusion on the Fourteenth Amendment's Equal Protection Clause.

. . .

... We have consistently held ... that some objectives, such as "a bare ... desire to harm a politically unpopular group," are not legitimate state interests. *Department of Agriculture v. Moreno, ...* See also *Cleburne v. Cleburne Living Center, ...; Romer v. Evans, ...* When a law exhibits such a desire to harm a politically unpopular group, we have applied a more searching form of rational basis review to strike down such laws under the Equal Protection Clause.

We have been most likely to apply rational basis review to hold a law unconstitutional under the Equal Protection Clause where, as here, the challenged legislation inhibits personal relationships. In *Department of Agriculture v. Moreno*, for example, we held that a law preventing those households containing an individual unrelated to any other member of the household from receiving food stamps violated equal protection because the purpose of the law was to " 'discriminate against hippies.' " ... The asserted governmental interest in preventing food stamp fraud was not deemed sufficient to satisfy rational basis review. ... In *Eisenstadt v. Baird*, 405 U.S. 438, 447–455 (1972), we refused to sanction a law that discriminated between married and unmarried persons by prohibiting the distribution of contraceptives to single persons. Likewise, in *Cleburne v. Cleburne Living Center*, ... we held that it was irrational for a State to require a home for the mentally disabled to obtain a special use permit when other residences—like fraternity houses and apartment buildings—did not have to obtain such a permit. And in *Romer v. Evans*, we disallowed a state statute that "impos[ed] a broad and undifferentiated disability on a single named group"—specifically, homosexuals. ...

... Sodomy between opposite-sex partners ... is not a crime in Texas. That is, Texas treats the same conduct differently based solely on the participants. Those harmed by this law are people who have a same-sex sexual orientation and thus are more likely to engage in behavior prohibited by § 21.06.

The Texas statute makes homosexuals unequal in the eyes of the law by making particular conduct—and only that conduct—subject to criminal sanction. ...

... Texas' sodomy law brands all homosexuals as criminals, thereby making it more difficult for homosexuals to be treated in the same manner as everyone else. ...

Texas attempts to justify its law, and the effects of the law, by arguing that the statute satisfies rational basis review because it furthers the legitimate governmental interest of the promotion of morality. In *Bowers*, we held that a state law criminalizing sodomy as applied to homosexual couples did not violate substantive due process. We rejected the argument that no rational basis existed to justify the law, pointing to the government's interest in promoting morality. . . . The only question in front of the Court in *Bowers* was whether the substantive component of the Due Process Clause protected a right to engage in homosexual sodomy. . . . *Bowers* did not hold that moral disapproval of a group is a rational basis under the Equal Protection Clause to criminalize homosexual sodomy when heterosexual sodomy is not punished.

This case raises a different issue than *Bowers:* whether, under the Equal Protection Clause, moral disapproval is a legitimate state interest to justify by itself a statute that bans homosexual sodomy, but not heterosexual sodomy. It is not. Moral disapproval of this group, like a bare desire to harm the group, is an interest that is insufficient to satisfy rational basis review under the Equal Protection Clause. . . . Indeed, we have never held that moral disapproval, without any other asserted state interest, is a sufficient rationale under the Equal Protection Clause to justify a law that discriminates among groups of persons.

Moral disapproval of a group cannot be a legitimate governmental interest under the Equal Protection Clause because legal classifications must not be "drawn for the purpose of disadvantaging the group burdened by the law." . . . Texas' invocation of moral disapproval as a legitimate state interest proves nothing more than Texas' desire to criminalize homosexual sodomy. But the Equal Protection Clause prevents a State from creating "a classification of persons undertaken for its own sake." . . . And because Texas so rarely enforces its sodomy law as applied to private, consensual acts, the law serves more as a statement of dislike and disapproval against homosexuals than as a tool to stop criminal behavior. The Texas sodomy law "raise[s] the inevitable inference that the disadvantage imposed is born of animosity toward the class of persons affected." . . .

Texas argues, however, that the sodomy law does not discriminate against homosexual persons. Instead, the State maintains that the law discriminates only against homosexual conduct. While it is true that the law applies only to conduct, the conduct targeted by this law is conduct that is closely correlated with being homosexual. Under such circumstances, Texas' sodomy law is targeted at more than conduct. It is instead directed toward gay persons as a class. . . . When a State makes homosexual conduct criminal, and not "deviate sexual intercourse" committed by persons of different sexes, "that declaration in and of itself is an invitation to subject homosexual persons to discrimination both in the public and in the private spheres."

Indeed, Texas law confirms that the sodomy statute is directed toward homosexuals as a class. In Texas, calling a person a homosexual is slander *per se* because the word "homosexual" "impute[s] the commission of a crime." . . . The State has admitted that because of the sodomy law, *being* homosexual carries the presumption of being a criminal. See *State v. Morales*, 826 S. W. 2d, at 202–203 ("[T]he statute brands lesbians and gay men as criminals and thereby legally sanctions discrimination against them in a variety of ways

(Arizona)

unrelated to the criminal law"). Texas' sodomy law therefore results in discrimination against homosexuals as a class in an array of areas outside the criminal law. . . . In *Romer v. Evans,* we refused to sanction a law that singled out homosexuals "for disfavored legal status." . . . The same is true here. The Equal Protection Clause " 'neither knows nor tolerates classes among citizens.' " . . . (quoting *Plessy v. Ferguson,* 163 U.S. 537, 559 (1896) (Harlan, J. dissenting)).

Singled out for same behavior (not conduct)

A State can of course assign certain consequences to a violation of its criminal law. But the State cannot single out one identifiable class of citizens for punishment that does not apply to everyone else, with moral disapproval as the only asserted state interest for the law. . . .

Whether a sodomy law that is neutral both in effect and application, see *Yick Wo v. Hopkins,* 118 U.S. 356 (1886), would violate the substantive component of the Due Process Clause is an issue that need not be decided today. I am confident, however, that so long as the Equal Protection Clause requires a sodomy law to apply equally to the private consensual conduct of homosexuals and heterosexuals alike, such a law would not long stand in our democratic society. . . .

rational basis + moral

(

That this law as applied to private, consensual conduct is unconstitutional under the Equal Protection Clause does not mean that other laws distinguishing between heterosexuals and homosexuals would similarly fail under rational basis review. Texas cannot assert any legitimate state interest here, such as national security or preserving the traditional institution of marriage. Unlike the moral disapproval of same-sex relations—the asserted state interest in this case—other reasons exist to promote the institution of marriage beyond mere moral disapproval of an excluded group.

A law branding one class of persons as criminal solely based on the State's moral disapproval of that class and the conduct associated with that class runs contrary to the values of the Constitution and the Equal Protection Clause, under any standard of review. I therefore concur in the Court's judgment that Texas' sodomy law banning "deviate sexual intercourse" between consenting adults of the same sex, but not between consenting adults of different sexes, is unconstitutional.

Justice Scalia, with whom the Chief Justice and Justice Thomas join, dissenting.

. . . .

no SS!

. . . [N]owhere does the Court's opinion declare that homosexual sodomy is a "fundamental right" under the Due Process Clause; nor does it subject the Texas law to the standard of review that would be appropriate (strict scrutiny) if homosexual sodomy *were* a "fundamental right." Thus, while overruling the *outcome* of *Bowers,* the Court leaves strangely untouched its central legal conclusion: "[R]espondent would have us announce . . . a fundamental right to engage in homosexual sodomy. This we are quite unwilling to do." . . . Instead the Court simply describes petitioners' conduct as "an exercise of their liberty"—which it undoubtedly is—and proceeds to apply an unheard-of form of rational-basis review that will have far-reaching implications beyond this case. . . .

I

... I do not myself believe in rigid adherence to *stare decisis* in constitutional cases; but I do believe that we should be consistent rather than manipulative in invoking the doctrine.... [T]hree Members of today's majority[,] in *Planned Parenthood v. Casey* ... when *stare decisis* meant preservation of judicially invented abortion rights, [found] the widespread criticism of *Roe* ... strong reason to *reaffirm* it....

Today, however, the widespread opposition to *Bowers*, a decision resolving an issue as "intensely divisive" as the issue in *Roe*, is offered as a reason in favor of *overruling* it....

Today's approach to *stare decisis* invites us to overrule an erroneously decided precedent ... *if:* (1) its foundations have been "eroded" by subsequent decisions; (2) it has been subject to "substantial and continuing" criticism.; and (3) it has not induced "individual or societal reliance" that counsels against overturning. The problem is that *Roe* itself—which today's majority surely has no disposition to overrule—satisfies these conditions to at least the same degree as *Bowers*.

(1) ...

I do not quarrel with the Court's claim that *Romer v. Evans*, 517 U.S. 620 (1996), "eroded" the "foundations" of *Bowers'* rational-basis holding. See *Romer*, ... (Scalia, J., dissenting). But *Roe* and *Casey* have been equally "eroded" by *Washington v. Glucksberg*, 521 U.S. 702, 721 (1997), which held that *only* fundamental rights which are " 'deeply rooted in this Nation's history and tradition' " qualify for anything other than rational basis scrutiny under the doctrine of "substantive due process." *Roe* and *Casey*, of course, subjected the restriction of abortion to heightened scrutiny without even attempting to establish that the freedom to abort *was* rooted in this Nation's tradition.

(2) *Bowers*, the Court says, has been subject to "substantial and continuing [criticism], disapproving of its reasoning in all respects, not just as to its historical assumptions." Exactly what those nonhistorical criticisms are, and whether the Court even agrees with them, are left unsaid ... Of course, *Roe* too (and by extension *Casey*) had been (and still is) subject to unrelenting criticism, including criticism from the two commentators cited by the Court today....

(3) That leaves, to distinguish the rock-solid, unamendable disposition of *Roe* from the readily overrulable *Bowers*, only the third factor.... It seems to me that the "societal reliance" on the principles confirmed in *Bowers* and discarded today has been overwhelming. Countless judicial decisions and legislative enactments have relied on the ancient proposition that a governing majority's belief that certain sexual behavior is "immoral and unacceptable" constitutes a rational basis for regulation.... State laws against bigamy, same-sex marriage, adult incest, prostitution, masturbation, adultery, fornication, bestiality, and obscenity are likewise sustainable only in light of *Bowers'* validation of laws based on moral choices. Every single one of these laws is called into question by today's decision; the Court makes no effort to cabin the scope of its decision to exclude them from its holding.... The impossibility of distinguishing homosexuality from other traditional "morals" offenses is precisely why *Bowers* rejected the rational-basis challenge. "The law," it said, "is

constantly based on notions of morality, and if all laws representing essentially moral choices are to be invalidated under the Due Process Clause, the courts will be very busy indeed." ...

What a massive disruption of the current social order, therefore, the overruling of *Bowers* entails. Not so the overruling of *Roe*, which would simply have restored the regime that existed for centuries before 1973, in which the permissibility of and restrictions upon abortion were determined legislatively State-by-State. ...

. . .

II

. . .

Texas Penal Code Ann. § 21.06(a) (2003) undoubtedly imposes constraints on liberty. So do laws prohibiting prostitution, recreational use of heroin, and, for that matter, working more than 60 hours per week in a bakery. But there is no right to "liberty" under the Due Process Clause, though today's opinion repeatedly makes that claim. ... The Fourteenth Amendment *expressly allows* States to deprive their citizens of "liberty," *so long as "due process of law"* is *provided*. ...

Like Lochner= no constitutional basis

Our opinions applying the doctrine known as "substantive due process" hold that the Due Process Clause prohibits States from infringing *fundamental* liberty interests, unless the infringement is narrowly tailored to serve a compelling state interest. *Washington v. Glucksberg*, 521 U.S., at 721. ... All other liberty interests may be abridged or abrogated pursuant to a validly enacted state law if that law is rationally related to a legitimate state interest.

Bowers held, first, that criminal prohibitions of homosexual sodomy are not subject to heightened scrutiny because they do not implicate a "fundamental right" under the Due Process Clause. ... Noting that "[p]roscriptions against that conduct have ancient roots," ... that "[s]odomy was a criminal offense at common law and was forbidden by the laws of the original 13 States when they ratified the Bill of Rights," ... and that many States had retained their bans on sodomy, ... *Bowers* concluded that a right to engage in homosexual sodomy was not " 'deeply rooted in this Nation's history and tradition,' " ....

The Court today does not overrule this holding. Not once does it describe homosexual sodomy as a "fundamental right" or a "fundamental liberty interest," nor does it subject the Texas statute to strict scrutiny. Instead, ... the Court concludes that the application of Texas's statute to petitioners' conduct fails the rational-basis test, and overrules *Bowers*' holding to the contrary. ...

. . .

III

. . .

After discussing the history of antisodomy laws, the Court proclaims that, "it should be noted that there is no longstanding history in this country of laws directed at homosexual conduct as a distinct matter." This observation in no way casts into doubt the "definitive [historical] conclusion," ... on which

Bowers relied: that our Nation has a longstanding history of laws prohibiting *sodomy in general*—regardless of whether it was performed by same-sex or opposite-sex couples:

> "It is obvious to us that neither of these formulations would extend a fundamental right to homosexuals to engage in acts of consensual sodomy. Proscriptions against that conduct have ancient roots. *Sodomy* was a criminal offense at common law and was forbidden by the laws of the original 13 States when they ratified the Bill of Rights. In 1868, when the Fourteenth Amendment was ratified, all but 5 of the 37 States in the Union had *criminal sodomy laws*. In fact, until 1961, all 50 States outlawed *sodomy*, and today, 24 States and the District of Columbia continue to provide criminal penalties for *sodomy* performed in private and between consenting adults. Against this background, to claim that a right to engage in such conduct is "deeply rooted in this Nation's history and tradition" or "implicit in the concept of ordered liberty" is, at best, facetious." ... (... emphasis added).

It is (as *Bowers* recognized) entirely irrelevant whether the laws in our long national tradition criminalizing homosexual sodomy were "directed at homosexual conduct as a distinct matter." Whether homosexual sodomy was prohibited by a law targeted at same-sex sexual relations or by a more general law prohibiting both homosexual and heterosexual sodomy, the only relevant point is that it *was criminalized*—which suffices to establish that homosexual sodomy is not a right "deeply rooted in our Nation's history and tradition." The Court today agrees that homosexual sodomy was criminalized and thus does not dispute the facts on which *Bowers actually* relied.

. . .

[T]he Court ... says: "[W]e think that our laws and traditions in the past half century are of most relevance here. These references show *an emerging awareness* that liberty gives substantial protection to adult persons in deciding how to conduct their private lives *in matters pertaining to sex*." (emphasis added). Apart from the fact that such an "emerging awareness" does not establish a "fundamental right," the statement is factually false. States continue to prosecute all sorts of crimes by adults "in matters pertaining to sex": prostitution, adult incest, adultery, obscenity, and child pornography. Sodomy laws, too, have been enforced "in the past half century," in which there have been 134 reported cases involving prosecutions for consensual, adult, homosexual sodomy.... In relying ... upon the American Law Institute's 1955 recommendation not to criminalize " 'consensual sexual relations conducted in private,' " the Court ignores the fact that this recommendation was "a point of resistance in most of the states that considered adopting the Model Penal Code." Gaylaw 159.

MPL resisted by States

In any event, an "emerging awareness" is by definition not "deeply rooted in this Nation's history and tradition[s]," as we have said "fundamental right" status requires. Constitutional entitlements do not spring into existence because some States choose to lessen or eliminate criminal sanctions on certain behavior. Much less do they spring into existence, as the Court seems to believe, because *foreign nations* decriminalize conduct.... The Court's discus-

"spring into existence"

sion of these foreign views (ignoring, of course, the many countries that have retained criminal prohibitions on sodomy) is therefore meaningless dicta. . . .

IV

I turn now to the ground on which the Court squarely rests its holding: the contention that there is no rational basis for the law here under attack. This proposition is so out of accord with our jurisprudence—indeed, with the jurisprudence of *any* society we know—that it requires little discussion.

The Texas statute undeniably seeks to further the belief of its citizens that certain forms of sexual behavior are "immoral and unacceptable," *Bowers* . . .—the same interest furthered by criminal laws against fornication, bigamy, adultery, adult incest, bestiality, and obscenity. *Bowers* held that this *was* a legitimate state interest. The Court today reaches the opposite conclusion. . . . This effectively decrees the end of all morals legislation. If, as the Court asserts, the promotion of majoritarian sexual morality is not even a *legitimate* state interest, none of the above-mentioned laws can survive rational-basis review.

V

Finally, I turn to petitioners' equal-protection challenge, which no Member of the Court save Justice O'Connor . . . embraces: On its face § 21.06(a) applies equally to all persons. Men and women, heterosexuals and homosexuals, are all subject to its prohibition of deviate sexual intercourse with someone of the same sex. To be sure, § 21.06 does distinguish between the sexes insofar as concerns the partner with whom the sexual acts are performed: men can violate the law only with other men, and women only with other women. But this cannot itself be a denial of equal protection, since it is precisely the same distinction regarding partner that is drawn in state laws prohibiting marriage with someone of the same sex while permitting marriage with someone of the opposite sex.

The objection is made, however, that the antimiscegenation laws invalidated in *Loving v. Virginia*, 388 U.S. 1, 8 (1967), similarly were applicable to whites and blacks alike, and only distinguished between the races insofar as the *partner* was concerned. In *Loving*, however, we correctly applied heightened scrutiny, rather than the usual rational-basis review, because the Virginia statute was "designed to maintain White Supremacy." . . . A racially discriminatory purpose is always sufficient to subject a law to strict scrutiny. . . . No purpose to discriminate against men or women as a class can be gleaned from the Texas law, so rational-basis review applies. That review is readily satisfied here by the same rational basis that satisfied it in *Bowers*—society's belief that certain forms of sexual behavior are "immoral and unacceptable," . . . . This is the same justification that supports many other laws regulating sexual behavior that make a distinction based upon the identity of the partner—for example, laws against adultery, fornication, and adult incest, and laws refusing to recognize homosexual marriage.

Justice O'Connor argues that the discrimination in this law which must be justified is not its discrimination with regard to the sex of the partner but its discrimination with regard to the sexual proclivity of the principal actor. . . .

Of course the same could be said of any law. A law against public nudity targets "the conduct that is closely correlated with being a nudist," and hence "is targeted at more than conduct"; it is "directed toward nudists as a class." But ... [e]ven if the Texas law *does* deny equal protection to "homosexuals as a class," that denial *still* does not need to be justified by anything more than a rational basis, which our cases show is satisfied by the enforcement of traditional notions of sexual morality.

Justice O'Connor simply decrees application of "a more searching form of rational basis review" to the Texas statute. The cases she cites do not recognize such a standard, and reach their conclusions only after finding, as required by conventional rational-basis analysis, that no conceivable legitimate state interest supports the classification at issue.... [She] must at least mean, however, that laws exhibiting " 'a ... desire to harm a politically unpopular group' " are invalid *even though* there may be a conceivable rational basis to support them.

This reasoning leaves on pretty shaky grounds state laws limiting marriage to opposite-sex couples. Justice O'Connor seeks to preserve them by the conclusory statement that "preserving the traditional institution of marriage" is a legitimate state interest. But "preserving the traditional institution of marriage" is just a kinder way of describing the State's *moral disapproval* of same-sex couples. Texas's interest in § 21.06 could be recast in similarly euphemistic terms: "preserving the traditional sexual mores of our society." In the jurisprudence Justice O'Connor has seemingly created, judges can validate laws by characterizing them as "preserving the traditions of society" (good); or invalidate them by characterizing them as "expressing moral disapproval" (bad).

* * *

Today's opinion is the product of a Court, which is the product of a law-profession culture, that has largely signed on to the so-called homosexual agenda, by which I mean the agenda promoted by some homosexual activists directed at eliminating the moral opprobrium that has traditionally attached to homosexual conduct. ...

One of the most revealing statements in today's opinion is the Court's grim warning that the criminalization of homosexual conduct is "an invitation to subject homosexual persons to discrimination both in the public and in the private spheres." It is clear from this that the Court has taken sides in the culture war, departing from its role of assuring, as neutral observer, that the democratic rules of engagement are observed. Many Americans do not want persons who openly engage in homosexual conduct as partners in their business, as scoutmasters for their children, as teachers in their children's schools, or as boarders in their home. They view this as protecting themselves and their families from a lifestyle that they believe to be immoral and destructive. The Court views it as "discrimination" which it is the function of our judgments to deter. So imbued is the Court with the law profession's anti-anti-homosexual culture, that it is seemingly unaware that the attitudes of that culture are not obviously "mainstream"; that in most States what the Court calls "discrimination" against those who engage in homosexual acts is perfectly legal; that proposals to ban such "discrimination" under Title VII have repeatedly been rejected by Congress, see Employment Non–Discrimination Act of 1994, S.

2238, 103d Cong., 2d Sess. (1994); Civil Rights Amendments, H. R. 5452, 94th Cong., 1st Sess. (1975); that in some cases such "discrimination" is *mandated* by federal statute, see 10 U.S.C. § 654(b)(1) (mandating discharge from the armed forces of any service member who engages in or intends to engage in homosexual acts); and that in some cases such "discrimination" is a constitutional right, see *Boy Scouts of America v. Dale*, 530 U.S. 640 (2000).

Court activism

Let me be clear that I have nothing against homosexuals, or any other group, promoting their agenda through normal democratic means.... But persuading one's fellow citizens is one thing, and imposing one's views in absence of democratic majority will is something else. I would no more *require* a State to criminalize homosexual acts—or, for that matter, display *any* moral disapprobation of them—than I would *forbid* it to do so. What Texas has chosen to do is well within the range of traditional democratic action, and its hand should not be stayed through the invention of a brand-new "constitutional right" by a Court that is impatient of democratic change. It is indeed true that "later generations can see that laws once thought necessary and proper in fact serve only to oppress"; and when that happens, later generations can repeal those laws. ...

One of the benefits of leaving regulation of this matter to the people rather than to the courts is that the people, unlike judges, need not carry things to their logical conclusion. The people may feel that their disapprobation of homosexual conduct is strong enough to disallow homosexual marriage, but not strong enough to criminalize private homosexual acts—and may legislate accordingly. The Court today pretends that it possesses a similar freedom of action, so that that we need not fear judicial imposition of homosexual marriage, as has recently occurred in Canada.... Do not believe it.... Today's opinion dismantles the structure of constitutional law that has permitted a distinction to be made between heterosexual and homosexual unions, insofar as formal recognition in marriage is concerned. If moral disapprobation of homosexual conduct is "no legitimate state interest" for purposes of proscribing that conduct; and if, as the Court coos (casting aside all pretense of neutrality), "[w]hen sexuality finds overt expression in intimate conduct with another person, the conduct can be but one element in a personal bond that is more enduring"; what justification could there possibly be for denying the benefits of marriage to homosexual couples exercising "[t]he liberty protected by the Constitution"? Surely not the encouragement of procreation, since the sterile and the elderly are allowed to marry. This case "does not involve" the issue of homosexual marriage only if one entertains the belief that principle and logic have nothing to do with the decisions of this Court....

. . .

Justice Thomas, dissenting.

... I write separately to note that the law before the Court today "is ... uncommonly silly." *Griswold v. Connecticut*, 381 U.S. 479, 527 (1965) (Stewart, J., dissenting). If I were a member of the Texas Legislature, I would vote to repeal it. Punishing someone for expressing his sexual preference through noncommercial consensual conduct with another adult does not appear to be a worthy way to expend valuable law enforcement resources.

Notwithstanding this, I recognize that as a member of this Court I am not empowered to help petitioners and others similarly situated.... [J]ust like Justice Stewart, I "can find [neither in the Bill of Rights nor any other part of the Constitution a] general right of privacy," ..., or as the Court terms it today, the "liberty of the person both in its spatial and more transcendent dimensions."

CHAPTER 10

THE EQUAL PROTECTION CLAUSE AND THE REVIEW OF THE REASONABLENESS OF LEGISLATION

SECTION 3. SUSPECT CLASSIFICATIONS

C. CLASSIFICATIONS BASED ON GENDER

Page 780. Replace Miller v. Albright with the following:

Nguyen v. Immigration and Naturalization Service

533 U.S. 53, 121 S.Ct. 2053, 150 L.Ed.2d 115 (2001).

Justice Kennedy delivered the opinion of the Court.

... Title 8 U.S.C. § 1409 governs the acquisition of United States citizenship by persons born to one United States citizen parent and one noncitizen parent when the parents are unmarried and the child is born outside of the United States or its possessions. The statute imposes different requirements for the child's acquisition of citizenship depending upon whether the citizen parent is the mother or the father. The question before us is whether the statutory distinction is consistent with the equal protection guarantee embedded in the Due Process Clause of the Fifth Amendment.

I

Petitioner Tuan Ahn Nguyen was born in Saigon, Vietnam, on September 11, 1969, to copetitioner Joseph Boulais and a Vietnamese citizen. Boulais and Nguyen's mother were not married. Boulais always has been a citizen of the United States, and he was in Vietnam under the employ of a corporation.... In June 1975, Nguyen, then almost six ..., came to the United States. He became a lawful permanent resident and was raised in Texas by Boulais.

In 1992, when Nguyen was 22, he pleaded guilty in a Texas state court to two counts of sexual assault on a child. He was sentenced to eight years in prison on each count. Three years later, the United States Immigration and Naturalization Service (INS) initiated deportation proceedings against Nguyen as an alien who had been convicted of two crimes involving moral turpitude, as well as an aggravated felony.... Though later he would change his position and argue he was a United States citizen, Nguyen testified at his deportation

68

hearing that he was a citizen of Vietnam. The Immigration Judge found him deportable.

Nguyen appealed to the Board of Immigration of Appeals and, in 1998, while the matter was pending, his father obtained an order of parentage from a state court, based on DNA testing. By this time, Nguyen was 28 years old. The Board dismissed Nguyen's appeal, rejecting his claim to United States citizenship because he had failed to establish compliance with 8 U.S.C. § 1409(a), which sets forth the requirements for one who was born out of wedlock and abroad to a citizen father and a noncitizen mother.

[On appeal] the Fifth Circuit ... rejected the constitutional challenge to § 1409(a).

. . .

... We [also] hold that § 1409(a) is consistent with the constitutional guarantee of equal protection.

II

[A] child born outside the United States ... to parents who are married, one of whom is a citizen and the other of whom is an alien, ... is also a citizen if, before the birth, the citizen parent had been physically present in the United States for a total of five years, at least two of which were after the parent turned 14 years of age.

As to an individual born under the same circumstances, save that the parents are unwed, § 1409(a) sets forth the following requirements where the father is the citizen parent and the mother is an alien:

"(1) a blood relationship between the person and the father is established by clear and convincing evidence,

"(2) the father had the nationality of the United States at the time of the person's birth,

"(3) the father (unless deceased) has agreed in writing to provide financial support for the person until the person reaches the age of 18 years, and

"(4) while the person is under the age of 18 years—

"(A) the person is legitimated under the law of the person's residence or domicile,

"(B) the father acknowledges paternity of the person in writing under oath, or

"(C) the paternity of the person is established by adjudication of a competent court."

In addition, § 1409(a) incorporates ..., as to the citizen parent, the [same] residency requirement.

. . .

When the citizen parent of the child born abroad and out of wedlock is the child's mother, the requirements for the transmittal of citizenship are described in § 1409(c):

"(c) Notwithstanding the provision of subsection (a) of this section, a person born ... outside the United States and out of wedlock shall be held to have acquired at birth the nationality status of his mother, if the mother had the nationality of the United States at the time of such person's birth, and if the mother had previously been physically present in the United States or one of its outlying possessions for a continuous period of one year...."

Section 1409(a) thus imposes a set of requirements on the children of citizen fathers born abroad and out of wedlock to a noncitizen mother that are not imposed under like circumstances when the citizen parent is the mother. All concede the requirements of §§ 1409(a)(3) and (a)(4), relating to a citizen father's acknowledgment of a child while he is under 18, were not satisfied in this case. We need not discuss § 1409(a)(3), however[, given that] our ruling respecting § 1409(a)(4) is dispositive of the case. As an individual seeking citizenship under § 1409(a) must meet all of its preconditions, the failure to satisfy § 1409(a)(4) renders Nguyen ineligible for citizenship.

For a gender-based classification to withstand equal protection scrutiny, it must be established " 'at least that the [challenged] classification serves "important governmental objectives and that the discriminatory means employed" are "substantially related to the achievement of those objectives." ' " United States v. Virginia.... For reasons to follow, we conclude § 1409 satisfies this standard. Given that determination, we need not decide whether some lesser degree of scrutiny pertains because the statute implicates Congress' immigration and naturalization power....

Before considering the important governmental interests advanced by the statute, two observations concerning the operation of the provision are in order. First, a citizen mother expecting a child and living abroad has the right to reenter the United States so the child can be born here and be a 14th Amendment citizen. From one perspective, then, the statute simply ensures equivalence between two expectant mothers who are citizens abroad if one chooses to reenter for the child's birth and the other chooses not to return, or does not have the means to do so. This equivalence is not a factor if the single citizen parent living abroad is the father. For, unlike the unmarried mother, the unmarried father as a general rule cannot control where the child will be born.

Second, although § 1409(a)(4) requires certain conduct to occur before the child of a citizen father, born out of wedlock and abroad, reaches 18 years of age, it imposes no limitations on when an individual who qualifies under the statute can claim citizenship. The statutory treatment of citizenship is identical in this respect whether the citizen parent is the mother or the father. A person born to a citizen parent of either gender may assert citizenship, assuming compliance with statutory preconditions, regardless of his or her age. And while the conditions necessary for a citizen mother to transmit citizenship under § 1409(c) exist at birth, citizen fathers and/or their children have 18 years to satisfy the requirements of § 1409(a)(4)....

The statutory distinction relevant in this case, then, is that § 1409(a)(4) requires one of three affirmative steps to be taken if the citizen parent is the father, but not if the citizen parent is the mother: legitimation; a declaration of paternity under oath by the father; or a court order of paternity. Congress' decision to impose requirements on unmarried fathers that differ from those on unmarried mothers is based on the significant difference between their respective relationships to the potential citizen at the time of birth. Specifically, the imposition of the requirement for a paternal relationship, but not a maternal one, is justified by two important governmental objectives. . . .

The first governmental interest to be served is the importance of assuring that a biological parent-child relationship exists. In the case of the mother, the relation is verifiable from the birth itself. The mother's status is documented in most instances by the birth certificate or hospital records and the witnesses who attest to her having given birth.

In the case of the father, the uncontestable fact is that he need not be present at the birth. . . . If he is present, furthermore, that circumstance is not incontrovertible proof of fatherhood. Fathers and mothers are not similarly situated with regard to the proof of biological parenthood. The imposition of a different set of rules for making that legal determination with respect to fathers and mothers is neither surprising nor troublesome from a constitutional perspective. . . . Section 1409(a)(4)'s provision of three options for a father seeking to establish paternity—legitimation, paternity oath, and court order of paternity—is designed to ensure an acceptable documentation of paternity.

Petitioners argue that the requirement of § 1409(a)(1), that a father provide clear and convincing evidence of parentage, is sufficient to achieve the end of establishing paternity, given the sophistication of modern DNA tests. . . . Section 1409(a)(1) does not actually mandate a DNA test, however. The Constitution, moreover, does not require that Congress elect one particular mechanism from among many possible methods of establishing paternity, even if that mechanism arguably might be the most scientifically advanced method. With respect to DNA testing, the expense, reliability, and availability of such testing in various parts of the world may have been of particular concern to Congress. . . . The requirement of § 1409(a)(4) represents a reasonable conclusion by the legislature that the satisfaction of one of several alternatives will suffice to establish the blood link between father and child required as a predicate to the child's acquisition of citizenship. . . . Given the proof of motherhood that is inherent in birth itself, it is unremarkable that Congress did not require the same affirmative steps of mothers.

Finally, to require Congress to speak without reference to the gender of the parent with regard to its objective of ensuring a blood tie between parent and child would be to insist on a hollow neutrality. . . . Congress could have required both mothers and fathers to prove parenthood within 30 days or, for that matter, 18 years, of the child's birth. . . . Given that the mother is always present at birth, but that the father need not be, the facially neutral rule would sometimes require fathers to take additional affirmative steps which would not be required of mothers, whose names will appear on the birth certificate as a result of their presence at the birth, and who will have the benefit of witnesses to the birth to call upon. The issue is not the use of gender specific terms instead of neutral ones. Just as neutral terms can mask discrimination that is unlawful, gender specific terms can mark a permissible distinction. The equal protection question is whether the distinction is lawful. Here, the use of gender specific terms takes into account a biological difference between the parents. The differential treatment is inherent in a sensible statutory scheme, given the unique relationship of the mother to the event of birth.

The second important governmental interest furthered in a substantial manner by § 1409(a)(4) is the determination to ensure that the child and the citizen parent have some demonstrated opportunity or potential to develop not just a relationship that is recognized, as a formal matter, by the law, but one that consists of the real, everyday ties that provide a connection between child and citizen parent and, in turn, the United States. . . . In the case of a citizen mother and a child born overseas, the opportunity for a meaningful relationship between citizen parent and child inheres in the very event of birth, an event so often critical to our constitutional and statutory understandings of citizenship. The mother knows that the child is in being and is hers and has an initial point of contact with him. There is at least an opportunity for mother and child to develop a real, meaningful relationship.

The same opportunity does not result from the event of birth, as a matter of biological inevitability, in the case of the unwed father. Given the 9–month interval between conception and birth, it is not always certain that a father will know that a child was conceived, nor is it always clear that even the mother will be sure of the father's identity. This fact takes on particular significance in the case of a child born overseas and out of wedlock. One concern in this context has always been with young people, men for the most part, who are on duty with the Armed Forces in foreign countries. . . .

[T]he passage of time has produced additional and even more substantial grounds to justify the statutory distinction. The ease of travel and the willingness of Americans to visit foreign countries have resulted in numbers of trips abroad that must be of real concern when we contemplate the prospect of accepting petitioners' argument, which would mandate, contrary to Congress' wishes, citizenship by male parentage subject to no condition save the father's previous length of residence in this country. In 1999 alone, Americans made almost 25 million trips abroad, excluding trips to Canada and Mexico. . . . Visits to Canada and Mexico add to this figure almost 34 million additional visits. . . .

Principles of equal protection do not require Congress to ignore this reality. To the contrary, these facts demonstrate the critical importance of the Government's interest in ensuring some opportunity for a tie between citizen father and foreign born child which is a reasonable substitute for the opportunity manifest between mother and child at the time of birth. Indeed, especially in light of the number of Americans who take short sojourns abroad, the prospect that a father might not even know of the conception is a realistic possibility. . . . Even if a father knows of the fact of conception, moreover, it does not follow that he will be present at the birth of the child. Thus, unlike the case of the mother, there is no assurance that the father and his biological child will ever meet. Without an initial point of contact with the child by a father who knows the child is his own, there is no opportunity for father and child to begin a relationship. Section 1409 takes the unremarkable step of ensuring that such an opportunity, inherent in the event of birth as to the mother-child relationship, exists between father and child before citizenship is conferred upon the latter.

The importance of the governmental interest at issue here is too profound to be satisfied merely by conducting a DNA test. . . . [S]cientific proof of biological paternity does nothing, by itself, to ensure contact between father and child during the child's minority.

Congress is well within its authority in refusing, absent proof of at least the opportunity for the development of a relationship between citizen parent and child, to commit this country to embracing a child as a citizen entitled as of birth to the full protection of the United States, to the absolute right to enter its borders, and to full participation in the political process. If citizenship is to be conferred by the unwitting means petitioners urge, so that its acquisition abroad bears little relation to the realities of the child's own ties and allegiances, it is for Congress, not this Court, to make that determination. Congress has ... instead chosen ... to ensure in the case of father and child the opportunity for a relationship to develop, an opportunity which the event of birth itself provides for the mother and child. It should be unobjectionable for Congress to require some evidence of a minimal opportunity for the development of a relationship with the child in terms the male can fulfill.

While the INS' brief contains statements indicating the governmental interest we here describe, ... it suggests other interests as well. Statements from the government's brief are not conclusive as to the objects of the statute, however, as we are concerned with the objectives of Congress, not those of the INS. We ascertain the purpose of a statute by drawing logical conclusions from its text, structure, and operation.

Petitioners and their amici argue in addition that, rather than fulfilling an important governmental interest, § 1409 merely embodies a gender-based stereotype. Although the above discussion should illustrate that, contrary to petitioners' assertions, § 1409 addresses an undeniable difference in the circumstance of the parents at the time a child is born, it should be noted, furthermore, that the difference does not result from some stereotype, defined as a frame of mind resulting from irrational or uncritical analysis. There is nothing irrational or improper in the recognition that at the moment of birth— a critical event in the statutory scheme and in the whole tradition of citizenship law—the mother's knowledge of the child and the fact of parenthood have been established in a way not guaranteed in the case of the unwed father. This is not a stereotype....

2

Having concluded that facilitation of a relationship between parent and child is an important governmental interest, the question remains whether the means Congress chose to further its objective—the imposition of certain additional requirements upon an unwed father—substantially relate to that end. Under this test, the means Congress adopted must be sustained.

First, it should be unsurprising that Congress decided to require that an opportunity for a parent-child relationship occur during the formative years of the child's minority....

Second, petitioners ... assert that, although a mother will know of her child's birth, "knowledge that one is a parent, no matter how it is acquired, does not guarantee a relationship with one's child." ... They thus maintain that the imposition of the additional requirements of § 1409(a)(4) only on the children of citizen fathers must reflect a stereotype that women are more likely than men to actually establish a relationship with their children....

[handwritten margin note: do the means substantially relate to facilitation of a relationship between parent and child]

This line of argument misconceives the nature of both the governmental interest at issue and the manner in which we examine statutes alleged to violate equal protection. As to the former, Congress would of course be entitled to advance the interest of ensuring an actual, meaningful relationship in every case before citizenship is conferred. Or Congress could excuse compliance with the formal requirements when an actual father-child relationship is proved. It did neither here, perhaps because of the subjectivity, intrusiveness, and difficulties of proof that might attend an inquiry into any particular bond or tie. Instead, Congress enacted an easily administered scheme to promote the different but still substantial interest of ensuring at least an opportunity for a parent-child relationship to develop. Petitioners' argument confuses the means and ends of the equal protection inquiry; § 1409(a)(4) should not be invalidated because Congress elected to advance an interest that is less demanding to satisfy than some other alternative.

Even if one conceives of the interest Congress pursues as the establishment of a real, practical relationship of considerable substance between parent and child in every case, as opposed simply to ensuring the potential for the relationship to begin, petitioners' misconception of the nature of the equal protection inquiry is fatal to their argument. A statute meets the equal protection standard we here apply so long as it is " 'substantially related to the achievement of' " the governmental objective in question.... It is almost axiomatic that a policy which seeks to foster the opportunity for meaningful parent-child bonds to develop has a close and substantial bearing on the governmental interest in the actual formation of that bond. None of our gender-based classification equal protection cases have required that the statute under consideration must be capable of achieving its ultimate objective in every instance.

In this difficult context of conferring citizenship on vast numbers of persons, the means adopted by Congress are in substantial furtherance of important governmental objectives. The fit between the means and the important end is "exceedingly persuasive." ...

C

In analyzing § 1409(a)(4), we are mindful that the obligation it imposes with respect to the acquisition of citizenship by the child of a citizen father is minimal.... Congress has not erected inordinate and unnecessary hurdles to the conferral of citizenship on the children of citizen fathers in furthering its important objectives. Only the least onerous of the three options provided for in § 1409(a)(4) must be satisfied.... The statute can be satisfied on the day of birth, or the next day, or for the next 18 years. In this case, the unfortunate, even tragic, circumstance is that Boulais did not pursue, or perhaps did not know of, these simple steps and alternatives. Any omission, however, does not nullify the statutory scheme.

Section 1409(a), moreover, is not the sole means by which the child of a citizen father can attain citizenship. An individual who fails to comply with § 1409(a), but who has substantial ties to the United States, can seek citizenship in his or her own right, rather than via reliance on ties to a citizen parent.... This option now may be foreclosed to Nguyen, but any bar is due to the serious nature of his criminal offenses not to an equal protection denial or to any supposed rigidity or harshness in the citizenship laws.

IV

... In light of our holding that there is no equal protection violation, ... we need not assess the implications of statements in our earlier cases regarding the wide deference afforded to Congress in the exercise of its immigration and naturalization power. See, e.g., Fiallo v. Bell, 430 U.S. 787, 792–793, and n. 4. . . .

V

To fail to acknowledge even our most basic biological differences—such as the fact that a mother must be present at birth but the father need not be—risks making the guarantee of equal protection superficial, and so disserving it. Mechanistic classification of all our differences as stereotypes would operate to obscure those misconceptions and prejudices that are real. The distinction embodied in the statutory scheme here at issue is not marked by misconception and prejudice, nor does it show disrespect for either class. The difference between men and women in relation to the birth process is a real one, and the principle of equal protection does not forbid Congress to address the problem at hand in a manner specific to each gender.

The judgment of the Court of Appeals is

Affirmed.[a]

Justice O'Connor, with whom Justice Souter, Justice Ginsburg, and Justice Breyer join, dissenting.

... Because the ... INS has not shown an exceedingly persuasive justification for the sex-based classification embodied in 8 U.S.C. § 1409(a)(4)—i.e., because it has failed to establish at least that the classification substantially relates to the achievement of important governmental objectives—I would reverse the judgment of the Court of Appeals.

. . .

II

. . .

[T]he majority hypothesizes about the interests served by the statute and fails adequately to inquire into the actual purposes of § 1409(a)(4). The Court also does not always explain adequately the importance of the interests that it claims to be served by the provision. The majority also fails carefully to consider whether the sex-based classification is being used impermissibly "as a 'proxy for other, more germane bases of classification,'" Mississippi Univ. for Women, ... and instead casually dismisses the relevance of available sex-neutral alternatives. And, contrary to the majority's conclusion, the fit between the means and ends of § 1409(a)(4) is far too attenuated for the provision to survive heightened scrutiny. In all, the majority opinion represents far less

a. Justice Scalia's concurring opinion, joined by Justice Thomas, is omitted.

than the rigorous application of heightened scrutiny that our precedents require.

A

According to the Court, "[t]he first governmental interest to be served is the importance of assuring that a biological parent-child relationship exists." The majority does not elaborate on the importance of this interest, which presumably lies in preventing fraudulent conveyances of citizenship. Nor does the majority demonstrate that this is one of the actual purposes of § 1409(a)(4)....

The gravest defect in the Court's reliance on this interest, however, is the insufficiency of the fit between § 1409(a)(4)'s discriminatory means and the asserted end. Section 1409(c) imposes no particular burden of proof on mothers wishing to convey citizenship to their children. By contrast, § 1409(a)(1), which petitioners do not challenge before this Court, requires that "a blood relationship between the person and the father [be] established by clear and convincing evidence." ... It is difficult to see what § 1409(a)(4) accomplishes in furtherance of "assuring that a biological parent-child relationship exists" that § 1409(a)(1) does not achieve on its own. The virtual certainty of a biological link that modern DNA testing affords reinforces the sufficiency of § 1409(a)(1)....

It is also difficult to see how § 1409(a)(4)'s limitation of the time allowed for obtaining proof of paternity substantially furthers the assurance of a blood relationship. Modern DNA testing, in addition to providing accuracy unmatched by other methods of establishing a biological link, essentially negates the evidentiary significance of the passage of time. Moreover, the application of § 1409(a)(1)'s "clear and convincing evidence" requirement can account for any effect that the passage of time has on the quality of the evidence.

... No one argues that § 1409(a)(1) mandates a DNA test. Legitimation or an adjudication of paternity, see §§ 1409(a)(4)(A), (C), may well satisfy the "clear and convincing" standard of § 1409(a)(1). (Satisfaction of § 1409(a)(4) by a written acknowledgment of paternity under oath, ... would seem to do little, if anything, to advance the assurance of a blood relationship, further stretching the means-end fit in this context). Likewise, petitioners' argument does not depend on the idea that one particular method of establishing paternity is constitutionally required. Petitioners' argument rests instead on the fact that, if the goal is to obtain proof of paternity, the existence of a statutory provision governing such proof, coupled with the efficacy and availability of modern technology, is highly relevant to the sufficiency of the tailoring between § 1409(a)(4)'s sex-based classification and the asserted end. Because § 1409(a)(4) adds little to the work that § 1409(a)(1) does on its own, it is difficult to say that § 1409(a)(4) "substantially furthers" an important governmental interest....

The majority concedes that Congress could achieve the goal of assuring a biological parent-child relationship in a sex-neutral fashion, but then, in a surprising turn, dismisses the availability of sex-neutral alternatives as irrelevant. As the Court suggests, "Congress could have required both mothers and fathers to prove parenthood within 30 days or, for that matter, 18 years, of the child's birth." ... As the majority seems implicitly to acknowledge at one point, a mother will not always have formal legal documentation of birth because a birth certificate may not issue or may subsequently be lost. Conversely, a father's name may well appear on a birth certificate. While it is doubtless true that a mother's blood relation to a child is uniquely "verifiable from the birth itself" to those present at birth, the majority has not shown that a mother's birth relation is uniquely verifiable by the INS, much less that any greater verifiability warrants a sex-based, rather than a sex-neutral, statute.

In our prior cases, the existence of comparable or superior sex-neutral alternatives has been a powerful reason to reject a sex-based classification.... The majority, however, turns this principle on its head by denigrating as "hollow" the very neutrality that the law requires.... While the majority trumpets the availability of superior sex-neutral alternatives as confirmation of § 1409(a)(4)'s validity, our precedents demonstrate that this fact is a decided strike against the law. Far from being "hollow," the avoidance of gratuitous sex-based distinctions is the hallmark of equal protection....

... [I]t will likely be easier for mothers to satisfy a sex-neutral proof of parentage requirement. But facially neutral laws that have a disparate impact are a different animal for purposes of constitutional analysis than laws that specifically provide for disparate treatment. We have long held that the differential impact of a facially neutral law does not trigger heightened scrutiny, see, e.g., Washington v. Davis, 426 U.S. 229 (1976), whereas we apply heightened scrutiny to laws that facially classify individuals on the basis of their sex....

. . .

B

... The majority's focus on "some demonstrated opportunity or potential to develop ... real, everyday ties," ... appears to be the type of hypothesized rationale that is insufficient under heightened scrutiny. ...

. . .

Assuming, as the majority does, that Congress was actually concerned about ensuring a "demonstrated opportunity" for a relationship, it is questionable whether such an opportunity qualifies as an "important" governmental interest apart from the existence of an actual relationship. By focusing on "opportunity" rather than reality, the majority presumably improves the chances of a sufficient means-end fit. But in doing so, it dilutes significantly the weight of the interest. It is difficult to see how, in this citizenship-conferral context, anyone profits from a "demonstrated opportunity" for a relationship in the absence of the fruition of an actual tie. Children who have an "opportunity" for such a tie with a parent, of course, may never develop an actual relationship with that parent.... Likewise, where there is an actual relationship, it is the actual relationship that does all the work in rendering appropriate a grant of citizenship, regardless of when and how the opportunity for that relationship arose.

... Even if it is important "to require that an opportunity for a parent-child relationship occur during the formative years of the child's minority," it is difficult to see how the requirement that proof of such opportunity be obtained before the child turns 18 substantially furthers the asserted interest. As the facts of this case demonstrate, it is entirely possible that a father and child will have the opportunity to develop a relationship and in fact will develop a relationship without obtaining the proof of the opportunity during the child's minority....

Further underscoring the gap between the discriminatory means and the asserted end is the possibility that "a child might obtain an adjudication of paternity 'absent any affirmative act by the father, and perhaps even over his express objection.' " [T]hat the means-end fit can break down so readily in theory, and not just in practice, is hardly characteristic of a "substantial" means-end relationship.

Moreover, available sex-neutral alternatives would at least replicate, and could easily exceed, whatever fit there is between § 1409(a)(4)'s discriminatory means and the majority's asserted end.... Congress could simply substitute for § 1409(a)(4) a requirement that the parent be present at birth or have knowledge of birth.... Congress could at least allow proof of such presence or knowledge to be one way of demonstrating an opportunity for a relationship. Under the present law, the statute on its face accords different treatment to a mother who is by nature present at birth and a father who is by choice present at birth even though those two individuals are similarly situated with respect to the "opportunity" for a relationship. The mother can transmit her citizenship at birth, but the father cannot do so in the absence of at least one other affirmative act. The different statutory treatment is solely on account of the sex of the similarly situated individuals. This type of treatment is patently inconsistent with the promise of equal protection of the laws. See, e.g., *Reed*....

Indeed, the idea that a mother's presence at birth supplies adequate assurance of an opportunity to develop a relationship while a father's presence at birth does not would appear to rest only on an overbroad sex-based generalization. A mother may not have an opportunity for a relationship if the child is removed from his or her mother on account of alleged abuse or neglect, or if the child and mother are separated by tragedy, such as disaster or war, of the sort apparently present in this case. There is no reason, other than stereotype, to say that fathers who are present at birth lack an opportunity for a relationship on similar terms. The "[p]hysical differences between men and women," *Virginia*, ... therefore do not justify § 1409(a)(4)'s discrimination.

[With respect to the majority's proposition that it] "is almost axiomatic that a policy which seeks to foster the opportunity for meaningful parent-child bonds to develop has a close and substantial bearing on the governmental interest in the actual formation of that bond"[, w]hether the classification indeed "has a close and substantial bearing" on the actual occurrence of the preferred result depends on facts and circumstances and must be proved by the classification's defender. Far from being a virtual axiom, the relationship between the intent to foster an opportunity and the fruition of the desired effect is merely a contingent proposition. The majority's sweeping claim is no surrogate for the careful application of heightened scrutiny to a particular classification.

The question that then remains is the sufficiency of the fit between § 1409(a)(4)'s discriminatory means and the goal of "establish[ing] ... a real, practical relationship of considerable substance." If Congress wishes to advance this end, it could easily do so by employing a sex-neutral classification that is a far "more germane bas[i]s of classification" than sex, *Craig*.... For example,

Congress could require some degree of regular contact between the child and the citizen parent over a period of time. . . .

. . . The Court admits that "Congress could excuse compliance with the formal requirements when an actual father-child relationship is proved," but speculates that Congress did not do so "perhaps because of the subjectivity, intrusiveness, and difficulties of proof that might attend an inquiry into any particular bond or tie." We have repeatedly rejected efforts to justify sex-based classifications on the ground of administrative convenience. . . . There is no reason to think that this is a case where administrative convenience concerns are so powerful that they would justify the sex-based discrimination, . . . especially where the use of sex as a proxy is so ill fit to the purported ends as it is here. And to the extent Congress might seek simply to ensure an "opportunity" for a relationship, little administrative inconvenience would seem to accompany a sex-neutral requirement of presence at birth, knowledge of birth, or contact between parent and child prior to a certain age.

The claim that § 1409(a)(4) substantially relates to the achievement of the goal of a "real, practical relationship" thus finds support not in biological differences but instead in a stereotype—i.e., "the generalization that mothers are significantly more likely than fathers . . . to develop caring relationships with their children." . . . Such a claim relies on "the very stereotype the law condemns," *J.E.B.* . . . , "lends credibility" to the generalization, *Mississippi Univ. for Women* . . . , and helps to convert that "assumption" into "a self-fulfilling prophecy," ibid. . . . Indeed, contrary to this stereotype, Boulais has reared Nguyen, while Nguyen apparently has lacked a relationship with his mother.

. . .

In denying petitioner's claim that § 1409(a)(4) rests on stereotypes, the majority articulates a misshapen notion of "stereotype" and its significance in our equal protection jurisprudence. The majority asserts that a "stereotype" is "defined as a frame of mind resulting from irrational or uncritical analysis." This Court has long recognized, however, that an impermissible stereotype may enjoy empirical support and thus be in a sense "rational." . . . Indeed, the stereotypes that underlie a sex-based classification "may hold true for many, even most, individuals." . . . But in numerous cases where a measure of truth has inhered in the generalization, "the Court has rejected official actions that classify unnecessarily and overbroadly by gender when more accurate and impartial functional lines can be drawn." . . .

Nor do stereotypes consist only of those overbroad generalizations that the reviewing court considers to "show disrespect" for a class. . . . The hallmark of a stereotypical sex-based classification under this Court's precedents is not whether the classification is insulting, but whether it "relie[s] upon the simplistic, outdated assumption that gender could be used as a 'proxy for other, more germane bases of classification.'" . . .

[W]hile our explanations of many decisions invalidating sex-based classifications have pointed to the problems of "stereotypes" and "overbroad generalizations," these explanations certainly do not mean that the burden is on the challenger of the classification to prove legislative reliance on such generalizations. Indeed, an arbitrary distinction between the sexes may rely on no identifiable generalization at all but may simply be a denial of opportunity out of pure caprice. Such a distinction, of course, would nonetheless be a classic equal protection violation....

C

... The history of sex discrimination in laws governing the transmission of citizenship and with respect to parental responsibilities for children born out of wedlock counsels at least some circumspection in discerning legislative purposes in this context....

. . .

Section 1409(a)(4) is ... paradigmatic of a historic regime that left women with responsibility, and freed men from responsibility, for nonmarital children. Under this law, as one advocate explained to Congress in a 1932 plea for a sex-neutral citizenship law, "when it comes to the illegitimate child, which is a great burden, then the mother is the only recognized parent, and the father is put safely in the background." ... Unlike § 1409(a)(4), our States' child custody and support laws no longer assume that mothers alone are "bound" to serve as "natural guardians" of nonmarital children.... The majority, however, rather than confronting the stereotypical notion that mothers must care for these children and fathers may ignore them, quietly condones the "very stereotype the law condemns," *J.E.B.* ...

. . .

The Court ... states that the obligation imposed by § 1409(a)(4) is "minimal" and does not present "inordinate and unnecessary hurdles" to the acquisition of citizenship by the nonmarital child of a citizen father. Even assuming that the burden is minimal (and the question whether the hurdle is "unnecessary" is quite different in kind from the question whether it is burdensome), it is well settled that "the 'absence of an insurmountable barrier' will not redeem an otherwise unconstitutionally discriminatory law." *Kirchberg*....

. . .

III

. . .

[With respect to "the implications of statements in our earlier cases regarding the wide deference afforded to Congress in the exercise of its immigration and naturalization power," the dissent said in relevant part:]

The instant case is not about the admission of aliens but instead concerns the logically prior question whether an individual is a citizen in the first place. A predicate for application of the deference commanded by *Fiallo* is that the individuals concerned be aliens. But whether that predicate obtains is the very matter at issue in this case.... Because §§ 1401 and 1409 govern the conferral of citizenship at birth, and not the admission of aliens, the ordinary standards of equal protection review apply....

* * *

... Today's decision ... represents a deviation from a line of cases in which we have vigilantly applied heightened scrutiny to [sex] classifications to determine whether a constitutional violation has occurred. I trust that the depth and vitality of these precedents will ensure that today's error remains an aberration. I respectfully dissent.

E. "BENIGN" DISCRIMINATION: AFFIRMATIVE ACTION, QUOTAS, PREFERENCES BASED ON GENDER OR RACE

2. CLASSIFICATIONS ADVANTAGING RACIAL MINORITIES

Pages 820–846. Omit Regents of the University of California v. Bakke:

Page 883. Add at end of subsection:

Grutter v. Bollinger

539 U.S. ___, 123 S.Ct. 2325, ___ L.Ed.2d ___ (2003).

Justice O'Connor delivered the opinion of the Court.

This case requires us to decide whether the use of race as a factor in student admissions by the University of Michigan Law School ... is unlawful.

I

A

The Law School['s admissions policy seeks an academically capable, diverse student body through efforts that sought to] compl[y] with this Court's most recent ruling on the use of race in university admissions. See *Regents of Univ. of Cal. v. Bakke,* 438 U.S. 265 (1978)....

The hallmark of that policy is its focus on academic ability coupled with a flexible assessment of applicants' talents, experiences, and potential "to contribute to the learning of those around them." ... The policy requires admissions officials to evaluate each applicant based on all the information available in the file, including a personal statement, letters of recommendation, and an essay describing the ways in which the applicant will contribute to the life and diversity of the Law School.... In reviewing an applicant's file, admissions officials must consider the applicant's undergraduate grade point average (GPA) and Law School Admissions Test (LSAT) score because they are important (if imperfect) predictors of academic success in law school.... The policy stresses that "no applicant should be admitted unless we expect that applicant to do well enough to graduate with no serious academic problems." ...

The policy makes clear, however, that even the highest possible score does not guarantee admission.... Nor does a low score automatically disqualify an applicant.... Rather, the policy requires admissions officials to look beyond grades and test scores to other criteria that are important to the Law School's educational objectives.... So-called " 'soft' variables" such as "the enthusiasm of recommenders, the quality of the undergraduate institution, the quality of the applicant's essay, and the areas and difficulty of undergraduate course selection" are all brought to bear in assessing an "applicant's likely contributions to the intellectual and social life of the institution." ...

The policy aspires to "achieve that diversity which has the potential to enrich everyone's education and thus make a law school class stronger than the sum of its parts." ... The policy does not restrict the types of diversity contributions eligible for "substantial weight" in the admissions process, but instead recognizes "many possible bases for diversity admissions." ... The policy does, however, reaffirm the Law School's longstanding commitment to "one particular type of diversity," that is, "racial and ethnic diversity with special reference to the inclusion of students from groups which have been historically discriminated against, like African–Americans, Hispanics and Native Americans, who without this commitment might not be represented in our student body in meaningful numbers." ... By enrolling a "'critical mass' of [underrepresented] minority students," the Law School seeks to "ensur[e] their ability to make unique contributions to the character of the Law School." ...

The policy does not define diversity "solely in terms of racial and ethnic status." ... Nor is the policy "insensitive to the competition among all students for admission to the [L]aw [S]chool." ... Rather, the policy seeks to guide admissions officers in "producing classes both diverse and academically outstanding, classes made up of students who promise to continue the tradition of outstanding contribution by Michigan Graduates to the legal profession." ...

B

Petitioner Barbara Grutter is a white Michigan resident who applied to the Law School in 1996 with a 3.8 grade point average and 161 LSAT score. The Law School [eventually] rejected her application [and she sued,] ... alleg[ing] that respondents discriminated against her on the basis of race in violation of the Fourteenth Amendment; Title VI of the Civil Rights Act of 1964, ... 42 U.S.C. § 2000d; and ... 42 U.S.C. § 1981.

Petitioner further alleged that her application was rejected because the Law School uses race as a "predominant" factor, giving applicants who belong to certain minority groups "a significantly greater chance of admission than students with similar credentials from disfavored racial groups." ...

. . .

... The District Court ... conduct[ed] a bench trial on the extent to which race was a factor in the Law School's admissions decisions, and whether the Law School's consideration of race in admissions decisions constituted a race-based double standard.

... [The] Director of Admissions ... testified that he did not direct his staff to admit a particular percentage or number of minority students, but rather to consider an applicant's race along with all other factors.... [He] testified that at the height of the admissions season, he would frequently consult the so-called "daily reports" that kept track of the racial and ethnic composition of the class (along with other information such as residency status and gender) ... to ensure that a critical mass of underrepresented minority students would be reached so as to realize the educational benefits of a diverse student body.... [He] stressed, however, that he did not seek to admit any particular number or percentage of underrepresented minority students....

Bakke - Powell

[A successor] Director of Admissions ... testified that " 'critical mass' " means " 'meaningful numbers' " or " 'meaningful representation,' " which she understood to mean a number that encourages underrepresented minority students to participate in the classroom and not feel isolated.... [She] stated there is no number, percentage, or range of numbers or percentages that constitute critical mass [and] that she must consider the race of applicants because a critical mass of underrepresented minority students could not be enrolled if admissions decisions were based primarily on undergraduate GPAs and LSAT scores....

The ... Dean of the Law School ... indicated that critical mass means numbers such that underrepresented minority students do not feel isolated or like spokespersons for their race.... In some cases, [he testified,] an applicant's race may play no role, while in others it may be a " 'determinative' " factor....

. . .

In an attempt to quantify the extent to which the Law School actually considers race in making admissions decisions, the parties introduced voluminous evidence at trial. [P]etitioner's expert ... generated and analyzed "admissions grids" for ... 1995–2000 ... show[ing] the number of applicants and the number of admittees for all combinations of GPAs and LSAT scores.... He concluded that membership in certain minority groups " 'is an extremely strong factor in the decision for acceptance,' " and that applicants from these minority groups " 'are given an extremely large allowance for admission' " as compared to applicants who are members of nonfavored groups.... [He] conceded, however, that race is not the predominant factor in the Law School's admissions calculus....

[T]he Law School's expert ... focused on the predicted effect of eliminating race as a factor in the Law School's admission process [and concluded that] a race-blind admissions system would have a " 'very dramatic,' " negative effect on underrepresented minority admissions.... He testified that in 2000, 35 percent of underrepresented minority applicants were admitted [and] predicted that if race were not considered, only 10 percent of those applicants would have been admitted.... Under this scenario, underrepresented minority students would have comprised 4 percent of the entering class in 2000 instead of the actual figure of 14.5 percent....

In the end, the District Court concluded that the Law School's use of race as a factor in admissions decisions was unlawful....

Sitting en banc, the Court of Appeals reversed[, four judges dissenting.] ...

. . .

We granted certiorari ... to resolve the disagreement among the Courts of Appeals on a question of national importance: Whether diversity is a compelling interest that can justify the narrowly tailored use of race in selecting applicants for admission to public universities. ...

Is diversity a "compelling interest"

II

A

We last addressed the use of race in public higher education over 25 years ago. In the landmark *Bakke* case, we reviewed a racial set-aside program that reserved 16 out of 100 seats in a medical school class for members of certain minority groups. 438 U.S. 265 (1978). The decision produced six separate opinions, none of which commanded a majority of the Court. Four Justices would have upheld the program against all attack on the ground that the government can use race to "remedy disadvantages cast on minorities by past racial prejudice." *Id.*, at 325 (joint opinion of Brennan, White, Marshall, and Blackmun, JJ., concurring in judgment in part and dissenting in part). Four other Justices avoided the constitutional question altogether and struck down the program on statutory grounds. *Id.*, at 408 (opinion of Stevens, J., joined by Burger, C. J., and Stewart and Rehnquist, JJ., concurring in judgment in part and dissenting in part). Justice Powell provided a fifth vote not only for invalidating the set-aside program, but also for reversing the state court's injunction against any use of race whatsoever. The only holding for the Court in *Bakke* was that a "State has a substantial interest that legitimately may be served by a properly devised admissions program involving the competitive consideration of race and ethnic origin." . . . Thus, we reversed that part of the lower court's judgment that enjoined the university "from any consideration of the race of any applicant." . . .

Since this Court's splintered decision in *Bakke*, Justice Powell's opinion announcing the judgment of the Court has served as the touchstone for constitutional analysis of race-conscious admissions policies. Public and private universities across the Nation have modeled their own admissions programs on Justice Powell's views on permissible race-conscious policies. . . . We therefore discuss Justice Powell's opinion in some detail.

Justice Powell began by stating that "[t]he guarantee of equal protection cannot mean one thing when applied to one individual and something else when applied to a person of another color. If both are not accorded the same protection, then it is not equal." . . . In Justice Powell's view, when governmental decisions "touch upon an individual's race or ethnic background, he is entitled to a judicial determination that the burden he is asked to bear on that basis is precisely tailored to serve a compelling governmental interest." . . . Under this exacting standard, only one of the interests asserted by the university survived Justice Powell's scrutiny.

First, Justice Powell rejected an interest in " 'reducing the historic deficit of traditionally disfavored minorities in medical schools and in the medical profession' " as an unlawful interest in racial balancing. . . . Second, Justice Powell rejected an interest in remedying societal discrimination because such measures would risk placing unnecessary burdens on innocent third parties "who bear no responsibility for whatever harm the beneficiaries of the special admissions program are thought to have suffered." . . . Third, Justice Powell rejected an interest in "increasing the number of physicians who will practice in communities currently underserved," concluding that even if such an interest could be compelling in some circumstances the program under review was not "geared to promote that goal." . . .

Justice Powell approved the university's use of race to further only one interest: "the attainment of a diverse student body." . . . With the important proviso that "constitutional limitations protecting individual rights may not be disregarded," Justice Powell grounded his analysis in the academic freedom that "long has been viewed as a special concern of the First Amendment." . . .

Justice Powell emphasized that nothing less than the " 'nation's future depends upon leaders trained through wide exposure' to the ideas and mores of students as diverse as this Nation of many peoples." ... In seeking the "right to select those students who will contribute the most to the 'robust exchange of ideas,' " a university seeks "to achieve a goal that is of paramount importance in the fulfillment of its mission." ... Both "tradition and experience lend support to the view that the contribution of diversity is substantial." ...

Justice Powell was, however, careful to emphasize that in his view race "is only one element in a range of factors a university properly may consider in attaining the goal of a heterogeneous student body." ... For Justice Powell, "[i]t is not an interest in simple ethnic diversity, in which a specified percentage of the student body is in effect guaranteed to be members of selected ethnic groups," that can justify the use of race.... Rather, "[t]he diversity that furthers a compelling state interest encompasses a far broader array of qualifications and characteristics of which racial or ethnic origin is but a single though important element." ...

Can't have quotas

. . .

... [F]or the reasons set out below, today we endorse Justice Powell's view that student body diversity is a compelling state interest that can justify the use of race in university admissions.

B

... Because the Fourteenth Amendment "protect[s] *persons*, not *groups*," all "governmental action based on race—a *group* classification long recognized as in most circumstances irrelevant and therefore prohibited—should be subjected to detailed judicial inquiry to ensure that the *personal* right to equal protection of the laws has not been infringed." *Adarand Constructors, Inc. v. Peã*, 515 U.S. 200, 227 (1995) (emphasis in original ...). ...

We have held that all racial classifications imposed by government "must be analyzed by a reviewing court under strict scrutiny." ... This means that such classifications are constitutional only if they are narrowly tailored to further compelling governmental interests. "Absent searching judicial inquiry into the justification for such race-based measures," we have no way to determine what "classifications are 'benign' or 'remedial' and what classifications are in fact motivated by illegitimate notions of racial inferiority or simple racial politics." *Richmond v. J. A. Croson Co.*, 488 U.S. 469, 493 (1989) (plurality opinion). We apply strict scrutiny to all racial classifications to " 'smoke out' illegitimate uses of race by assuring that [government] is pursuing a goal important enough to warrant use of a highly suspect tool." ...

racial classifications reviewed under strict scrutiny

reason for strict scrutiny

Strict scrutiny is not "strict in theory, but fatal in fact." *Adarand* ... Although all governmental uses of race are subject to strict scrutiny, not all are invalidated by it. ... When race-based action is necessary to further a compelling governmental interest, such action does not violate the constitutional guarantee of equal protection so long as the narrow-tailoring requirement is also satisfied.

Context matters when reviewing race-based governmental action under the Equal Protection Clause.... Not every decision influenced by race is equally objectionable and strict scrutiny is designed to provide a framework for carefully examining the importance and the sincerity of the reasons advanced by the governmental decisionmaker for the use of race in that particular context.

III

A

With these principles in mind, we turn to the question whether the Law School's use of race is justified by a compelling state interest. [R]espondents assert only one justification for their use of race in the admissions process: obtaining "the educational benefits that flow from a diverse student body." ... In other words, the Law School asks us to recognize, in the context of higher education, a compelling state interest in student body diversity.

We first wish to dispel the notion that the Law School's argument has been foreclosed, either expressly or implicitly, by our affirmative-action cases decided since *Bakke*. It is true that some language in those opinions might be read to suggest that remedying past discrimination is the only permissible justification for race-based governmental action. See, *e.g.*, *Richmond v. J. A. Croson Co.*, *supra*, at 493 (plurality opinion) (stating that unless classifications based on race are "strictly reserved for remedial settings, they may in fact promote notions of racial inferiority and lead to a politics of racial hostility' "). But we have never held that the only governmental use of race that can survive strict scrutiny is remedying past discrimination. Nor, since *Bakke*, have we directly addressed the use of race in the context of public higher education. Today, we hold that the Law School has a compelling interest in attaining a diverse student body.

The Law School's educational judgment that such diversity is essential to its educational mission is one to which we defer. The Law School's assessment that diversity will, in fact, yield educational benefits is substantiated by respondents and their *amici*. Our scrutiny of the interest asserted by the Law School is no less strict for taking into account complex educational judgments in an area that lies primarily within the expertise of the university. Our holding today is in keeping with our tradition of giving a degree of deference to a university's academic decisions, within constitutionally prescribed limits....

We have long recognized that, given the important purpose of public education and the expansive freedoms of speech and thought associated with the university environment, universities occupy a special niche in our constitutional tradition.... In announcing the principle of student body diversity as a compelling state interest, Justice Powell invoked our cases recognizing a constitutional dimension, grounded in the First Amendment, of educational autonomy: "The freedom of a university to make its own judgments as to education includes the selection of its student body." *Bakke* .... From this premise, Justice Powell reasoned that by claiming "the right to select those students who will contribute the most to the "robust exchange of ideas," a university "seek[s] to achieve a goal that is of paramount importance in the fulfillment of its mission." ... Our conclusion that the Law School has a compelling interest in a diverse student body is informed by our view that attaining a diverse student body is at the heart of the Law School's proper institutional mission, and that "good faith" on the part of a university is "presumed" absent "a showing to the contrary." ...

As part of its goal of "assembling a class that is both exceptionally academically qualified and broadly diverse," the Law School seeks to "enroll a 'critical mass' of minority students." ... The Law School's interest is not simply "to assure within its student body some specified percentage of a particular group merely because of its race or ethnic origin." *Bakke*, ... (opinion of Powell, J.). That would amount to outright racial balancing, which is patently unconstitutional. ... Rather, the Law School's concept of critical mass is defined by reference to the educational benefits that diversity is designed to produce.

These benefits are substantial. As the District Court emphasized, the Law School's admissions policy promotes "cross-racial understanding," helps to break down racial stereotypes, and "enables [students] to better understand persons of different races." ... These benefits are "important and laudable," because "classroom discussion is livelier, more spirited, and simply more enlightening and interesting" when the students have "the greatest possible variety of backgrounds." ...

The Law School's claim of a compelling interest is further bolstered by its *amici*, who point to the educational benefits that flow from student body diversity. In addition to the expert studies and reports entered into evidence at trial, numerous studies show that student body diversity promotes learning outcomes, and "better prepares students for an increasingly diverse workforce and society, and better prepares them as professionals." Brief for American Educational Research Association et al. as *Amici Curiae* 3; see, *e.g.*, W. Bowen & D. Bok, The Shape of the River (1998); Diversity Challenged: Evidence on the Impact of Affirmative Action (G. Orfield & M. Kurlaender eds. 2001); Compelling Interest: Examining the Evidence on Racial Dynamics in Colleges and Universities (M. Chang, D. Witt, J. Jones, & K. Hakuta eds. 2003).

These benefits are not theoretical but real, as major American businesses have made clear that the skills needed in today's increasingly global marketplace can only be developed through exposure to widely diverse people, cultures, ideas, and viewpoints. Brief for 3M et al. as *Amici Curiae* 5; Brief for General Motors Corp. as *Amicus Curiae* 3–4. What is more, high-ranking retired officers and civilian leaders of the United States military assert that, "[b]ased on [their] decades of experience," a "highly qualified, racially diverse officer corps ... is essential to the military's ability to fulfill its principle mission to provide national security." Brief for Julius W. Becton, Jr. et al. as *Amici Curiae* 27. The primary sources for the Nation's officer corps are the service academies and the Reserve Officers Training Corps (ROTC), the latter comprising students already admitted to participating colleges and universities.... At present, "the military cannot achieve an officer corps that is *both* highly qualified *and* racially diverse unless the service academies and the ROTC used limited race-conscious recruiting and admissions policies." *Ibid.* (emphasis in original). To fulfill its mission, the military "must be selective in admissions for training and education for the officer corps, *and* it must train and educate a highly qualified, racially diverse officer corps in a racially diverse setting." ... (emphasis in original). We agree that "[i]t requires only a small step from this analysis to conclude that our country's other most selective institutions must remain both diverse and selective." *Ibid.*

We have repeatedly acknowledged the overriding importance of preparing students for work and citizenship, describing education as pivotal to "sustaining our political and cultural heritage" with a fundamental role in maintaining the fabric of society. *Plyler v. Doe*, 457 U.S. 202, 221 (1982). This Court has long recognized that "education ... is the very foundation of good citizenship." *Brown v. Board of Education*, 347 U.S. 483, 493 (1954). For this reason, the diffusion of knowledge and opportunity through public institutions of higher education must be accessible to all individuals regardless of race or ethnicity. The United States, as *amicus curiae*, affirms that "[e]nsuring that public institutions are open and available to all segments of American society, including people of all races and ethnicities, represents a paramount government objective." ... And, "[n]owhere is the importance of such openness more acute than in the context of higher education." ... Effective participation by members of all racial and ethnic groups in the civic life of our Nation is essential if the dream of one Nation, indivisible, is to be realized.

Moreover, universities, and in particular, law schools, represent the training ground for a large number of our Nation's leaders. *Sweatt v. Painter*, 339 U.S. 629, 634 (1950) (describing law school as a "proving ground for legal learning and practice"). Individuals with law degrees occupy roughly half the state governorships, more than half the seats in the United States Senate, and more than a third of the seats in the United States House of Representatives.... The pattern is even more striking when it comes to highly selective law schools. A handful of these schools accounts for 25 of the 100 United States Senators, 74 United States Courts of Appeals judges, and nearly 200 of the more than 600 United States District Court judges....

In order to cultivate a set of leaders with legitimacy in the eyes of the citizenry, it is necessary that the path to leadership be visibly open to talented and qualified individuals of every race and ethnicity. All members of our heterogeneous society must have confidence in the openness and integrity of the educational institutions that provide this training. [L]aw schools "cannot be effective in isolation from the individuals and institutions with which the law interacts." See *Sweatt v. Painter*.... Access to legal education (and thus the legal profession) must be inclusive of talented and qualified individuals of every race and ethnicity, so that all members of our heterogeneous society may participate in the educational institutions that provide the training and education necessary to succeed in America.

The Law School does not premise its need for critical mass on "any belief that minority students always (or even consistently) express some characteristic minority viewpoint on any issue." ... To the contrary, diminishing the force of such stereotypes is both a crucial part of the Law School's mission, and one that it cannot accomplish with only token numbers of minority students. Just as growing up in a particular region or having particular professional experiences is likely to affect an individual's views, so too is one's own, unique experience of being a racial minority in a society, like our own, in which race unfortunately still matters. The Law School has determined, based on its experience and expertise, that a "critical mass" of underrepresented minorities is necessary to further its compelling interest in securing the educational benefits of a diverse student body.

B

Even in the limited circumstance when drawing racial distinctions is permissible to further a compelling state interest, government is still "constrained in how it may pursue that end: [T]he means chosen to accomplish the [government's] asserted purpose must be specifically and narrowly framed to accomplish that purpose." *Shaw v. Hunt*, 517 U.S. 899, 908 (1996) .... The purpose of the narrow tailoring requirement is to ensure that "the means chosen 'fit' ... th[e] compelling goal so closely that there is little or no possibility that the motive for the classification was illegitimate racial prejudice or stereotype." *Richmond v. J. A. Croson Co.*, 488 U.S., at 493 (plurality opinion).

Since *Bakke*, we have had no occasion to define the contours of the narrow-tailoring inquiry with respect to race-conscious university admissions programs. That inquiry must be calibrated to fit the distinct issues raised by the use of race to achieve student body diversity in public higher education. Contrary to Justice Kennedy's assertions, we do not "abandon[] strict scrutiny." Rather, ... we adhere to *Adarand*'s teaching that the very purpose of strict scrutiny is to take such "relevant differences into account." ...

To be narrowly tailored, a race-conscious admissions program cannot use a quota system—it cannot "insulat[e] each category of applicants with certain desired qualifications from competition with all other applicants." *Bakke*, ... (opinion of Powell, J.). Instead, a university may consider race or ethnicity only as a " 'plus' in a particular applicant's file," without "insulat[ing] the individual from comparison with all other candidates for the available seats." ... In other words, an admissions program must be "flexible enough to consider all pertinent elements of diversity in light of the particular qualifications of each applicant, and to place them on the same footing for consideration, although not necessarily according them the same weight." ...

We find that the Law School's admissions program bears the hallmarks of a narrowly tailored plan. As Justice Powell made clear in *Bakke*, truly individualized consideration demands that race be used in a flexible, nonmechanical way. It follows from this mandate that universities cannot establish quotas for members of certain racial groups or put members of those groups on separate admissions tracks.... Nor can universities insulate applicants who belong to certain racial or ethnic groups from the competition for admission.... Universities can, however, consider race or ethnicity more flexibly as a "plus" factor in the context of individualized consideration of each and every applicant....

We are satisfied that the Law School's admissions program, like the Harvard plan described by Justice Powell, does not operate as a quota. Properly understood, a "quota" is a program in which a certain fixed number or proportion of opportunities are "reserved exclusively for certain minority groups." ... Quotas " 'impose a fixed number or percentage which must be attained, or which cannot be exceeded,' " ... and "insulate the individual from comparison with all other candidates for the available seats." ... In contrast, "a permissible goal ... require[s] only a good-faith effort ... to come within a range demarcated by the goal itself," ... and permits consideration of race as a "plus" factor in any given case while still ensuring that each candidate "compete[s] with all other qualified applicants,' " ....

Justice Powell's distinction between the medical school's rigid 16–seat quota and Harvard's flexible use of race as a "plus" factor is instructive. Harvard certainly had minimum *goals* for minority enrollment, even if it had no specific number firmly in mind. See *Bakke,* . . . (opinion of Powell, J.) ("10 or 20 black students could not begin to bring to their classmates and to each other the variety of points of view, backgrounds and experiences of blacks in the United States"). What is more, Justice Powell flatly rejected the argument that Harvard's program was "the functional equivalent of a quota" merely because it had some " 'plus' " for race, or gave greater "weight" to race than to some other factors, in order to achieve student body diversity. . . .

The Law School's goal of attaining a critical mass of underrepresented minority students does not transform its program into a quota. As the Harvard plan described by Justice Powell recognized, there is of course "some relationship between numbers and achieving the benefits to be derived from a diverse student body, and between numbers and providing a reasonable environment for those students admitted." . . . "[S]ome attention to numbers," without more, does not transform a flexible admissions system into a rigid quota. . . . Nor, as Justice Kennedy posits, does the Law School's consultation of the "daily reports,' " which keep track of the racial and ethnic composition of the class (as well as of residency and gender), "suggest [] there was no further attempt at individual review save for race itself" during the final stages of the admissions process. To the contrary, the Law School's admissions officers testified without contradiction that they never gave race any more or less weight based on the information contained in these reports. . . . Moreover, as Justice Kennedy concedes, between 1993 and 2000, the number of African–American, Latino, and Native–American students in each class at the Law School varied from 13.5 to 20.1 percent, a range inconsistent with a quota.

The Chief Justice believes that the Law School's policy conceals an attempt to achieve racial balancing, and cites admissions data to contend that the Law School discriminates among different groups within the critical mass. But, as the Chief Justice concedes, the number of underrepresented minority students who ultimately enroll in the Law School differs substantially from their representation in the applicant pool and varies considerably for each group from year to year. . . .

That a race-conscious admissions program does not operate as a quota does not, by itself, satisfy the requirement of individualized consideration. When using race as a "plus" factor in university admissions, a university's admissions program must remain flexible enough to ensure that each applicant is evaluated as an individual and not in a way that makes an applicant's race or ethnicity the defining feature of his or her application. The importance of this individualized consideration in the context of a race-conscious admissions program is paramount. . . .

Here, the Law School engages in a highly individualized, holistic review of each applicant's file, giving serious consideration to all the ways an applicant might contribute to a diverse educational environment. The Law School affords this individualized consideration to applicants of all races. There is no policy, either *de jure* or *de facto*, of automatic acceptance or rejection based on any single "soft" variable. Unlike the program at issue in *Gratz v. Bollinger*, [539 U.S. ___ (2003),] the Law School awards no mechanical, predetermined diversi-

ty "bonuses" based on race or ethnicity. See [*Gratz*] (distinguishing a race-conscious admissions program that automatically awards 20 points based on race from the Harvard plan, which considered race but "did not contemplate that any single characteristic automatically ensured a specific and identifiable contribution to a university's diversity"). Like the Harvard plan, the Law School's admissions policy "is flexible enough to consider all pertinent elements of diversity in light of the particular qualifications of each applicant, and to place them on the same footing for consideration, although not necessarily according them the same weight." ...

We also find that, like the Harvard plan Justice Powell referenced in *Bakke*, the Law School's race-conscious admissions program adequately ensures that all factors that may contribute to student body diversity are meaningfully considered alongside race in admissions decisions. With respect to the use of race itself, all underrepresented minority students admitted by the Law School have been deemed qualified. By virtue of our Nation's struggle with racial inequality, such students are both likely to have experiences of particular importance to the Law School's mission, and less likely to be admitted in meaningful numbers on criteria that ignore those experiences....

The Law School does not, however, limit in any way the broad range of qualities and experiences that may be considered valuable contributions to student body diversity. To the contrary, the [admissions] policy makes clear "[t]here are many possible bases for diversity admissions," and provides examples of admittees who have lived or traveled widely abroad, are fluent in several languages, have overcome personal adversity and family hardship, have exceptional records of extensive community service, and have had successful careers in other fields.... The Law School seriously considers each "applicant's promise of making a notable contribution to the class by way of a particular strength, attainment, or characteristic—*e.g.*, an unusual intellectual achievement, employment experience, nonacademic performance, or personal background." ... All applicants have the opportunity to highlight their own potential diversity contributions through the submission of a personal statement, letters of recommendation, and an essay describing the ways in which the applicant will contribute to the life and diversity of the Law School.

What is more, the Law School actually gives substantial weight to diversity factors besides race. The Law School frequently accepts nonminority applicants with grades and test scores lower than underrepresented minority applicants (and other nonminority applicants) who are rejected.... This shows that the Law School seriously weighs many other diversity factors besides race that can make a real and dispositive difference for nonminority applicants as well. By this flexible approach, the Law School sufficiently takes into account, in practice as well as in theory, a wide variety of characteristics besides race and ethnicity that contribute to a diverse student body. Justice Kennedy speculates that "race is likely outcome determinative for many members of minority groups" who do not fall within the upper range of LSAT scores and grades.... But the same could be said of the Harvard plan discussed approvingly by Justice Powell in *Bakke*, and indeed of any plan that uses race as one of many factors....

Petitioner and the United States argue that the Law School's plan is not narrowly tailored because race-neutral means exist to obtain the educational benefits of student body diversity that the Law School seeks. We disagree. Narrow tailoring does not require exhaustion of every conceivable race-neutral alternative. Nor does it require a university to choose between maintaining a reputation for excellence or fulfilling a commitment to provide educational opportunities to members of all racial groups. . . . Narrow tailoring does, however, require serious, good faith consideration of workable race-neutral alternatives that will achieve the diversity the university seeks. . . .

We agree with the Court of Appeals that the Law School sufficiently considered workable race-neutral alternatives. The District Court took the Law School to task for failing to consider race-neutral alternatives such as "using a lottery system" or "decreasing the emphasis for all applicants on undergraduate GPA and LSAT scores." . . . But these alternatives would require a dramatic sacrifice of diversity, the academic quality of all admitted students, or both.

The Law School's current admissions program considers race as one factor among many, in an effort to assemble a student body that is diverse in ways broader than race. Because a lottery would make that kind of nuanced judgment impossible, it would effectively sacrifice all other educational values, not to mention every other kind of diversity. So too with the suggestion that the Law School simply lower admissions standards for all students, a drastic remedy that would require the Law School to become a much different institution and sacrifice a vital component of its educational mission. The United States advocates "percentage plans," recently adopted by public undergraduate institutions in Texas, Florida, and California to guarantee admission to all students above a certain class-rank threshold in every high school in the State. . . . The United States does not, however, explain how such plans could work for graduate and professional schools. Moreover, even assuming such plans are race-neutral, they may preclude the university from conducting the individualized assessments necessary to assemble a student body that is not just racially diverse, but diverse along all the qualities valued by the university. We are satisfied that the Law School adequately considered race-neutral alternatives currently capable of producing a critical mass without forcing the Law School to abandon the academic selectivity that is the cornerstone of its educational mission.

We acknowledge that "there are serious problems of justice connected with the idea of preference itself." *Bakke,* . . . (opinion of Powell, J.). Narrow tailoring, therefore, requires that a race-conscious admissions program not unduly harm members of any racial group. . . .

We are satisfied that the Law School's admissions program does not. Because the Law School considers "all pertinent elements of diversity," it can (and does) select nonminority applicants who have greater potential to enhance student body diversity over underrepresented minority applicants. . . . As Justice Powell recognized in *Bakke,* so long as a race-conscious admissions program uses race as a "plus" factor in the context of individualized consideration, a rejected applicant

> "will not have been foreclosed from all consideration for that seat simply because he was not the right color or had the wrong surname. . . . His qualifications would have been weighed fairly and competitively, and he

would have no basis to complain of unequal treatment under the Fourteenth Amendment." . . .

We agree that, in the context of its individualized inquiry into the possible diversity contributions of all applicants, the Law School's race-conscious admissions program does not unduly harm nonminority applicants.

We are mindful, however, that "[a] core purpose of the Fourteenth Amendment was to do away with all governmentally imposed discrimination based on race." *Palmore v. Sidoti,* 466 U.S. 429, 432 (1984). Accordingly, race-conscious admissions policies must be limited in time. This requirement reflects that racial classifications, however compelling their goals, are potentially so dangerous that they may be employed no more broadly than the interest demands. Enshrining a permanent justification for racial preferences would offend this fundamental equal protection principle. We see no reason to exempt race-conscious admissions programs from the requirement that all governmental use of race must have a logical end point. The Law School, too, concedes that all "race-conscious programs must have reasonable durational limits." . . . .

In the context of higher education, the durational requirement can be met by sunset provisions in race-conscious admissions policies and periodic reviews to determine whether racial preferences are still necessary to achieve student body diversity. Universities in California, Florida, and Washington State, where racial preferences in admissions are prohibited by state law, are currently engaged in experimenting with a wide variety of alternative approaches. Universities in other States can and should draw on the most promising aspects of these race-neutral alternatives as they develop. . . .

The requirement that all race-conscious admissions programs have a termination point "assure[s] all citizens that the deviation from the norm of equal treatment of all racial and ethnic groups is a temporary matter, a measure taken in the service of the goal of equality itself." *Richmond v. J. A. Croson Co.,* . . . .

We take the Law School at its word that it would "like nothing better than to find a race-neutral admissions formula" and will terminate its race-conscious admissions program as soon as practicable. . . . It has been 25 years since Justice Powell first approved the use of race to further an interest in student body diversity in the context of public higher education. Since that time, the number of minority applicants with high grades and test scores has indeed increased. . . . We expect that 25 years from now, the use of racial preferences will no longer be necessary to further the interest approved today.

IV

In summary, the Equal Protection Clause does not prohibit the Law School's narrowly tailored use of race in admissions decisions to further a compelling interest in obtaining the educational benefits that flow from a diverse student body. Consequently, petitioner's statutory claims based on Title VI and 42 U.S.C. § 1981 also fail. See *Bakke, supra,* at 287 (opinion of Powell, J.) ("Title VI . . . proscribe[s] only those racial classifications that would violate the Equal Protection Clause or the Fifth Amendment"); *General Building Contractors Assn., Inc. v. Pennsylvania,* 458 U.S. 375, 389–391 (1982) (the prohibition against discrimination in § 1981 is co-extensive with the Equal

Protection Clause). The judgment of the Court of Appeals for the Sixth Circuit, accordingly, is affirmed.

. . .

Justice Ginsburg, with whom Justice Breyer joins, concurring.

. . .

The Court . . . observes that "[i]t has been 25 years since Justice Powell [in *Regents of Univ. of Cal. v. Bakke,* 438 U.S. 265 (1978)] first approved the use of race to further an interest in student body diversity in the context of public higher education." For at least part of that time, however, the law could not fairly be described as "settled," and in some regions of the Nation, overtly race-conscious admissions policies have been proscribed. . . . Moreover, it was only 25 years before *Bakke* that this Court declared public school segregation unconstitutional, a declaration that, after prolonged resistance, yielded an end to a law-enforced racial caste system, itself the legacy of centuries of slavery. . . .

It is well documented that conscious and unconscious race bias, even rank discrimination based on race, remain alive in our land, impeding realization of our highest values and ideals. . . . As to public education, data for the years 2000–2001 show that 71.6% of African–American children and 76.3% of Hispanic children attended a school in which minorities made up a majority of the student body. . . . And schools in predominantly minority communities lag far behind others measured by the educational resources available to them. . . .

However strong the public's desire for improved education systems may be, . . . it remains the current reality that many minority students encounter markedly inadequate and unequal educational opportunities. Despite these inequalities, some minority students are able to meet the high threshold requirements set for admission to the country's finest undergraduate and graduate educational institutions. As lower school education in minority communities improves, an increase in the number of such students may be anticipated. From today's vantage point, one may hope, but not firmly forecast, that over the next generation's span, progress toward nondiscrimination and genuinely equal opportunity will make it safe to sunset affirmative action.

Chief Justice Rehnquist, with whom Justice Scalia, Justice Kennedy, and Justice Thomas join, dissenting.

. . . I do not believe . . . that the University of Michigan Law School's . . . means are narrowly tailored to the interest it asserts. The Law School claims it must take the steps it does to achieve a " 'critical mass' " of underrepresented minority students. . . . But its actual program bears no relation to this asserted goal. Stripped of its "critical mass" veil, the Law School's program is revealed as a naked effort to achieve racial balancing.

. . . Our cases establish that . . . respondents must demonstrate that their methods of using race " 'fit' " a compelling state interest "with greater precision than any alternative means." . . .

Before the Court's decision today, we consistently applied the same strict scrutiny analysis regardless of the government's purported reason for using race and regardless of the setting in which race was being used. . . . Indeed, even in the specific context of higher education, we emphasized that "constitutional limitations protecting individual rights may not be disregarded." *Bakke*, ...

Although the Court recites the language of our strict scrutiny analysis, its application of that review is unprecedented in its deference.

. . .

In practice, the Law School's program bears little or no relation to its asserted goal of achieving "critical mass." Respondents explain that the Law School seeks to accumulate a "critical mass" of *each* underrepresented minority group. . . . But the record demonstrates that the Law School's admissions practices with respect to these groups differ dramatically and cannot be defended under any consistent use of the term "critical mass."

From 1995 through 2000, the Law School admitted between 1,130 and 1,310 students. Of those, between 13 and 19 were Native American, between 91 and 108 were African–Americans, and between 47 and 56 were Hispanic. If the Law School is admitting between 91 and 108 African–Americans in order to achieve "critical mass," thereby preventing African–American students from feeling "isolated or like spokespersons for their race," one would think that a number of the same order of magnitude would be necessary to accomplish the same purpose for Hispanics and Native Americans. Similarly, even if all of the Native American applicants admitted in a given year matriculate, which the record demonstrates is not at all the case, how can this possibly constitute a "critical mass" of Native Americans in a class of over 350 students? In order for this pattern of admission to be consistent with the Law School's explanation of "critical mass," one would have to believe that the objectives of "critical mass" offered by respondents are achieved with only half the number of Hispanics and one-sixth the number of Native Americans as compared to African-Americans. But respondents offer no race-specific reasons for such disparities. Instead, they simply emphasize the importance of achieving "critical mass," without any explanation of why that concept is applied differently among the three underrepresented minority groups.

These different numbers, moreover, come only as a result of substantially different treatment among the three underrepresented minority groups, as is apparent in an example offered by the Law School and highlighted by the Court: The school asserts that it "frequently accepts nonminority applicants with grades and test scores lower than underrepresented minority applicants (and other nonminority applicants) who are rejected." . . . Specifically, the Law School states that "[s]ixty-nine minority applicants were rejected between 1995 and 2000 with at least a 3.5 [Grade Point Average (GPA)] and a [score of] 159 or higher on the [Law School Admissions Test (LSAT)]" while a number of Caucasian and Asian–American applicants with similar or lower scores were admitted. . . .

Review of the record reveals only 67 such individuals. Of these 67 individuals, *56* were Hispanic, while only 6 were African–American, and only 5 were Native American. This discrepancy reflects a consistent practice. For example, in 2000, 12 Hispanics who scored between a 159–160 on the LSAT and earned a GPA of 3.00 or higher applied for admission and only 2 were admitted. . . . Meanwhile, 12 African–Americans in the same range of qualifications applied for admission and all 12 were admitted.... Likewise, that same year, 16 Hispanics who scored between a 151–153 on the LSAT and earned a 3.00 or higher applied for admission and only 1 of those applicants was admitted.... Twenty-three similarly qualified African–Americans applied for admission and 14 were admitted....

These statistics have a significant bearing on petitioner's case. Respondents have *never* offered any race-specific arguments explaining why significantly more individuals from one underrepresented minority group are needed in order to achieve "critical mass" or further student body diversity. They certainly have not explained why Hispanics, who they have said are among "the groups most isolated by racial barriers in our country," should have their admission capped out in this manner.... [T]he Law School's disparate admissions practices with respect to these minority groups demonstrate that its alleged goal of "critical mass" is simply a sham.... Surely strict scrutiny cannot permit these sort of disparities without at least some explanation.

Only when the "critical mass" label is discarded does a likely explanation for these numbers emerge....

[T]he correlation between the percentage of the Law School's pool of applicants who are members of the three minority groups and the percentage of the admitted applicants who are members of these same groups is far too precise to be dismissed as merely the result of the school paying "some attention to [the] numbers." ... [F]rom 1995 through 2000 the percentage of admitted applicants who were members of these minority groups closely tracked the percentage of individuals in the school's applicant pool who were from the same groups.

. . .

For example, in 1995, when 9.7% of the applicant pool was African–American, 9.4% of the admitted class was African–American. By 2000, only 7.5% of the applicant pool was African–American, and 7.3% of the admitted class was African–American. This correlation is striking. Respondents themselves emphasize that the number of underrepresented minority students admitted to the Law School would be significantly smaller if the race of each applicant were not considered.... But, as the examples above illustrate, the measure of the decrease would differ dramatically among the groups. The tight correlation between the percentage of applicants and admittees of a given race, therefore, must result from careful race based planning by the Law School. It suggests a formula for admission based on the aspirational assumption that all applicants are equally qualified academically, and therefore that the proportion of each group admitted should be the same as the proportion of that group in the applicant pool....

Not only do respondents fail to explain this phenomenon, they attempt to obscure it.... ("The Law School's minority enrollment percentages ... diverged from the percentages in the applicant pool by as much as 17.7% from 1995–2000"). But the divergence between the percentages of underrepresented minorities in the applicant pool and in the *enrolled* classes is not the only relevant comparison. In fact, it may not be the most relevant comparison. The Law School cannot precisely control which of its admitted applicants decide to attend the university. But it can and, as the numbers demonstrate, clearly does employ racial preferences in extending offers of admission. Indeed, the ostensibly flexible nature of the Law School's admissions program that the Court finds appealing appears to be, in practice, a carefully managed program designed to ensure proportionate representation of applicants from selected minority groups.

I do not believe that the Constitution gives the Law School such free rein in the use of race. The Law School has offered no explanation for its actual admissions practices and, unexplained, we are bound to conclude that the Law School has managed its admissions program, not to achieve a "critical mass," but to extend offers of admission to members of selected minority groups in proportion to their statistical representation in the applicant pool. But this is precisely the type of racial balancing that the Court itself calls "patently unconstitutional."

Finally, I believe that the Law School's program fails strict scrutiny because it is devoid of any reasonably precise time limit on the Law School's use of race in admissions....

The Court suggests a possible 25–year limitation on the Law School's current program. Respondents, on the other hand, remain more ambiguous, explaining that "the Law School of course recognizes that race-conscious programs must have reasonable durational limits, and the Sixth Circuit properly found such a limit in the Law School's resolve to cease considering race when genuine race-neutral alternatives become available." ... These discussions of a time limit are the vaguest of assurances. In truth, they permit the Law School's use of racial preferences on a seemingly permanent basis. Thus, an important component of strict scrutiny—that a program be limited in time—is casually subverted.

The Court, in an unprecedented display of deference under our strict scrutiny analysis, upholds the Law School's program despite its obvious flaws. We have said that when it comes to the use of race, the connection between the ends and the means used to attain them must be precise. But here the flaw is deeper than that; it is not merely a question of "fit" between ends and means. Here the means actually used are forbidden by the Equal Protection Clause of the Constitution.

Justice Kennedy, dissenting.

The separate opinion by Justice Powell in *Regents of Univ. of Cal. v. Bakke* is based on the principle that a university admissions program may take account of race as one, nonpredominant factor in a system designed to consider each applicant as an individual, provided the program can meet the test of strict scrutiny by the judiciary. ... This is a unitary formulation. If strict scrutiny is abandoned or manipulated to distort its real and accepted meaning, the Court lacks authority to approve the use of race even in this modest, limited way. The opinion by Justice Powell, in my view, states the correct rule for resolving this case. The Court, however, does not apply strict scrutiny. By trying to say otherwise, it undermines both the test and its own controlling precedents.

Justice Powell's approval of the use of race in university admissions reflected a tradition, grounded in the First Amendment, of acknowledging a university's conception of its educational mission.... Our precedents provide a basis for the Court's acceptance of a university's considered judgment that racial diversity among students can further its educational task, when supported by empirical evidence....

It is unfortunate, however, that the Court takes the first part of Justice Powell's rule but abandons the second. Having approved the use of race as a factor in the admissions process, the majority proceeds to nullify the essential safeguard Justice Powell insisted upon as the precondition of the approval [—] rigorous judicial review, with strict scrutiny as the controlling standard.... The Court confuses deference to a university's definition of its educational objective with deference to the implementation of this goal. In the context of university admissions the objective of racial diversity can be accepted based on empirical data known to us, but deference is not to be given with respect to the methods by which it is pursued....

The Court, in a review that is nothing short of perfunctory, accepts the University of Michigan Law School's assurances that its admissions process meets with constitutional requirements. The majority fails to confront the reality of how the Law School's admissions policy is implemented. The dissenting opinion by the Chief Justice, which I join in full, demonstrates beyond question why the concept of critical mass is a delusion used by the Law School to mask its attempt to make race an automatic factor in most instances and to achieve numerical goals indistinguishable from quotas.... It remains to point out how critical mass becomes inconsistent with individual consideration in some more specific aspects of the admissions process.

About 80 to 85 percent of the places in the entering class are given to applicants in the upper range of Law School Admissions Test scores and grades. An applicant with these credentials likely will be admitted without consideration of race or ethnicity. With respect to the remaining 15 to 20 percent of the seats, race is likely outcome determinative for many members of minority groups. That is where the competition becomes tight and where any given applicant's chance of admission is far smaller if he or she lacks minority status. At this point the numerical concept of critical mass has the real potential to compromise individual review.

The Law School has not demonstrated how individual consideration is, or can be, preserved at this stage of the application process given the instruction to attain what it calls critical mass. In fact the evidence shows otherwise. There was little deviation among admitted minority students during the years from 1995 to 1998. The percentage of enrolled minorities fluctuated only by 0.3%, from 13.5% to 13.8%. The number of minority students to whom offers were extended varied by just a slightly greater magnitude of 2.2%, from the high of 15.6% in 1995 to the low of 13.4% in 1998.

The District Court relied on this uncontested fact to draw an inference that the Law School's pursuit of critical mass mutated into the equivalent of a quota.... Admittedly, there were greater fluctuations among enrolled minorities in the preceding years, 1987–1994, by as much as 5 or 6%. The percentage of minority offers, however, at no point fell below 12%, historically defined by the Law School as the bottom of its critical mass range. The greater variance during the earlier years, in any event, does not dispel suspicion that the school engaged in racial balancing. The data would be consistent with an inference that the Law School modified its target only twice, in 1991 (from 13% to 19%), and then again in 1995 (back from 20% to 13%). The intervening year, 1993, when the percentage dropped to 14.5%, could be an aberration, caused by the school's miscalculation as to how many applicants with offers would accept or by its redefinition, made in April 1992, of which minority groups were entitled to race-based preference. . . .

The narrow fluctuation band raises an inference that the Law School subverted individual determination, and strict scrutiny requires the Law School to overcome the inference. . . .

. . . At the very least, the constancy of admitted minority students and the close correlation between the racial breakdown of admitted minorities and the composition of the applicant pool . . . require the Law School either to produce a convincing explanation or to show it has taken adequate steps to ensure individual assessment. The Law School does neither.

The obvious tension between the pursuit of critical mass and the requirement of individual review increased by the end of the admissions season. Most of the decisions where race may decide the outcome are made during this period. . . .

The consultation of daily reports during the last stages in the admissions process suggests there was no further attempt at individual review save for race itself. The admissions officers could use the reports to recalibrate the plus factor given to race depending on how close they were to achieving the Law School's goal of critical mass. The bonus factor of race would then become divorced from individual review; it would be premised instead on the numerical objective set by the Law School.

The Law School made no effort to guard against this danger. It provided no guidelines to its admissions personnel on how to reconcile individual assessment with the directive to admit a critical mass of minority students. The admissions program could have been structured to eliminate at least some of the risk that the promise of individual evaluation was not being kept. The daily consideration of racial breakdown of admitted students is not a feature of affirmative-action programs used by other institutions of higher learning. . . .

To be constitutional, a university's compelling interest in a diverse student body must be achieved by a system where individual assessment is safeguarded through the entire process. There is no constitutional objection to the goal of considering race as one modest factor among many others to achieve diversity, but an educational institution must ensure, through sufficient procedures, that each applicant receives individual consideration and that race does not become a predominant factor in the admissions decisionmaking. . . .

. . . By deferring to the law schools' choice of minority admissions programs, the courts will lose the talents and resources of the faculties and administrators in devising new and fairer ways to ensure individual consideration. Constant and rigorous judicial review forces the law school faculties to undertake their responsibilities as state employees in this most sensitive of areas with utmost fidelity to the mandate of the Constitution. . . . Prospective students, the courts, and the public can demand that the State and its law schools prove their process is fair and constitutional in every phase of implementation.

It is difficult to assess the Court's pronouncement that race-conscious admissions programs will be unnecessary 25 years from now. If it is intended to mitigate the damage the Court does to the concept of strict scrutiny, neither petitioners nor other rejected law school applicants will find solace in knowing the basic protection put in place by Justice Powell will be suspended for a full quarter of a century. Deference is antithetical to strict scrutiny, not consistent with it.

As to the interpretation that the opinion contains its own self-destruct mechanism, the majority's abandonment of strict scrutiny undermines this objective. Were the courts to apply a searching standard to race-based admissions schemes, that would force educational institutions to seriously explore race-neutral alternatives. The Court, by contrast, is willing to be satisfied by the Law School's profession of its own good faith....

If universities are given the latitude to administer programs that are tantamount to quotas, they will have few incentives to make the existing minority admissions schemes transparent and protective of individual review. The unhappy consequence will be to perpetuate the hostilities that proper consideration of race is designed to avoid. The perpetuation, of course, would be the worst of all outcomes. Other programs do exist which will be more effective in bringing about the harmony and mutual respect among all citizens that our constitutional tradition has always sought. They, and not the program under review here, should be the model, even if the Court defaults by not demanding it.

It is regrettable the Court's important holding allowing racial minorities to have their special circumstances considered in order to improve their educational opportunities is accompanied by a suspension of the strict scrutiny which was the predicate of allowing race to be considered in the first place. If the Court abdicates its constitutional duty to give strict scrutiny to the use of race in university admissions, it negates my authority to approve the use of race in pursuit of student diversity. The Constitution cannot confer the right to classify on the basis of race even in this special context absent searching judicial review. For these reasons, though I reiterate my approval of giving appropriate consideration to race in this one context, I must dissent in the present case.

Justice Scalia, with whom Justice Thomas joins, concurring in part and dissenting in part.

I join the opinion of the Chief Justice. As he demonstrates, the University of Michigan Law School's mystical "critical mass" justification for its discrimination by race challenges even the most gullible mind. The admissions statistics show it to be a sham to cover a scheme of racially proportionate admissions.

I also join Parts I through VII of Justice Thomas's opinion. I find particularly unanswerable his central point: that the allegedly "compelling state interest" at issue here is not the incremental "educational benefit" that emanates from the fabled "critical mass" of minority students, but rather Michigan's interest in maintaining a "prestige" law school whose normal admissions standards disproportionately exclude blacks and other minorities. If that is a compelling state interest, everything is.

I add the following: The "educational benefit" that the University of Michigan seeks to achieve by racial discrimination consists, according to the Court, of " 'cross-racial understanding,' " and " 'better prepar[ation of] students for an increasingly diverse workforce and society,' " all of which is necessary not only for work, but also for good "citizenship." ... If it is appropriate for the University of Michigan Law School to use racial discrimination for the purpose of putting together a "critical mass" that will convey generic lessons in socialization and good citizenship, surely it is no less appropriate—indeed, *particularly* appropriate—for the civil service system of the State of Michigan to do so.... And surely private employers cannot be criticized—indeed, should be praised—if they also "teach" good citizenship to their adult employees through a patriotic, all-American system of racial discrimination in hiring. The nonminority individuals who are deprived of a legal education, a civil service job, or any job at all by reason of their skin color will surely understand.

Unlike a clear constitutional holding that racial preferences in state educational institutions are impermissible, or even a clear anticonstitutional holding that racial preferences in state educational institutions are OK, today's *Grutter–Gratz* split double header seems perversely designed to prolong the controversy and the litigation. Some future lawsuits will presumably focus on whether the discriminatory scheme in question contains enough evaluation of the applicant "as an individual" and sufficiently avoids "separate admissions tracks" to fall under *Grutter* rather than *Gratz*. Some will focus on whether a university has gone beyond the bounds of a " 'good faith effort' " and has so zealously pursued its "critical mass" as to make it an unconstitutional *de facto* quota system, rather than merely " 'a permissible goal.' " ... Other lawsuits may focus on whether, in the particular setting at issue, any educational benefits flow from racial diversity.... Still other suits may challenge the bona fides of the institution's expressed commitment to the educational benefits of diversity that immunize the discriminatory scheme in *Grutter*.... And still other suits may claim that the institution's racial preferences have gone below or above the mystical *Grutter*-approved "critical mass." Finally, litigation can be expected on behalf of minority groups intentionally short changed in the institution's composition of its generic minority "critical mass." I do not look forward to any of these cases. The Constitution proscribes government discrimination on the basis of race, and state-provided education is no exception.

Justice Thomas, with whom Justice Scalia joins as to Parts I–VII, concurring in part and dissenting in part.

... I believe blacks can achieve in every avenue of American life without the meddling of university administrators....

No one would argue that a university could set up a lower general admission standard and then impose heightened requirements only on black applicants. Similarly, a university may not maintain a high admission standard and grant exemptions to favored races. The Law School, of its own choosing, and for its own purposes, maintains an exclusionary admissions system that it knows produces racially disproportionate results. Racial discrimination is not a permissible solution to the self-inflicted wounds of this elitist admissions policy.

. . .

I

The majority agrees that the Law School's racial discrimination should be subjected to strict scrutiny....

... A majority of the Court has validated only two circumstances where "pressing public necessity" or a "compelling state interest" can possibly justify racial discrimination by state actors. First, the lesson of *Korematsu* is that national security constitutes a "pressing public necessity," though the government's use of race to advance that objective must be narrowly tailored. Second, the Court has recognized as a compelling state interest a government's effort to remedy past discrimination for which it is responsible. *Richmond v. J. A. Croson Co.*, 488 U.S. 469, 504 (1989).

. . .

... In *Palmore v. Sidoti*, 466 U.S. 429 (1984), the Court held that even the best interests of a child did not constitute a compelling state interest that would allow a state court to award custody to the father because the mother was in a mixed-race marriage....

. . .

Where the Court has accepted only national security, and rejected even the best interests of a child, as a justification for racial discrimination, I conclude that only those measures the State must take to provide a bulwark against anarchy, or to prevent violence, will constitute a "pressing public necessity."
...

[handwritten margin note: prevention of violence and anarchy only compelling state interest]

. . .

II

Unlike the majority, I seek to define with precision the interest being asserted by the Law School before determining whether that interest is so compelling as to justify racial discrimination....

... Attaining "diversity," whatever it means, is the mechanism by which the Law School obtains educational benefits, not an end of itself. ...

... It is the *educational benefits* that are the end, or allegedly compelling state interest, not "diversity."

One must also consider the Law School's refusal to entertain changes to its current admissions system that might produce the same educational benefits. The Law School adamantly disclaims any race-neutral alternative that would reduce "academic selectivity," which would in turn "require the Law School to become a very different institution, and to sacrifice a core part of its educational mission." ... In other words, the Law School seeks to improve marginally the education it offers without sacrificing too much of its exclusivity and elite status.[4]

---

4. The Law School believes both that the educational benefits of a racially engineered student body are large and that adjusting its overall admissions standards to achieve the same racial mix would require it to sacrifice its elite status. If the Law School is correct that the educational benefits of "diversity" are so great, then achieving them by altering admissions standards should not compromise its elite status. The Law School's

The proffered interest that the majority vindicates today, then, is not simply "diversity." Instead the Court upholds the use of racial discrimination as a tool to advance the Law School's interest in offering a marginally superior education while maintaining an elite institution. Unless each constituent part of this state interest is of pressing public necessity, the Law School's use of race is unconstitutional. I find each of them to fall far short of this standard.

pressing public necessity

III

A

A close reading of the Court's opinion reveals that all of its legal work is done through one conclusory statement: The Law School has a "compelling interest in securing the educational benefits of a diverse student body." ...

Justice Powell's opinion in *Bakke* and the Court's decision today rest on the fundamentally flawed proposition that racial discrimination can be contextualized so that a goal, such as classroom aesthetics, can be compelling in one context but not in another. This "we know it when we see it" approach to evaluating state interests is not capable of judicial application. Today, the Court insists on radically expanding the range of permissible uses of race to something as trivial (by comparison) as the assembling of a law school class. I can only presume that the majority's failure to justify its decision by reference to any principle arises from the absence of any such principle. See Part VI, *infra.*

B

Under the proper standard, there is no pressing public necessity in maintaining a public law school at all and, it follows, certainly not an elite law school. Likewise, marginal improvements in legal education do not qualify as a compelling state interest.

1

While legal education at a public university may be good policy or otherwise laudable, it is obviously not a pressing public necessity....

2

... Michigan has no compelling interest in having a law school at all, much less an *elite* one. Still, even assuming that a State may, under appropriate circumstances, demonstrate a cognizable interest in having an elite law school, Michigan has failed to do so here.

· · ·

... The only interests that can satisfy the Equal Protection Clause's demands are those found within a State's jurisdiction.

The only cognizable state interests vindicated by operating a public law school are, therefore, the education of that State's citizens and the training of that State's lawyers....

reluctance to do this suggests that the edu- or do not exist at all.
cational benefits it alleges are not significant

The Law School today, however, does precious little training of those attorneys who will serve the citizens of Michigan. In 2002, graduates of the University of Michigan Law School made up less than 6% of applicants to the Michigan bar. . . .

In sum, the Law School trains few Michigan residents and overwhelmingly serves students, who, as lawyers, leave the State of Michigan. By contrast, Michigan's other public law school, Wayne State University Law School, sends 88% of its graduates on to serve the people of Michigan. . . . It does not take a social scientist to conclude that it is precisely the Law School's status as an elite institution that causes it to be a way-station for the rest of the country's lawyers, rather than a training ground for those who will remain in Michigan. The Law School's decision to be an elite institution does little to advance the welfare of the people of Michigan or any cognizable interest of the State of Michigan.

[Also,] that few States choose to maintain elite law schools raises a strong inference that there is nothing compelling about elite status. . . .

3

Finally, even if the Law School's racial tinkering produces tangible educational benefits, a marginal improvement in legal education cannot justify racial discrimination where the Law School has no compelling interest in either its existence or in its current educational and admissions policies.

IV

The interest in remaining elite and exclusive that the majority thinks so obviously critical requires the use of admissions "standards" that, in turn, create the Law School's "need" to discriminate on the basis of race. The Court validates these admissions standards by concluding that alternatives that would require "a dramatic sacrifice of . . . the academic quality of all admitted students" need not be considered before racial discrimination can be employed. . . .

With the adoption of different admissions methods, such as accepting all students who meet minimum qualifications, see Brief for United States as *Amicus Curiae* 13–14, the Law School could achieve its vision of the racially aesthetic student body without the use of racial discrimination. . . . [E]ven if its "academic selectivity" must be maintained at all costs along with racial discrimination, the Court ignores the fact that other top law schools have succeeded in meeting their aesthetic demands without racial discrimination.

. . .

The Court's deference to the Law School's conclusion that its racial experimentation leads to educational benefits will, if adhered to, have serious collateral consequences. The Court relies heavily on social science evidence to justify its deference. . . . The Court never acknowledges, however, the growing evidence that racial (and other sorts) of heterogeneity actually impairs learning among black students. See, *e.g.,* Flowers & Pascarella, Cognitive Effects of College Racial Composition on African American Students After 3 Years of College, 40 J. of College Student Development 669, 674 (1999) (concluding that black students experience superior cognitive development at Historically Black

Colleges (HBCs) and that, even among blacks, "a substantial diversity moderates the cognitive effects of attending an HBC"); Allen, The Color of Success: African–American College Student Outcomes at Predominantly White and Historically Black Public Colleges and Universities, 62 Harv. Educ. Rev. 26, 35 (1992) (finding that black students attending HBCs report higher academic achievement than those attending predominantly white colleges).

. . .

The majority grants deference to the Law School's "assessment that diversity will, in fact, yield educational benefits." It follows, therefore, that an HBC's assessment that racial homogeneity will yield educational benefits would similarly be given deference. An HBC's rejection of white applicants in order to maintain racial homogeneity seems permissible, therefore, under the majority's view of the Equal Protection Clause. . . .

Moreover one would think, in light of the Court's decision in *United States v. Virginia,* 518 U.S. 515 (1996), that before being given license to use racial discrimination, the Law School would be required to radically reshape its admissions process, even to the point of sacrificing some elements of its character. In *Virginia,* a majority of the Court, without a word about academic freedom, accepted the all-male Virginia Military Institute's (VMI) representation that some changes in its "adversative" method of education would be required with the admission of women, . . . but did not defer to VMI's judgment that these changes would be too great. Instead, the Court concluded that they were "manageable." . . . That case involved sex discrimination, which is subjected to intermediate, not strict, scrutiny. . . . So in *Virginia,* where the standard of review dictated that greater flexibility be granted to VMI's educational policies than the Law School deserves here, this Court gave no deference. Apparently where the status quo being defended is that of the elite establishment—here the Law School—rather than a less fashionable Southern military institution, the Court will defer without serious inquiry and without regard to the applicable legal standard.

. . .

Virginia is also notable for the fact that the Court relied on the "experience" of formerly single-sex institutions, such as the service academies, to conclude that admission of women to VMI would be "manageable." . . . Today, however, the majority ignores the "experience" of those institutions that have been forced to abandon explicit racial discrimination in admissions.

The sky has not fallen at Boalt Hall at the University of California, Berkeley, for example. Prior to Proposition 209's adoption of Cal. Const., Art. 1, § 31(a), which bars the State from "grant[ing] preferential treatment . . . on the basis of race . . . in the operation of . . . public education," Boalt Hall enrolled 20 blacks and 28 Hispanics in its first-year class for 1996. In 2002, without deploying express racial discrimination in admissions, Boalt's entering class enrolled 14 blacks and 36 Hispanics. . . . Total underrepresented minority student enrollment at Boalt Hall now exceeds 1996 levels. Apparently [Michigan] Law School cannot be counted on to be as resourceful. The Court is willfully blind to the very real experience in California and elsewhere, which raises the inference that institutions with "reputation[s] for excellence" rivaling the Law School's have satisfied their sense of mission without resorting to prohibited racial discrimination.

V

. . .

[T]here is nothing ancient, honorable, or constitutionally protected about "selective" admissions . . .

. . . Since its inception, selective admissions has been the vehicle for racial, ethnic, and religious tinkering and experimentation by university administrators. The initial driving force for the relocation of the selective function from the high school to the universities was the same desire to select racial winners and losers that the Law School exhibits today. Columbia, Harvard, and others infamously determined that they had "too many" Jews, just as today the Law School argues it would have "too many" whites if it could not discriminate in its admissions process. . . .

Columbia employed intelligence tests precisely because Jewish applicants, who were predominantly immigrants, scored worse on such tests. . . . In other words, the tests were adopted with full knowledge of their disparate impact. Cf. *DeFunis v. Odegaard*, 416 U.S. 312, 335 (1974) *(per curiam)* (Douglas, J., dissenting).

Similarly no modern law school can claim ignorance of the poor performance of blacks, relatively speaking, on the Law School Admissions Test (LSAT). Nevertheless, law schools continue to use the test and then attempt to "correct" for black underperformance by using racial discrimination in admissions so as to obtain their aesthetic student body. The Law School's continued adherence to measures it knows produce racially skewed results is not entitled to deference by this Court. . . .

Having decided to use the LSAT, the Law School must accept the constitutional burdens that come with this decision. The Law School may freely continue to employ the LSAT and other allegedly merit-based standards in whatever fashion it likes. What the Equal Protection Clause forbids, but the Court today allows, is the use of these standards hand-in-hand with racial discrimination. . . .

The Court will not even deign to make the Law School try other methods, however, preferring instead to grant a 25–year license to violate the Constitution. . . .

VI

. . . I believe what lies beneath the Court's decision today are the benighted notions that one can tell when racial discrimination benefits (rather than hurts) minority groups, . . . and that racial discrimination is necessary to remedy general societal ills. This Court's precedents supposedly settled both issues, but clearly the majority still cannot commit to the principle that racial classifications are *per se* harmful and that almost no amount of benefit in the eye of the beholder can justify such classifications.

Putting aside what I take to be the Court's implicit rejection of *Adarand*'s holding that beneficial and burdensome racial classifications are equally invalid,

I must contest the notion that the Law School's discrimination benefits those admitted as a result of it.... [N]owhere in any of the filings in this Court is any evidence that the purported "beneficiaries" of this racial discrimination prove themselves by performing at (or even near) the same level as those students who receive no preferences. Cf. Thernstrom & Thernstrom, Reflections on the Shape of the River, 46 UCLA L. Rev. 1583, 1605–1608 (1999) (discussing the failure of defenders of racial discrimination in admissions to consider the fact that its "beneficiaries" are underperforming in the classroom).

The silence in this case is deafening to those of us who view higher education's purpose as imparting knowledge and skills to students, rather than a communal, rubber-stamp, credentialing process. The Law School is not looking for those students who, despite a lower LSAT score or undergraduate grade point average, will succeed in the study of law. The Law School seeks only a facade—it is sufficient that the class looks right, even if it does not perform right.

. . .

Beyond the harm the Law School's racial discrimination visits upon its test subjects, no social science has disproved the notion that this discrimination "engender[s] attitudes of superiority or, alternatively, provoke[s] resentment among those who believe that they have been wronged by the government's use of race." *Adarand*, . . . (Thomas, J., concurring in part and concurring in judgment). "These programs stamp minorities with a badge of inferiority and may cause them to develop dependencies or to adopt an attitude that they are 'entitled' to preferences." . . .

. . . The majority of blacks are admitted to the Law School because of discrimination, and because of this policy all are tarred as undeserving. This problem of stigma does not depend on determinacy as to whether those stigmatized are actually the "beneficiaries" of racial discrimination. When blacks take positions in the highest places of government, industry, or academia, it is an open question today whether their skin color played a part in their advancement. The question itself is the stigma—because either racial discrimination did play a role, in which case the person may be deemed "otherwise unqualified," or it did not, in which case asking the question itself unfairly marks those blacks who would succeed without discrimination. Is this what the Court means by "visibly open"?

Finally, the Court's disturbing reference to the importance of the country's law schools as training grounds meant to cultivate "a set of leaders with legitimacy in the eyes of the citizenry" through the use of racial discrimination deserves discussion. [T]he Court has soundly rejected the remedying of societal discrimination as a justification for governmental use of race. *Wygant*, 476 U.S., at 276 (plurality opinion); *Croson*, 488 U.S., at 497 (plurality opinion); *id.*, at 520–521 (Scalia, J., concurring in judgment). For those who believe that every racial disproportionality in our society is caused by some kind of racial discrimination, there can be no distinction between remedying societal discrimination and erasing racial disproportionalities in the country's leadership caste. And if the lack of proportional racial representation among our leaders is not caused by societal discrimination, then "fixing" it is even less of a pressing public necessity.

. . .

VII

As the foregoing makes clear, I believe the Court's opinion to be, in most respects, erroneous. I do, however, find two points on which I agree.

A

First, I note that the issue of unconstitutional racial discrimination among the groups the Law School prefers is not presented in this case, because petitioner has never argued that the Law School engages in such a practice, and the Law School maintains that it does not.... I join the Court's opinion insofar as it confirms that this type of racial discrimination remains unlawful.... [T]he Law School may not discriminate in admissions between similarly situated blacks and Hispanics, or between whites and Asians. This is so because preferring black to Hispanic applicants, for instance, does nothing to further the interest recognized by the majority today.[12] Indeed, the majority describes such racial balancing as "patently unconstitutional." Like the Court, I express no opinion as to whether the Law School's current admissions program runs afoul of this prohibition.

B

The Court also holds that racial discrimination in admissions should be given another 25 years before it is deemed no longer narrowly tailored to the Law School's fabricated compelling state interest. While I agree that in 25 years the practices of the Law School will be illegal, they are, for the reasons I have given, illegal now.... No one can seriously contend, and the Court does not, that the racial gap in academic credentials will disappear in 25 years. Nor is the Court's holding that racial discrimination will be unconstitutional in 25 years made contingent on the gap closing in that time.

. . .

I ... understand the imposition of a 25–year time limit only as a holding that the deference the Court pays to the Law School's educational judgments and refusal to change its admissions policies will itself expire.... The Court defines this time limit in terms of narrow tailoring, but I believe this arises from its refusal to define rigorously the broad state interest vindicated today. ... With these observations, I join the last sentence of Part III of the opinion of the Court.

. . .

12. That interest depends on enrolling a "critical mass" of underrepresented minority students, as the majority repeatedly states.... As it relates to the Law School's racial discrimination, the Court clearly approves of only one use of race—the distinction between underrepresented minority applicants and those of all other races. A relative preference awarded to a black applicant over, for example, a similarly situated Native American applicant, does not lead to the enrollment of even one more underrepresented minority student, but only balances the races within the "critical mass."

Gratz v. Bollinger

__ U.S. __, 123 S.Ct. 2411, __ L.Ed.2d __ (2003).

Chief Justice Rehnquist delivered the opinion of the Court.

We granted certiorari in this case to decide whether "the University of Michigan's use of racial preferences in undergraduate admissions violate[s] the Equal Protection Clause of the Fourteenth Amendment, Title VI of the Civil Rights Act of 1964 (42 U.S.C. § 2000d), or 42 U.S.C. § 1981." ... Because we find that the manner in which the University considers the race of applicants in its undergraduate admissions guidelines violates these constitutional and statutory provisions, we reverse that portion of the District Court's decision upholding the guidelines.

I

[Petitioners Gratz and Hamacher, white residents of Michigan, applied to the University of Michigan's College of Literature, Science, and the Arts (LSA) and were eventually denied admission. They brought a class-action lawsuit challenging the University's use of race in its admissions system.]

... The University's Office of Undergraduate Admissions (OUA)[—i]n order to promote consistency in the review of the large number of applications received[—]uses written guidelines.... Admissions counselors make admissions decisions in accordance with these guidelines.

OUA considers a number of factors in making admissions decisions, including high school grades, standardized test scores, high school quality, curriculum strength, geography, alumni relationships, and leadership. OUA also considers race. During all periods relevant to this litigation, the University has considered African–Americans, Hispanics, and Native Americans to be "underrepresented minorities," and it is undisputed that the University admits "virtually every qualified ... applicant" from these groups....

During 1995 and 1996, OUA counselors evaluated applications according to grade point average combined with what were referred to as the "SCUGA" factors. These factors included the quality of an applicant's high school (S), the strength of an applicant's high school curriculum (C), an applicant's unusual circumstances (U), an applicant's geographical residence (G), and an applicant's alumni relationships (A). After these scores were combined to produce an applicant's "GPA 2" score, the reviewing admissions counselors referenced a set of "Guidelines" tables, which listed GPA 2 ranges on the vertical axis, and American College Test/Scholastic Aptitude Test (ACT/SAT) scores on the horizontal axis. Each table was divided into cells that included one or more courses of action to be taken, including admit, reject, delay for additional information, or postpone for reconsideration.

In both years, applicants with the same GPA 2 score and ACT/SAT score were subject to different admissions outcomes based upon their racial or ethnic status. For example, as a Caucasian in-state applicant, Gratz's GPA 2 score and ACT score placed her within a cell calling for a postponed decision on her application. An in-state or out-of-state minority applicant with Gratz's scores would have fallen within a cell calling for admission.

In 1997, the University modified its admissions procedure. Specifically, the formula for calculating an applicant's GPA 2 score was restructured to include additional point values under the "U" category in the SCUGA factors. Under this new system, applicants could receive points for underrepresented minority status, socioeconomic disadvantage, or attendance at a high school with a predominantly underrepresented minority population, or underrepresentation in the unit to which the student was applying (for example, men who sought to pursue a career in nursing). Under the 1997 procedures, Hamacher's GPA 2 score and ACT score placed him in a cell on the in-state applicant table calling for postponement of a final admissions decision. An underrepresented minority applicant placed in the same cell would generally have been admitted.

Beginning with the 1998 academic year, the OUA dispensed with the Guidelines tables and the SCUGA point system in favor of a "selection index," on which an applicant could score a maximum of 150 points. This index was divided linearly into ranges generally calling for admissions dispositions as follows: 100–150 (admit); 95–99 (admit or postpone); 90–94 (postpone or admit); 75–89 (delay or postpone); 74 and below (delay or reject).

Each application received points based on high school grade point average, standardized test scores, academic quality of an applicant's high school, strength or weakness of high school curriculum, in-state residency, alumni relationship, personal essay, and personal achievement or leadership. Of particular significance here, under a "miscellaneous" category, an applicant was entitled to 20 points based upon his or her membership in an underrepresented racial or ethnic minority group. The University explained that the " 'development of the selection index for admissions in 1998 changed only the mechanics, not the substance of how race and ethnicity were considered in admissions.' "

. . .

In all application years from 1995 to 1998, the guidelines provided that qualified applicants from underrepresented minority groups be admitted as soon as possible in light of the University's belief that such applicants were more likely to enroll if promptly notified of their admission. Also from 1995 through 1998, the University carefully managed its rolling admissions system to permit consideration of certain applications submitted later in the academic year through the use of "protected seats." Specific groups—including athletes, foreign students, ROTC candidates, and underrepresented minorities—were "protected categories" eligible for these seats. A committee called the Enrollment Working Group (EWG) projected how many applicants from each of these protected categories the University was likely to receive after a given date and then paced admissions decisions to permit full consideration of expected applications from these groups. If this space was not filled by qualified candidates from the designated groups toward the end of the admissions season, it was then used to admit qualified candidates remaining in the applicant pool, including those on the waiting list.

During 1999 and 2000, the OUA used the selection index, under which every applicant from an underrepresented racial or ethnic minority group was awarded 20 points. Starting in 1999, however, the University established an Admissions Review Committee (ARC), to provide an additional level of consideration for some applications. Under the new system, counselors may, in their discretion, "flag" an application for the ARC to review after determining that the applicant (1) is academically prepared to succeed at the University, (2) has achieved a minimum selection index score, and (3) possesses a quality or characteristic important to the University's composition of its freshman class, such as high class rank, unique life experiences, challenges, circumstances, interests or talents, socioeconomic disadvantage, and underrepresented race, ethnicity, or geography. After reviewing "flagged" applications, the ARC determines whether to admit, defer, or deny each applicant.

. . .

[On cross-motions for summary judgment, the District Court granted petitioners' motion for summary judgment with respect to the LSA's admissions programs in existence from 1995 through 1998, and respondents' motion with respect to the LSA's admissions programs for 1999 and 2000. On interlocutory appeal, the Sixth Circuit heard the case en banc on the same day as *Grutter* v. *Bollinger* and later issued its opinion in *Grutter*. The Supreme Court then granted certiorari in this case as well as in *Grutter*, despite the fact that the Court of Appeals had not yet rendered a judgment here, so that the Court] could address the constitutionality of the consideration of race in university admissions in a wider range of circumstances. . . .

II

. . .

Petitioners . . . contend that this Court has only sanctioned the use of racial classifications to remedy identified discrimination, a justification on which respondents have never relied. . . . Petitioners further argue that "diversity as a basis for employing racial preferences is simply too open-ended, ill-defined, and indefinite to constitute a compelling interest capable of supporting narrowly-tailored means." . . . But for the reasons set forth today in *Grutter v. Bollinger,* the Court has rejected these arguments of petitioners.

Petitioners alternatively argue that even if the University's interest in diversity can constitute a compelling state interest, the District Court erroneously concluded that the University's use of race in its current freshman admissions policy is narrowly tailored to achieve such an interest. Petitioners argue that the guidelines the University began using in 1999 do not "remotely resemble the kind of consideration of race and ethnicity that Justice Powell endorsed in *Bakke*." . . . Respondents reply that the University's current admissions program *is* narrowly tailored and avoids the problems of the Medical School of the University of California at Davis program (U. C. Davis) rejected by Justice Powell.[18] They claim that their program "hews closely" to

---

18. U.C. Davis set aside 16 of the 100 seats available in its first year medical school program for "economically and/or educationally disadvantaged" applicants who were also members of designated "minority groups" as defined by the university. "To the extent that there existed a pool of at least minimally qualified minority applicants to fill the 16 special admissions seats, white applicants could compete only for 84 seats in the entering class, rather than the 100 open to minori-

ty applicants." *Regents of Univ. of Cal. v. Bakke*, 438 U.S. 265, 274, 289 (1978) (principal opinion). Justice Powell found that the program employed an impermissible two-track system that 'disregard[ed] . . . individual rights as guaranteed by the Fourteenth Amendment.' *Id.*, at 315. He reached this conclusion even though the university argued that 'the reservation of a specified number of seats in each class for individuals from the both the admissions program described by Justice Powell as well as the Harvard College admissions program that he endorsed.... Specifically, respondents contend that the LSA's policy provides the individualized consideration that "Justice Powell considered a hallmark of a constitutionally appropriate admissions program." ... For the reasons set out below, we do not agree.

It is by now well established that "all racial classifications reviewable under the Equal Protection Clause must be strictly scrutinized." *Adarand Constructors, Inc. v. Peã,* 515 U.S. 200, 224 (1995)....

To withstand our strict scrutiny analysis, respondents must demonstrate that the University's use of race in its current admission program employs "narrowly tailored measures that further compelling governmental interests." *Id.,*.... We find that the University's policy, which automatically distributes 20 points, or one-fifth of the points needed to guarantee admission, to every single "underrepresented minority" applicant solely because of race, is not narrowly tailored to achieve the interest in educational diversity that respondents claim justifies their program.

In *Bakke,* Justice Powell reiterated that "[p]referring members of any one group for no reason other than race or ethnic origin is discrimination for its own sake." ... He then explained, however, that in his view it would be permissible for a university to employ an admissions program in which "race or ethnic background may be deemed a 'plus' in a particular applicant's file." ... He explained that such a program might allow for "[t]he file of a particular black applicant [to] be examined for his potential contribution to diversity without the factor of race being decisive when compared, for example, with that of an applicant identified as an Italian-American if the latter is thought to exhibit qualities more likely to promote beneficial educational pluralism." ... Such a system, in Justice Powell's view, would be "flexible enough to consider all pertinent elements of diversity in light of the particular qualifications of each applicant." ...

Justice Powell's opinion in *Bakke* emphasized the importance of considering each particular applicant as an individual, assessing all of the qualities that individual possesses, and in turn, evaluating that individual's ability to contribute to the unique setting of higher education. The admissions program Justice Powell described, however, did not contemplate that any single characteristic automatically ensured a specific and identifiable contribution to a university's diversity. ... Instead, under the approach Justice Powell described, each characteristic of a particular applicant was to be considered in assessing the applicant's entire application.

The current LSA policy does not provide such individualized consideration. The LSA's policy automatically distributes 20 points to every single applicant from an "underrepresented minority" group, as defined by the University. The only consideration that accompanies this distribution of points is a factual review of an application to determine whether an individual is a member of one of these minority groups. Moreover, unlike Justice Powell's example, where the race of a "particular black applicant" could be considered without being

preferred ethnic groups' was 'the only effective means of serving the interest of diversity.' *Ibid.* Justice Powell concluded that such

arguments misunderstood the very nature of the diversity he found to be compelling. See *ibid.*

decisive, ... the LSA's automatic distribution of 20 points has the effect of making "the factor of race ... decisive" for virtually every minimally qualified underrepresented minority applicant....[19]

Also instructive in our consideration of the LSA's system is the example provided in the description of the Harvard College Admissions Program, which Justice Powell both discussed in, and attached to, his opinion in *Bakke*. The example was included to "illustrate the kind of significance attached to race" under the Harvard College program.... It provided as follows:

> "The Admissions Committee, with only a few places left to fill, might find itself forced to choose between A, the child of a successful black physician in an academic community with promise of superior academic performance, and B, a black who grew up in an inner-city ghetto of semi-literate parents whose academic achievement was lower but who had demonstrated energy and leadership as well as an apparently abiding interest in black power. If a good number of black students much like A but few like B had already been admitted, the Committee might prefer B; and vice versa. If C, a white student with extraordinary artistic talent, were also seeking one of the remaining places, his unique quality might give him an edge over both A and B. Thus, the critical criteria are often individual qualities or experience *not dependent upon race but sometimes associated with it.*" ... (emphasis added).

This example further demonstrates the problematic nature of the LSA's admissions system. Even if student C's "extraordinary artistic talent" rivaled that of Monet or Picasso, the applicant would receive, at most, five points under the LSA's system.... At the same time, every single underrepresented minority applicant, including students A and B, would automatically receive 20 points for submitting an application. Clearly, the LSA's system does not offer applicants the individualized selection process described in Harvard's example. Instead of considering how the differing backgrounds, experiences, and characteristics of students A, B, and C might benefit the University, admissions counselors reviewing LSA applications would simply award both A and B 20 points because their applications indicate that they are African–American, and student C would receive up to 5 points for his "extraordinary talent."[20]

Respondents emphasize the fact that the LSA has created the possibility of an applicant's file being flagged for individualized consideration by the ARC. We think that the flagging program only emphasizes the flaws of the University's system as a whole when compared to that described by Justice Powell. Again, students A, B, and C illustrate the point. First, student A would never be flagged. This is because, as the University has conceded, the effect of automatically awarding 20 points is that virtually every qualified underrepresented minority applicant is admitted. Student A, an applicant "with promise of superior academic performance," would certainly fit this description. Thus, the

---

19. Justice Souter recognizes that the LSA's use of race is decisive in practice, but he attempts to avoid that fact through unsupported speculation about the self-selection of minorities in the applicant pool.

20. Justice Souter is therefore wrong when he contends that "applicants to the undergraduate college are [not] denied individualized consideration." As Justice O'Connor explains in her concurrence, the LSA's program "ensures that the diversity contributions of applicants cannot be individually assessed."

result of the automatic distribution of 20 points is that the University would never consider student A's individual background, experiences, and characteristics to assess his individual "potential contribution to diversity,".... Instead, every applicant like student A would simply be admitted.

It is possible that students B and C would be flagged and considered as individuals. This assumes that student B was not already admitted because of the automatic 20–point distribution, and that student C could muster at least 70 additional points. But the fact that the "review committee can look at the applications individually and ignore the points," once an application is flagged, ... is of little comfort under our strict scrutiny analysis. The record does not reveal precisely how many applications are flagged for this individualized consideration, but it is undisputed that such consideration is the exception and not the rule in the operation of the LSA's admissions program.... Additionally, this individualized review is only provided *after* admissions counselors automatically distribute the University's version of a "plus" that makes race a decisive factor for virtually every minimally qualified underrepresented minority applicant.

Respondents contend that "[t]he volume of applications and the presentation of applicant information make it impractical for [LSA] to use the ... admissions system" upheld by the Court today in *Grutter*.... But the fact that the implementation of a program capable of providing individualized consideration might present administrative challenges does not render constitutional an otherwise problematic system....

We conclude, therefore, that because the University's use of race in its current freshman admissions policy is not narrowly tailored to achieve respondents' asserted compelling interest in diversity, the admissions policy violates the Equal Protection Clause of the Fourteenth Amendment.[22] We further find that the admissions policy also violates Title VI and 42 U.S.C. § 1981. Accordingly, we reverse that portion of the District Court's decision granting respondents summary judgment....

Justice O'Connor, concurring.*

I

Unlike the law school admissions policy the Court upholds today in *Grutter v. Bollinger*, the procedures employed by [OUA] do not provide for a meaningful individualized review of applicants. Cf. *Regents of Univ. of Cal. v. Bakke*,

---

22. Justice Ginsburg in her dissent observes that "[o]ne can reasonably anticipate ... that colleges and universities will seek to maintain their minority enrollment ... whether or not they can do so in full candor through adoption of affirmative action plans of the kind here at issue." She goes on to say that "[i]f honesty is the best policy, surely Michigan's accurately described, fully disclosed College affirmative action program is preferable to achieving similar numbers through winks, nods, and disguises." These observations are remarkable for two reasons.

First, they suggest that universities—to whose academic judgment we are told in *Grutter v. Bollinger* we should defer—will pursue their affirmative-action programs whether or not they violate the United States Constitution. Second, they recommend that these violations should be dealt with, not by requiring the universities to obey the Constitution, but by changing the Constitution so that it conforms to the conduct of the universities.

* Justice Breyer joins this opinion, except for the last sentence.

438 U.S. 265 (1978) (principal opinion of Powell, J.). The law school considers the various diversity qualifications of each applicant, including race, on a case-by-case basis.... By contrast, [OUA] relies on the selection index to assign *every* underrepresented minority applicant the same, *automatic* 20–point bonus without consideration of the particular background, experiences, or qualities of each individual applicant. And this mechanized selection index score, by and large, automatically determines the admissions decision for each applicant. The selection index thus precludes admissions counselors from conducting the type of individualized consideration the Court's opinion in *Grutter*... requires: consideration of each applicant's individualized qualifications, including the contribution each individual's race or ethnic identity will make to the diversity of the student body, taking into account diversity within and among all racial and ethnic groups....

. . .

II

Although [OUA] does assign 20 points to some "soft" variables other than race, the points available for other diversity contributions, such as leadership and service, personal achievement, and geographic diversity, are capped at much lower levels. Even the most outstanding national high school leader could never receive more than five points for his or her accomplishments—a mere quarter of the points automatically assigned to an underrepresented minority solely based on the fact of his or her race. Of course, as Justice Powell made clear in *Bakke*, a university need not "necessarily accor[d]" all diversity factors "the same weight," ... and the "weight attributed to a particular quality may vary from year to year depending on the 'mix' both of the student body and the applicants for the incoming class,".... But the selection index, by setting up automatic, predetermined point allocations for the soft variables, ensures that the diversity contributions of applicants cannot be individually assessed. This policy stands in sharp contrast to the law school's admissions plan, which enables admissions officers to make nuanced judgments with respect to the contributions each applicant is likely to make to the diversity of the incoming class. See *Grutter v. Bollinge*....

The only potential source of individualized consideration appears to be the Admissions Review Committee. The evidence in the record, however, reveals very little about how the review committee actually functions. And what evidence there is indicates that the committee is a kind of afterthought, rather than an integral component of a system of individualized review.... Review by the committee thus represents a necessarily limited exception to [OUA's] general reliance on the selection index. Indeed, the record does not reveal how many applications admissions counselors send to the review committee each year, and the University has not pointed to evidence demonstrating that a meaningful percentage of applicants receives this level of discretionary review. In addition, eligibility for consideration by the committee is itself based on automatic cut-off levels determined with reference to selection index scores. And there is no evidence of how the decisions are actually made—what type of individualized consideration is or is not used. Given these circumstances, the addition of the Admissions Review Committee to the admissions process cannot offset the apparent absence of individualized consideration from [OUA's] general practices.

For these reasons, the record before us does not support the conclusion that the ... admissions program for [LSA]—to the extent that it considers race—provides the necessary individualized consideration. The University, of course, remains free to modify its system so that it does so.... But the current system, as I understand it, is a nonindividualized, mechanical one. As a result, I join the Court's opinion reversing the decision of the District Court.

Justice Thomas, concurring.

I join the Court's opinion because I believe it correctly applies our precedents, including today's decision in *Grutter v. Bollinger*. For similar reasons to those given in my separate opinion in that case, however, I would hold that a State's use of racial discrimination in higher education admissions is categorically prohibited by the Equal Protection Clause.

... The ... admissions policy that the Court today invalidates does not suffer from the additional constitutional defect of allowing racial "discriminat[ion] among [the] groups" included within its definition of underrepresented minorities, ... because it awards all underrepresented minorities the same racial preference. The LSA policy falls, however, because it does not sufficiently allow for the consideration of nonracial distinctions among underrepresented minority applicants. Under today's decisions, a university may not racially discriminate between the groups constituting the critical mass.... An admissions policy, however, must allow for consideration of these nonracial distinctions among applicants on both sides of the single permitted racial classification....

Justice Breyer, concurring in the judgment.

... I join Justice O'Connor's opinion except insofar as it joins that of the Court. I join Part I of Justice Ginsburg's dissenting opinion, but I do not dissent from the Court's reversal of the District Court's decision. I agree with Justice Ginsburg that, in implementing the Constitution's equality instruction, government decisionmakers may properly distinguish between policies of inclusion and exclusion, for the former are more likely to prove consistent with the basic constitutional obligation that the law respect each individual equally, see U.S. Const., Amdt. 14.[a]

Justice Souter, with whom Justice Ginsburg joins as to Part II, dissenting.

... [B]ecause a majority of the Court has chosen to address the merits, I also add a word to say that even if the merits were reachable, I would dissent from the Court's judgment.

. . .

a. A dissenting opinion by Justice Stevens, joined by Justice Souter, urging dismissal for lack of jurisdiction and not reaching the merits, is omitted.

II

The cases now contain two pointers toward the line between the valid and the unconstitutional in race-conscious admissions schemes. *Grutter* reaffirms the permissibility of individualized consideration of race to achieve a diversity of students, at least where race is not assigned a preordained value in all cases. On the other hand, Justice Powell's opinion in *Regents of Univ. of Cal. v. Bakke,* 438 U.S. 265 (1978), rules out a racial quota or set-aside, in which race is the sole fact of eligibility for certain places in a class. Although the freshman admissions system here is subject to argument on the merits, I think it is closer to what *Grutter* approves than to what *Bakke* condemns, and should not be held unconstitutional on the current record.

The record does not describe a system with a quota like the one struck down in *Bakke....*

The plan here ... lets all applicants compete for all places and values an applicant's offering for any place not only on grounds of race, but on grades, test scores, strength of high school, quality of course of study, residence, alumni relationships, leadership, personal character, socioeconomic disadvantage, athletic ability, and quality of a personal essay. A nonminority applicant who scores highly in these other categories can readily garner a selection index exceeding that of a minority applicant who gets the 20–point bonus....

Subject to one qualification ..., this scheme of considering, through the selection index system, all of the characteristics that the college thinks relevant to student diversity for every one of the student places to be filled fits Justice Powell's description of a constitutionally acceptable program: one that considers "all pertinent elements of diversity in light of the particular qualifications of each applicant" and places each element "on the same footing for consideration, although not necessarily according them the same weight....

The one qualification ... is that membership in an underrepresented minority is given a weight of 20 points on the 150–point scale. On the face of things, however, this assignment of specific points does not set race apart from all other weighted considerations. Nonminority students may receive 20 points for athletic ability, socioeconomic disadvantage, attendance at a socioeconomically disadvantaged or predominantly minority high school, or at the Provost's discretion; they may also receive 10 points for being residents of Michigan, 6 for residence in an underrepresented Michigan county, 5 for leadership and service, and so on.

The Court['s] ... objection goes to the use of points to quantify and compare characteristics, or to the number of points awarded due to race, but on either reading the objection is mistaken.

The very nature of a college's permissible practice of awarding value to racial diversity means that race must be considered in a way that increases some applicants' chances for admission. Since college admission is not left entirely to inarticulate intuition, it is hard to see what is inappropriate in assigning some stated value to a relevant characteristic, whether it be reasoning ability, writing style, running speed, or minority race. Justice Powell's plus factors necessarily are assigned some values. The college simply does by a numbered scale what the law school accomplishes in its "holistic review," *Grutter* ...; the distinction does not imply that applicants to the undergraduate college are denied individualized consideration or a fair chance to compete on the basis of all the various merits their applications may disclose.

Nor is it possible to say that the 20 points convert race into a decisive factor comparable to reserving minority places as in *Bakke*. Of course we can conceive of a point system in which the "plus" factor given to minority applicants would be so extreme as to guarantee every minority applicant a higher rank than every nonminority applicant in the university's admissions system. . . . But petitioners do not have a convincing argument that the freshman admissions system operates this way. The present record obviously shows that nonminority applicants may achieve higher selection point totals than minority applicants owing to characteristics other than race, and the fact that the university admits "virtually every qualified under-represented minority applicant," . . . may reflect nothing more than the likelihood that very few qualified minority applicants apply, . . . as well as the possibility that self-selection results in a strong minority applicant pool. It suffices . . . that there are no *Bakke*-like set-asides and that consideration of an applicant's whole spectrum of ability is no more ruled out by giving 20 points for race than by giving the same points for athletic ability or socioeconomic disadvantage.

Any argument that the "tailoring" amounts to a set-aside, then, boils down to the claim that a plus factor of 20 points makes some observers suspicious, where a factor of 10 points might not. But suspicion does not carry petitioners' ultimate burden of persuasion in this constitutional challenge, . . . and it surely does not warrant condemning the college's admissions scheme on this record. [T]he District Court . . . made only limited and general findings on other characteristics of the university's admissions practice, such as the conduct of individualized review by the Admissions Review Committee. . . . The point system cannot operate as a *de facto* set-aside if the greater admissions process, including review by the committee, results in individualized review sufficient to meet the Court's standards. Since the record is quiet, if not silent, on the case-by-case work of the committee, the Court would be on more defensible ground by vacating and remanding for evidence about the committee's specific determinations.[3]

. . . Drawing on admissions systems used at public universities in California, Florida, and Texas, the United States contends that Michigan could get student diversity in satisfaction of its compelling interest by guaranteeing admission to a fixed percentage of the top students from each high school in Michigan. . . .

While there is nothing unconstitutional about such a practice, it nonetheless suffers from a serious disadvantage.[4] It is the disadvantage of deliberate obfuscation. The "percentage plans" are just as race conscious as the point scheme (and fairly so), but they get their racially diverse results without saying directly what they are doing or why they are doing it. In contrast, Michigan states its purpose directly and, if this were a doubtful case for me, I would be

---

3. The Court surmises that the committee does not contribute meaningfully to the University's individualized review of applications. The Court should not take it upon itself to apply a newly-formulated legal standard to an undeveloped record. . . .

4. Of course it might be pointless in the State of Michigan, where minorities are a much smaller fraction of the population than in California, Florida, or Texas. . . .

tempted to give Michigan an extra point of its own for its frankness. Equal protection cannot become an exercise in which the winners are the ones who hide the ball.

. . .

Justice Ginsburg, with whom Justice Souter joins, dissenting. *

I

... [T]he Court once again maintains that the same standard of review controls judicial inspection of all official race classifications.... This insistence on "consistency," *Adarand*, ... would be fitting were our Nation free of the vestiges of rank discrimination long reinforced by law .... But we are not far distant from an overtly discriminatory past, and the effects of centuries of law-sanctioned inequality remain painfully evident in our communities and schools.

. . .

... [G]overnment decisionmakers may properly distinguish between policies of exclusion and inclusion.... Actions designed to burden groups long denied full citizenship stature are not sensibly ranked with measures taken to hasten the day when entrenched discrimination and its after effects have been extirpated....

Our jurisprudence ranks race a "suspect" category, "not because [race] is inevitably an impermissible classification, but because it is one which usually, to our national shame, has been drawn for the purpose of maintaining racial inequality." *Norwalk Core v. Norwalk Redevelopment Agency*, 395 F. 2d 920, 931–932 (C.A.2 1968).... But where race is considered "for the purpose of achieving equality," ... no automatic proscription is in order. For, as insightfully explained, "[t]he Constitution is both color blind and color conscious. To avoid conflict with the equal protection clause, a classification that denies a benefit, causes harm, or imposes a burden must not be based on race. In that sense, the Constitution is color blind. But the Constitution is color conscious to prevent discrimination being perpetuated and to undo the effects of past discrimination." *United States v. Jefferson County Bd. of Ed.*, 372 F. 2d 836, 876 (C.A.5 1966) (Wisdom, J.).... Contemporary human rights documents draw just this line; they distinguish between policies of oppression and measures designed to accelerate *de facto* equality. See ... the United Nations-initiated Conventions on the Elimination of All Forms of Racial Discrimination and on the Elimination of All Forms of Discrimination against Women....

. . .

II

... Every applicant admitted under the current plan, petitioners do not here dispute, is qualified to attend the College.... The racial and ethnic groups to which the College accords special consideration (African–Americans, Hispanics, and Native-Americans) historically have been relegated to inferior status by law and social practice; their members continue to experience class-based discrimination to this day.... There is no suggestion that the College adopted

---

* Justice Breyer joins Part I of this opinion.

its current policy in order to limit or decrease enrollment by any particular racial or ethnic group, and no seats are reserved on the basis of race.... Nor has there been any demonstration that the College's program unduly constricts admissions opportunities for students who do not receive special consideration based on race....[10]

... [C]olleges and universities will seek to maintain their minority enrollment—and the networks and opportunities thereby opened to minority graduates—whether or not they can do so in full candor through adoption of affirmative action plans of the kind here at issue. Without recourse to such plans, institutions of higher education may resort to camouflage. For example, schools may encourage applicants to write of their cultural traditions in the essays they submit, or to indicate whether English is their second language. Seeking to improve their chances for admission, applicants may highlight the minority group associations to which they belong, or the Hispanic surnames of their mothers or grandparents. In turn, teachers' recommendations may emphasize who a student is as much as what he or she has accomplished.... If honesty is the best policy, surely Michigan's accurately described, fully disclosed College affirmative action program is preferable to achieving similar numbers through winks, nods, and disguises.

. . .

10. The United States points to the "percentage plans" used in California, Florida, and Texas as one example of a "race-neutral alternativ[e]" that would permit the College to enroll meaningful numbers of minority students. ... Calling such 10 or 20% plans "race-neutral" seems to me disingenuous, for they "unquestionably were adopted with the specific purpose of increasing representation of African–Americans and Hispanics in the public higher education system." ... Percentage plans depend for their effectiveness on continued racial segregation at the secondary school level: They can ensure significant minority enrollment in universities only if the majority-minority high school population is large enough to guarantee that, in many schools, most of the students in the top 10 or 20% are minorities. Moreover, because such plans link college admission to a single criterion—high school class rank—they create perverse incentives. They encourage parents to keep their children in low-performing segregated schools, and discourage students from taking challenging classes that might lower their grade point averages.... And even if percentage plans could boost the sheer numbers of minority enrollees at the undergraduate level, they do not touch enrollment in graduate and professional schools.

G. WHAT OTHER CLASSIFICATIONS WILL PROVOKE HEIGHTENED SCRUTINY?

2. CLASSIFICATIONS DISADVANTAGING THE RETARDED, HOMOSEXUALS, THE ELDERLY, THE POOR, ETC.

Page 920. Add after Romer v. Evans:

Lawrence v. Texas, ___ U.S. ___, 123 S.Ct. 2472 (2003). The report in this case appears supra at p. 50.

SECTION 4. PROTECTION OF PERSONAL LIBERTIES

B. VOTING AND ELECTIONS

2. LEGISLATIVE DISTRICTING

can't do SJ

Page 982. Add at end of subsection:

EASLEY v. CROMARTIE (II), 532 U.S. 234 (2001). On remand from the reversal of summary judgment in Hunt v. Cromartie, supra p. 980, the three-judge District Court held a 3–day trial and again concluded, over one dissent, that the North Carolina legislature unconstitutionally had used race as the "predominant factor" in drawing the 1997 boundaries of its 12th Congressional District. On direct appeal, the Supreme Court again reversed, this time finding the District Court's findings "clearly erroneous." Calling the issue "evidentiary," and engaging in "extensive review," Justice Breyer's majority opinion "concede[d that] the record contains a modicum of evidence offering support for the District Court's conclusion[,]" but concluded that the "evidence, taken together, . . . does not show that racial considerations predominated in the drawing of District 12's boundaries . . . because race in this case correlates closely with political behavior." He continued:

dirt ct found following racial lines to max dem voters

"The basic question is whether the legislature drew District 12's boundaries because of race *rather than* because of political behavior (coupled with traditional, nonracial districting considerations). It is not, as the dissent contends, whether a legislature may defend its districting decisions based on a 'stereotype' about African–American voting behavior. And given the fact that the party attacking the legislature's decision bears the burden of proving that racial considerations are 'dominant and controlling,' *Miller* . . ., given the 'demanding' nature of that burden of proof, id. . . . (O'Connor, J., concurring), and given the sensitivity, the 'extraordinary caution,' that district courts must show to avoid treading upon legislative prerogatives, id. . . . (majority opinion), the attacking party has not successfully shown that race, rather than politics, predominantly accounts for the result. The record leaves us with the 'definite and firm conviction,' . . . that the District Court erred in finding to the contrary. . . .

"... [M]ore generally ...: In a case such as this one where majority-minority districts (or the approximate equivalent) are at issue and where racial identification correlates highly with political affiliation, the party attacking the legislatively drawn boundaries must show at the least that

new stadad →
the legislature could have achieved its legitimate political objectives in alternative ways that are comparably consistent with traditional districting principles. That party must also show that those districting alternatives would have brought about significantly greater racial balance. Appellees failed to make any such showing here. . . ."

dissent

Justice Thomas, joined by Chief Justice Rehnquist and Justices Scalia and Kennedy, dissented. Objecting that "the Court ignores its role as a reviewing court and engages in its own factfinding enterprise[,]" he concluded that "[i]f I were the District Court, I might have reached the same conclusion that the Court does[,]" but that "[i]n light of the direct evidence of racial motive and the inferences that may be drawn from the circumstantial evidence, I am satisfied that the District Court's finding was permissible, even if not compelled by the record." In the course of his opinion, he expressed the view that it was "[un]necessary to impose a new burden on appellees to show districting alternatives would have brought about 'significantly greater racial balance.'" He also said that

"the District Court was assigned the task of determining *whether*, not *why*, race predominated. As I see it, this inquiry is sufficient to answer the constitutional question because racial gerrymandering offends the Constitution whether the motivation is malicious or benign. It is not a defense that the legislature merely may have drawn the district based on the stereotype that blacks are reliable Democratic voters."

to the extent that lines look racial,
could also be Dem-Rep.
Can use race to gerrymander?
- Just didn't meet burden of proof.
- Can't draw lines where predominant factor is race

APPLICATION OF THE POST CIVIL WAR AMENDMENTS TO PRIVATE CONDUCT: CONGRESSIONAL POWER TO ENFORCE THE AMENDMENTS

SECTION 2. APPLICATION OF THE CONSTITUTION TO "PRIVATE" CONDUCT

B. GOVERNMENTAL ENFORCEMENT OF "PRIVATE" DECISIONS

Page 1139.   Add at end of subsection:

Brentwood Academy v. Tennessee Secondary School Athletic Association

531 U.S. 288, 121 S.Ct. 924, 148 L.Ed.2d 807 (2001).

Justice Souter delivered the opinion of the Court.

The issue is whether a statewide association incorporated to regulate interscholastic athletic competition among public and private secondary schools may be regarded as engaging in state action when it enforces a rule against a member school. The association in question here includes most public schools located within the State, acts through their representatives, draws its officers from them, is largely funded by their dues and income received in their stead, and has historically been seen to regulate in lieu of the State Board of Education's exercise of its own authority. We hold that the association's regulatory activity may and should be treated as state action owing to the pervasive entwinement of state school officials in the structure of the association, there being no offsetting reason to see the association's acts in any other way.

I

Respondent Tennessee Secondary School Athletic Association (Association) is a not-for-profit membership corporation organized to regulate interscholastic sport among the public and private high schools in Tennessee that belong to it. No school is forced to join, but without any other authority actually regulating interscholastic athletics, it enjoys the memberships of almost all the State's public high schools (some 290 of them or 84% of the Association's voting

123

membership), far outnumbering the 55 private schools that belong. A member school's team may play or scrimmage only against the team of another member, absent a dispensation.

The Association's rulemaking arm is its legislative council, while its board of control tends to administration. The voting membership of each of these nine-person committees is limited under the Association's bylaws to high school principals, assistant principals, and superintendents elected by the member schools, and the public school administrators who so serve typically attend meetings during regular school hours. Although the Association's staff members are not paid by the State, they are eligible to join the State's public retirement system for its employees. Member schools pay dues to the Association, though the bulk of its revenue is gate receipts at member teams' football and basketball tournaments, many of them held in public arenas rented by the Association.

The constitution, bylaws, and rules of the Association set standards of school membership and the eligibility of students to play in interscholastic games. . . .

Ever since the Association was incorporated in 1925, Tennessee's State Board of Education (State Board) has (to use its own words) acknowledged the corporation's functions "in providing standards, rules and regulations for interscholastic competition in the public schools of Tennessee," . . . More recently, . . . in 1972, it went so far as to adopt a rule expressly "designat[ing]" the Association as "the organization to supervise and regulate the athletic activities in which the public junior and senior high schools in Tennessee participate on an interscholastic basis." . . . In 1996, however, the State Board dropped the original Rule . . . expressly designating the Association as regulator; it substituted a statement "recogniz[ing] the value of participation in interscholastic athletics and the role of [the Association] in coordinating interscholastic athletic competition," while "authoriz[ing] the public schools of the state to voluntarily maintain membership in [the Association]." . . .

The action before us responds to a 1997 regulatory enforcement proceeding brought against petitioner, Brentwood Academy, a private parochial high school member of the Association. The Association's board of control found that Brentwood violated a rule prohibiting "undue influence" in recruiting athletes, when it wrote to incoming students and their parents about spring football practice. The Association accordingly placed Brentwood's athletic program on probation for four years, declared its football and boys' basketball teams ineligible to compete in playoffs for two years, and imposed a $3,000 fine. When these penalties were imposed, all the voting members of the board of control and legislative council were public school administrators.

Brentwood sued the Association and its executive director in federal court under . . . 42 U.S.C. § 1983, claiming that enforcement of the Rule was state action and a violation of the First and Fourteenth Amendments. The District Court entered summary judgment for Brentwood. . . .

The United States Court of Appeals for the Sixth Circuit reversed. . . . Rehearing en banc was later denied over the dissent of two judges. . . .

We granted certiorari, . . . and now reverse.

Our cases try to plot a line between state action subject to Fourteenth Amendment scrutiny and private conduct (however exceptionable) that is not. . . . If the Fourteenth Amendment is not to be displaced . . . its ambit cannot be a simple line between States and people operating outside formally governmental organizations, and the deed of an ostensibly private organization or individual is to be treated sometimes as if a State had caused it to be performed. . . .

What is fairly attributable is a matter of normative judgment, and the criteria lack rigid simplicity. From the range of circumstances that could point toward the State behind an individual face, no one fact can function as a necessary condition across the board for finding state action; nor is any set of circumstances absolutely sufficient, for there may be some countervailing reason against attributing activity to the government. . . .

Our cases have identified a host of facts that can bear on the fairness of such an attribution. . . .

Amidst such variety, examples may be the best teachers, and examples from our cases are unequivocal in showing that the character of a legal entity is determined neither by its expressly private characterization in statutory law, nor by the failure of the law to acknowledge the entity's inseparability from recognized government officials or agencies.... Pennsylvania v. Board of Directors of City Trusts of Philadelphia . . . held the privately endowed Gerard College to be a state actor and enforcement of its private founder's limitation of admission to whites attributable to the State, because, consistent with the terms of the settlor's gift, the college's board of directors was a state agency established by state law. Ostensibly the converse situation occurred in Evans v. Newton, . . . which held that private trustees to whom a city had transferred a park were nonetheless state actors barred from enforcing racial segregation, since the park served the public purpose of providing community recreation, and "the municipality remain[ed] entwined in [its] management [and] control," . . .

These examples of public entwinement in the management and control of ostensibly separate trusts or corporations foreshadow this case, as this Court itself anticipated in [National Collegiate Athletic Assn. v. Tarkanian, 488 U.S. 179 (1988)]. *Tarkanian* arose when an undoubtedly state actor, the University of Nevada, suspended its basketball coach, Tarkanian, in order to comply with rules and recommendations of the National Collegiate Athletic Association (NCAA). The coach charged the NCAA with state action, arguing that the state university had delegated its own functions to the NCAA, clothing the latter with authority to make and apply the university's rules, the result being joint action making the NCAA a state actor.

To be sure, it is not the strict holding in *Tarkanian* that points to our view of this case, for we found no state action on the part of the NCAA. We could see, on the one hand, that the university had some part in setting the NCAA's rules, and the Supreme Court of Nevada had gone so far as to hold that the NCAA had been delegated the university's traditionally exclusive public authority over personnel. . . . But on the other side, the NCAA's policies were shaped not by the University of Nevada alone, but by several hundred member institutions, most of them having no connection with Nevada, and exhibiting no color of Nevada law. . . . Since it was difficult to see the NCAA, not as a collective membership, but as surrogate for the one State, we held the organiza-

tion's connection with Nevada too insubstantial to ground a state action claim.
. . .

But dictum in *Tarkanian* pointed to a contrary result on facts like ours, with an organization whose member public schools are all within a single State. "The situation would, of course, be different if the [Association's] membership consisted entirely of institutions located within the same State, many of them public institutions created by the same sovereign.". . . .

B

Just as we foresaw in *Tarkanian*, the "necessarily fact-bound inquiry," . . . leads to the conclusion of state action here. The nominally private character of the Association is overborne by the pervasive entwinement of public institutions and public officials in its composition and workings, and there is no substantial reason to claim unfairness in applying constitutional standards to it.

The Association is not an organization of natural persons acting on their own, but of schools, and of public schools to the extent of 84% of the total. . . .

. . . Interscholastic athletics obviously play an integral part in the public education of Tennessee. . . . Since a pickup system of interscholastic games would not do, these public teams need some mechanism to produce rules and regulate competition. The mechanism is an organization overwhelmingly composed of public school officials who select representatives (all of them public officials at the time in question here), who in turn adopt and enforce the rules that make the system work. Thus, by giving these jobs to the Association, the 290 public schools of Tennessee belonging to it can sensibly be seen as exercising their own authority to meet their own responsibilities. Unsurprisingly, then, the record indicates that half the council or board meetings documented here were held during official school hours, and that public schools have largely provided for the Association's financial support. A small portion of the Association's revenue comes from membership dues paid by the schools, and the principal part from gate receipts at tournaments among the member schools. Unlike mere public buyers of contract services, whose payments for services rendered do not convert the service providers into public actors, . . . the schools here obtain membership in the service organization and give up sources of their own income to their collective association. The Association thus exercises the authority of the predominantly public schools to charge for admission to their games; the Association does not receive this money from the schools, but enjoys the schools' moneymaking capacity as its own.

In sum, to the extent of 84% of its membership, the Association is an organization of public schools represented by their officials acting in their official capacity to provide an integral element of secondary public schooling. There would be no recognizable Association, legal or tangible, without the public school officials, who do not merely control but overwhelmingly perform all but the purely ministerial acts by which the Association exists and functions in practical terms. Only the 16% minority of private school memberships prevents this entwinement of the Association and the public school system from being total and their identities totally indistinguishable.

To complement the entwinement of public school officials with the Association from the bottom up, the State of Tennessee has provided for entwinement from top down. State Board members are assigned ex officio to serve as members of the board of control and legislative council, and the Association's ministerial employees are treated as state employees to the extent of being eligible for membership in the state retirement system.

It is, of course, true that the time is long past when the close relationship between the surrogate association and its public members and public officials acting as such was attested frankly. As mentioned, the terms of the State Board's Rule expressly designating the Association as regulator of interscholastic athletics in public schools was deleted in 1996, the year after a Federal District Court held that the Association was a state actor . . .

But the removal of the designation language . . . affected nothing but words. . . . The District Court spoke to this point in finding that because of "custom and practice," "the conduct of the parties has not materially changed" since 1996, "the connections between TSSAA and the State [being] still pervasive and entwined."

The entwinement down from the State Board is therefore unmistakable, just as the entwinement up from the member public schools is overwhelming. Entwinement will support a conclusion that an ostensibly private organization ought to be charged with a public character and judged by constitutional standards; entwinement to the degree shown here requires it.

C

Entwinement is also the answer to the Association's several arguments offered to persuade us that the facts would not support a finding of state action under various criteria applied in other cases. These arguments are beside the point, simply because the facts justify a conclusion of state action under the criterion of entwinement, a conclusion in no sense unsettled merely because other criteria of state action may not be satisfied by the same facts.

The Association places great stress, for example, on the application of a public function test, as exemplified in Rendell–Baker v. Kohn, 457 U.S. 830 (1982). There, an apparently private school provided education for students whose special needs made it difficult for them to finish high school. . . . [W]e held that the performance of such a public function did not permit a finding of state action on the part of the school unless the function performed was exclusively and traditionally public, as it was not in that case. The Association argues that application of the public function criterion would produce the same result here, and we will assume, arguendo, that it would. But this case does not turn on a public function test, any more than Rendell–Baker had anything to do with entwinement of public officials in the special school.

For the same reason, it avails the Association nothing to stress that the State neither coerced nor encouraged the actions complained of. "Coercion" and "encouragement" are like "entwinement" in referring to kinds of facts that can justify characterizing an ostensibly private action as public instead. Facts that address any of these criteria are significant, but no one criterion must necessarily be applied. When, therefore, the relevant facts show pervasive entwinement to the point of largely overlapping identity, the implication of state action is not affected by pointing out that the facts might not loom large under a different test.

D

This is not to say that all of the Association's arguments are rendered beside the point by the public officials' involvement in the Association, for after application of the entwinement criterion, or any other, there is a further potential issue.... Even facts that suffice to show public action (or, standing alone, would require such a finding) may be outweighed in the name of some value at odds with finding public accountability in the circumstances. ...

. . .

The judgment of the Court of Appeals for the Sixth Circuit is reversed, and the case is remanded for further proceedings consistent with this opinion.

It is so ordered.

Justice Thomas, with whom the Chief Justice, Justice Scalia, and Justice Kennedy join, dissenting.

We have never found state action based upon mere "entwinement." Until today, we have found a private organization's acts to constitute state action only when the organization performed a public function; was created, coerced, or encouraged by the government; or acted in a symbiotic relationship with the government. ... I respectfully dissent.

... Although we have used many different tests to identify state action, they all have a common purpose. Our goal in every case is to determine whether an action "can fairly be attributed to the State." ...

A

Regardless of these various tests for state action, common sense dictates that the TSSAA's actions cannot fairly be attributed to the State, and thus cannot constitute state action.... The TSSAA's rules are enforced not by a state agency but by its own board of control, which comprises high school principals, assistant principals, and superintendents, none of whom must work at a public school. Of course, at the time the recruiting rule was enforced in this case, all of the board members happened to be public school officials. However, each board member acts in a representative capacity on behalf of all the private and public schools in his region of Tennessee, and not simply his individual school.

The State of Tennessee did not create the TSSAA. The State does not fund the TSSAA and does not pay its employees. ... The only state pronouncement acknowledging the TSSAA's existence is a rule providing that the State Board of Education permits public schools to maintain membership in the TSSAA if they so choose.

Moreover, the State of Tennessee has never had any involvement in the particular action taken by the TSSAA in this case: the enforcement of the TSSAA's recruiting rule prohibiting members from using "undue influence" on students or their parents or guardians "to secure or to retain a student for athletic purposes." There is no indication that the State has ever had any interest in how schools choose to regulate recruiting. . . .

B

. . .

The TSSAA has not performed a function that has been "traditionally exclusively reserved to the State." . . . The TSSAA no doubt serves the public, particularly the public schools, but the mere provision of a service to the public does not render such provision a traditional and exclusive public function. . . .

. . . It is also obvious that the TSSAA is not an entity created and controlled by the government for the purpose of fulfilling a government objective. . . . Indeed, no one claims that the State of Tennessee played any role in the creation of the TSSAA as a private corporation in 1925. . . .

In addition, the State of Tennessee has not "exercised coercive power or . . . provided such significant encouragement [to the TSSAA], either overt or covert," . . . To be sure, public schools do provide a small portion of the TSSAA's funding through their membership dues, but no one argues that these dues are somehow conditioned on the TSSAA's enactment and enforcement of recruiting rules. Likewise, even if the TSSAA were dependent on state funding to the extent of 90%, as was the case in Blum, instead of less than 4%, mere financial dependence on the State does not convert the TSSAA's actions into acts of the State. . . . Furthermore, there is no evidence of "joint participation," . . . between the State and the TSSAA in the TSSAA's enforcement of its recruiting rule. The TSSAA's board of control enforces its recruiting rule solely in accordance with the authority granted to it under the contract that each member signs.

. . .

Because I do not believe that the TSSAA's action of enforcing its recruiting rule is fairly attributable to the State of Tennessee, I would affirm.

II

Although the TSSAA's enforcement activities cannot be considered state action as a matter of common sense or under any of this Court's existing theories of state action, the majority presents a new theory. Under this theory, the majority holds that the combination of factors it identifies evidences "entwinement" of the State with the TSSAA, and that such entwinement converts private action into state action. . . .

. . . [I]n *City Trusts*, we did not consider entwinement when we addressed the question whether an agency established by state law was a state actor. . . .

. . . Evans v. Newton . . . lends no more support to an "entwinement" theory . . . [W]e did not discuss entwinement as a distinct concept, let alone one sufficient to transform a private entity into a state actor when traditional theories of state action do not. On the contrary, our analysis rested on the recognition that the subject of the dispute, a park, served a "public function," much like a fire department or a police department. . . . Because the park served public functions, the private trustees operating the park were considered to be state actors.

.   .   .

* * *

Because the majority never defines "entwinement," the scope of its holding is unclear. If we are fortunate, the majority's fact-specific analysis will have little bearing beyond this case. But if the majority's new entwinement test develops in future years, it could affect many organizations that foster activities, enforce rules, and sponsor extracurricular competition among high schools—not just in athletics, but in such diverse areas as agriculture, mathematics, music, marching bands, forensics, and cheerleading. Indeed, this entwinement test may extend to other organizations that are composed of, or controlled by, public officials or public entities, such as firefighters, policemen, teachers, cities, or counties. I am not prepared to say that any private organization that permits public entities and public officials to participate acts as the State in anything or everything it does, and our state-action jurisprudence has never reached that far. The state-action doctrine was developed to reach only those actions that are truly attributable to the State, not to subject private citizens to the control of federal courts hearing § 1983 actions.

I respectfully dissent.

SECTION 6.   THE SCOPE OF CONGRESSIONAL POWER TO REDEFINE THE AMENDMENTS

B.   "INTERPRETIVE" POWER

Page 1195.   Add after Kimel v. Florida Board of Regents:

Board of Trustees of the University of Alabama v. Garrett

531 U.S. 356, 121 S.Ct. 955, 148 L.Ed.2d 866 (2001).

Chief Justice Rehnquist delivered the opinion of the Court.

We decide here whether employees of the State of Alabama may recover money damages by reason of the State's failure to comply with the provisions of Title I of the Americans with Disabilities Act of 1990 (ADA or Act). . . .[1] We hold that such suits are barred by the Eleventh Amendment.

The ADA prohibits certain employers, including the States, from "discriminat[ing] against a qualified individual with a disability because of the disability of such individual in regard to job application procedures, the hiring, advancement, or discharge of employees, employee compensation, job training, and

---

1. . . . Title II of the ADA, [deals] with the "services, programs, or activities of a public entity," . . . . We are not disposed to decide the constitutional issue whether Title II, which has somewhat different remedial provisions from Title I, is appropriate legislation under § 5 of the Fourteenth Amendment. . . .

other terms, conditions, and privileges of employment." ... To this end, the Act requires employers to "mak[e] reasonable accommodations to the known physical or mental limitations of an otherwise qualified individual with a disability who is an applicant or employee, unless [the employer] can demonstrate that the accommodation would impose an undue hardship on the operation of the [employer's] business." ...

Respondent Patricia Garrett, a registered nurse, was employed as the Director of Nursing, OB/Gyn/Neonatal Services, for the University of Alabama in Birmingham Hospital. In 1994, Garrett was diagnosed with breast cancer and subsequently underwent a lumpectomy, radiation treatment, and chemotherapy. Garrett's treatments required her to take substantial leave from work. Upon returning to work in July 1995, Garrett's supervisor informed Garrett that she would have to give up her Director position. Garrett then applied for and received a transfer to another, lower paying position as a nurse manager.

Respondent Milton Ash worked as a security officer for the Alabama Department of Youth Services (Department). Upon commencing this employment, Ash informed the Department that he suffered from chronic asthma and that his doctor recommended he avoid carbon monoxide and cigarette smoke, and Ash requested that the Department modify his duties to minimize his exposure to these substances. Ash was later diagnosed with sleep apnea and requested, again pursuant to his doctor's recommendation, that he be reassigned to daytime shifts to accommodate his condition. Ultimately, the Department granted none of the requested relief. Shortly after Ash filed a discrimination claim with the Equal Employment Opportunity Commission, he noticed that his performance evaluations were lower than those he had received on previous occasions.

Garrett and Ash filed separate lawsuits in the District Court, both seeking money damages under the ADA. Petitioners moved for summary judgment, claiming that the ADA exceeds Congress' authority to abrogate the State's Eleventh Amendment immunity. ... [T]he District Court agreed with petitioners' position and granted their motions for summary judgment.... The Court of Appeals reversed....

. . .

I

. . .

We have recognized ... that Congress may abrogate the States' Eleventh Amendment immunity when it both unequivocally intends to do so and "act[s] pursuant to a valid grant of constitutional authority." ...

Congress may not ... base its abrogation of the States' Eleventh Amendment immunity upon the powers enumerated in Article I. ... Congress may subject nonconsenting States to suit in federal court when it does so pursuant to a valid exercise of its [Fourteenth Amendment] § 5 power. ... Accordingly, the ADA can apply to the States only to the extent that the statute is appropriate § 5 legislation.[3]

. . .

---

3. It is clear that Congress intended to invoke § 5 as one of its bases for enacting the ADA. ...

City of Boerne ... confirmed ... the long-settled principle that it is the responsibility of this Court, not Congress, to define the substance of constitutional guarantees. ... Accordingly, § 5 legislation reaching beyond the scope of § 1's actual guarantees must exhibit "congruence and proportionality between the injury to be prevented or remedied and the means adopted to that end."
...

II

The first step in applying these now familiar principles is to identify with some precision the scope of the constitutional right at issue. Here, that inquiry requires us to examine the limitations § 1 of the Fourteenth Amendment places upon States' treatment of the disabled. As we did last Term in *Kimel*, ... we look to our prior decisions under the Equal Protection Clause dealing with this issue.

In Cleburne v. Cleburne Living Center, Inc., 473 U.S. 432 (1985), we considered an equal protection challenge to a city ordinance requiring a special use permit for the operation of a group home for the mentally retarded. The specific question before us was whether ... mental retardation qualified as a "quasi-suspect" classification under our equal protection jurisprudence.... We ... [concluded] instead that such legislation incurs only the minimum "rational-basis" review applicable to general social and economic legislation.[4] ... In a statement that today seems quite prescient, we explained that

> "if the large and amorphous class of the mentally retarded were deemed quasi-suspect for the reasons given by the Court of Appeals, it would be difficult to find a principled way to distinguish a variety of other groups who have perhaps immutable disabilities setting them off from others, who cannot themselves mandate the desired legislative responses, and who can claim some degree of prejudice from at least part of the public at large. One need mention in this respect only the aging, the disabled, the mentally ill, and the infirm. We are reluctant to set out on that course, and we decline to do so." ...

Under rational-basis review, where a group possesses "distinguishing characteristics relevant to interests the State has the authority to implement," a State's decision to act on the basis of those differences does not give rise to a constitutional violation. ...

Justice Breyer suggests that *Cleburne* stands for the broad proposition that state decisionmaking reflecting "negative attitudes" or "fear" necessarily runs afoul of the Fourteenth Amendment. Although such biases may often accompany irrational (and therefore unconstitutional) discrimination, their presence alone does not a constitutional violation make. As we noted in *Cleburne*: "[M]ere negative attitudes, or fear, unsubstantiated by factors which are properly cognizable in a zoning proceeding, are not permissible bases for treating a home for the mentally retarded differently...." ... This language, read in context, simply states the unremarkable and widely acknowledged tenet

---

4. Applying the basic principles of rationality review, *Cleburne* struck down the city ordinance in question. ... The Court's reasoning was that the city's purported justifications for the ordinance made no sense in light of how the city treated other groups similarly situated ...

of this Court's equal protection jurisprudence that state action subject to rational-basis scrutiny does not violate the Fourteenth Amendment when it "rationally furthers the purpose identified by the State." Massachusetts Bd. of Retirement v. Murgia, 427 U.S. 307 (1976) (per curiam).

Thus, the result of *Cleburne* is that States are not required by the Fourteenth Amendment to make special accommodations for the disabled, so long as their actions towards such individuals are rational. They could quite hard headedly—and perhaps hardheartedly—hold to job-qualification requirements which do not make allowance for the disabled. If special accommodations for the disabled are to be required, they have to come from positive law and not through the Equal Protection Clause.[5]

III

Once we have determined the metes and bounds of the constitutional right in question, we examine whether Congress identified a history and pattern of unconstitutional employment discrimination by the States against the disabled. Just as § 1 of the Fourteenth Amendment applies only to actions committed "under color of state law," Congress' § 5 authority is appropriately exercised only in response to state transgressions. ... The legislative record of the ADA, however, simply fails to show that Congress did in fact identify a pattern of irrational state discrimination in employment against the disabled.

Respondents contend that the inquiry as to unconstitutional discrimination should extend not only to States themselves, but to units of local governments, such as cities and counties. All of these, they say, are "state actors" for purposes of the Fourteenth Amendment. This is quite true, but the Eleventh Amendment does not extend its immunity to units of local government. ... These entities are subject to private claims for damages under the ADA without Congress' ever having to rely on § 5 of the Fourteenth Amendment to render them so. It would make no sense to consider constitutional violations on their part, as well as by the States themselves, when only the States are the beneficiaries of the Eleventh Amendment.

Congress made a general finding in the ADA that "historically, society has tended to isolate and segregate individuals with disabilities, and, despite some improvements, such forms of discrimination against individuals with disabilities continue to be a serious and pervasive social problem." ... The record assembled by Congress includes many instances to support such a finding. But the great majority of these incidents do not deal with the activities of States.

Respondents in their brief cite half a dozen examples from the record that did involve States. A department head at the University of North Carolina refused to hire an applicant for the position of health administrator because he was blind; similarly, a student at a state university in South Dakota was denied an opportunity to practice teach because the dean at that time was convinced that blind people could not teach in public schools. A microfilmer at the Kansas Department of Transportation was fired because he had epilepsy; deaf workers

---

5. It is worth noting that by the time that Congress enacted the ADA in 1990, every State in the Union had enacted such measures. At least one Member of Congress remarked that "this is probably one of the few times where the States are so far out in front of the Federal Government, it's not funny." ... A number of these provisions, however, did not go as far as the ADA did in requiring accommodation.

at the University of Oklahoma were paid a lower salary than those who could hear. The Indiana State Personnel Office informed a woman with a concealed disability that she should not disclose it if she wished to obtain employment.

Several of these incidents undoubtedly evidence an unwillingness on the part of state officials to make the sort of accommodations for the disabled required by the ADA. Whether they were irrational under our decision in *Cleburne* is more debatable, particularly when the incident is described out of context. But even if it were to be determined that each incident upon fuller examination showed unconstitutional action on the part of the State, these incidents taken together fall far short of even suggesting the pattern of unconstitutional discrimination on which § 5 legislation must be based. ... In 1990, the States alone employed more than 4.5 million people. ... It is telling, we think, that given these large numbers, Congress assembled only such minimal evidence of unconstitutional state discrimination in employment against the disabled.

Justice Breyer maintains that Congress applied Title I of the ADA to the States in response to a host of incidents representing unconstitutional state discrimination in employment against persons with disabilities. A close review of the relevant materials, however, undercuts that conclusion. Justice Breyer's Appendix C consists not of legislative findings, but of unexamined, anecdotal accounts of "adverse, disparate treatment by state officials." Of course, as we have already explained, "adverse, disparate treatment" often does not amount to a constitutional violation where rational-basis scrutiny applies. These accounts, moreover, were submitted not directly to Congress but to the Task Force on the Rights and Empowerment of Americans with Disabilities, which made no findings on the subject of state discrimination in employment. ... And, had Congress truly understood this information as reflecting a pattern of unconstitutional behavior by the States, one would expect some mention of that conclusion in the Act's legislative findings. There is none. . . .

Even were it possible to squeeze out of these examples a pattern of unconstitutional discrimination by the States, the rights and remedies created by the ADA against the States would raise the same sort of concerns as to congruence and proportionality as were found in *City of Boerne*, supra. For example, whereas it would be entirely rational (and therefore constitutional) for a state employer to conserve scarce financial resources by hiring employees who are able to use existing facilities, the ADA requires employers to "mak[e] existing facilities used by employees readily accessible to and usable by individuals with disabilities." ... The ADA does except employers from the "reasonable accommodatio[n]" requirement where the employer "can demonstrate that the accommodation would impose an undue hardship on the operation of the business of such covered entity." ... However, even with this exception, the accommodation duty far exceeds what is constitutionally required in that it makes unlawful a range of alternate responses that would be reasonable but would fall short of imposing an "undue burden" upon the employer. ...

The ADA also forbids "utilizing standards, criteria, or methods of administration" that disparately impact the disabled, without regard to whether such conduct has a rational basis. ... Although disparate impact may be relevant evidence of racial discrimination, ... such evidence alone is insufficient even where the Fourteenth Amendment subjects state action to strict scrutiny. ...

The ADA's constitutional shortcomings are apparent when the Act is compared to Congress' efforts in the Voting Rights Act of 1965 to respond to a serious pattern of constitutional violations. In South Carolina v. Katzenbach, 383 U.S. 301 (1966), ... we noted that "[b]efore enacting the measure, Congress explored with great care the problem of racial discrimination in voting." ...

In that Act, Congress documented a marked pattern of unconstitutional action by the States. State officials, Congress found, routinely applied voting tests in order to exclude African–American citizens from registering to vote. ... Congress also determined that litigation had proved ineffective and that there persisted an otherwise inexplicable 50–percentage-point gap in the registration of white and African–American voters in some States. ... Congress' response was to promulgate in the Voting Rights Act a detailed but limited remedial scheme designed to guarantee meaningful enforcement of the Fifteenth Amendment in those areas of the Nation where abundant evidence of States' systematic denial of those rights was identified.

... The contrast between this kind of evidence, and the evidence that Congress considered in the present case, is stark. Congressional enactment of the ADA represents its judgment that there should be a "comprehensive national mandate for the elimination of discrimination against individuals with disabilities." ... Congress is the final authority as to desirable public policy, but in order to authorize private individuals to recover money damages against the States, there must be a pattern of discrimination by the States which violates the Fourteenth Amendment, and the remedy imposed by Congress must be congruent and proportional to the targeted violation. Those requirements are not met here, and to uphold the Act's application to the States would allow Congress to rewrite the Fourteenth Amendment law laid down by this Court in Cleburne. Section 5 does not so broadly enlarge congressional authority. The judgment of the Court of Appeals is therefore Reversed.

Justice Kennedy, with whom Justice O'Connor joins, concurring.

Prejudice, we are beginning to understand, rises not from malice or hostile animus alone. ... There can be little doubt ... that persons with mental or physical impairments are confronted with prejudice which can stem from indifference or insecurity as well as from malicious ill will.

... I do not doubt that the Americans with Disabilities Act of 1990 will be a milestone on the path to a more decent, tolerant, progressive society.

It is a question of quite a different order, however, to say that the States in their official capacities, the States as governmental entities, must be held in violation of the Constitution on the assumption that they embody the misconceived or malicious perceptions of some of their citizens. ... The failure of a State to revise policies now seen as incorrect under a new understanding of proper policy does not always constitute the purposeful and intentional action required to make out a violation of the Equal Protection Clause. ...

. . .

It must be noted, moreover, that what is in question is not whether the Congress, acting pursuant to a power granted to it by the Constitution, can compel the States to act. What is involved is only the question whether the

States can be subjected to liability in suits brought not by the Federal Government (to which the States have consented, . . . but by private persons seeking to collect moneys from the state treasury without the consent of the State). The predicate for money damages against an unconsenting State in suits brought by private persons must be a federal statute enacted upon the documentation of patterns of constitutional violations committed by the State in its official capacity. That predicate . . . has not been established. With these observations, I join the Court's opinion.

Justice Breyer, with whom Justice Stevens, Justice Souter and Justice Ginsberg join, dissenting.

. . .

. . . In my view, Congress reasonably could have concluded that the remedy before us constitutes an "appropriate" way to enforce this basic equal protection requirement. And that is all the Constitution requires.

I

The Court says that its primary problem with this statutory provision is one of legislative evidence. It says that "Congress assembled only . . . minimal evidence of unconstitutional state discrimination in employment." In fact, Congress compiled a vast legislative record documenting " 'massive, society-wide discrimination' " against persons with disabilities. . . .

The powerful evidence of discriminatory treatment throughout society in general, including discrimination by private persons and local governments, implicates state governments as well, for state agencies form part of that same larger society. There is no particular reason to believe that they are immune from the "stereotypic assumptions" and pattern of "purposeful unequal treatment" that Congress found prevalent. The Court claims that it "make[s] no sense" to take into consideration constitutional violations committed by local governments. But the substantive obligation that the Equal Protection Clause creates applies to state and local governmental entities alike. . . . Local governments often work closely with, and under the supervision of, state officials, and in general, state and local government employers are similarly situated. . . .

. . .

The congressionally appointed task force collected numerous specific examples, provided by persons with disabilities themselves, of adverse, disparate treatment by state officials. They reveal, not what the Court describes as "half a dozen" instances of discrimination, but hundreds of instances of adverse treatment at the hands of state officials—instances in which a person with a disability found it impossible to obtain a state job, to retain state employment, to use the public transportation that was readily available to others in order to get to work, or to obtain a public education, which is often a prerequisite to obtaining employment. . . .

As the Court notes, those who presented instances of discrimination rarely provided additional, independent evidence sufficient to prove in court that, in each instance, the discrimination they suffered lacked justification from a judicial standpoint. Perhaps this explains the Court's view that there is "minimal evidence of unconstitutional state discrimination." But a legislature is not a court of law. And Congress, unlike courts, must, and does, routinely draw general conclusions . . .

Regardless, Congress expressly found substantial unjustified discrimination against persons with disabilities. . . . In making these findings, Congress followed our decision in *Cleburne*, which established that not only discrimination against persons with disabilities that rests upon "a bare . . . desire to harm a politically unpopular group," . . . violates the Fourteenth Amendment, but also discrimination that rests solely upon "negative attitude [s]," "fea[r]," . . . or "irrational prejudice,". . . .

The evidence in the legislative record bears out Congress' finding that the adverse treatment of persons with disabilities was often arbitrary or invidious in this sense, and thus unjustified. . . .

II

The Court's failure to find sufficient evidentiary support may well rest upon its decision to hold Congress to a strict, judicially created evidentiary standard, particularly in respect to lack of justification. . . .

The problem with the Court's approach is that neither the "burden of proof" that favors States nor any other rule of restraint applicable to judges applies to Congress when it exercises its § 5 power. "Limitations stemming from the nature of the judicial process . . . have no application to Congress." . . . Rational-basis review—with its presumptions favoring constitutionality—is "a paradigm of judicial restraint." . . . And the Congress of the United States is not a lower court.

Indeed, the Court in *Cleburne* drew this very institutional distinction. We emphasized that "courts have been very reluctant, as they should be in our federal system and with our respect for the separation of powers, to closely scrutinize legislative choices." . . .

There is simply no reason to require Congress, seeking to determine facts relevant to the exercise of its § 5 authority, to adopt rules or presumptions that reflect a court's institutional limitations. Unlike courts, Congress can readily gather facts from across the Nation, assess the magnitude of a problem, and more easily find an appropriate remedy. . . . Unlike courts, Congress directly reflects public attitudes and beliefs, enabling Congress better to understand where, and to what extent, refusals to accommodate a disability amount to behavior that is callous or unreasonable to the point of lacking constitutional justification. Unlike judges, Members of Congress can directly obtain information from constituents who have first-hand experience with discrimination and related issues.

Moreover, unlike judges, Members of Congress are elected. . . . To apply a rule designed to restrict courts as if it restricted Congress' legislative power is to stand the underlying principle—a principle of judicial restraint—on its head. But without the use of this burden of proof rule or some other unusually stringent standard of review, it is difficult to see how the Court can find the legislative record here inadequate. Read with a reasonably favorable eye, the record indicates that state governments subjected those with disabilities to seriously adverse, disparate treatment. And Congress could have found, in a significant number of instances, that this treatment violated the substantive principles of justification—shorn of their judicial-restraint-related presumptions—that this Court recognized in *Cleburne*.

III

The Court argues in the alternative that the statute's damage remedy is not "congruent" with and "proportional" to the equal protection problem that Congress found. . . .

[W]hat is wrong with a remedy that, in response to unreasonable employer behavior, requires an employer to make accommodations that are reasonable? Of course, what is "reasonable" in the statutory sense and what is "unreasonable" in the constitutional sense might differ. In other words, the requirement may exceed what is necessary to avoid a constitutional violation. But it is just that power—the power to require more than the minimum that § 5 grants to Congress, as this Court has repeatedly confirmed. . . .

. . .

. . . [E]ven today, the Court purports to apply, not to depart from, these standards. But the Court's analysis and ultimate conclusion deprive its declarations of practical significance. The Court "sounds the word of promise to the ear but breaks it to the hope."

IV

The Court's harsh review of Congress' use of its § 5 power is reminiscent of the similar (now-discredited) limitation that it once imposed upon Congress' Commerce Clause power. Compare Carter v. Carter Coal Co., 298 U.S. 238 (1936), with United States v. Darby, 312 U.S. 100 (1941) (rejecting *Carter Coal's* rationale). I could understand the legal basis for such review were we judging a statute that discriminated against those of a particular race or gender . . ., or a statute that threatened a basic constitutionally protected liberty such as free speech, . . . The legislation before us, however, does not discriminate against anyone, nor does it pose any threat to basic liberty. And it is difficult to understand why the Court, which applies "minimum 'rational-basis' review" to statutes that burden persons with disabilities, subjects to far stricter scrutiny a statute that seeks to help those same individuals.

. . . Rules for interpreting § 5 that would provide States with special protection . . . run counter to the very object of the Fourteenth Amendment. . . . I doubt that today's decision serves any constitutionally based federalism interest.

The Court, through its evidentiary demands, its non-deferential review, and its failure to distinguish between judicial and legislative constitutional competencies, improperly invades a power that the Constitution assigns to Congress. . . . Whether the Commerce Clause does or does not enable Congress to enact this provision, . . . in my view, § 5 gives Congress the necessary authority.

For the reasons stated, I respectfully dissent.

Nevada Department of Human Resources v. Hibbs

___ U.S. ___, 123 S.Ct. 1972, ___ L.Ed.2d ___ (2003).

Chief Justice Rehnquist delivered the opinion of the Court.

The Family and Medical Leave Act of 1993 (FMLA or Act) entitles eligible employees to take up to 12 work weeks of unpaid leave annually for any of several reasons, including the onset of a "serious health condition" in an employee's spouse, child, or parent. ... The Act creates a private right of action to seek both equitable relief and money damages "against any employer (including a public agency) in any Federal or State court of competent jurisdiction," ... should that employer "interfere with, restrain, or deny the exercise of" FMLA rights ... We hold that employees of the State of Nevada may recover money damages in the event of the State's failure to comply with the family-care provision of the Act.

... Respondent ... worked for the Department's Welfare Division. In April and May 1997, he sought leave under the FMLA to care for his ailing wife, who was recovering from a car accident and neck surgery. The Department granted his request for the full 12 weeks of FMLA leave.... In October 1997, the Department informed respondent that he had exhausted his FMLA leave, that no further leave would be granted, and that he must report to work by November 12, 1997. Respondent failed to do so and was terminated.

Respondent sued petitioners in the United States District Court seeking damages and injunctive and declaratory relief for ... violations of [FMLA]. The District Court awarded petitioners summary judgment on the grounds that the FMLA claim was barred by the Eleventh Amendment and that respondent's Fourteenth Amendment rights had not been violated. ... The Ninth Circuit reversed.

. . .

Congress may ... abrogate ... immunity in federal court if it makes its intention to abrogate unmistakably clear in the language of the statute and acts pursuant to a valid exercise of its power under § 5 of the Fourteenth Amendment. ... This case turns, then, on whether Congress acted within its constitutional authority when it sought to abrogate the States' immunity for purposes of the FMLA's family-leave provision.

In enacting the FMLA, Congress relied on two of the powers vested in it by the Constitution: its Article I commerce power and its power under § 5 of the Fourteenth Amendment to enforce that Amendment's guarantees. Congress may not abrogate the States' sovereign immunity pursuant to its Article I power over commerce. ... Congress may, however, abrogate States' sovereign immunity through a valid exercise of its § 5 power ...

Two provisions of the Fourteenth Amendment are relevant here: Section 5 grants Congress the power "to enforce" the substantive guarantees of § 1— among them, equal protection of the laws—by enacting "appropriate legislation." Congress may, in the exercise of its § 5 power, do more than simply proscribe conduct that we have held unconstitutional. "Congress' power 'to enforce' the Amendment includes the authority both to remedy and to deter violation of rights guaranteed thereunder by prohibiting a somewhat broader swath of conduct, including that which is not itself forbidden by the Amendment's text." ... In other words, Congress may enact so-called prophylactic legislation that proscribes facially constitutional conduct, in order to prevent and deter unconstitutional conduct.

City of Boerne also confirmed, however, that it falls to this Court, not Congress, to define the substance of constitutional guarantees. ... We distinguish appropriate prophylactic legislation from "substantive redefinition of the Fourteenth Amendment right at issue," ... by applying the test set forth in *City of Boerne:* Valid § 5 legislation must exhibit "congruence and proportionality between the injury to be prevented or remedied and the means adopted to that end." ...

The FMLA aims to protect the right to be free from gender-based discrimination in the workplace. We have held that statutory classifications that distinguish between males and females are subject to heightened scrutiny. ... For a gender-based classification to withstand such scrutiny, it must "serv[e] important governmental objectives," and "the discriminatory means employed [must be] substantially related to the achievement of those objectives." ... The State's justification for such a classification "must not rely on overbroad generalizations about the different talents, capacities, or preferences of males and females." ... We now inquire whether Congress had evidence of a pattern of constitutional violations on the part of the States in this area.

The history of the many state laws limiting women's employment opportunities is chronicled in—and, until relatively recently, was sanctioned by—this Court's own opinions.

. . .

Congress responded to this history of discrimination by abrogating States' sovereign immunity in Title VII of the Civil Rights Act of 1964 ... But state gender discrimination did not cease. ... According to evidence that was before Congress when it enacted the FMLA, States continue to rely on invalid gender stereotypes in the employment context, specifically in the administration of leave benefits. Reliance on such stereotypes cannot justify the States' gender discrimination in this area. ... The long and extensive history of sex discrimination prompted us to hold that measures that differentiate on the basis of gender warrant heightened scrutiny; here ... the persistence of such unconstitutional discrimination by the States justifies Congress' passage of prophylactic § 5 legislation.

As the FMLA's legislative record reflects, a 1990 Bureau of Labor Statistics (BLS) survey stated that 37 percent of surveyed private-sector employees were covered by maternity leave policies, while only 18 percent were covered by paternity leave policies. ...

Congress also heard testimony that "[p]arental leave for fathers ... is rare. Even ... [w]here child-care leave policies do exist, men, *both in the public and private sectors*, receive notoriously discriminatory treatment in their requests for such leave." ...

Finally, Congress had evidence that, even where state laws and policies were not facially discriminatory, they were applied in discriminatory ways. ...

In spite of all of the above evidence, Justice Kennedy argues in dissent that Congress' passage of the FMLA was unnecessary because "the States appear to have been ahead of Congress in providing gender-neutral family leave benefits," and points to Nevada's leave policies in particular. However, it was only "[s]ince Federal family leave legislation was first introduced" that the States had even "begun to consider similar family leave initiatives." . . .

Furthermore, the dissent's statement that some States "had adopted some form of family-care leave" before the FMLA's enactment glosses over important shortcomings of some state policies. First, seven States had childcare leave provisions that applied to women only. . . . These laws reinforced the very stereotypes that Congress sought to remedy through the FMLA. Second, 12 States provided their employees no family leave, beyond an initial childbirth or adoption, to care for a seriously ill child or family member. Third, many States provided no statutorily guaranteed right to family leave, offering instead only voluntary or discretionary leave programs. Three States left the amount of leave time primarily in employers' hands. Congress could reasonably conclude that such discretionary family-leave programs would do little to combat the stereotypes about the roles of male and female employees that Congress sought to eliminate. Finally, four States provided leave only through administrative regulations or personnel policies, which Congress could reasonably conclude offered significantly less firm protection than a federal law. Against the above backdrop of limited state leave policies, no matter how generous petitioner's own may have been, Congress was justified in enacting the FMLA as remedial legislation.

In sum, the States' record of unconstitutional participation in, and fostering of, gender-based discrimination in the administration of leave benefits is weighty enough to justify the enactment of prophylactic § 5 legislation.

We reached the opposite conclusion in *Garrett* and *Kimel*. In those cases, the § 5 legislation under review responded to a purported tendency of state officials to make age-or disability-based distinctions. Under our equal protection case law, discrimination on the basis of such characteristics is not judged under a heightened review standard . . .

Here, however, Congress directed its attention to state gender discrimination, which triggers a heightened level of scrutiny. . . . Because the standard for demonstrating the constitutionality of a gender-based classification is more difficult to meet than our rational-basis test . . . it was easier for Congress to show a pattern of state constitutional violations. Congress was similarly successful in South Carolina v. Katzenbach, 383 U.S. 301, 308–313 (1966), where we upheld the Voting Rights Act of 1965: Because racial classifications are presumptively invalid, most of the States' acts of race discrimination violated the Fourteenth Amendment.

. . .

Stereotypes about women's domestic roles are reinforced by parallel stereotypes presuming a lack of domestic responsibilities for men. Because employers continued to regard the family as the woman's domain, they often denied men similar accommodations or discouraged them from taking leave. These mutually reinforcing stereotypes created a self-fulfilling cycle of discrimination that forced women to continue to assume the role of primary family caregiver, and fostered employers' stereotypical views about women's commitment to work and their value as employees. Those perceptions, in turn, Congress reasoned, lead to subtle discrimination that may be difficult to detect on a case-by-case basis.

. . .

By creating an across-the-board, routine employment benefit for all eligible employees, Congress sought to ensure that family-care leave would no longer be stigmatized as an inordinate drain on the workplace caused by female employees, and that employers could not evade leave obligations simply by hiring men. By setting a minimum standard of family leave for *all* eligible employees, irrespective of gender, the FMLA attacks the formerly state-sanctioned stereotype that only women are responsible for family caregiving, thereby reducing employers' incentives to engage in discrimination by basing hiring and promotion decisions on stereotypes.

The dissent characterizes the FMLA as a "substantive entitlement program" rather than a remedial statute because it establishes a floor of 12 weeks' leave. In the dissent's view, in the face of evidence of gender-based discrimination by the States in the provision of leave benefits, Congress could do no more in exercising its § 5 power than simply proscribe such discrimination. But this position cannot be squared with our recognition that Congress "is not confined to the enactment of legislation that merely parrots the precise wording of the Fourteenth Amendment," but may prohibit "a somewhat broader swath of conduct, including that which is not itself forbidden by the Amendment's text." . . . For example, this Court has upheld certain prophylactic provisions of the Voting Rights Act as valid exercises of Congress' § 5 power, including the literacy test ban and preclearance requirements for changes in States' voting procedures. . . .

Indeed, in light of the evidence before Congress, a statute mirroring Title VII, that simply mandated gender equality in the administration of leave benefits, would not have achieved Congress' remedial object. Such a law would allow States to provide for no family leave at all. Where "[t]wo-thirds of the nonprofessional caregivers for older, chronically ill, or disabled persons are working women," . . . and state practices continue to reinforce the stereotype of women as caregivers, such a policy would exclude far more women than men from the workplace.

Unlike the statutes at issue in *City of Boerne*, *Kimel*, and *Garrett*, which applied broadly to every aspect of state employers' operations, the FMLA is narrowly targeted at the fault line between work and family—precisely where sex-based overgeneralization has been and remains strongest—and affects only one aspect of the employment relationship. . . .

. . .

For the above reasons, we conclude that [FMLA] is congruent and proportional to its remedial object, and can "be understood as responsive to, or designed to prevent, unconstitutional behavior." . . .

The judgment of the Court of Appeals is therefore

Affirmed.

Justice Souter, with whom Justice Ginsburg and Justice Breyer join, concurring.

... I join the Court's opinion here without conceding the dissenting ... views expressed in Seminole Tribe of Fla. v. Florida ...

Justice Stevens, concurring in the judgment.

Because I have never been convinced that an Act of Congress can amend the Constitution and because I am uncertain whether the congressional enactment before us was truly " 'needed to secure the guarantees of the Fourteenth Amendment,' " I write separately to explain why I join the Court's judgment. ...

... As long as it clearly expresses its intent, Congress may abrogate that common-law defense pursuant to its power to regulate commerce "among the several States." ... The family-care provision of the Family and Medical Leave Act of 1993 is unquestionably a valid exercise of a power that is "broad enough to support federal legislation regulating the terms and conditions of state employment." ...

Justice Scalia, dissenting.

I join Justice Kennedy's dissent, and add one further observation: The constitutional violation that is a prerequisite to "prophylactic" congressional action to "enforce" the Fourteenth Amendment is a violation by the State against which the enforcement action is taken. There is no guilt by association, enabling the sovereignty of one State to be abridged under § 5 of the Fourteenth Amendment because of violations by another State, or by most other States, or even by 49 other States. Congress has sometimes displayed awareness of this self-evident limitation. That is presumably why the most sweeping provisions of the Voting Rights Act of 1965—which we upheld in *City of Rome v. United States,* 446 U.S. 156 (1980), as a valid exercise of congressional power under § 2 of the Fifteenth Amendment—were restricted to States "with a demonstrable history of intentional racial discrimination in voting," ...

Today's opinion for the Court does not even attempt to demonstrate that each one of the 50 States ... was in violation of the Fourteenth Amendment. It treats "the States" as some sort of collective entity which is guilty or innocent as a body. ...

... [T]he court may, if asked, proceed to analyze whether the statute ... can be validly applied to the litigant. In the context of § 5 prophylactic legislation applied against a State, this would entail examining whether the State has itself engaged in discrimination sufficient to support the exercise of Congress's prophylactic power.

... I think Nevada will be entitled to assert that the mere facts that (1) it is a State, and (2) some States are bad actors, is not enough; it can demand that *it* be shown to have been acting in violation of the Fourteenth Amendment.

Justice Kennedy, with whom Justice Scalia and Justice Thomas join, dissenting.

... [T]he family leave provision of the Act ... is invalid to the extent it allows for private suits against the unconsenting States.

Congress does not have authority to define the substantive content of the Equal Protection Clause; it may only shape the remedies warranted by the violations of that guarantee. *City of Boerne, supra* ... This requirement has special force in the context of the Eleventh Amendment, which protects a State's fiscal integrity from federal intrusion by vesting the States with immunity from private actions for damages pursuant to federal laws. The Commerce Clause likely would permit the National Government to enact an entitlement program such as this one; but when Congress couples the entitlement with the authorization to sue the States for monetary damages, it blurs the line of accountability the State has to its own citizens. ...

The Court is unable to show that States have engaged in a pattern of unlawful conduct which warrants the remedy of opening state treasuries to private suits. The inability to adduce evidence of alleged discrimination, coupled with the inescapable fact that the federal scheme is not a remedy but a benefit program, demonstrate the lack of the requisite link between any problem Congress has identified and the program it mandated.

... All would agree that women historically have been subjected to conditions in which their employment opportunities are more limited than those available to men. As the Court acknowledges, however, Congress responded to this problem by abrogating States' sovereign immunity in Title VII of the Civil Rights Act of 1964 ... The provision now before us ... has a different aim than Title VII. It seeks to ensure that eligible employees, irrespective of gender, can take a minimum amount of leave time to care for an ill relative.

The relevant question, as the Court seems to acknowledge, is whether, notwithstanding the passage of Title VII and similar state legislation, the States continued to engage in widespread discrimination on the basis of gender in the provision of family leave benefits. ... The evidence to substantiate this charge must be far more specific, however, than a simple recitation of a general history of employment discrimination against women. ...

Respondents fail to make the requisite showing. ...

As the Court seems to recognize, the evidence considered by Congress concerned discriminatory practices of the private sector, not those of state employers. ...

. . .

The Court's reliance on evidence suggesting States provided men and women with the parenting leave of different length ... concerns the Act's grant of parenting leave, ... and is too attenuated to justify the family leave provision. The Court of Appeals' conclusion to the contrary was based on an assertion that "if states discriminate along gender lines regarding the one kind of leave, then they are likely to do so regarding the other." The charge that a State has engaged in a pattern of unconstitutional discrimination against its citizens is a most serious one. It must be supported by more than conjecture.

The Court maintains the evidence pertaining to the parenting leave is relevant because both parenting and family leave provisions respond to "the same gender stereotype: that women's family duties trump those of the workplace." This sets the contours of the inquiry at too high a level of abstraction. The question is not whether the family leave provision is a congruent and proportional response to general gender-based stereotypes in employment ...; the question is whether it is a proper remedy to an alleged pattern of unconstitutional discrimination by States in the grant of family leave. The evidence of gender-based stereotypes is too remote to support the required showing.

The Court next argues that "even where state laws and policies were not facially discriminatory, they were applied in discriminatory ways."

Even if there were evidence that individual state employers, in the absence of clear statutory guidelines, discriminated in the administration of leave benefits, this circumstance alone would not support a finding of a state-sponsored pattern of discrimination. The evidence could perhaps support the charge of disparate impact, but not a charge that States have engaged in a pattern of intentional discrimination prohibited by the Fourteenth Amendment. ...

The federal-state equivalence upon which the Court places such emphasis is a deficient rationale at an even more fundamental level, however; for the States appear to have been ahead of Congress in providing gender-neutral family leave benefits. Thirty States, the District of Columbia, and Puerto Rico had adopted some form of family-care leave in the years preceding the Act's adoption. ... At the very least, the history of the Act suggests States were in the process of solving any existing gender-based discrimination in the provision of family leave.

The Court acknowledges that States have adopted family leave programs prior to federal intervention, but argues these policies suffered from serious imperfections. Even if correct, this observation proves, at most, that programs more generous and more effective than those operated by the States were feasible. That the States did not devise the optimal programs is not, however, evidence that the States were perpetuating unconstitutional discrimination. Given that the States assumed a pioneering role in the creation of family leave schemes, it is not surprising these early efforts may have been imperfect. This is altogether different, however, from purposeful discrimination.

. . .

Our concern with gender discrimination, which is subjected to heightened scrutiny, as opposed to age-or disability-based distinctions, which are reviewed under rational standard, ... does not alter this conclusion. The application of heightened scrutiny is designed to ensure gender-based classifications are not based on the entrenched and pervasive stereotypes which inhibit women's progress in the workplace. ... Given the insufficiency of the evidence that States discriminated in the provision of family leave, the unfortunate fact that stereotypes about women continue to be a serious and pervasive social problem would not alone support the charge that a State has engaged in a practice designed to deny its citizens the equal protection of the laws.

The paucity of evidence to support the case the Court tries to make demonstrates that Congress was not responding with a congruent and proportional remedy to a perceived course of unconstitutional conduct. Instead, it enacted a substantive entitlement program of its own. If Congress had been concerned about different treatment of men and women with respect to family leave, a congruent remedy would have sought to ensure the benefits of any leave program enacted by a State are available to men and women on an equal basis. Instead, the Act imposes, across the board, a requirement that States grant a minimum of 12 weeks of leave per year. . . .

. . .

To be sure, the Nevada scheme did not track that devised by the Act in all respects. The provision of unpaid leave was discretionary and subject to a possible reporting requirement. . . . A congruent remedy to any discriminatory exercise of discretion, however, is the requirement that the grant of leave be administered on a gender-equal basis, not the displacement of the State's scheme by a federal one. The scheme enacted by the Act does not respect the States' autonomous power to design their own social benefits regime.

Were more proof needed to show that this is an entitlement program, not a remedial statute, it should suffice to note that the Act does not even purport to bar discrimination in some leave programs the States do enact and administer. Under the Act, a State is allowed to provide women with, say, 24 weeks of family leave per year but provide only 12 weeks of leave to men. As the counsel for the United States conceded during the argument, a law of this kind might run afoul of the Equal Protection Clause or Title VII, but it would not constitute a violation of the Act. The Act on its face is not drawn as a remedy to gender-based discrimination in family leave.

. . . The dual requirement that Congress identify a pervasive pattern of unconstitutional state conduct and that its remedy be proportional and congruent to the violation is designed to separate permissible exercises of congressional power from instances where Congress seeks to enact a substantive entitlement under the guise of its § 5 authority.

The Court's precedents upholding the Voting Rights Act of 1965 as a proper exercise of Congress' remedial power are instructive. In South Carolina v. Katzenbach, 383 U.S. 301 (1966), the Court concluded that the Voting Rights Act's prohibition on state literacy tests was an appropriate method of enforcing the constitutional protection against racial discrimination in voting. This measure was justified because "Congress documented a marked pattern of unconstitutional action by the States." This scheme was both congruent, because it "aimed at areas where voting discrimination has been most flagrant," . . . and proportional, because it was necessary to "banish the blight of racial discrimination in voting, which has infected the electoral process in parts of our country for nearly a century," . . .

. . .

. . . The family leave benefit conferred by the Act is, by contrast, a substantive benefit Congress chose to confer upon state employees. . . .

. . .

PART IV

Constitutional Protection of Expression and Conscience

CHAPTER 13

Governmental Control of the Content of Expression

SECTION 2.   Intermezzo: An Introduction to the Concepts of Vagueness, Overbreadth and Prior Restraint

A.   Vagueness and Overbreadth

Page 1256.   Add at end of subsection:

Virginia v. Hicks

___ U.S. ___, 123 S.Ct. 2191, ___ L.Ed.2d ___ (2003).

Justice Scalia delivered the opinion of the Court.

The issue presented in this case is whether the Richmond Redevelopment and Housing Authority's trespass policy is facially invalid under the First Amendment's overbreadth doctrine.

I

A

The Richmond Redevelopment and Housing Authority (RRHA) owns and operates a housing development for low-income residents called Whitcomb Court. Until June 23, 1997, the city of Richmond owned the streets within Whitcomb Court. The city council decided, however, to "privatize" these streets in an effort to combat rampant crime and drug dealing in Whitcomb Court— much of it committed and conducted by nonresidents. . . . The city then conveyed these streets by a recorded deed to the RRHA (which is a political subdivision of the Commonwealth of Virginia). . . . [T]he RRHA posted red-and-white signs on each apartment building—and every 100 feet along the streets— of Whitcomb Court, which state: "NO TRESPASSING[.] PRIVATE PROPER-TY[.] . . . " The RRHA also enacted a policy authorizing the Richmond police

> "to serve notice, either orally or in writing, to any person who is found on Richmond Redevelopment and Housing Authority property when such person is not a resident, employee, or such person cannot demonstrate *a legitimate business or social purpose* for being on the premises. Such notice shall forbid the person from returning to the property. Finally, Richmond Redevelopment and Housing Authority authorizes Richmond Police Department officers to arrest any person for trespassing after such person, having been duly notified, either stays upon or returns to Richmond Redevelopment and Housing Authority property."

Persons who trespass after being notified not to return are subject to prosecution under Va. Code Ann. § 18.2–119 (1996):

> "If any person without authority of law goes upon or remains upon the lands, buildings or premises of another, or any portion or area thereof, after having been forbidden to do so, either orally or in writing, by the owner, lessee, custodian or other person lawfully in charge thereof . . . he shall be guilty of a Class 1 misdemeanor."

B

Respondent Kevin Hicks, a nonresident of Whitcomb Court, has been convicted on two prior occasions of trespassing there and once of damaging property there. Those convictions are not at issue in this case. While the property-damage charge was pending, the RRHA gave Hicks written notice barring him from Whitcomb Court, and Hicks signed this notice in the presence of a police officer. Twice after receiving this notice Hicks asked for permission to return; twice the Whitcomb Court housing manager said "no." That did not stop Hicks; in January 1999 he again trespassed at Whitcomb Court and was arrested and convicted under § 18.2–119.

At trial, Hicks maintained that the RRHA's policy limiting access to Whitcomb Court was both unconstitutionally overbroad and void for vagueness. On appeal of his conviction, . . . the Virginia Supreme Court . . . found the policy defective because it vested too much discretion in Whitcomb Court's manager to determine whether an individual's presence at Whitcomb Court is "authorized," allowing her to "prohibit speech that she finds personally distasteful or offensive even though such speech may be protected by the First Amendment." . . .

II

A

Hicks does not contend that he was engaged in constitutionally protected conduct when arrested; nor does he challenge the validity of the trespass *statute* under which he was convicted. Instead he claims that the RRHA *policy* barring him from Whitcomb Court is overbroad under the First Amendment, and cannot be applied to him—or anyone else. The First Amendment doctrine of overbreadth is an exception to our normal rule regarding the standards for facial challenges. . . .

. . .

B

Petitioner asks this Court to impose restrictions on "the use of overbreadth standing," limiting the availability of facial overbreadth challenges to those whose *own conduct* involved some sort of expressive activity. The United States as *amicus curiae* makes the same proposal, and urges that Hicks' facial challenge to the RRHA trespass policy "should not have been entertained." The problem with these proposals is that we are reviewing here the decision of a *State* Supreme Court; our standing rules limit only the *federal* courts' jurisdiction over certain claims. "[S]tate courts are not bound by the limitations of a case or controversy or other federal rules of justiciability even when they address issues of federal law." . . . Whether Virginia's courts should have *entertained* this overbreadth challenge is entirely a matter of state law.

This Court may, however, review the Virginia Supreme Court's holding that the RRHA policy violates the First Amendment. We may examine, in particular, whether the claimed overbreadth in the RRHA policy is sufficiently "substantial" to produce facial invalidity. These questions involve not standing, but "the determination of [a] First Amendment challenge on the merits." . . . Because it is the Commonwealth of Virginia, not Hicks, that has invoked the authority of the federal courts by petitioning for a writ of certiorari, our jurisdiction to review the First Amendment merits question is clear . . . The Commonwealth has suffered, as a consequence of the Virginia Supreme Court's "final judgment altering tangible legal rights," an actual injury in fact—inability to prosecute Hicks for trespass—that is sufficiently "distinct and palpable" to confer standing under Article III . . . We accordingly proceed to that merits inquiry, leaving for another day the question whether our ordinary rule that a litigant may not rest a claim to relief on the legal rights or interests of third parties . . . would exclude a case such as this from initiation in federal court.

C

The Virginia Supreme Court found that the RRHA policy allowed Gloria S. Rogers, the manager of Whitcomb Court, to exercise "unfettered discretion" in determining who may use the RRHA's property. . . . Specifically, the court faulted an "unwritten" rule that persons wishing to hand out flyers on the sidewalks of Whitcomb Court need to obtain Rogers' permission. This unwritten portion of the RRHA policy, the court concluded, unconstitutionally allows Rogers to "prohibit speech that she finds personally distasteful or offensive."

... The Virginia Supreme Court, based on its objection to the "unwritten" requirement that demonstrators and leafleters obtain advance permission, declared the *entire* RRHA trespass policy overbroad and void—including the written rule that those who return after receiving a barment notice are subject to arrest. Whether these provisions are severable is of course a matter of state law, ... and the Virginia Supreme Court has implicitly decided that they are not—that all components of the RRHA trespass policy must stand or fall together. It could not properly decree that they fall by reason of the overbreadth doctrine, however, unless the trespass policy, *taken as a whole*, is substantially overbroad judged in relation to its plainly legitimate sweep. ...

Hicks has not made such a showing with regard to the RRHA policy taken as a whole ... Consider the "no-return" notice served on nonresidents who have no "legitimate business or social purpose" in Whitcomb Court: Hicks has failed to demonstrate that this notice would even be given to anyone engaged in constitutionally protected speech. ... Hicks has failed to demonstrate that *any* First Amendment activity falls outside the "legitimate business or social purpose[s]" that permit entry. As far as appears, until one receives a barment notice, entering for a First Amendment purpose is not a trespass.

As for the written provision authorizing the police to arrest those who return to Whitcomb Court after receiving a barment notice: That certainly does not violate the First Amendment as applied to persons whose postnotice entry is not for the purpose of engaging in constitutionally protected speech. And Hicks has not even established that it would violate the First Amendment as applied to persons whose postnotice entry *is* for that purpose. ... [T]he notice-barment rule subjects to arrest those who reenter after trespassing and after being warned not to return—*regardless* of whether, upon their return, they seek to engage in speech. Neither the basis for the barment sanction (the prior trespass) nor its purpose (preventing future trespasses) has anything to do with the First Amendment. Punishing its violation by a person who wishes to engage in free speech no more implicates the First Amendment than would the punishment of a person who has (pursuant to lawful regulation) been banned from a public park after vandalizing it, and who ignores the ban in order to take part in a political demonstration. Here, as there, it is Hicks' nonexpressive *conduct*—his entry in violation of the notice-barment rule—not his speech, for which he is punished as a trespasser.

Most importantly, both the notice-barment rule and the 'legitimate business or social purpose' rule apply to *all* persons who enter the streets of Whitcomb Court, not just to those who seek to engage in expression. ... Applications of the RRHA policy that violate the First Amendment can still be remedied through as-applied litigation, but the Virginia Supreme Court should not have used the 'strong medicine' of overbreadth to invalidate the entire RRHA trespass policy. Whether respondent may challenge his conviction on other grounds—and whether those claims have been properly preserved—are issues we leave open on remand.

. . .

Justice Souter, with whom Justice Breyer joins, concurring.

I join the Court's opinion and add this afterword to flag an issue of no consequence here, but one on which a future case might turn. In comparing invalid applications against valid ones for purposes of the First Amendment overbreadth doctrine, the Supreme Court of Virginia apparently assumed that the appropriate focus of the analysis was the "unwritten" element of the housing authority's trespass policy, that is, the requirement that nonresidents distributing literature or demonstrating on the property obtain prior authorization. ... We, on the other hand, take a broader view of the relevant law, by looking to the potential applications of the entire trespass policy, written and unwritten. It does not matter here, however, which position one takes on the appropriate "law" whose overbreadth is to be assessed, for there is no substantial overbreadth either way. ... But in other circumstances, the scope of the law chosen for comparison with invalid applications might decide the case. It might be dispositive whether, say, a city's speech ordinance for a public park is analyzed alone or as one element of the combined policies governing expression in public schoolyards, municipal cemeteries, and the city council chamber. Suffice it to say that today's decision does not address how to go about identifying the scope of the relevant law for purposes of overbreadth analysis.

B. PRIOR RESTRAINT

Page 1262. Replace last sentence of first paragraph:

Thomas v. Chicago Park District, 534 U.S. 316 (2002), held that *Freedman*'s requirement that licensing officials seek prompt judicial review was not applicable to content-neutral denial of parade and demonstration permits. ("Such a traditional exercise of authority does not raise the censorship concerns that prompted us to impose the extraordinary procedural safeguards on the film licensing process in *Freedman*.")

Page 1263. Add at end of section:

Watchtower Bible and Tract Society of New York v. Village of Stratton

536 U.S. 150, 122 S.Ct. 2080, 153 L.Ed.2d 205 (2002).

Justice Stevens delivered the opinion of the Court.

Petitioners contend that a village ordinance making it a misdemeanor to engage in door-to-door advocacy without first registering with the mayor and receiving a permit violates the First Amendment. Through this facial challenge, we consider the door-to-door canvassing regulation not only as it applies to religious proselytizing, but also to anonymous political speech and the distribution of handbills.

I

Petitioner Watchtower Bible and Tract Society of New York, Inc., coordinates the preaching activities of Jehovah's Witnesses throughout the United States and publishes Bibles and religious periodicals that are widely distributed. Petitioner Wellsville, Ohio, Congregation of Jehovah's Witnesses, Inc., supervises the activities of approximately 59 members in a part of Ohio that includes the Village of Stratton (Village). Petitioners offer religious literature without cost to anyone interested in reading it. They allege that they do not solicit contributions or orders for the sale of merchandise or services, but they do accept donations.

Petitioners brought this action against the Village and its mayor in the United States District Court for the Southern District of Ohio, seeking an injunction against the enforcement of several sections of Ordinance No. 1998–5 regulating uninvited peddling and solicitation on private property in the Village. Petitioners' complaint alleged that the ordinance violated several constitutional rights, including the free exercise of religion, free speech, and the freedom of the press. The District Court conducted a bench trial at which evidence of the administration of the ordinance and its effect on petitioners was introduced.

Section 116.01 prohibits "canvassers" and others from "going in and upon" private residential property for the purpose of promoting any "cause" without first having obtained a permit pursuant to § 116.03. That section provides that any canvasser who intends to go on private property to promote a cause, must obtain a "Solicitation Permit" from the office of the mayor; there is no charge for the permit, and apparently one is issued routinely after an applicant fills out a fairly detailed "Solicitor's Registration Form." The canvasser is then authorized to go upon premises that he listed on the registration form, but he must carry the permit upon his person and exhibit it whenever requested to do so by a police officer or by a resident. The ordinance sets forth grounds for the denial or revocation of a permit, but the record before us does not show that any application has been denied or that any permit has been revoked. Petitioners did not apply for a permit.

A section of the ordinance that petitioners do not challenge establishes a procedure by which a resident may prohibit solicitation even by holders of permits. If the resident files a "No Solicitation Registration Form" with the mayor, and also posts a "No Solicitation" sign on his property, no uninvited canvassers may enter his property, unless they are specifically authorized to do so in the "No Solicitation Registration Form" itself. Only 32 of the Village's 278 residents filed such forms. Each of the forms in the record contains a list of 19 suggested exceptions; on one form, a resident checked 17 exceptions, thereby excluding only "Jehovah's Witnesses" and "Political Candidates" from the list of invited canvassers. Although Jehovah's Witnesses do not consider themselves to be "solicitors" because they make no charge for their literature or their teaching, leaders of the church testified at trial that they would honor "no solicitation" signs in the Village. They also explained at trial that they did not apply for a permit because they derive their authority to preach from Scripture. "For us to seek a permit from a municipality to preach we feel would almost be an insult to God."

Petitioners introduced some evidence that the ordinance was the product of the mayor's hostility to their ministry, but the District Court credited the mayor's testimony that it had been designed to protect the privacy rights of the Village residents, specifically to protect them "from 'flim flam' con artists who prey on small town populations." Nevertheless, the court concluded that the terms of the ordinance applied to the activities of petitioners as well as to "business or political canvassers."

The District Court . . . held the ordinance constitutionally valid as applied to petitioners and dismissed the case.

The Court of Appeals for the Sixth Circuit affirmed. . . .

. . .

We granted certiorari to decide the following question: "Does a municipal ordinance that requires one to obtain a permit prior to engaging in the door-to-door advocacy of a political cause and to display upon demand the permit, which contains one's name, violate the First Amendment protection accorded to anonymous pamphleteering or discourse?"

II

For over 50 years, the Court has invalidated restrictions on door-to-door canvassing and pamphleteering. It is more than historical accident that most of these cases involved First Amendment challenges brought by Jehovah's Witnesses, because door-to-door canvassing is mandated by their religion. As we noted in *Murdock v. Pennsylvania*, 319 U.S. 105, 108 (1943), the Jehovah's Witnesses "claim to follow the example of Paul, teaching 'publicly, and from house to house.' . . . In doing so they believe that they are obeying a commandment of God." . . .

Although our past cases involving Jehovah's Witnesses, most of which were decided shortly before and during World War II, do not directly control the question we confront today, they provide both a historical and analytical backdrop for consideration of petitioners' First Amendment claim that the breadth of the Village's ordinance offends the First Amendment. Those cases involved petty offenses that raised constitutional questions of the most serious magnitude—questions that implicated the free exercise of religion, the freedom of speech, and the freedom of the press. From these decisions, several themes emerge that guide our consideration of the ordinance at issue here.

First, the cases emphasize the value of the speech involved. For example, in *Murdock v. Pennsylvania*, the Court noted that "hand distribution of religious tracts is an age-old form of missionary evangelism—as old as the history of printing presses. . . . It has the same claim to protection as the more orthodox and conventional exercises of religion. It also has the same claim as the others to the guarantees of freedom of speech and freedom of the press." . . .

In addition, the cases discuss extensively the historical importance of door-to-door canvassing and pamphleteering as vehicles for the dissemination of ideas. In *Schneider v. State (Town of Irvington)*, 308 U.S. 147 (1939), the petitioner was a Jehovah's Witness who had been convicted of canvassing without a permit based on evidence that she had gone from house to house offering to leave books or booklets. Writing for the Court, Justice Roberts stated that "pamphlets have proved most effective instruments in the dissemination of opinion. . . . To require a censorship through license which makes impossible the *free and unhampered* distribution of pamphlets strikes at the very heart of the constitutional guarantees." . . .

Despite the emphasis on the important role that door-to-door canvassing and pamphleteering has played in our constitutional tradition of free and open discussion, these early cases also recognized the interests a town may have in some form of regulation, particularly when the solicitation of money is involved. In *Cantwell v. Connecticut,* 310 U.S. 296 (1940), the Court held that an ordinance requiring Jehovah's Witnesses to obtain a license before soliciting door to door was invalid because the issuance of the license depended on the exercise of discretion by a city official. Our opinion recognized that "a State may protect its citizens from fraudulent solicitation by requiring a stranger in the community, before permitting him publicly to solicit funds for any purpose, to establish his identity and his authority to act for the cause which he purports to represent." *Id.,* at 306. Similarly, in Martin v. City of Struthers, the Court recognized crime prevention as a legitimate interest served by these ordinances and noted that "burglars frequently pose as canvassers, either in order that they may have a pretense to discover whether a house is empty and hence ripe for burglary, or for the purpose of spying out the premises in order that they may return later." 319 U.S., at 144. Despite recognition of these interests as legitimate, our precedent is clear that there must be a balance between these interests and the effect of the regulations on First Amendment rights. . . .

Finally, the cases demonstrate that efforts of the Jehovah's Witnesses to resist speech regulation have not been a struggle for their rights alone. In *Martin*, after cataloging the many groups that rely extensively upon this method of communication, the Court summarized that "[d]oor to door distribution of circulars is essential to the poorly financed causes of little people." 319 U.S., at 144–146.

That the Jehovah's Witnesses are not the only "little people" who face the risk of silencing by regulations like the Village's is exemplified by our cases involving nonreligious speech. . . . In *Thomas* [v. Collins, 323 U. S. 516 (1945)], the issue was whether a labor leader could be required to obtain a permit before delivering a speech to prospective union members. After reviewing the Jehovah's Witnesses cases discussed above, the Court observed:

> "As a matter of principle a requirement of registration in order to make a public speech would seem generally incompatible with an exercise of the rights of free speech and free assembly. . . .

> . . .

> "If the exercise of the rights of free speech and free assembly cannot be made a crime, we do not think this can be accomplished by the device of requiring previous registration as a condition for exercising them and making such a condition the foundation for restraining in advance their exercise and for imposing a penalty for violating such a restraining order. So long as no more is involved than exercise of the rights of free speech and free assembly, it is immune to such a restriction. If one who solicits support for the cause of labor may be required to register as a condition to the exercise of his right to make a public speech, so may he who seeks to rally support for any social, business, religious or political cause. We think a requirement that one must register before he undertakes to make a public speech to enlist support for a lawful movement is quite incompatible with the requirements of the First Amendment." *Id.,* at 539–540.

Although these World War II-era cases provide guidance for our consideration of the question presented, they do not answer one preliminary issue that the parties adamantly dispute. That is, what standard of review ought we use in assessing the constitutionality of this ordinance. We find it unnecessary, however, to resolve that dispute because the breadth of speech affected by the ordinance and the nature of the regulation make it clear that the Court of Appeals erred in upholding it.

III

The Village argues that three interests are served by its ordinance: the prevention of fraud, the prevention of crime, and the protection of residents' privacy. We have no difficulty concluding, in light of our precedent, that these are important interests that the Village may seek to safeguard through some form of regulation of solicitation activity. We must also look, however, to the amount of speech covered by the ordinance and whether there is an appropriate balance between the affected speech and the governmental interests that the ordinance purports to serve.

The text of the Village's ordinance prohibits "canvassers" from going on private property for the purpose of explaining or promoting any "cause," unless they receive a permit and the residents visited have not opted for a "no solicitation" sign. Had this provision been construed to apply only to commercial activities and the solicitation of funds, arguably the ordinance would have been tailored to the Village's interest in protecting the privacy of its residents and preventing fraud. Yet, even though the Village has explained that the ordinance was adopted to serve those interests, it has never contended that it should be so narrowly interpreted. To the contrary, the Village's administration of its ordinance unquestionably demonstrates that the provisions apply to a significant number of noncommercial "canvassers" promoting a wide variety of "causes." Indeed, on the "No Solicitation Forms" provided to the residents, the canvassers include "Camp Fire Girls," "Jehovah's Witnesses," "Political Candidates," "Trick or Treaters during Halloween Season," and "Persons Affiliated with Stratton Church." The ordinance unquestionably applies, not only to religious causes, but to political activity as well. It would seem to extend to "residents casually soliciting the votes of neighbors," or ringing doorbells to enlist support for employing a more efficient garbage collector.

The mere fact that the ordinance covers so much speech raises constitutional concerns. It is offensive—not only to the values protected by the First Amendment, but to the very notion of a free society—that in the context of everyday public discourse a citizen must first inform the government of her desire to speak to her neighbors and then obtain a permit to do so. Even if the issuance of permits by the mayor's office is a ministerial task that is performed promptly and at no cost to the applicant, a law requiring a permit to engage in such speech constitutes a dramatic departure from our national heritage and constitutional tradition. Three obvious examples illustrate the pernicious effect of such a permit requirement.

First, as our cases involving distribution of unsigned handbills demonstrate, there are a significant number of persons who support causes anonymously. ..., the Court of Appeals erred in concluding that the ordinance does not implicate anonymity interests. ... The badge requirement that we invalidated in *Buckley* [v. American Constitutional Law Foundation, Inc., 525 U.S. 182 (1999)] applied to petition circulators seeking signatures in face-to-face interactions. ... In the Village, strangers to the resident certainly maintain their anonymity, and the ordinance may preclude such persons from canvassing for unpopular causes. Such preclusion may well be justified in some situations—for example, by the special state interest in protecting the integrity of a ballot-initiative process, see *ibid.*, or by the interest in preventing fraudulent commercial transactions. The Village ordinance, however, sweeps more broadly, covering unpopular causes unrelated to commercial transactions or to any special interest in protecting the electoral process.

Second, requiring a permit as a prior condition on the exercise of the right to speak imposes an objective burden on some speech of citizens holding religious or patriotic views. As our World War II-era cases dramatically demonstrate, there are a significant number of persons whose religious scruples will prevent them from applying for such a license. There are no doubt other patriotic citizens, who have such firm convictions about their constitutional right to engage in uninhibited debate in the context of door-to-door advocacy, that they would prefer silence to speech licensed by a petty official.

Third, there is a significant amount of spontaneous speech that is effectively banned by the ordinance. A person who made a decision on a holiday or a weekend to take an active part in a political campaign could not begin to pass out handbills until after he or she obtained the required permit. Even a spontaneous decision to go across the street and urge a neighbor to vote against the mayor could not lawfully be implemented without first obtaining the mayor's permission. ...

The breadth and unprecedented nature of this regulation does not alone render the ordinance invalid. ...[I]t is not tailored to the Village's stated interests. Even if the interest in preventing fraud could adequately support the ordinance insofar as it applies to commercial transactions and the solicitation of funds, that interest provides no support for its application to petitioners, to political campaigns, or to enlisting support for unpopular causes. The Village, however, argues that the ordinance is nonetheless valid because it serves the two additional interests of protecting the privacy of the resident and the prevention of crime.

With respect to the former, it seems clear that § 107 of the ordinance, which provides for the posting of "No Solicitation" signs and which is not challenged in this case, coupled with the resident's unquestioned right to refuse to engage in conversation with unwelcome visitors, provides ample protection for the unwilling listener. *Schaumburg*, 444 U.S., at 639 ("[T]he provision permitting homeowners to bar solicitors from their property by posting [no solicitation] signs ... suggest[s] the availability of less intrusive and more effective measures to protect privacy"). The annoyance caused by an uninvited knock on the front door is the same whether or not the visitor is armed with a permit.

With respect to the latter, it seems unlikely that the absence of a permit would preclude criminals from knocking on doors and engaging in conversations not covered by the ordinance. They might, for example, ask for directions or permission to use the telephone, or pose as surveyers or census takers. Or they might register under a false name with impunity because the ordinance contains no provision for verifying an applicant's identity or organizational credentials. Moreover, the Village did not assert an interest in crime prevention below, and there is an absence of any evidence of a special crime problem related to door-to-door solicitation in the record before us.

The rhetoric used in the World War II-era opinions that repeatedly saved petitioners' co-religionists from petty prosecutions reflected the Court's evaluation of the First Amendment freedoms that are implicated in this case. The value judgment that then motivated a united democratic people fighting to defend those very freedoms from totalitarian attack is unchanged. It motivates our decision today.

The judgment of the Court of Appeals is reversed, and the case is remanded for further proceedings consistent with this opinion.

It is so ordered.

Justice Breyer, with whom Justice Souter and Justice Ginsburg join, concurring.

While joining the Court's opinion, I write separately to note that the dissent's "crime prevention" justification for this ordinance is not a strong one. For one thing, there is no indication that the legislative body that passed the ordinance considered this justification. . . .

. . . I can only conclude that if the village of Stratton thought preventing burglaries and violent crimes was an important justification for this ordinance, it would have said so.

.   .   .

Justice Scalia, with whom Justice Thomas joins, concurring in the judgment.

I concur in the judgment, for many but not all of the reasons set forth in the opinion for the Court. I do not agree, for example, that one of the causes of the invalidity of Stratton's ordinance is that some people have a religious objection to applying for a permit . . .

.   .   .

As for the Court's fairy-tale category of "patriotic citizens," who would rather be silenced than licensed in a manner that the Constitution (but for their "patriotic" objection) would permit: If our free-speech jurisprudence is to be determined by the predicted behavior of such crackpots, we are in a sorry state indeed.

Chief Justice Rehnquist, dissenting.

Stratton is a village of 278 people located along the Ohio River where the borders of Ohio, West Virginia, and Pennsylvania converge. It is strung out along a multilane highway connecting it with the cities of East Liverpool to the north and Steubenville and Weirton, West Virginia, to the south. One may doubt how much legal help a village of this size has available in drafting an ordinance such as the present one, but even if it had availed itself of a battery of constitutional lawyers, they would have been of little use in the town's effort. For the Court today ignores the cases on which those lawyers would have relied, and comes up with newly fashioned doctrine. . . .

More than half a century ago we recognized that canvassers, "whether selling pots or distributing leaflets, may lessen the peaceful enjoyment of a home," and that "burglars frequently pose as canvassers, either in order that they may have a pretense to discover whether a house is empty and hence ripe for burglary, or for the purpose of spying out the premises in order that they may return later." *Martin v. City of Struthers*, 319 U.S. 141, 144 (1943). These problems continue to be associated with door-to-door canvassing, as are even graver ones.

. . .

The town had little reason to suspect that the negligible burden of having to obtain a permit runs afoul of the First Amendment. For over 60 years, we have categorically stated that a permit requirement for door-to-door canvassers, which gives no discretion to the issuing authority, is constitutional. The District Court and Court of Appeals, relying on our cases, upheld the ordinance. The Court today, however, abruptly changes course and invalidates the ordinance.

. . . Our early decisions in this area expressly sanction a law that merely requires a canvasser to register. In *Cantwell v. Connecticut*, 310 U.S. 296, 306 (1940), we stated that "[w]ithout doubt a State may protect its citizens from fraudulent solicitation by requiring a stranger in the community, before permitting him publicly to solicit funds for any purpose, to establish his identity and his authority to act for the cause which he purports to represent." In *Murdock v. Pennsylvania*, 319 U.S. 105, 116 (1943), we contrasted the license tax struck down in that case with "merely a registration ordinance calling for an identification of the solicitors so as to give the authorities some basis for investigating strangers coming into the community." And *Martin, supra,* at 148, states that a "city can punish those who call at a home in defiance of the previously expressed will of the occupant and, in addition, can by identification devices control the abuse of the privilege by criminals posing as canvassers."

It is telling that Justices Douglas and Black, perhaps the two Justices in this Court's history most identified with an expansive view of the First Amendment, authored, respectively, *Murdock* and *Martin.* Their belief in the constitutionality of the permit requirement that the Court strikes down today demonstrates just how far the Court's present jurisprudence has strayed from the core concerns of the First Amendment.

. . .

The Stratton ordinance suffers from none of the defects deemed fatal in these earlier decisions. The ordinance does not prohibit door-to-door canvassing; it merely requires that canvassers fill out a form and receive a permit. Cf. *Martin, supra.* The mayor does not exercise any discretion in deciding who receives a permit; approval of the permit is automatic upon proper completion of the form. Cf. *Cantwell, supra.* And petitioners do not contend in this Court that the ordinance is vague. . . .

Just as troubling . . . is the difficulty of discerning from the Court's opinion what exactly it is about the Stratton ordinance that renders it unconstitutional. It is not clear what test the Court is applying, or under which part of that indeterminate test the ordinance fails. . . . Under a straightforward application of the applicable First Amendment framework, however, the ordinance easily passes muster.

There is no support in our case law for applying anything more stringent than intermediate scrutiny to the ordinance. The ordinance is content neutral and does not bar anyone from going door-to-door in Stratton. It merely regulates the manner in which one must canvass: A canvasser must first obtain a permit. ... Earlier this Term, the Court reaffirmed that this test applies to content-neutral time, place, or manner restrictions on speech in public forums. See Thomas v. Chicago Park Dist., 534 U.S. 316 (2002).

... [I]t would be puzzling if regulations of speech taking place on *another citizen's* private property warranted greater scrutiny than regulations of speech taking place in public forums. Common sense and our precedent say just the opposite....

. . .

The next question is whether the ordinance serves the important interests of protecting privacy and preventing fraud and crime. With respect to the interest in protecting privacy, the Court concludes that "[t]he annoyance caused by an uninvited knock on the front door is the same whether or not the visitor is armed with a permit." True, but that misses the key point: the permit requirement results in fewer uninvited knocks. Those who have complied with the permit requirement are less likely to visit residences with no trespassing signs, as it is much easier for the authorities to track them down.

The Court also fails to grasp how the permit requirement serves Stratton's interest in preventing crime. We have approved of permit requirements for those engaging in protected First Amendment activity because of a common-sense recognition that their existence both deters and helps detect wrongdoing. . . .

The ordinance prevents and detects serious crime by making it a crime not to register. ...

Of course, the Stratton ordinance does not guarantee that no canvasser will ever commit a burglary or violent crime. ... In order to survive intermediate scrutiny, however, a law need not solve the crime problem, it need only further the interest in preventing crime. Some deterrence of serious criminal activity is more than enough to survive intermediate scrutiny.

. . .

... A discretionless permit requirement for canvassers does not violate the First Amendment. Today, the Court elevates its concern with what is, at most, a negligible burden on door-to-door communication above this established proposition. Ironically, however, today's decision may result in less of the door-to-door communication that the Court extols. As the Court recognizes, any homeowner may place a "No Solicitation" sign on his or her property, and it is a crime to violate that sign. In light of today's decision depriving Stratton residents of the degree of accountability and safety that the permit requirement provides, more and more residents may decide to place these signs in their yards and cut off door-to-door communication altogether.

SECTION 3.   SPEECH CONFLICTING WITH OTHER COMMUNITY VALUES: GOVERNMENT CONTROL OF THE CONTENT OF SPEECH

A.   PROTECTION OF INDIVIDUAL REPUTATION AND PRIVACY

Page 1287.   Add after The Florida Star v. B.J.F.:

Bartnicki v. Vopper

532 U.S. 514, 121 S.Ct. 1753, 149 L.Ed.2d 787 (2001).

Justice Stevens delivered the opinion of the Court.

These cases raise an important question concerning what degree of protection, if any, the First Amendment provides to speech that discloses the contents of an illegally intercepted communication. . . .

The suit at hand involves the repeated intentional disclosure of an illegally intercepted cellular telephone conversation about a public issue. The persons who made the disclosures did not participate in the interception, but they did know—or at least had reason to know—that the interception was unlawful. Accordingly, these cases present a conflict between interests of the highest order—on the one hand, the interest in the full and free dissemination of information concerning public issues, and, on the other hand, the interest in individual privacy and, more specifically, in fostering private speech. . . . [W]e are firmly convinced that the disclosures made by respondents in this suit are protected by the First Amendment.

I

During 1992 and most of 1993, the Pennsylvania State Education Association, a union representing the teachers at the Wyoming Valley West High School, engaged in collective-bargaining negotiations with the school board. Petitioner Kane, then the president of the local union, testified that the negotiations were " 'contentious' and received 'a lot of media attention.' " In May 1993, petitioner Bartnicki, who was acting as the union's "chief negotiator," used the cellular phone in her car to call Kane and engage in a lengthy conversation about the status of the negotiations. An unidentified person intercepted and recorded that call.

. . . At one point, Kane said: "If they're not gonna move for three percent, we're gonna have to go to their, their homes. . . . To blow off their front porches, we'll have to do some work on some of those guys. (PAUSES). Really, uh, really and truthfully because this is, you know, this is bad news. (UNDECIPHERABLE)."

In the early fall of 1993, the parties accepted a non-binding arbitration proposal that was generally favorable to the teachers. In connection with news reports about the settlement, respondent Vopper, a radio commentator who had been critical of the union in the past, played a tape of the intercepted conversation on his public affairs talk show. Another station also broadcast the tape, and local newspapers published its contents. After filing suit against Vopper and other representatives of the media, Bartnicki and Kane (hereinafter petitioners) learned through discovery that Vopper had obtained the tape from Jack Yocum, the head of a local taxpayers' organization that had opposed the union's demands throughout the negotiations. Yocum, who was added as a defendant, testified that he had found the tape in his mailbox shortly after the interception and recognized the voices of Bartnicki and Kane. Yocum played the tape for some members of the school board, and later delivered the tape itself to Vopper.

II

In their amended complaint, petitioners alleged that their telephone conversation had been surreptitiously intercepted by an unknown person using an electronic device, that Yocum had obtained a tape of that conversation, and that he intentionally disclosed it to Vopper, as well as other individuals and media representatives. Thereafter, Vopper and other members of the media repeatedly published the contents of that conversation. The amended complaint alleged that each of the defendants "knew or had reason to know" that the recording of the private telephone conversation had been obtained by means of an illegal interception. Relying on both federal and Pennsylvania statutory provisions, petitioners sought actual damages, statutory damages, punitive damages, and attorney's fees and costs.

. . . [T]he District Court rejected respondents' First Amendment defense
. . .

Thereafter, the District Court granted a motion for an interlocutory appeal, [certifying] as controlling questions of law: "(1) whether the imposition of liability on the media Defendants under the [wiretapping statutes] solely for broadcasting the newsworthy tape on the Defendant [Vopper's] radio/public affairs program, when the tape was illegally intercepted and recorded by unknown persons who were not agents of [the] Defendants, violates the First Amendment; and (2) whether imposition of liability under the aforesaid [wiretapping] statutes on Defendant Jack Yocum solely for providing the anonymously intercepted and recorded tape to the media Defendants violates the First Amendment." . . .

. . . [T]he majority [of the Court of Appeals] concluded that the statutes were invalid because they deterred significantly more speech than necessary to protect the privacy interests at stake. The court remanded the case with instructions to enter summary judgment for respondents. . . .

III

. . . One of the stated purposes of [Title III of the Omnibus Crime Control and Safe Streets Act of 1968, entitled Wiretapping and Electronic Surveillance] was "to protect effectively the privacy of wire and oral communications." . . . In addition to authorizing and regulating electronic surveillance for law enforcement purposes, Title III also regulated private conduct. . . . Subsection (c), the original version of the provision most directly at issue in this case, applied to any person who "willfully discloses, or endeavors to disclose, to any other person the contents of any wire or oral communication, knowing or having reason to know that the information was obtained through the interception of a wire or oral communication in violation of this subsection." The oral communications protected by the Act were only those "uttered by a person exhibiting an expectation that such communication is not subject to interception under circumstances justifying such expectation." . . .

. . . As enacted in 1968, Title III did not apply to the monitoring of radio transmissions. In the Electronic Communications Privacy Act of 1986, . . . however, Congress enlarged the coverage of Title III to prohibit the interception of "electronic" as well as oral and wire communications. By reason of that amendment, as well as a 1994 amendment which applied to cordless telephone communications, . . . Title III now applies to the interception of conversations over both cellular and cordless phones. . . .

IV

The constitutional question before us concerns the validity of the statutes as applied to the specific facts of this case. Because of the procedural posture of the case, it is appropriate to make certain important assumptions about those facts. We accept petitioners' submission that the interception was intentional, and therefore unlawful, and that, at a minimum, respondents "had reason to know" that it was unlawful. Accordingly, the disclosure of the contents of the intercepted conversation by Yocum to school board members and to representatives of the media, as well as the subsequent disclosures by the media defendants to the public, violated the federal and state statutes. Under the provisions of the federal statute, as well as its Pennsylvania analog, petitioners are thus entitled to recover damages from each of the respondents. The only question is whether the application of these statutes in such circumstances violates the First Amendment.[8]

In answering that question, we accept respondents' submission on three factual matters that serve to distinguish most of the cases that have arisen under § 2511. First, respondents played no part in the illegal interception. Rather, they found out about the interception only after it occurred, and in fact never learned the identity of the person or persons who made the interception. Second, their access to the information on the tapes was obtained lawfully, even though the information itself was intercepted unlawfully by someone else. . . . Third, the subject matter of the conversation was a matter of public concern. If the statements about the labor negotiations had been made in a public arena— during a bargaining session, for example—they would have been newsworthy. This would also be true if a third party had inadvertently overheard Bartnicki making the same statements to Kane when the two thought they were alone.

V

We agree with petitioners that § 2511(1)(c), as well as its Pennsylvania analog, is in fact a content-neutral law of general applicability. . . . In determining whether a regulation is content based or content neutral, we look to the purpose behind the regulation . . . In this case, the basic purpose of the statute at issue is to "protec[t] the privacy of wire[, electronic,] and oral communica-

---

8. In answering this question, we draw no distinction between the media respondents and Yocum. See, e.g., New York Times Co. v. Sullivan, 376 U.S. 254 (1964); First Nat. Bank of Boston v. Bellotti, 435 U.S. 765, 777 (1978).

tions." . . . The statute does not distinguish based on the content of the intercepted conversations, nor is it justified by reference to the content of those conversations. Rather, the communications at issue are singled out by virtue of the fact that they were illegally intercepted—by virtue of the source, rather than the subject matter.

On the other hand, the naked prohibition against disclosures is fairly characterized as a regulation of pure speech. Unlike the prohibition against the "use" of the contents of an illegal interception in § 2511(1)(d), subsection (c) is not a regulation of conduct. It is true that the delivery of a tape recording might be regarded as conduct, but given that the purpose of such a delivery is to provide the recipient with the text of recorded statements, it is like the delivery of a handbill or a pamphlet, and as such, it is the kind of "speech" that the First Amendment protects. . . . As a general matter, "state action to punish the publication of truthful information seldom can satisfy constitutional standards." Smith v. Daily Mail Publishing Co., 443 U.S. 97, 102 (1979). . . .

. . .

. . . New York Times Co. v. United States, 403 U.S. 713 (1971) . . . raised, but did not resolve the question "whether, in cases where information has been acquired unlawfully by a newspaper or by a source, government may ever punish not only the unlawful acquisition, but the ensuing publication as well." . . . The question here, however, is a narrower version of that still-open question. Simply put, the issue here is this: "Where the punished publisher of information has obtained the information in question in a manner lawful in itself but from a source who has obtained it unlawfully, may the government punish the ensuing publication of that information based on the defect in a chain?" . . .

. . .

The Government identifies two interests served by the statute—first, the interest in removing an incentive for parties to intercept private conversations, and second, the interest in minimizing the harm to persons whose conversations have been illegally intercepted. We assume that those interests adequately justify the prohibition in § 2511(1)(d) against the interceptor's own use of information that he or she acquired by violating § 2511(1)(a), but it by no means follows that punishing disclosures of lawfully obtained information of public interest by one not involved in the initial illegality is an acceptable means of serving those ends.

The normal method of deterring unlawful conduct is to impose an appropriate punishment on the person who engages in it. If the sanctions that presently attach to a violation of § 2511(1)(a) do not provide sufficient deterrence, perhaps those sanctions should be made more severe. But it would be quite remarkable to hold that speech by a law-abiding possessor of information can be suppressed in order to deter conduct by a non-law-abiding third party. . . . With only a handful of exceptions, the violations of § 2511(1)(a) that have been described in litigated cases have been motivated by either financial gain or domestic disputes. In virtually all of those cases, the identity of the person or persons intercepting the communication has been known. Moreover, petitioners cite no evidence that Congress viewed the prohibition against disclosures as a response to the difficulty of identifying persons making improper use of scanners and other surveillance devices and accordingly of deterring such conduct, and there is no empirical evidence to support the assumption that the prohibition against disclosures reduces the number of illegal interceptions.

Although this case demonstrates that there may be an occasional situation in which an anonymous scanner will risk criminal prosecution by passing on information without any expectation of financial reward or public praise, surely this is the exceptional case. Moreover, there is no basis for assuming that imposing sanctions upon respondents will deter the unidentified scanner from continuing to engage in surreptitious interceptions. Unusual cases fall far short of a showing that there is a "need of the highest order" for a rule supplementing the traditional means of deterring antisocial conduct.

The Government's second argument, however, is considerably stronger. Privacy of communication is an important interest, ... and Title III's restrictions are intended to protect that interest, thereby "encouraging the uninhibited exchange of ideas and information among private parties...." Moreover, the fear of public disclosure of private conversations might well have a chilling effect on private speech.

... [T]here are important interests to be considered on both sides of the constitutional calculus. In considering that balance, we acknowledge that some intrusions on privacy are more offensive than others, and that the disclosure of the contents of a private conversation can be an even greater intrusion on privacy than the interception itself. As a result, there is a valid independent justification for prohibiting such disclosures by persons who lawfully obtained access to the contents of an illegally intercepted message, even if that prohibition does not play a significant role in preventing such interceptions from occurring in the first place.

We need not decide whether that interest is strong enough to justify the application of § 2511(c) to disclosures of trade secrets or domestic gossip or other information of purely private concern. ... In other words, the outcome of the case does not turn on whether § 2511(1)(c) may be enforced with respect to most violations of the statute without offending the First Amendment. The enforcement of that provision in this case, however, implicates the core purposes of the First Amendment because it imposes sanctions on the publication of truthful information of public concern.

... In this case, privacy concerns give way when balanced against the interest in publishing matters of public importance. As Warren and Brandeis stated in their classic law review article: "The right of privacy does not prohibit any publication of matter which is of public or general interest." The Right to Privacy, 4 Harv. L.Rev. 193, 214 (1890). One of the costs associated with participation in public affairs is an attendant loss of privacy. ...

. . .

We think it clear that parallel reasoning requires the conclusion that a stranger's illegal conduct does not suffice to remove the First Amendment shield from speech about a matter of public concern. The months of negotiations over the proper level of compensation for teachers at the Wyoming Valley West High School were unquestionably a matter of public concern, and respondents were clearly engaged in debate about that concern. That debate may be more mundane than the Communist rhetoric that inspired Justice Brandeis' classic opinion in Whitney v. California, 274 U.S., at 372, but it is no less worthy of constitutional protection.

The judgment is affirmed.

It is so ordered.

Justice Breyer, with whom Justice O'Connor joins, concurring.

I join the Court's opinion because I agree with its "narrow" holding, limited to the special circumstances present here: (1) the radio broadcasters acted lawfully (up to the time of final public disclosure); and (2) the information publicized involved a matter of unusual public concern, namely a threat of potential physical harm to others. I write separately to explain why, in my view, the Court's holding does not imply a significantly broader constitutional immunity for the media.

. . .

I would ask whether the statutes strike a reasonable balance between their speech-restricting and speech-enhancing consequences. Or do they instead impose restrictions on speech that are disproportionate when measured against their corresponding privacy and speech-related benefits, taking into account the kind, the importance, and the extent of these benefits, as well as the need for the restrictions in order to secure those benefits? What this Court has called "strict scrutiny"—with its strong presumption against constitutionality—is normally out of place where, as here, important competing constitutional interests are implicated. . . .

The statutory restrictions before us directly enhance private speech. . . . The statutes ensure the privacy of telephone conversations much as a trespass statute ensures privacy within the home. That assurance of privacy helps to overcome our natural reluctance to discuss private matters when we fear that our private conversations may become public. And the statutory restrictions consequently encourage conversations that otherwise might not take place.

. . . At the same time, these statutes restrict public speech directly, deliberately, and of necessity. They include media publication within their scope not simply as a means, say, to deter interception, but also as an end. Media dissemination of an intimate conversation to an entire community will often cause the speakers serious harm over and above the harm caused by an initial disclosure to the person who intercepted the phone call. . . . And the threat of that widespread dissemination can create a far more powerful disincentive to speak privately than the comparatively minor threat of disclosure to an interceptor and perhaps to a handful of others. Insofar as these statutes protect private communications against that widespread dissemination, they resemble laws that would award damages caused through publication of information obtained by theft from a private bedroom. See generally Warren & Brandeis, The Right to Privacy, 4 Harv. L.Rev. 193 (1890) . . . See also Restatement (Second) of Torts § 652D (1977).

As a general matter, despite the statutes' direct restrictions on speech, the Federal Constitution must tolerate laws of this kind because of the importance of these privacy and speech-related objectives. . . . Rather than broadly forbid this kind of legislative enactment, the Constitution demands legislative efforts to tailor the laws in order reasonably to reconcile media freedom with personal, speech-related privacy.

Nonetheless, looked at more specifically, the statutes, as applied in these circumstances, do not reasonably reconcile the competing constitutional objectives. Rather, they disproportionately interfere with media freedom. For one thing, the broadcasters here engaged in no unlawful activity other than the ultimate publication of the information another had previously obtained. . . .

For another thing, the speakers had little or no legitimate interest in maintaining the privacy of the particular conversation. That conversation involved a suggestion about "blow[ing] off . . . front porches" and "do[ing] some work on some of these guys," thereby raising a significant concern for the safety of others. . . . Even where the danger may have passed by the time of publication, that fact cannot legitimize the speaker's earlier privacy expectation. Nor should editors, who must make a publication decision quickly, have to determine present or continued danger before publishing this kind of threat.

Further, the speakers themselves, the president of a teacher's union and the union's chief negotiator, were "limited public figures," for they voluntarily engaged in a public controversy. They thereby subjected themselves to somewhat greater public scrutiny and had a lesser interest in privacy than an individual engaged in purely private affairs. . . .

This is not to say that the Constitution requires anyone, including public figures, to give up entirely the right to private communication, i.e., communication free from telephone taps or interceptions. But the subject matter of the conversation at issue here is far removed from that in situations where the media publicizes truly private matters. . . .

Thus, in finding a constitutional privilege to publish unlawfully intercepted conversations of the kind here at issue, the Court does not create a "public interest" exception that swallows up the statutes' privacy-protecting general rule. Rather, it finds constitutional protection for publication of intercepted information of a special kind. Here, the speakers' legitimate privacy expectations are unusually low, and the public interest in defeating those expectations is unusually high. Given these circumstances, along with the lawful nature of respondents' behavior, the statutes' enforcement would disproportionately harm media freedom.

I emphasize the particular circumstances before us because, in my view, the Constitution permits legislatures to respond flexibly to the challenges future technology may pose to the individual's interest in basic personal privacy. Clandestine and pervasive invasions of privacy, unlike the simple theft of documents from a bedroom, are genuine possibilities as a result of continuously advancing technologies. Eavesdropping on ordinary cellular phone conversations in the street (which many callers seem to tolerate) is a very different matter from eavesdropping on encrypted cellular phone conversations or those carried on in the bedroom. But the technologies that allow the former may come to permit the latter. And statutes that may seem less important in the former context may turn out to have greater importance in the latter. Legislatures also may decide to revisit statutes such as those before us, creating better tailored provisions designed to encourage, for example, more effective privacy-protecting technologies.

For these reasons, we should avoid adopting overly broad or rigid constitutional rules, which would unnecessarily restrict legislative flexibility. I consequently agree with the Court's holding that the statutes as applied here violate the Constitution, but I would not extend that holding beyond these present circumstances.

Chief Justice Rehnquist, with whom Justice Scalia and Justice Thomas join, dissenting.

... In an attempt to prevent some of the most egregious violations of privacy, the United States, the District of Columbia, and 40 States have enacted laws prohibiting the intentional interception and knowing disclosure of electronic communications. The Court holds that all of these statutes violate the First Amendment insofar as the illegally intercepted conversation touches upon a matter of "public concern," an amorphous concept that the Court does not even attempt to define. But the Court's decision diminishes, rather than enhances, the purposes of the First Amendment: chilling the speech of the millions of Americans who rely upon electronic technology to communicate each day.

. . .

... [T]he *Daily Mail* cases upon which the Court relies do not address the question presented here. Our decisions themselves made this clear: "The *Daily Mail* principle does not settle the issue whether, in cases where information has been acquired unlawfully by a newspaper or by a source, the government may ever punish not only the unlawful acquisition, but the ensuing publication as well." ... The transmission of the intercepted communication from the eavesdropper to the third party is itself illegal; and where, as here, the third party then knowingly discloses that communication, another illegal act has been committed. The third party in this situation cannot be likened to the reporters in the *Daily Mail* cases, who lawfully obtained their information through consensual interviews or public documents.

. . .

Congress and the overwhelming majority of States reasonably have concluded that sanctioning the knowing disclosure of illegally intercepted communications will deter the initial interception itself, a crime which is extremely difficult to detect. ...

. . .

... Were there no prohibition on disclosure, an unlawful eavesdropper who wanted to disclose the conversation could anonymously launder the interception through a third party and thereby avoid detection. Indeed, demand for illegally obtained private information would only increase if it could be disclosed without repercussion. The law against interceptions, which the Court agrees is valid, would be utterly ineffectual without these antidisclosure provisions.

At base, the Court's decision to hold these statutes unconstitutional rests upon nothing more than the bald substitution of its own prognostications in place of the reasoned judgment of 41 legislative bodies and the United States Congress. . . .

. . .

. . . The Constitution should not protect the involuntary broadcast of personal conversations. Even where the communications involve public figures or concern public matters, the conversations are nonetheless private and worthy of protection. Although public persons may have forgone the right to live their lives screened from public scrutiny in some areas, it does not and should not follow that they also have abandoned their right to have a private conversation without fear of it being intentionally intercepted and knowingly disclosed.

B.   CONTROL OF OBSCENITY AND PORNOGRAPHY

Page 1297.   Replace New York v. Ferber:

Ashcroft v. The Free Speech Coalition

535 U.S. 234, 122 S.Ct. 1389, 152 L.Ed.2d 403 (2002).

Justice Kennedy delivered the opinion of the Court.

We consider in this case whether the Child Pornography Prevention Act of 1996 (CPPA), 18 U.S.C. § 2251 et seq., abridges the freedom of speech. The CPPA extends the federal prohibition against child pornography to sexually explicit images that appear to depict minors but were produced without using any real children. The statute prohibits, in specific circumstances, possessing or distributing these images, which may be created by using adults who look like minors or by using computer imaging. The new technology, according to Congress, makes it possible to create realistic images of children who do not exist. . . .

By prohibiting child pornography that does not depict an actual child, the statute goes beyond New York v. Ferber, 458 U.S. 747 (1982), which distinguished child pornography from other sexually explicit speech because of the State's interest in protecting the children exploited by the production process. . . . As a general rule, pornography can be banned only if obscene, but under *Ferber*, pornography showing minors can be proscribed whether or not the images are obscene under the definition set forth in Miller v. California . . .

While we have not had occasion to consider the question, we may assume that the apparent age of persons engaged in sexual conduct is relevant to whether a depiction offends community standards. Pictures of young children engaged in certain acts might be obscene where similar depictions of adults, or perhaps even older adolescents, would not. The CPPA, however, is not directed at speech that is obscene . . . Like the law in *Ferber*, the CPPA seeks to reach beyond obscenity, and it makes no attempt to conform to the *Miller* standard. For instance, the statute would reach visual depictions, such as movies, even if they have redeeming social value.

The principal question to be resolved, then, is whether the CPPA is constitutional where it proscribes a significant universe of speech that is neither obscene under *Miller* nor child pornography under *Ferber*.

I

Before 1996, Congress defined child pornography as the type of depictions at issue in *Ferber*, images made using actual minors. . . . The CPPA retains that prohibition at 18 U.S.C. § 2256(8)(A) and adds three other prohibited categories of speech, of which the first, § 2256(8)(B), and the third, § 2256(8)(D), are at issue in this case. Section 2256(8)(B) prohibits "any visual depiction, including any photograph, film, video, picture, or computer or computer-generated image or picture" that "is, or appears to be, of a minor engaging in sexually explicit conduct." The prohibition on "any visual depiction" does not depend at all on how the image is produced. The section captures a range of depictions, sometimes called "virtual child pornography," which include computer-generated images, as well as images produced by more traditional means. For instance, the literal terms of the statute embrace a Renaissance painting depicting a scene from classical mythology, a "picture" that "appears to be, of a minor engaging in sexually explicit conduct." The statute also prohibits Hollywood movies, filmed without any child actors, if a jury believes an actor "appears to be" a minor engaging in "actual or simulated . . . sexual intercourse." § 2256(2).

These images do not involve, let alone harm, any children in the production process; but Congress decided the materials threaten children in other, less direct, ways. Pedophiles might use the materials to encourage children to participate in sexual activity. . . . Furthermore, pedophiles might "whet their own sexual appetites" with the pornographic images, "thereby increasing the creation and distribution of child pornography and the sexual abuse and exploitation of actual children." . . . Under these rationales, harm flows from the content of the images, not from the means of their production. In addition, Congress identified another problem created by computer-generated images: Their existence can make it harder to prosecute pornographers who do use real minors. . . . As imaging technology improves, Congress found, it becomes more difficult to prove that a particular picture was produced using actual children.
. . .

Section 2256(8)(C) prohibits a more common and lower tech means of creating virtual images, known as computer morphing. Rather than creating original images, pornographers can alter innocent pictures of real children so that the children appear to be engaged in sexual activity. Although morphed images may fall within the definition of virtual child pornography, they implicate the interests of real children and are in that sense closer to the images in *Ferber*. Respondents do not challenge this provision, and we do not consider it.

Respondents do challenge § 2256(8)(D). Like the text of the "appears to be" provision, the sweep of this provision is quite broad. Section 2256(8)(D) defines child pornography to include any sexually explicit image that was "advertised, promoted, presented, described, or distributed in such a manner that conveys the impression" it depicts "a minor engaging in sexually explicit conduct." One Committee Report identified the provision as directed at sexually explicit images pandered as child pornography. . . . The statute is not so limited in its reach, however, as it punishes even those possessors who took no part in pandering. Once a work has been described as child pornography, the taint remains on the speech in the hands of subsequent possessors, making possession unlawful even though the content otherwise would not be objectionable.

Fearing that the CPPA threatened the activities of its members, respondent Free Speech Coalition and others challenged the statute in the United States District Court for the Northern District of California. The Coalition, a California trade association for the adult-entertainment industry, alleged that its members did not use minors in their sexually explicit works, but they believed some of these materials might fall within the CPPA's expanded definition of child pornography. The other respondents are Bold Type, Inc., the publisher of a book advocating the nudist lifestyle; Jim Gingerich, a painter of nudes; and Ron Raffaelli, a photographer specializing in erotic images. Respondents alleged that the "appears to be" and "conveys the impression" provisions are overbroad and vague, chilling them from producing works protected by the First Amendment. The District Court disagreed and granted summary judgment to the Government. . . .

The Court of Appeals for the Ninth Circuit reversed. . . .

. . .

II

. . . [A] law imposing criminal penalties on protected speech is a stark example of speech suppression. The CPPA's penalties are indeed severe. A first offender may be imprisoned for 15 years. . . . A repeat offender faces a prison sentence of not less than 5 years and not more than 30 years in prison. . . . While even minor punishments can chill protected speech, . . . this case provides a textbook example of why we permit facial challenges to statutes that burden expression. With these severe penalties in force, few legitimate movie producers or book publishers, or few other speakers in any capacity, would risk distributing images in or near the uncertain reach of this law. The Constitution gives significant protection from overbroad laws that chill speech within the First Amendment's vast and privileged sphere. Under this principle, the CPPA is unconstitutional on its face if it prohibits a substantial amount of protected expression. . . .

. . .

. . . [S]peech may not be prohibited because it concerns subjects offending our sensibilities. . . .

As a general principle, the First Amendment bars the government from dictating what we see or read or speak or hear. The freedom of speech has its limits; it does not embrace certain categories of speech, including defamation, incitement, obscenity, and pornography produced with real children. . . . While these categories may be prohibited without violating the First Amendment, none of them includes the speech prohibited by the CPPA. . . .

As we have noted, the CPPA is much more than a supplement to the existing federal prohibition on obscenity. . . . The CPPA . . ., extends to images that appear to depict a minor engaging in sexually explicit activity without regard to the *Miller* requirements. . . . Any depiction of sexually explicit activity, no matter how it is presented, is proscribed. The CPPA applies to a picture in a psychology manual, as well as a movie depicting the horrors of sexual abuse. . . .

. . . The statute proscribes the visual depiction of an idea—that of teenagers engaging in sexual activity—that is a fact of modern society and has been a theme in art and literature throughout the ages. Under the CPPA, images are prohibited so long as the persons appear to be under 18 years of age. This is higher than the legal age for marriage in many States, as well as the age at which persons may consent to sexual relations. . . .

. . . Both themes—teenage sexual activity and the sexual abuse of children—have inspired countless literary works. William Shakespeare created the most famous pair of teenage lovers, one of whom is just 13 years of age. . . . The work has inspired no less than 40 motion pictures, some of which suggest that the teenagers consummated their relationship. . . .

Contemporary movies pursue similar themes. Last year's Academy Awards featured the movie, *Traffic*, which was nominated for Best Picture. . . . The film portrays a teenager, identified as a 16–year-old, who becomes addicted to drugs. The viewer sees the degradation of her addiction, which in the end leads her to a filthy room to trade sex for drugs. The year before, *American Beauty* won the Academy Award for Best Picture. . . . In the course of the movie, a teenage girl engages in sexual relations with her teenage boyfriend, and another yields herself to the gratification of a middle-aged man. . . .

. . . Whether or not the films we mention violate the CPPA, they explore themes within the wide sweep of the statute's prohibitions. If these films, or hundreds of others of lesser note that explore those subjects, contain a single graphic depiction of sexual activity within the statutory definition, the possessor of the film would be subject to severe punishment without inquiry into the work's redeeming value. This is inconsistent with an essential First Amendment rule: The artistic merit of a work does not depend on the presence of a single explicit scene. . . .

The Government seeks to address this deficiency by arguing that speech prohibited by the CPPA is virtually indistinguishable from child pornography, which may be banned without regard to whether it depicts works of value. . . . *Ferber* recognized that the State had an interest in stamping it out without regard to any judgment about its content. . . . The production of the work, not its content, was the target of the statute. The fact that a work contained serious literary, artistic, or other value did not excuse the harm it caused to its child participants. . . .

. . . First, as a permanent record of a child's abuse, the continued circulation itself would harm the child who had participated. Like a defamatory statement, each new publication of the speech would cause new injury to the child's reputation and emotional well-being. . . . Second, because the traffic in child pornography was an economic motive for its production, the State had an interest in closing the distribution network. . . . Under either rationale, the speech had what the Court in effect held was a proximate link to the crime from which it came.

Later, in Osborne v. Ohio, 495 U.S. 103 (1990), the Court ruled that these same interests justified a ban on the possession of pornography produced by using children. . . . It did not suggest that, absent this concern, other governmental interests would suffice.

. . . [T]he CPPA prohibits speech that records no crime and creates no victims by its production. Virtual child pornography is not "intrinsically related" to the sexual abuse of children, as were the materials in *Ferber*. . . . While the Government asserts that the images can lead to actual instances of child abuse, . . . the causal link is contingent and indirect. The harm does not necessarily follow from the speech, but depends upon some unquantified potential for subsequent criminal acts.

The Government says these indirect harms are sufficient because, as *Ferber* acknowledged, child pornography rarely can be valuable speech. . . . This argument, however, suffers from two flaws. First, *Ferber*'s judgment about child pornography was based upon how it was made, not on what it communicated. . . .

The second flaw in the Government's position is that *Ferber* did not hold that child pornography is by definition without value. On the contrary, the Court recognized some works in this category might have significant value, . . . but relied on virtual images—the very images prohibited by the CPPA—as an alternative and permissible means of expression . . . *Ferber*, then, not only referred to the distinction between actual and virtual child pornography, it relied on it as a reason supporting its holding. *Ferber* provides no support for a statute that eliminates the distinction and makes the alternative mode criminal as well.

III

. . . The Government . . . argues that the CPPA is necessary because pedophiles may use virtual child pornography to seduce children. . . . The Government, of course, may punish adults who provide unsuitable materials to children, see Ginsberg v. New York, 390 U.S. 629 (1968), and it may enforce criminal penalties for unlawful solicitation. The precedents establish, however, that speech within the rights of adults to hear may not be silenced completely in an attempt to shield children from it. . . .

Here, the Government wants to keep speech from children not to protect them from its content but to protect them from those who would commit other crimes. The principle, however, remains the same: The Government cannot ban speech fit for adults simply because it may fall into the hands of children. The evil in question depends upon the actor's unlawful conduct, conduct defined as criminal quite apart from any link to the speech in question. This establishes that the speech ban is not narrowly drawn. The objective is to prohibit illegal conduct, but this restriction goes well beyond that interest by restricting the speech available to law-abiding adults.

The Government submits further that virtual child pornography whets the appetites of pedophiles and encourages them to engage in illegal conduct. This rationale cannot sustain the provision in question. The mere tendency of speech to encourage unlawful acts is not a sufficient reason for banning it. . . . First Amendment freedoms are most in danger when the government seeks to control thought or to justify its laws for that impermissible end. The right to think is the beginning of freedom, and speech must be protected from the government because speech is the beginning of thought.

... There is here no attempt, incitement, solicitation, or conspiracy. The Government has shown no more than a remote connection between speech that might encourage thoughts or impulses and any resulting child abuse. Without a significantly stronger, more direct connection, the Government may not prohibit speech on the ground that it may encourage pedophiles to engage in illegal conduct.

The Government next argues that its objective of eliminating the market for pornography produced using real children necessitates a prohibition on virtual images as well. Virtual images, the Government contends, are indistinguishable from real ones; they are part of the same market and are often exchanged. In this way, it is said, virtual images promote the trafficking in works produced through the exploitation of real children. The hypothesis is somewhat implausible. If virtual images were identical to illegal child pornography, the illegal images would be driven from the market by the indistinguishable substitutes. Few pornographers would risk prosecution by abusing real children if fictional, computerized images would suffice.

In the case of the material covered by *Ferber*, the creation of the speech is itself the crime of child abuse; the prohibition deters the crime by removing the profit motive. ...[H]ere, there is no underlying crime at all. Even if the Government's market deterrence theory were persuasive in some contexts, it would not justify this statute.

Finally, the Government says that the possibility of producing images by using computer imaging makes it very difficult for it to prosecute those who produce pornography by using real children. Experts, we are told, may have difficulty in saying whether the pictures were made by using real children or by using computer imaging. The necessary solution, the argument runs, is to prohibit both kinds of images. The argument, in essence, is that protected speech may be banned as a means to ban unprotected speech. This analysis turns the First Amendment upside down.

The Government may not suppress lawful speech as the means to suppress unlawful speech. Protected speech does not become unprotected merely because it resembles the latter. The Constitution requires the reverse.... The overbreadth doctrine prohibits the Government from banning unprotected speech if a substantial amount of protected speech is prohibited or chilled in the process.

To avoid the force of this objection, the Government would have us read the CPPA not as a measure suppressing speech but as a law shifting the burden to the accused to prove the speech is lawful. In this connection, the Government relies on an affirmative defense under the statute, which allows a defendant to avoid conviction for nonpossession offenses by showing that the materials were produced using only adults and were not otherwise distributed in a manner conveying the impression that they depicted real children. ...

The Government raises serious constitutional difficulties by seeking to impose on the defendant the burden of proving his speech is not unlawful.... If the evidentiary issue is a serious problem for the Government, as it asserts, it will be at least as difficult for the innocent possessor....

We need not decide, however, whether the Government could impose this burden on a speaker. Even if an affirmative defense can save a statute from First Amendment challenge, here the defense is incomplete and insufficient, even on its own terms.... A defendant charged with possessing, as opposed to distributing, proscribed works may not defend on the ground that the film depicts only adult actors. ... So while the affirmative defense may protect a movie producer from prosecution for the act of distribution, that same producer, and all other persons in the subsequent distribution chain, could be liable for possessing the prohibited work. Furthermore, the affirmative defense provides no protection to persons who produce speech by using computer imaging, or through other means that do not involve the use of adult actors who appear to be minors. ... In these cases, the defendant can demonstrate no children were harmed in producing the images, yet the affirmative defense would not bar the prosecution. For this reason, the affirmative defense cannot save the statute, for it leaves unprotected a substantial amount of speech not tied to the Government's interest in distinguishing images produced using real children from virtual ones.

. . .

IV

Respondents challenge § 2256(8)(D) as well. This provision bans depictions of sexually explicit conduct that are "advertised, promoted, presented, described, or distributed in such a manner that conveys the impression that the material is or contains a visual depiction of a minor engaging in sexually explicit conduct."....

... The CPPA prohibits sexually explicit materials that "convey[s] the impression" they depict minors. While that phrase may sound like the "appears to be" prohibition in § 2256(8)(B), it requires little judgment about the content of the image. Under § 2256(8)(D), the work must be sexually explicit, but otherwise the content is irrelevant. Even if a film contains no sexually explicit scenes involving minors, it could be treated as child pornography if the title and trailers convey the impression that the scenes would be found in the movie. The determination turns on how the speech is presented, not on what is depicted. ...

The Government does not offer a serious defense of this provision ... The materials, for instance, are not likely to be confused for child pornography in a criminal trial. The Court has recognized that pandering may be relevant, as an evidentiary matter, to the question whether particular materials are obscene. See Ginzburg v. United States, 383 U.S. 463, 474 (1966) ...

... Section 2256(8)(D), however, prohibits a substantial amount of speech that falls outside Ginzburg's rationale. Materials falling within the proscription are tainted and unlawful in the hands of all who receive it, though they bear no responsibility for how it was marketed, sold, or described. The statute, furthermore, does not require that the context be part of an effort at "commercial exploitation." ... § 2256(8)(D) is substantially overbroad ...

V

... [T]he prohibitions of §§ 2256(8)(B) and 2256(8)(D) are overbroad and unconstitutional. ...

The judgment of the Court of Appeals is affirmed.

. . .

Justice Thomas, concurring in the judgment.

In my view, the Government's most persuasive asserted interest in support of the [CCPA] is the prosecution rationale—that persons who possess and disseminate pornographic images of real children may escape conviction by claiming that the images are computer-generated, thereby raising a reasonable doubt as to their guilt. At this time, however, the Government asserts only that defendants raise such defenses, not that they have done so successfully. In fact, the Government points to no case in which a defendant has been acquitted based on a "computer-generated images" defense. While this speculative interest cannot support the broad reach of the CPPA, technology may evolve to the point where it becomes impossible to enforce actual child pornography laws because the Government cannot prove that certain pornographic images are of real children. In the event this occurs, the Government should not be foreclosed from enacting a regulation of virtual child pornography that contains an appropriate affirmative defense or some other narrowly drawn restriction.

. . . [I]f technological advances thwart prosecution of "unlawful speech," the Government may well have a compelling interest in barring or otherwise regulating some narrow category of "lawful speech" in order to enforce effectively laws against pornography made through the abuse of real children.

. . .

Justice O'Connor, with whom The Chief Justice and Justice Scalia join as to Part II, concurring in the judgment in part and dissenting in part.

. . .

This litigation involves a facial challenge to the CPPA's prohibitions of pornographic images that "appea[r] to be . . . of a minor" and of material that "conveys the impression" that it contains pornographic images of minors. While I agree with the Court's judgment that the First Amendment requires that the latter prohibition be struck down, I disagree with its decision to strike down the former prohibition in its entirety. . . . I would strike down the prohibition of pornography that "appears to be" of minors only insofar as it is applied to the class of youthful-adult pornography.

I

. . . The Government . . . requests that the Court exclude youthful-adult and virtual-child pornography from the protection of the First Amendment.

I agree with the Court's decision not to grant this request. . . . [W]hat the Government asks this Court to rule is that it may . . . prohibit youthful-adult and virtual-adult pornography that is merely indecent. . . . Although such pornography looks like the material at issue in New York v. Ferber, . . . no children are harmed in the process of creating such pornography. . . . Therefore, *Ferber* does not support the Government's ban on youthful-adult and virtual-child pornography. . . . The Court correctly concludes that the causal connection between pornographic images that "appear" to include minors and actual child abuse is not strong enough to justify withdrawing First Amendment protection for such speech.

I also agree with the Court's decision to strike down the CPPA's ban on material presented in a manner that "conveys the impression" that it contains pornographic depictions of actual children ("actual-child pornography"). . . . The Court concludes that § 2256(8)(D) is overbroad, but its reasoning also persuades me that the provision is not narrowly tailored. The provision therefore fails strict scrutiny. . . .

Finally, I agree with Court that that the CPPA's ban on youthful-adult pornography is overbroad. The Court provides several examples of movies that, although possessing serious literary, artistic or political value and employing only adult actors to perform simulated sexual conduct, fall under the CPPA's proscription . . .

II

I disagree with the Court, however, that the CPPA's prohibition of virtual-child pornography is overbroad. Before I reach that issue, there are two preliminary questions: whether the ban on virtual-child pornography fails strict scrutiny and whether that ban is unconstitutionally vague. I would answer both in the negative.

. . . [G]iven the rapid pace of advances in computer-graphics technology, the Government's concern is reasonable. . . .

Respondents argue that, even if the Government has a compelling interest to justify banning virtual-child pornography, the "appears to be . . . of a minor" language is not narrowly tailored to serve that interest. . . . They assert that the CPPA would capture even cartoon-sketches or statues of children that were sexually suggestive. Such images surely could not be used, for instance, to seduce children. I agree. A better interpretation of "appears to be . . . of" is "virtually indistinguishable from"—an interpretation that would not cover the examples respondents provide. . . .

Reading the statute only to bar images that are virtually indistinguishable from actual children would not only assure that the ban on virtual-child pornography is narrowly tailored, but would also assuage any fears that the "appears to be . . . of a minor" language is vague. . . .

The Court concludes that the CPPA's ban on virtual-child pornography is overbroad. . . . Respondents provide no examples of films or other materials that are wholly computer-generated and contain images that "appea[r] to be . . . of minors" engaging in indecent conduct, but that have serious value or do not facilitate child abuse. Their overbreadth challenge therefore fails.

III

Although in my view the CPPA's ban on youthful-adult pornography appears to violate the First Amendment, the ban on virtual-child pornography does not. It is true that both bans are authorized by the same text. . . . Invalidating a statute due to overbreadth, however, is an extreme remedy, one that should be employed "sparingly and only as a last resort." . . .

Heeding this caution, I would strike the "appears to be" provision only insofar as it is applied to the subset of cases involving youthful-adult pornography. . . .

. . . Drawing a line around, and striking just, the CPPA's ban on youthful-child pornography . . . preserves the CPPA's prohibition of the material that Congress found most dangerous to children.

. . .

Chief Justice Rehnquist, with whom Justice Scalia joins in part, dissenting.

I agree with Part II of Justice O'Connor's opinion . . . Congress has a compelling interest in ensuring the ability to enforce prohibitions of actual child pornography, and we should defer to its findings that rapidly advancing technology soon will make it all but impossible to do so. . . .

I also agree with Justice O'Connor that serious First Amendment concerns would arise were the Government ever to prosecute someone for simple distribution or possession of a film with literary or artistic value, such as "Traffic" or "American Beauty." I write separately, however, because the . . . (CPPA) . . . need not be construed to reach such materials.

We normally do not strike down a statute on First Amendment grounds "when a limiting instruction has been or could be placed on the challenged statute." . . .

Other than computer generated images that are virtually indistinguishable from real children engaged in sexually explicit conduct, the CPPA can be limited so as not to reach any material that was not already unprotected before the CPPA . . .

Indeed, we should be loath to construe a statute as banning film portrayals of Shakespearian tragedies, without some indication—from text or legislative history—that such a result was intended. . . .

. . .

Page 1310.   Add after United States v. Playboy Entertainment Group, Inc.:

Ashcroft v. ACLU

535 U.S. 564, 122 S.Ct. 1700, 152 L.Ed.2d 771 (2002).

Justice Thomas announced the judgment of the Court and delivered the opinion of the Court with respect to Parts I, II, and IV, an opinion with respect to Parts III–A, III–C, and III–D, in which THE Chief Justice and Justice Scalia join, and an opinion with respect to Part III–B, in which THE Chief Justice, Justice O'Connor, and Justice Scalia join.

This case presents the narrow question whether the Child Online Protection Act's (COPA or Act) use of "community standards" to identify "material that is harmful to minors" violates the First Amendment. We hold that this aspect of COPA does not render the statute facially unconstitutional.

I

... While "surfing" the World Wide Web, ... individuals can access material about topics ranging from aardvarks to Zoroastrianism. One can use the Web to read thousands of newspapers published around the globe, purchase tickets for a matinee at the neighborhood movie theater, or follow the progress of any Major League Baseball team on a pitch-by-pitch basis.

The Web also contains a wide array of sexually explicit material, including hardcore pornography. ... In 1998, for instance, there were approximately 28,000 adult sites promoting pornography on the Web. ...[C]hildren may discover this pornographic material either by deliberately accessing pornographic Web sites or by stumbling upon them. ...

Congress first attempted to protect children from exposure to pornographic material on the Internet by enacting the Communications Decency Act of 1996 (CDA) ... The CDA prohibited the knowing transmission over the Internet of obscene or indecent messages to any recipient under 18 years of age. ... It also forbade any individual from knowingly sending over or displaying on the Internet certain "patently offensive" material in a manner available to persons under 18 years of age. ... The prohibition specifically extended to "any comment, request, suggestion, proposal, image, or other communication that, in context, depict [ed] or describ[ed], in terms patently offensive as measured by contemporary community standards, sexual or excretory activities or organs."
...

The CDA provided two affirmative defenses to those prosecuted under the statute. The first protected individuals who took "good faith, reasonable, effective, and appropriate actions" to restrict minors from accessing obscene, indecent, and patently offensive material over the Internet. ... The second shielded those who restricted minors from accessing such material "by requiring use of a verified credit card, debit account, adult access code, or adult personal identification number." ...

Notwithstanding these affirmative defenses, in Reno v. American Civil Liberties Union, [521 U.S. 844 (1997),] we held that the CDA's regulation of indecent transmissions, ... and the display of patently offensive material, ... ran afoul of the First Amendment. We concluded that "the CDA lack[ed] the precision that the First Amendment requires when a statute regulates the content of speech" because, "[i]n order to deny minors access to potentially harmful speech, the CDA effectively suppress[ed] a large amount of speech that adults ha[d] a constitutional right to receive and to address to one another."
...

Our holding was based on three crucial considerations. First, "existing technology did not include any effective method for a sender to prevent minors from obtaining access to its communications on the Internet without also denying access to adults." ... Second, "[t]he breadth of the CDA's coverage [was] wholly unprecedented." ... "Its open-ended prohibitions embrace[d]," not only commercial speech or commercial entities, but also "all nonprofit entities and individuals posting indecent messages or displaying them on their own computers in the presence of minors." *Ibid.* In addition, because the CDA did not define the terms "indecent" and "patently offensive," the statute "cover[ed] large amounts of nonpornographic material with serious educational or other value." ... As a result, regulated subject matter under the CDA extended to "discussions about prison rape or safe sexual practices, artistic images that include nude subjects, and arguably the card catalog of the Carnegie Library." ... Third, we found that neither affirmative defense set forth in the CDA "constitute[d] the sort of 'narrow tailoring' that [would] save an otherwise patently invalid unconstitutional provision." ... Consequently, only the CDA's ban on the knowing transmission of obscene messages survived scrutiny because obscene speech enjoys no First Amendment protection. ...

After our decision in Reno v. American Civil Liberties Union, Congress explored other avenues for restricting minors' access to pornographic material on the Internet. In particular, Congress passed and the President signed into law the Child Online Protection Act, 112 Stat. 2681–736 (codified in 47 U.S.C. § 231 (1994 ed., Supp. V)). COPA prohibits any person from "knowingly and with knowledge of the character of the material, in interstate or foreign commerce by means of the World Wide Web, mak[ing] any communication for commercial purposes that is available to any minor and that includes any material that is harmful to minors." 47 U.S.C. § 231(a)(1).

Apparently responding to our objections to the breadth of the CDA's coverage, Congress limited the scope of COPA's coverage in at least three ways. First, while the CDA applied to communications over the Internet as a whole, including, for example, e-mail messages, COPA applies only to material displayed on the World Wide Web. Second, unlike the CDA, COPA covers only communications made "for commercial purposes." ... And third, while the CDA prohibited "indecent" and "patently offensive" communications, COPA restricts only the narrower category of "material that is harmful to minors." ...

Drawing on the three-part test for obscenity set forth in *Miller v. California,* 413 U.S. 15, 93 S.Ct. 2607, 37 L.Ed.2d 419 (1973), COPA defines "material that is harmful to minors" as

"any communication, picture, image, graphic image file, article, recording, writing, or other matter of any kind that is obscene or that—

"(A) the average person, applying contemporary community standards, would find, taking the material as a whole and with respect to minors, is designed to appeal to, or is designed to pander to, the prurient interest;

"(B) depicts, describes, or represents, in a manner patently offensive with respect to minors, an actual or simulated sexual act or sexual contact, an actual or simulated normal or perverted sexual act, or a lewd exhibition of the genitals or post-pubescent female breast; and

"(C) taken as a whole, lacks serious literary, artistic, political, or scientific value for minors." 47 U.S.C. § 231(e)(6).

Like the CDA, COPA also provides affirmative defenses to those subject to prosecution under the statute. An individual may qualify for a defense if he, "in good faith, has restricted access by minors to material that is harmful to minors—(A) by requiring the use of a credit card, debit account, adult access code, or adult personal identification number; (B) by accepting a digital certificate that verifies age; or (C) by any other reasonable measures that are feasible under available technology." § 231(c)(1). Persons violating COPA are subject to both civil and criminal sanctions. A civil penalty of up to $50,000 may be imposed for each violation of the statute. Criminal penalties consist of up to six months in prison and/or a maximum fine of $50,000. An additional fine of $50,000 may be imposed for any intentional violation of the statute. § 231(a).

One month before COPA was scheduled to go into effect, respondents filed a lawsuit challenging the constitutionality of the statute in the United States District Court for the Eastern District of Pennsylvania. Respondents are a diverse group of organizations, most of which maintain their own Web sites. While the vast majority of content on their Web sites is available for free, respondents all derive income from their sites. Some, for example, sell advertising that is displayed on their Web sites, while others either sell goods directly over their sites or charge artists for the privilege of posting material. All respondents either post or have members that post sexually oriented material on the Web. Respondents' Web sites contain "resources on obstetrics, gynecology, and sexual health; visual art and poetry; resources designed for gays and lesbians; information about books and stock photographic images offered for sale; and online magazines."

In their complaint, respondents alleged that, although they believed that the material on their Web sites was valuable for adults, they feared that they would be prosecuted under COPA because some of that material "could be construed as 'harmful to minors' in some communities." . . .

The District Court granted respondents' motion for a preliminary injunction, barring the Government from enforcing the Act until the merits of respondents' claims could be adjudicated. . . .

. . . The United States Court of Appeals for the Third Circuit affirmed. . . .

We . . . now vacate the Court of Appeals' judgment.

II

. . .

Ending over a decade of turmoil, this Court in *Miller* set forth the governing three-part test for assessing whether material is obscene and thus unprotected by the First Amendment . . .

. . . The Court preserved the use of community standards in formulating the *Miller* test, explaining that they furnish a valuable First Amendment safeguard: "[T]he primary concern . . . is to be certain that . . . [material] will be judged by its impact on an average person, rather than a particularly susceptible or sensitive person—or indeed a totally insensitive one." . . .

III

The Court of Appeals, however, concluded that this Court's prior community standards jurisprudence "has no applicability to the Internet and the Web" because "Web publishers are currently without the ability to control the geographic scope of the recipients of their communications." We therefore must decide whether this technological limitation renders COPA's reliance on community standards constitutionally infirm.

A

In addressing this question, the parties first dispute the nature of the community standards that jurors will be instructed to apply when assessing, in prosecutions under COPA, whether works appeal to the prurient interest of minors and are patently offensive with respect to minors. Respondents contend that jurors will evaluate material using "local community standards," while petitioner maintains that jurors will not consider the community standards of any particular geographic area, but rather will be "instructed to consider the standards of the adult community as a whole, without geographic specification."

In the context of this case, which involves a facial challenge to a statute that has never been enforced, we do not think it prudent to engage in speculation as to whether certain hypothetical jury instructions would or would not be consistent with COPA, and deciding this case does not require us to do so. It is sufficient to note that community standards need not be defined by reference to a precise geographic area. . . .

B

Because juries would apply different standards across the country, and Web publishers currently lack the ability to limit access to their sites on a geographic basis, the Court of Appeals feared that COPA's "community standards" component would effectively force all speakers on the Web to abide by the "most puritan" community's standards.

In evaluating the constitutionality of the CDA, this Court expressed a similar concern over that statute's use of community standards to identify patently offensive material on the Internet. We noted that "the 'community standards' criterion as applied to the Internet means that any communication available to a nationwide audience will be judged by the standards of the community most likely to be offended by the message." *Reno,* . . .

The CDA's use of community standards to identify patently offensive material, however, was particularly problematic in light of that statute's unprecedented breadth and vagueness. The statute covered communications depicting or describing "sexual or excretory activities or organs" that were "patently offensive as measured by contemporary community standards"—a standard somewhat similar to the second prong of *Miller*'s three-prong test. But the CDA did not include any limiting terms resembling *Miller*'s additional two prongs. . . . It neither contained any requirement that restricted material appeal to the prurient interest nor excluded from the scope of its coverage works with serious literary, artistic, political, or scientific value. . . . The tremendous breadth of the CDA magnified the impact caused by differences in community standards across the country, restricting Web publishers from openly displaying a significant amount of material that would have constituted protected speech in some communities across the country but run afoul of community standards in others.

COPA, by contrast, does not appear to suffer from the same flaw because it applies to significantly less material than did the CDA and defines the harmful-to-minors material restricted by the statute in a manner parallel to the *Miller* definition of obscenity. To fall within the scope of COPA, works must not only "depic[t], describ[e], or represen[t], in a manner patently offensive with respect to minors," particular sexual acts or parts of the anatomy, they must also be designed to appeal to the prurient interest of minors and "taken as a whole, lac[k] serious literary, artistic, political, or scientific value for minors." ...

These additional two restrictions substantially limit the amount of material covered by the statute. Material appeals to the prurient interest, for instance, only if it is in some sense erotic. ... Of even more significance, however, is COPA's exclusion of material with serious value for minors. ... In *Reno*, we emphasized that the serious value "requirement is particularly important because, unlike the 'patently offensive' and 'prurient interest' criteria, it is not judged by contemporary community standards." ...

C

When the scope of an obscenity statute's coverage is sufficiently narrowed by a "serious value" prong and a "prurient interest" prong, we have held that requiring a speaker disseminating material to a national audience to observe varying community standards does not violate the First Amendment. ... Hamling v. United States, 418 U.S. 87 (1974) ...

Like respondents here, the dissenting opinion in *Hamling* argued that it was unconstitutional for a federal statute to rely on community standards to regulate speech. ...

This Court, however, rejected Justice Brennan's argument that the federal mail statute unconstitutionally compelled speakers choosing to distribute materials on a national basis to tailor their messages to the least tolerant community ...

Fifteen years later, *Hamling*'s holding was reaffirmed in Sable Communications of Cal., Inc. v. FCC, 492 U.S. 115 (1989). *Sable* addressed the constitutionality of ... a statutory provision prohibiting the use of telephones to make obscene or indecent communications for commercial purposes. The petitioner in that case, a "dial-a-porn" operator, challenged, in part, that portion of the statute banning obscene phone messages. Like respondents here, the "dial-a-porn" operator argued that reliance on community standards to identify obscene material impermissibly compelled "message senders ... to tailor all their messages to the least tolerant community." ... Relying on *Hamling*, however, this Court once again rebuffed this attack on the use of community standards in a federal statute of national scope: "There is no constitutional barrier under *Miller* to prohibiting communications that are obscene in some communities under local standards even though they are not obscene in others. *If Sable's audience is comprised of different communities with different local standards, Sable ultimately bears the burden of complying with the prohibition on obscene messages.*" ... (emphasis added).

The Court of Appeals below concluded that *Hamling* and *Sable* "are easily distinguished from the present case" because in both of those cases "the defendants had the ability to control the distribution of controversial material with respect to the geographic communities into which they released it" whereas "Web publishers have no such comparable control." In neither *Hamling* nor *Sable*, however, was the speaker's ability to target the release of material into particular geographic areas integral to the legal analysis. In

Hamling, the ability to limit the distribution of material to targeted communities was not mentioned, let alone relied upon, and in *Sable,* a dial-a-porn operator's ability to screen incoming calls from particular areas was referenced only as a supplemental point . . . In the latter case, this Court made no effort to evaluate how burdensome it would have been for dial-a-porn operators to tailor their messages to callers from thousands of different communities across the Nation, instead concluding that the burden of complying with the statute rested with those companies. . . .

While Justice Kennedy and Justice Stevens question the applicability of this Court's community standards jurisprudence to the Internet, we do not believe that the medium's "unique characteristics" justify adopting a different approach than that set forth in *Hamling* and *Sable.* If a publisher chooses to send its material into a particular community, this Court's jurisprudence teaches that it is the publisher's responsibility to abide by that community's standards. The publisher's burden does not change simply because it decides to distribute its material to every community in the Nation. . . . If a publisher wishes for its material to be judged only by the standards of particular communities, then it need only take the simple step of utilizing a medium that enables it to target the release of its material into those communities.

Respondents offer no other grounds upon which to distinguish this case from *Hamling* and *Sable.* While those cases involved obscenity rather than material that is harmful to minors, we have no reason to believe that the practical effect of varying community standards under COPA, given the statute's definition of "material that is harmful to minors," is significantly greater than the practical effect of varying community standards under federal obscenity statutes. . . . [I]f we were to hold COPA unconstitutional *because of* its use of community standards, federal obscenity statutes would likely also be unconstitutional as applied to the Web . . .

D

. . . Because Congress has narrowed the range of content restricted by COPA in a manner analogous to *Miller*'s definition of obscenity, we conclude, consistent with our holdings in *Hamling* and *Sable,* that any variance caused by the statute's reliance on community standards is not substantial enough to violate the First Amendment.

IV

The scope of our decision today is quite limited. We hold only that COPA's reliance on community standards to identify "material that is harmful to minors" does not *by itself* render the statute substantially overbroad for purposes of the First Amendment. We do not express any view as to whether COPA suffers from substantial overbreadth for other reasons, whether the statute is unconstitutionally vague, or whether the District Court correctly concluded that the statute likely will not survive strict scrutiny analysis once adjudication of the case is completed below. While respondents urge us to resolve these questions at this time, prudence dictates allowing the Court of Appeals to first examine these difficult issues.

Petitioner does not ask us to vacate the preliminary injunction entered by the District Court, and in any event, we could not do so without addressing matters yet to be considered by the Court of Appeals. As a result, the Government remains enjoined from enforcing COPA absent further action by the Court of Appeals or the District Court.

. . .

Justice O'Connor, concurring in part and concurring in the judgment.

I agree with the plurality that even if obscenity on the Internet is defined in terms of local community standards, respondents have not shown that the Child Online Protection Act (COPA) is overbroad solely on the basis of the variation in the standards of different communities. Like Justice Breyer, however, I write separately to express my views on the constitutionality and desirability of adopting a national standard for obscenity for regulation of the Internet.

The plurality's opinion argues that, even under local community standards, the variation between the most and least restrictive communities is not so great with respect to the narrow category of speech covered by COPA as to, alone, render the statute substantially overbroad. I agree, given respondents' failure to provide examples of materials that lack literary, artistic, political, and scientific value for minors, which would nonetheless result in variation among communities judging the other elements of the test. . . .

But respondents' failure to prove substantial overbreadth on a facial challenge in this case still leaves open the possibility that the use of local community standards will cause problems for regulation of obscenity on the Internet, for adults as well as children, in future cases. In an as-applied challenge, for instance, individual litigants may still dispute that the standards of a community more restrictive than theirs should apply to them. And in future facial challenges to regulation of obscenity on the Internet, litigants may make a more convincing case for substantial overbreadth. Where adult speech is concerned, for instance, there may in fact be a greater degree of disagreement about what is patently offensive or appeals to the prurient interest.

Nor do I think such future cases can be resolved by application of the approach we took in *Hamling* . . . and *Sable* . . . I agree with Justice Kennedy that, given Internet speakers' inability to control the geographic location of their audience, expecting them to bear the burden of controlling the recipients of their speech, as we did in *Hamling* and *Sable,* may be entirely too much to ask, and would potentially suppress an inordinate amount of expression. For these reasons, adoption of a national standard is necessary in my view for any reasonable regulation of Internet obscenity.

. . .

While I would prefer that the Court resolve the issue before it by explicitly adopting a national standard for defining obscenity on the Internet, given respondents' failure to demonstrate substantial overbreadth due solely to the variation between local communities, I join Parts I, II, III–B, and IV of Justice Thomas' opinion and the judgment.

Justice Breyer, concurring in part and concurring in the judgment.

I write separately because I believe that Congress intended the statutory word "community" to refer to the Nation's adult community taken as a whole, not to geographically separate local areas. The statutory language does not explicitly describe the specific "community" to which it refers. It says only that the "average person, applying contemporary community standards" must find that the "material as a whole and with respect to minors, is designed to appeal to, or is designed to pander to, the prurient interest...." ...

. . .

... [T]his view of the statute avoids the need to examine the serious First Amendment problem that would otherwise exist. ... To read the statute as adopting the community standards of every locality in the United States would provide the most puritan of communities with a heckler's Internet veto affecting the rest of the Nation. The technical difficulties associated with efforts to confine Internet material to particular geographic areas make the problem particularly serious. ...

... I do not join Part III of Justice Thomas' opinion, although I agree with much of the reasoning set forth in Parts III–B and III–D, insofar as it explains ... that variation reflecting application of the same national standard by different local juries does not violate the First Amendment.

Justice Kennedy, with whom Justice Souter and Justice Ginsburg join, concurring in the judgment.

I

... COPA is a major federal statute, enacted in the wake of our previous determination that its predecessor violated the First Amendment. ... Congress and the President were aware of our decision, and we should assume that in seeking to comply with it they have given careful consideration to the constitutionality of the new enactment. For these reasons, even if this facial challenge appears to have considerable merit, the Judiciary must proceed with caution and identify overbreadth with care before invalidating the Act.

. . .

... To observe only that community standards vary across the country is to ignore the antecedent question: community standards as to what? Whether the national variation in community standards produces overbreadth requiring invalidation of COPA, ... depends on the breadth of COPA's coverage and on what community standards are being invoked. Only by identifying the universe of speech burdened by COPA is it possible to discern whether national variation in community standards renders the speech restriction overbroad. ...

... Some examination of the group of covered speakers and the categories of covered speech is necessary in order to comprehend the extent of the alleged overbreadth.

... I join the judgment of the Court vacating the opinion of the Court of Appeals and remanding for consideration of the statute as a whole. Unlike Justice Thomas, however, I would not assume that the Act is narrow enough to render the national variation in community standards unproblematic. Indeed, if the District Court correctly construed the statute across its other dimensions, then the variation in community standards might well justify enjoining enforcement of the Act. I would leave that question to the Court of Appeals in the first instance.

II

... The nub of the problem is, as the Court has said, that "the 'community standards' criterion as applied to the Internet means that any communication available to a nationwide audience will be judged by the standards of the community most likely to be offended by the message." ... This observation was the linchpin of the Court of Appeals' analysis, and we must now consider whether it alone suffices to support the holding below.

The quoted sentence from *Reno* was not casual dicta; rather, it was one rationale for the holding of the case. ... Variation in community standards rendered the statute broader than the scope of the Government's own expressed compelling interest.

It is true, as Justice Thomas points out, that requiring a speaker addressing a national audience to meet varying community standards does not always violate the First Amendment. See *Hamling* ...; *Sable* ... These cases, however, are of limited utility in analyzing the one before us, because each mode of expression has its own unique characteristics ... Indeed, when Congress purports to abridge the freedom of a new medium, we must be particularly attentive to its distinct attributes ... The economics and the technology of each medium affect both the burden of a speech restriction and the Government's interest in maintaining it.

... [I]n upholding a ban on obscene phone messages, we emphasized that the speaker could "hire operators to determine the source of the calls or engag[e] with the telephone company to arrange for the screening and blocking of out-of-area calls or fin[d] another means for providing messages compatible with community standards." ... And if we did not make the same point in *Hamling,* that is likely because it is so obvious that mailing lends itself to geographic restriction. ...

The economics and technology of Internet communication differ in important ways from those of telephones and mail. Paradoxically, as the District Court found, it is easy and cheap to reach a worldwide audience on the Internet, but expensive if not impossible to reach a geographic subset. A Web publisher in a community where avant garde culture is the norm may have no desire to reach a national market; he may wish only to speak to his neighbors; nevertheless, if an eavesdropper in a more traditional, rural community chooses to listen in, there is nothing the publisher can do. As a practical matter, COPA makes the eavesdropper the arbiter of propriety on the Web. And it is no answer to say that the speaker should "take the simple step of utilizing a [different] medium." ...

. . .

... [W]e need not decide whether the statute invokes local or national community standards to conclude that vacatur and remand are in order. If the statute does incorporate some concept of national community standards, the actual standard applied is bound to vary by community nevertheless, as the Attorney General concedes.

For this reason the Court of Appeals was correct to focus on COPA's incorporation of varying community standards; and it may have been correct as well to conclude that in practical effect COPA imposes the most puritanical community standard on the entire country. ... In striking down COPA's predecessor, the *Reno* Court identified this precise problem, and if the *Hamling* and *Sable* Courts did not find the problem fatal, that is because those cases involved quite different media. The national variation in community standards constitutes a particular burden on Internet speech.

III

The question that remains is whether this observation *"by itself"* suffices to enjoin the Act. I agree with the Court that it does not. We cannot know whether variation in community standards renders the Act substantially over-broad without first assessing the extent of the speech covered and the variations in community standards with respect to that speech.

. . . As this case comes to us, once it is accepted that we cannot strike down the Act based merely on the phrase "contemporary community standards," we should go no further than to vacate and remand for a more comprehensive analysis of the Act.

. . .

Justice Stevens, dissenting.

Appeals to prurient interests are commonplace on the Internet, as in older media. Many of those appeals lack serious value for minors as well as adults. Some are offensive to certain viewers but welcomed by others. For decades, our cases have recognized that the standards for judging their acceptability vary from viewer to viewer and from community to community. Those cases developed the requirement that communications should be protected if they do not violate contemporary community standards. In its original form, the community standard provided a shield for communications that are offensive only to the least tolerant members of society. . . . In the context of the Internet, however, community standards become a sword, rather than a shield. If a prurient appeal is offensive in a puritan village, it may be a crime to post it on the World Wide Web.

. . .

We have . . . repeatedly rejected the position that the free speech rights of adults can be limited to what is acceptable for children. See . . . *Butler v. Michigan,* 352 U.S. 380, 383 (1957).

. . . Like the . . . ban against selling adult books found impermissible in *Butler,* COPA seeks to limit protected speech that is not targeted at children, simply because it can be obtained by them while surfing the Web. In evaluating the overbreadth of such a statute, we should be mindful of Justice Frankfurter's admonition not to "burn the house to roast the pig," *Butler,* 352 U.S., at 383.

COPA not only restricts speech that is made available to the general public, it also covers a medium in which speech cannot be segregated to avoid communities where it is likely to be considered harmful to minors. . . .

If the material were forwarded through the mails, as in *Hamling,* or over the telephone, as in *Sable,* the sender could avoid destinations with the most restrictive standards. . . . In light of this fundamental difference in technologies, the rules applicable to the mass mailing of an obscene montage or to obscene dial-a-porn should not be used to judge the legality of messages on the World Wide Web.

. . .

Justice Thomas points to several other provisions in COPA to argue that any overbreadth will be rendered insubstantial by the rest of the statute. These provisions afford little reassurance, however, as they only marginally limit the sweep of the statute. . . .

. . .

Justice Kennedy makes a similar misstep when he ties the overbreadth inquiry to questions about the scope of the other provisions of the statute. . . . These other provisions may reduce the absolute number of Web pages covered by the statute, but even the narrowest version of the statute abridges a substantial amount of protected speech that many communities would not find harmful to minors. Because Web speakers cannot limit access to those specific communities, the statute is substantially overbroad regardless of how its other provisions are construed.

Justice Thomas acknowledges, and petitioner concedes, that juries across the country will apply different standards and reach different conclusions about whether particular works are harmful to minors. . . .

. . . Because communities differ widely in their attitudes toward sex, particularly when minors are concerned, the Court of Appeals was correct to conclude that, regardless of how COPA's other provisions are construed, applying community standards to the Internet will restrict a substantial amount of protected speech that would not be considered harmful to minors in many communities.

Whether that consequence is appropriate depends, of course, on the content of the message. The kind of hard-core pornography involved in *Hamling*, which I assume would be obscene under any community's standard, does not belong on the Internet. Perhaps "teasers" that serve no function except to invite viewers to examine hardcore materials, or the hidden terms written into a Web site's "metatags" in order to dupe unwitting Web surfers into visiting pornographic sites, deserve the same fate. But COPA extends to a wide range of prurient appeals in advertisements, online magazines, Web-based bulletin boards and chat rooms, stock photo galleries, Web diaries, and a variety of illustrations encompassing a vast number of messages that are unobjectionable in most of the country and yet provide no "serious value" for minors. It is quite wrong to allow the standards of a minority consisting of the least tolerant communities to regulate access to relatively harmless messages in this burgeoning market.

. . . I would affirm the judgment of the Court of Appeals . . .

C.   CONTROL OF "FIGHTING WORDS" AND OFFENSIVE SPEECH

Page 1317.   Replace RAV v. City of St. Paul:

Virginia v. Black

___ U.S. ___, 123 S.Ct. 1536, 155 L.Ed.2d 535 (2003).

Justice O'Connor announced the judgment of the Court and delivered the opinion of the Court with respect to Parts I, II, and III, and

an opinion with respect to Parts IV and V, in which the Chief Justice, Justice Stevens, and Justice Breyer join.

In this case we consider whether the Commonwealth of Virginia's statute banning cross burning with "an intent to intimidate a person or group of persons" violates the First Amendment. Va.Code Ann. § 18.2–423 (1996). We conclude that while a State, consistent with the First Amendment, may ban cross burning carried out with the intent to intimidate, the provision in the Virginia statute treating any cross burning as prima facie evidence of intent to intimidate renders the statute unconstitutional in its current form.

I

Respondents Barry Black, Richard Elliott, and Jonathan O'Mara were convicted separately of violating Virginia's cross-burning statute, § 18.2–423. That statute provides:

> "It shall be unlawful for any person or persons, with the intent of intimidating any person or group of persons, to burn, or cause to be burned, a cross on the property of another, a highway or other public place. Any person who shall violate any provision of this section shall be guilty of a Class 6 felony.

> "Any such burning of a cross shall be prima facie evidence of an intent to intimidate a person or group of persons."

On August 22, 1998, Barry Black led a Ku Klux Klan rally in Carroll County, Virginia. Twenty-five to thirty people attended this gathering, which occurred on private property with the permission of the owner, who was in attendance. The property was located on an open field just off Brushy Fork Road (State Highway 690) in Cana, Virginia.

When the sheriff of Carroll County learned that a Klan rally was occurring in his county, he went to observe it from the side of the road. During the approximately one hour that the sheriff was present, about 40 to 50 cars passed the site, a "few" of which stopped to ask the sheriff what was happening on the property. Eight to ten houses were located in the vicinity of the rally. Rebecca Sechrist ... "sat and watched to see wha[t][was] going on" from the lawn of her in-laws' house. She looked on as the Klan prepared for the gathering and subsequently conducted the rally itself. During the rally, Sechrist heard Klan members speak about "what they were" and "what they believed in." The speakers "talked real bad about the blacks and the Mexicans." One speaker told the assembled gathering that "he would love to take a .30/.30 and just random[ly] shoot the blacks." The speakers also talked about "President Clinton and Hillary Clinton," and about how their tax money "goes to ... the black people." Sechrist testified that this language made her "very ... scared."

At the conclusion of the rally, the crowd circled around a 25–to 30–foot cross. The cross was between 300 and 350 yards away from the road. According to the sheriff, the cross "then all of a sudden ... went up in a flame." As the cross burned, the Klan played Amazing Grace over the loudspeakers. Sechrist stated that the cross burning made her feel "awful" and "terrible."

... The sheriff ... entered the rally, and asked "who was responsible for burning the cross." ... Black responded, "I guess I am because I'm the head of the rally." ...

Black was charged with burning a cross with the intent of intimidating a person or group of persons, in violation of § 18.2–423. At his trial, the jury was instructed that "intent to intimidate means the motivation to intentionally put a person or a group of persons in fear of bodily harm. Such fear must arise from the willful conduct of the accused rather than from some mere temperamental timidity of the victim." The trial court also instructed the jury that "the burning of a cross by itself is sufficient evidence from which you may infer the required intent." . . . The Court of Appeals of Virginia affirmed Black's conviction.

On May 2, 1998, respondents Richard Elliott and Jonathan O'Mara, as well as a third individual, attempted to burn a cross on the yard of James Jubilee. Jubilee, an African–American, was Elliott's next-door neighbor in Virginia Beach, Virginia. Four months prior to the incident, Jubilee and his family had moved from California to Virginia Beach. Before the cross burning, Jubilee spoke to Elliott's mother to inquire about shots being fired from behind the Elliott home. Elliott's mother explained to Jubilee that her son shot firearms as a hobby, and that he used the backyard as a firing range.

On the night of May 2, respondents drove a truck onto Jubilee's property, planted a cross, and set it on fire. Their apparent motive was to "get back" at Jubilee for complaining about the shooting in the backyard. Respondents were not affiliated with the Klan. The next morning, as Jubilee was pulling his car out of the driveway, he noticed the partially burned cross approximately 20 feet from his house. After seeing the cross, Jubilee was "very nervous" because he "didn't know what would be the next phase," and because "a cross burned in your yard . . . tells you that it's just the first round."

Elliott and O'Mara were charged with attempted cross burning and conspiracy to commit cross burning. O'Mara pleaded guilty to both counts, reserving the right to challenge the constitutionality of the cross-burning statute. The judge sentenced O'Mara to 90 days in jail and fined him $2,500. The judge also suspended 45 days of the sentence and $1,000 of the fine.

At Elliott's trial, the judge originally ruled that the jury would be instructed "that the burning of a cross by itself is sufficient evidence from which you may infer the required intent." At trial, however, the court instructed the jury that the Commonwealth must prove that "the defendant intended to commit cross burning," that "the defendant did a direct act toward the commission of the cross burning," and that "the defendant had the intent of intimidating any person or group of persons." . . . The jury found Elliott guilty of attempted cross burning and acquitted him of conspiracy to commit cross burning. It sentenced Elliott to 90 days in jail and a $2,500 fine. The Court of Appeals of Virginia affirmed the convictions of both Elliott and O'Mara.

Each respondent appealed to the Supreme Court of Virginia, arguing that § 18.2–423 is facially unconstitutional. The Supreme Court of Virginia consolidated all three cases, and held that the statute is unconstitutional on its face. It held that the Virginia cross-burning statute "is analytically indistinguishable from the ordinance found unconstitutional in *R.A.V.* [*v. St. Paul*, 505 U.S. 377 (1992)]." . . .

. . .

II

. . .

Often, the Klan used cross burnings as a tool of intimidation and a threat of impending violence. . . .

. . .

Throughout the history of the Klan, cross burnings have also remained potent symbols of shared group identity and ideology. . . .

At Klan gatherings across the country, cross burning became the climax of the rally or the initiation. . . .

. . . In short, a burning cross has remained a symbol of Klan ideology and of Klan unity.

. . . [W]hile cross burning sometimes carries no intimidating message, at other times the intimidating message is the *only* message conveyed. For example, when a cross burning is directed at a particular person not affiliated with the Klan, the burning cross often serves as a message of intimidation, designed to inspire in the victim a fear of bodily harm. Moreover, the history of violence associated with the Klan shows that the possibility of injury or death is not just hypothetical. The person who burns a cross directed at a particular person often is making a serious threat, meant to coerce the victim to comply with the Klan's wishes unless the victim is willing to risk the wrath of the Klan. Indeed, as the cases of respondents Elliott and O'Mara indicate, individuals without Klan affiliation who wish to threaten or menace another person sometimes use cross burning because of this association between a burning cross and violence.

In sum, while a burning cross does not inevitably convey a message of intimidation, often the cross burner intends that the recipients of the message fear for their lives. And when a cross burning is used to intimidate, few if any messages are more powerful.

III

A

. . .

. . . The First Amendment permits "restrictions upon the content of speech in a few limited areas, which are 'of such slight social value as a step to truth that any benefit that may be derived from them is clearly outweighed by the social interest in order and morality.' " R.A.V. v. City of St. Paul, *supra,* at 382–383, (quoting Chaplinsky v. New Hampshire, [313 U.S. 568] at 572).

. . . [T]he First Amendment . . . permits a State to ban a "true threat." . . . ("[T]hreats of violence are outside the First Amendment"); Madsen v. Women's Health Center, Inc., 512 U.S. 753 (1994); Schenck v. Pro–Choice Network of Western N. Y., 519 U.S. 357, 373 (1997).

"True threats" encompass those statements where the speaker means to communicate a serious expression of an intent to commit an act of unlawful violence to a particular individual or group of individuals. . . . The speaker need not actually intend to carry out the threat. Rather, a prohibition on true threats "protect[s] individuals from the fear of violence" and "from the disruption that fear engenders," in addition to protecting people "from the possibility that the threatened violence will occur." ... Intimidation in the constitutionally proscribable sense of the word is a type of true threat, where a speaker directs a threat to a person or group of persons with the intent of placing the victim in fear of bodily harm or death. Respondents do not contest that some cross burnings fit within this meaning of intimidating speech, and rightly so. As noted in Part II, *supra,* the history of cross burning in this country shows that cross burning is often intimidating, intended to create a pervasive fear in victims that they are a target of violence.

B

... It is true, as the Supreme Court of Virginia held, that the burning of a cross is symbolic expression. The reason why the Klan burns a cross at its rallies, or individuals place a burning cross on someone else's lawn, is that the burning cross represents the message that the speaker wishes to communicate. Individuals burn crosses as opposed to other means of communication because cross burning carries a message in an effective and dramatic manner.

The fact that cross burning is symbolic expression, however, does not resolve the constitutional question. The Supreme Court of Virginia relied upon R.A.V. v. City of St. Paul, *supra,* to conclude that once a statute discriminates on the basis of this type of content, the law is unconstitutional. We disagree.

In *R.A.V.,* we held that a local ordinance that banned certain symbolic conduct, including cross burning, when done with the knowledge that such conduct would " 'arouse anger, alarm or resentment in others on the basis of race, color, creed, religion or gender' " was unconstitutional ... We held that the ordinance did not pass constitutional muster because it discriminated on the basis of content by targeting only those individuals who "provoke violence" on a basis specified in the law. ... The ordinance did not cover "[t]hose who wish to use 'fighting words' in connection with other ideas—to express hostility, for example, on the basis of political affiliation, union membership, or homosexuality." ... This content-based discrimination was unconstitutional because it allowed the city "to impose special prohibitions on those speakers who express views on disfavored subjects." ...

We did not hold in *R.A.V.* that the First Amendment prohibits *all* forms of content-based discrimination within a proscribable area of speech. Rather, we specifically stated that some types of content discrimination did not violate the First Amendment:

> "When the basis for the content discrimination consists entirely of the very reason the entire class of speech at issue is proscribable, no significant danger of idea or viewpoint discrimination exists. Such a reason, having been adjudged neutral enough to support exclusion of the entire class of speech from First Amendment protection, is also neutral enough to form the basis of distinction within the class." ...

Indeed, we noted that it would be constitutional to ban only a particular type of threat: "[T]he Federal Government can criminalize only those threats of violence that are directed against the President ... since the reasons why threats of violence are outside the First Amendment ... have special force when applied to the person of the President." ... And a State may "choose to prohibit only that obscenity which is the most patently offensive *in its prurience—i.e.*, that which involves the most lascivious displays of sexual activity." ... Consequently, while the holding of *R.A.V.* does not permit a State to ban only obscenity based on "offensive *political* messages," or "only those threats against the President that mention his policy on aid to inner cities," the First Amendment permits content discrimination "based on the very reasons why the particular class of speech at issue ... is proscribable," ...

Similarly, Virginia's statute does not run afoul of the First Amendment insofar as it bans cross burning with intent to intimidate. Unlike the statute at issue in *R.A.V.*, the Virginia statute does not single out for opprobrium only that speech directed toward "one of the specified disfavored topics." ... It does not matter whether an individual burns a cross with intent to intimidate because of the victim's race, gender, or religion, or because of the victim's "political affiliation, union membership, or homosexuality." Moreover, as a factual matter it is not true that cross burners direct their intimidating conduct solely to racial or religious minorities.... Indeed, in the case of Elliott and O'Mara, it is at least unclear whether the respondents burned a cross due to racial animus. ...

The First Amendment permits Virginia to outlaw cross burnings done with the intent to intimidate because burning a cross is a particularly virulent form of intimidation. Instead of prohibiting all intimidating messages, Virginia may choose to regulate this subset of intimidating messages in light of cross burning's long and pernicious history as a signal of impending violence. Thus, just as a State may regulate only that obscenity which is the most obscene due to its prurient content, so too may a State choose to prohibit only those forms of intimidation that are most likely to inspire fear of bodily harm. A ban on cross burning carried out with the intent to intimidate is fully consistent with our holding in *R.A.V.* and is proscribable under the First Amendment.

IV

The Supreme Court of Virginia ruled in the alternative that Virginia's cross-burning statute was unconstitutionally overbroad due to its provision stating that "[a]ny such burning of a cross shall be prima facie evidence of an intent to intimidate a person or group of persons." ... In this Court, as in the Supreme Court of Virginia, respondents do not argue that the prima facie evidence provision is unconstitutional as applied to any one of them. Rather, they contend that the provision is unconstitutional on its face.

The Supreme Court of Virginia has not ruled on the meaning of the prima facie evidence provision. It has, however, stated that "the act of burning a cross alone, with no evidence of intent to intimidate, will nonetheless suffice for arrest and prosecution and will insulate the Commonwealth from a motion to strike the evidence at the end of its case-in-chief." The jury in the case of Richard Elliott did not receive any instruction on the prima facie evidence provision, and the provision was not an issue in the case of Jonathan O'Mara because he pleaded guilty. The court in Barry Black's case, however, instructed the jury that the provision means: "The burning of a cross, by itself, is sufficient evidence from which you may infer the required intent." ...

The prima facie evidence provision, as interpreted by the jury instruction, renders the statute unconstitutional. Because this jury instruction is the Model Jury Instruction, and because the Supreme Court of Virginia had the opportunity to expressly disavow the jury instruction, the jury instruction's construction of the prima facie provision "is a ruling on a question of state law that is as binding on us as though the precise words had been written into" the statute. ... As construed by the jury instruction, the prima facie provision strips away the very reason why a State may ban cross burning with the intent to intimidate. The prima facie evidence provision permits a jury to convict in every cross-burning case in which defendants exercise their constitutional right not to put on a defense. And even where a defendant like Black presents a defense, the prima facie evidence provision makes it more likely that the jury will find an intent to intimidate regardless of the particular facts of the case. The provision permits the Commonwealth to arrest, prosecute, and convict a person based solely on the fact of cross burning itself.

It is apparent that the provision as so interpreted " 'would create an unacceptable risk of the suppression of ideas.' " ... The act of burning a cross may mean that a person is engaging in constitutionally proscribable intimidation. But that same act may mean only that the person is engaged in core political speech. The prima facie evidence provision in this statute blurs the line between these two meanings of a burning cross. As interpreted by the jury instruction, the provision chills constitutionally protected political speech because of the possibility that a State will prosecute—and potentially convict— somebody engaging only in lawful political speech at the core of what the First Amendment is designed to protect.

As the history of cross burning indicates, a burning cross is not always intended to intimidate. Rather, sometimes the cross burning is a statement of ideology, a symbol of group solidarity. It is a ritual used at Klan gatherings, and it is used to represent the Klan itself. ... Indeed, occasionally a person who burns a cross does not intend to express either a statement of ideology or intimidation. Cross burnings have appeared in movies such as Mississippi Burning, and in plays such as the stage adaptation of Sir Walter Scott's The Lady of the Lake.

The prima facie provision makes no effort to distinguish among these different types of cross burnings. It does not distinguish between a cross burning done with the purpose of creating anger or resentment and a cross burning done with the purpose of threatening or intimidating a victim. It does not distinguish between a cross burning at a public rally or a cross burning on a neighbor's lawn. It does not treat the cross burning directed at an individual differently from the cross burning directed at a group of like-minded believers. ... I agree with Justice Souter that the prima facie evidence provision can "skew jury deliberations toward conviction in cases where the evidence of intent to intimidate is relatively weak and arguably consistent with a solely ideological reason for burning."

It may be true that a cross burning, even at a political rally, arouses a sense of anger or hatred among the vast majority of citizens who see a burning cross. But this sense of anger or hatred is not sufficient to ban all cross burnings. As Gerald Gunther has stated, "The lesson I have drawn from my childhood in Nazi Germany and my happier adult life in this country is the need to walk the sometimes difficult path of denouncing the bigot's hateful ideas with all my power, yet at the same time challenging any community's attempt to suppress hateful ideas by force of law." Casper, Gerry, 55 Stan. L.Rev. 647, 649 (2002) (internal quotation marks omitted). The prima facie evidence provision in this case ignores all of the contextual factors that are necessary to decide whether a particular cross burning is intended to intimidate. The First Amendment does not permit such a shortcut.

For these reasons, the prima facie evidence provision, as interpreted through the jury instruction and as applied in Barry Black's case, is unconstitutional on its face. ... Unlike Justice Scalia, we refuse to speculate on whether *any* interpretation of the prima facie evidence provision would satisfy the First Amendment. Rather, all we hold is that because of the interpretation of the prima facie evidence provision given by the jury instruction, the provision makes the statute facially invalid at this point. We also recognize the theoretical possibility that the court, on remand, could interpret the provision in a manner different from that so far set forth in order to avoid the constitutional objections we have described. We leave open that possibility. We also leave open the possibility that the provision is severable, and if so, whether Elliott and O'Mara could be retried under § 18.2–423.

V

With respect to Barry Black, we agree with the Supreme Court of Virginia that his conviction cannot stand, and we affirm the judgment of the Supreme Court of Virginia. With respect to Elliott and O'Mara, we vacate the judgment of the Supreme Court of Virginia, and remand the case for further proceedings.*

. . .

Justice Scalia, with whom Justice Thomas joins as to Parts I and II, concurring in part, concurring in the judgment in part, and dissenting in part.

I agree with the Court that, under our decision in *R.A.V. v. St. Paul,* 505 U.S. 377 (1992), a State may, without infringing the First Amendment, prohibit cross burning carried out with the intent to intimidate. Accordingly, I join Parts I–III of the Court's opinion. I also agree that we should vacate and remand the judgment of the Virginia Supreme Court so that that Court can have an opportunity authoritatively to construe the prima-facie-evidence provision ... I write separately, however, to describe what I believe to be the correct interpretation of § 18.2–423, and to explain why I believe there is no justification for the plurality's apparent decision to invalidate that provision on its face.

I

Section 18.2–423 provides that the burning of a cross in public view "shall be prima facie evidence of an intent to intimidate." In order to determine whether this component of the statute violates the Constitution, it is necessary, first, to establish precisely what the presentation of prima facie evidence accomplishes.

. . .

* A concurring opinion by Justice Stevens is omitted.

The established meaning in Virginia, then, of the term "prima facie evidence" appears to be perfectly orthodox: It is evidence that suffices, on its own, to establish a particular fact. But . . . this is true only to the extent that the evidence goes unrebutted. . . .

. . .

It is important to note that the Virginia Supreme Court did not suggest (as did the trial court's jury instructions in respondent Black's case) that a jury may, in light of the prima-facie-evidence provision, ignore any rebuttal evidence that has been presented and, solely on the basis of a showing that the defendant burned a cross, find that he intended to intimidate. Nor, crucially, did that court say that the presentation of prima facie evidence is always sufficient to get a case to a jury . . . That is, presentation of evidence that a defendant burned a cross in public view is automatically sufficient, on its own, to support an inference that the defendant intended to intimidate *only until* the defendant comes forward with some evidence in rebuttal.

II

The question presented, then, is whether, given this understanding of the term "prima facie evidence," the cross-burning statute is constitutional. . . .

. . . We have never held that the mere threat that individuals who engage in protected conduct will be subject to arrest and prosecution suffices to render a statute overbroad. Rather, our overbreadth jurisprudence has consistently focused on whether *the prohibitory terms* of a particular statute extend to protected conduct; that is, we have inquired whether individuals who engage in protected conduct can be *convicted* under a statute, not whether they might be subject to arrest and prosecution. . . .

. . .

. . . [T]he plurality cannot claim that improper convictions will result from the operation of the prima-facie-evidence provision *alone*. As the plurality concedes, the only persons who might impermissibly be convicted by reason of that provision are those who adopt a particular trial strategy, to wit, abstaining from the presentation of a defense.

. . .

Conceding (quite generously, in my view) that this class of persons exists, it cannot possibly give rise to a viable facial challenge, not even with the aid of our First Amendment overbreadth doctrine. For this Court has emphasized repeatedly that "where a statute regulates expressive conduct, the scope of the statute does not render it unconstitutional unless its overbreadth is not only real, but *substantial* as well, judged in relation to the statute's plainly legitimate sweep." Osborne v. Ohio, 495 U.S. 103, 112 (1990). . . .

. . .

. . . [T]he plurality holds out the possibility that the Virginia Supreme Court will offer some saving construction of the statute. It should go without saying that if a saving construction of § 18.2–423 is possible, then facial invalidation is inappropriate. . . . So, what appears to have happened is that the plurality has facially invalidated not § 18.2–423, but its own hypothetical interpretation of § 18.2–423, and has then remanded to the Virginia Supreme Court to learn the *actual* interpretation of § 18.2–423. Words cannot express my wonderment at this virtuoso performance.

III

. . . I believe the prima-facie-evidence provision in Virginia's cross-burning statute is constitutionally unproblematic. Nevertheless, because the Virginia Supreme Court has not yet offered an authoritative construction of § 18.2–423, I concur in the Court's decision to vacate and remand the judgment with respect to respondents Elliott and O'Mara. I also agree that respondent Black's conviction cannot stand. . . . Because I believe the constitutional defect in Black's conviction is rooted in a jury instruction and not in the statute itself, I would not dismiss the indictment and would permit the Commonwealth to retry Black if it wishes to do so. . . .

Justice Souter, with whom Justice Kennedy and Justice Ginsburg join, concurring in the judgment in part and dissenting in part.

I agree with the majority that the Virginia statute makes a content-based distinction within the category of punishable intimidating or threatening expression, the very type of distinction we considered in R.A.V. v. St. Paul, 505 U.S. 377 (1992). I disagree that any exception should save Virginia's law from unconstitutionality under the holding in *R.A.V.* or any acceptable variation of it.

I

The ordinance struck down in *R.A.V.*, as it had been construed by the State's highest court, prohibited the use of symbols (including but not limited to a burning cross) as the equivalent of generally proscribable fighting words, but the ordinance applied only when the symbol was provocative " 'on the basis of race, color, creed, religion or gender.' " Although the Virginia statute in issue here contains no such express "basis of" limitation on prohibited subject matter, the specific prohibition of cross burning with intent to intimidate selects a symbol with particular content from the field of all proscribable expression meant to intimidate. . . .

. . . [T]he *R.A.V.* . . . opinion [identified] an exception for content discrimination on a basis that "consists entirely of the very reason the entire class of speech at issue is proscribable." *R.A.V., supra,* at 388, 112 S.Ct. 2538. This is the exception the majority speaks of here as covering statutes prohibiting "particularly virulent" proscribable expression.

I do not think that the Virginia statute qualifies for this virulence exception as *R.A.V.* explained it. The statute fits poorly with the illustrative examples given in *R.A.V.*, none of which involves communication generally associated with a particular message . . .

II

. . . I thus read *R.A.V.* . . . as covering prohibitions that are not clearly associated with a particular viewpoint, and that are consequently different from the Virginia statute. On that understanding of things, I necessarily read the majority opinion as treating *R.A.V.*'s virulence exception in a more flexible, pragmatic manner . . .

III

My concern here, in any event, is not with the merit of a pragmatic doctrinal move. For whether or not the Court should conceive of exceptions to *R.A.V.*'s general rule in a more practical way, no content-based statute should survive even under a pragmatic recasting of *R.A.V.* without a high probability that no "official suppression of ideas is afoot," *R.A.V., supra,* at 390. I believe the prima facie evidence provision stands in the way of any finding of such a high probability here.

. . .

As I see the likely significance of the evidence provision, its primary effect is to skew jury deliberations toward conviction in cases where the evidence of intent to intimidate is relatively weak and arguably consistent with a solely ideological reason for burning. an initiation ceremony or political rally visible to the public. In such a case, if the factfinder is aware of the prima facie evidence provision, as the jury was in respondent Black's case, the provision will have the practical effect of tilting the jury's thinking in favor of the prosecution. What is significant is not that the provision permits a factfinder's conclusion that the defendant acted with proscribable and punishable intent without any further indication, because some such indication will almost always be presented. What is significant is that the provision will encourage a factfinder to err on the side of a finding of intent to intimidate when the evidence of circumstances fails to point with any clarity either to the criminal intent or to the permissible one. . . .

To the extent the prima facie evidence provision skews prosecutions, then, it skews the statute toward suppressing ideas. . . .

. . .

Justice Thomas, dissenting.

In every culture, certain things acquire meaning well beyond what outsiders can comprehend. That goes for both the sacred, see Texas v. Johnson, 491 U.S. 397, 422–429 (1989) (Rehnquist, C. J., dissenting) (describing the unique position of the American flag in our Nation's 200 years of history), and the profane. I believe that cross burning is the paradigmatic example of the latter.

I

. . . I believe that the majority errs in imputing an expressive component to the activity in question. In my view, whatever expressive value cross burning has, the legislature simply wrote it out by banning only intimidating conduct undertaken by a particular means. A conclusion that the statute prohibiting cross burning with intent to intimidate sweeps beyond a prohibition on certain conduct into the zone of expression overlooks not only the words of the statute but also reality.

A

... To me, the majority's brief history of the Ku Klux Klan only reinforces this common understanding of the Klan as a terrorist organization, which, in its endeavor to intimidate, or even eliminate those its dislikes, uses the most brutal of methods.

Such methods typically include cross burning—"a tool for the intimidation and harassment of racial minorities, Catholics, Jews, Communists, and any other groups hated by the Klan." ... For those not easily frightened, cross burning has been followed by more extreme measures, such as beatings and murder. ... As the Solicitor General points out, the association between acts of intimidating cross burning and violence is well documented in recent American history. ...

But the perception that a burning cross is a threat and a precursor of worse things to come is not limited to blacks. Because the modern Klan expanded the list of its enemies beyond blacks and "radical[s]," to include Catholics, Jews, most immigrants, and labor unions, a burning cross is now widely viewed as a signal of impending terror and lawlessness. ...

In our culture, cross burning has almost invariably meant lawlessness and understandably instills in its victims well-grounded fear of physical violence.

B

. . .

It strains credulity to suggest that a state legislature that adopted a litany of segregationist laws self-contradictorily intended to squelch the segregationist message. Even for segregationists, violent and terroristic conduct, the Siamese twin of cross burning, was intolerable. The ban on cross burning with intent to intimidate demonstrates that even segregationists understood the difference between intimidating and terroristic conduct and racist expression. It is simply beyond belief that, in passing the statute now under review, the Virginia legislature was concerned with anything but penalizing conduct it must have viewed as particularly vicious.

Accordingly, this statute prohibits only conduct, not expression. And, just as one cannot burn down someone's house to make a political point and then seek refuge in the First Amendment, those who hate cannot terrorize and intimidate to make their point. In light of my conclusion that the statute here addresses only conduct, there is no need to analyze it under any of our First Amendment tests.

II

Even assuming that the statute implicates the First Amendment, in my view, the fact that the statute permits a jury to draw an inference of intent to intimidate from the cross burning itself presents no constitutional problems. Therein lies my primary disagreement with the plurality.

. . .

B

... The plurality fears the chill on expression because, according to the plurality, the inference permits "the Commonwealth to arrest, prosecute and convict a person based solely on the fact of cross burning itself." First, it is, at the very least, unclear that the inference comes into play during arrest and initiation of a prosecution, that is, prior to the instructions stage of an actual trial. Second, ... the inference is rebuttable and, as the jury instructions given in this case demonstrate, Virginia law still requires the jury to find the existence of each element, including intent to intimidate, beyond a reasonable doubt.

Moreover, even in the First Amendment context, the Court has upheld such regulations where conduct that initially appears culpable, ultimately results in dismissed charges. A regulation of pornography is one such example. ... [P]ornographers trafficking in images of adults who look like minors, may be not only deterred but also arrested and prosecuted for possessing what a jury might find to be legal materials. This "chilling" effect has not, however, been a cause for grave concern with respect to overbreadth of such statutes among the members of this Court.

That the First Amendment gives way to other interests is not a remarkable proposition. What is remarkable is that, under the plurality's analysis, the determination of whether an interest is sufficiently compelling depends not on the harm a regulation in question seeks to prevent, but on the area of society at which it aims. For instance, in Hill v. Colorado, 530 U.S. 703 (2000), the Court upheld a restriction on protests near abortion clinics, explaining that the State had a legitimate interest, which was sufficiently narrowly tailored, in protecting those seeking services of such establishments "from unwanted advice" and "unwanted communication" ... In so concluding, the Court placed heavy reliance on the "vulnerable physical and emotional conditions" of patients. ... Thus, when it came to the rights of those seeking abortions, the Court deemed restrictions on "unwanted advice," which, notably, can be given only from a distance of at least 8 feet from a prospective patient, justified by the counter-vailing interest in obtaining abortion. Yet, here, the plurality strikes down the statute because one day an individual might wish to burn a cross, but might do so without an intent to intimidate anyone. That cross burning subjects its targets, and, sometimes, an unintended audience, ... to extreme emotional distress, and is virtually never viewed merely as "unwanted communication," but rather, as a physical threat, is of no concern to the plurality. Henceforth, under the plurality's view, physical safety will be valued less than the right to be free from unwanted communications.

III

Because I would uphold the validity of this statute, I respectfully dissent.

Page 1344.   Add before 44 Liquormart, Inc. v. Rhode Island:

CHARITABLE SOLICITATION

Constitutionally protected commercial speech is not limited to advertising. In Schaumburg v. Citizens for a Better Environment, 444 U.S. 620 (1980), the Court invalidated an ordinance that prohibited solicitation for charities that received less than 75 percent of the receipts. Riley v. National Federation of Blind of N. C., Inc., 487 U.S. 781 (1988), held that it was unconstitutional to require solicitors to disclose the percentage of funds raised that would go to charities before asking for money. (The Court concluded that there were "less burdensome" alternatives available, such as state publication of financial disclosure forms that professional fundraisers were required to file. See also Secretary of State of Maryland v. Joseph H. Munson Co., 467 U.S. 947 (1984).) Illinois v. Telemarketing Associates, Inc., 123 S.Ct. 1829 (2003), involved a state court action for fraud that the state attorney general filed against a corporation which retained more than 85 percent of the gross receipts from its solicitation of contributions to a charity. In permitting the action to proceed, the Court emphasized that the defendant was charged with making affirmatively false or misleading representations, that were not protected by the First Amendment. The Court's earlier cases would be relevant if the complaint had merely alleged that the defendant's fundraising campaign was fraudulent only because so little money went to the charity. In this case, however, the complaint alleged that the defendant's telemarketers made affirmatively false statements to potential donors, leading them to believe that a substantial portion of their contributions would reach the charity.

D. REGULATION OF COMMERCIAL SPEECH

Page 1358. Add at end of chapter:

Lorillard Tobacco Co. v. Reilly

533 U.S. 525, 121 S.Ct. 2404, 150 L.Ed.2d 532 (2001).

Justice O'Connor delivered the opinion of the Court.

In January 1999, the Attorney General of Massachusetts promulgated comprehensive regulations governing the advertising and sale of cigarettes, smokeless tobacco, and cigars. ... Petitioners, a group of cigarette, smokeless tobacco, and cigar manufacturers and retailers, filed suit in Federal District Court claiming that the regulations violate federal law and the United States Constitution. In large measure, the District Court determined that the regulations are valid and enforceable. The United States Court of Appeals for the First Circuit affirmed in part and reversed in part, concluding that the regulations are not pre empted by federal law and do not violate the First Amendment. The first question presented for our review is whether certain cigarette advertising regulations are pre-empted by the Federal Cigarette Labeling and Advertising Act (FCLAA), ... 15 U.S.C. § 1331 et seq. The second question presented is whether certain regulations governing the advertising and sale of tobacco products violate the First Amendment.

I

In November 1998, Massachusetts, along with over 40 other States, reached a landmark agreement with major manufacturers in the cigarette industry. The signatory States settled their claims against these companies in exchange for monetary payments and permanent injunctive relief. ... At the press conference covering Massachusetts' decision to sign the agreement, then-

Attorney General Scott Harshbarger announced that as one of his last acts in office, he would create consumer protection regulations to restrict advertising and sales practices for tobacco products. He explained that the regulations were necessary in order to "close holes" in the settlement agreement and "to stop Big Tobacco from recruiting new customers among the children of Massachusetts."

In January 1999, pursuant to his authority to prevent unfair or deceptive practices in trade, . . . the Massachusetts Attorney General (Attorney General) promulgated regulations governing the sale and advertisement of cigarettes, smokeless tobacco, and cigars. . . . The regulations have a broader scope than the master settlement agreement, reaching advertising, sales practices, and members of the tobacco industry not covered by the agreement. The regulations place a variety of restrictions on outdoor advertising, point-of-sale advertising, retail sales transactions, transactions by mail, promotions, sampling of products, and labels for cigars.

. . .

II

[The Court held that the State's outdoor and point-of-sale advertising regulations for cigarettes were pre-empted.]

III

By its terms, the FCLAA's pre-emption provision only applies to cigarettes. Accordingly, we must evaluate the smokeless tobacco and cigar petitioners' First Amendment challenges to the State's outdoor and point-of-sale advertising regulations. The cigarette petitioners did not raise a pre-emption challenge to the sales practices regulations. Thus, we must analyze the cigarette as well as the smokeless tobacco and cigar petitioners' claim that certain sales practices regulations for tobacco products violate the First Amendment.

A

. . .

Petitioners urge us to reject the *Central Hudson* analysis and apply strict scrutiny. . . . But here, as in Greater New Orleans [Broadcasting Assn., Inc. v. United States], 527 U.S. 173, 184 (1999), we see "no need to break new ground. *Central Hudson*, as applied in our more recent commercial speech cases, provides an adequate basis for decision." . . .

Only the last two steps of *Central Hudson*'s four-part analysis are at issue here. The Attorney General has assumed for purposes of summary judgment that petitioners' speech is entitled to First Amendment protection. With respect to the second step, none of the petitioners contests the importance of the State's interest in preventing the use of tobacco products by minors.

The third step of *Central Hudson* concerns the relationship between the harm that underlies the State's interest and the means identified by the State to advance that interest. . . .

The last step of the *Central Hudson* analysis . . . requires a reasonable " 'fit between the legislature's ends and the means chosen to accomplish those ends, ... a means narrowly tailored to achieve the desired objective.' " ... Focusing on the third and fourth steps of the *Central Hudson* analysis, we first address the outdoor advertising and point-of-sale advertising regulations for smokeless tobacco and cigars. We then address the sales practices regulations for all tobacco products.

B

The outdoor advertising regulations prohibit smokeless tobacco or cigar advertising within a 1,000–foot radius of a school or playground. ...

1

The smokeless tobacco and cigar petitioners contend that the Attorney General's regulations do not satisfy *Central Hudson*'s third step. They maintain that although the Attorney General may have identified a problem with underage cigarette smoking, he has not identified an equally severe problem with respect to underage use of smokeless tobacco or cigars. ... The cigar petitioners catalogue a list of differences between cigars and other tobacco products, including the characteristics of the products and marketing strategies. The petitioners finally contend that the Attorney General cannot prove that advertising has a causal link to tobacco use such that limiting advertising will materially alleviate any problem of underage use of their products.

In previous cases, we have acknowledged the theory that product advertising stimulates demand for products, while suppressed advertising may have the opposite effect. ... The Attorney General cites numerous studies to support this theory in the case of tobacco products.

. . .

Our review of the record reveals that the Attorney General has provided ample documentation of the problem with underage use of smokeless tobacco and cigars. In addition, we disagree with petitioners' claim that there is no evidence that preventing targeted campaigns and limiting youth exposure to advertising will decrease underage use of smokeless tobacco and cigars. On this record and in the posture of summary judgment, we are unable to conclude that the Attorney General's decision to regulate advertising of smokeless tobacco and cigars in an effort to combat the use of tobacco products by minors was based on mere "speculation [and] conjecture." ...

2

Whatever the strength of the Attorney General's evidence to justify the outdoor advertising regulations, however, we conclude that the regulations do not satisfy the fourth step of the *Central Hudson* analysis. The final step of the *Central Hudson* analysis, the "critical inquiry in this case," requires a reasonable fit between the means and ends of the regulatory scheme. ... The Attorney General's regulations do not meet this standard. The broad sweep of the regulations indicates that the Attorney General did not "carefully calculat[e] the costs and benefits associated with the burden on speech imposed" by the regulations. ...

The outdoor advertising regulations prohibit any smokeless tobacco or cigar advertising within 1,000 feet of schools or playgrounds. ... [T]he Court of

Appeals concluded that the regulations prohibit advertising in a substantial portion of the major metropolitan areas of Massachusetts. . . .

The substantial geographical reach of the Attorney General's outdoor advertising regulations is compounded by other factors. "Outdoor" advertising includes not only advertising located outside an establishment, but also advertising inside a store if that advertising is visible from outside the store. The regulations restrict advertisements of any size and the term advertisement also includes oral statements. . . .

In some geographical areas, these regulations would constitute nearly a complete ban on the communication of truthful information about smokeless tobacco and cigars to adult consumers. The breadth and scope of the regulations, and the process by which the Attorney General adopted the regulations, do not demonstrate a careful calculation of the speech interests involved.

First, the Attorney General did not seem to consider the impact of the 1,000–foot restriction on commercial speech in major metropolitan areas. . . . The uniformly broad sweep of the geographical limitation demonstrates a lack of tailoring.

In addition, the range of communications restricted seems unduly broad. For instance, it is not clear from the regulatory scheme why a ban on oral communications is necessary to further the State's interest. Apparently that restriction means that a retailer is unable to answer inquiries about its tobacco products if that communication occurs outdoors. Similarly, a ban on all signs of any size seems ill suited to target the problem of highly visible billboards, as opposed to smaller signs. To the extent that studies have identified particular advertising and promotion practices that appeal to youth, tailoring would involve targeting those practices while permitting others. As crafted, the regulations make no distinction among practices on this basis.

. . .

The State's interest in preventing underage tobacco use is substantial, and even compelling, but it is no less true that the sale and use of tobacco products by adults is a legal activity. We must consider that tobacco retailers and manufacturers have an interest in conveying truthful information about their products to adults, and adults have a corresponding interest in receiving truthful information about tobacco products. . . . As the State protects children from tobacco advertisements, tobacco manufacturers and retailers and their adult consumers still have a protected interest in communication. . . .

. . .

. . . [A] retailer in Massachusetts may have no means of communicating to passersby on the street that it sells tobacco products because alternative forms of advertisement, like newspapers, do not allow that retailer to propose an instant transaction in the way that onsite advertising does. The ban on any indoor advertising that is visible from the outside also presents problems in establishments like convenience stores, which have unique security concerns that counsel in favor of full visibility of the store from the outside. It is these sorts of considerations that the Attorney General failed to incorporate into the regulatory scheme.

We conclude that the Attorney General has failed to show that the outdoor advertising regulations for smokeless tobacco and cigars are not more extensive than necessary to advance the State's substantial interest in preventing under-age tobacco use. Justice Stevens urges that the Court remand the case for further development of the factual record. We believe that a remand is inappropriate in this case because the State had ample opportunity to develop a record with respect to tailoring (as it had to justify its decision to regulate advertising), and additional evidence would not alter the nature of the scheme before the Court.

A careful calculation of the costs of a speech regulation does not mean that a State must demonstrate that there is no incursion on legitimate speech interests, but a speech regulation cannot unduly impinge on the speaker's ability to propose a commercial transaction and the adult listener's opportunity to obtain information about products. After reviewing the outdoor advertising regulations, we find the calculation in this case insufficient for purposes of the First Amendment.

C

Massachusetts has also restricted indoor, point-of-sale advertising for smokeless tobacco and cigars. Advertising cannot be "placed lower than five feet from the floor of any retail establishment which is located within a one thousand foot radius of" any school or playground. . . .

We conclude that the point-of-sale advertising regulations fail both the third and fourth steps of the *Central Hudson* analysis. . . . [T]he State's goal is to prevent minors from using tobacco products and to curb demand for that activity by limiting youth exposure to advertising. The 5 foot rule does not seem to advance that goal. Not all children are less than 5 feet tall, and those who are certainly have the ability to look up and take in their surroundings.

By contrast to Justice Stevens, we do not believe this regulation can be construed as a mere regulation of conduct under United States v. O'Brien, 391 U.S. 367 (1968). To qualify as a regulation of communicative action governed by the scrutiny outlined in *O'Brien*, the State's regulation must be unrelated to expression. . . . Here, Massachusetts' height restriction is an attempt to regu-late directly the communicative impact of indoor advertising.

Massachusetts may wish to target tobacco advertisements and displays that entice children, much like floor-level candy displays in a convenience store, but the blanket height restriction does not constitute a reasonable fit with that goal. . . . There is no de minimis exception for a speech restriction that lacks sufficient tailoring or justification. We conclude that the restriction on the height of indoor advertising is invalid under *Central Hudson*'s third and fourth prongs.

D

The Attorney General also promulgated a number of regulations that restrict sales practices by cigarette, smokeless tobacco, and cigar manufacturers and retailers. Among other restrictions, the regulations bar the use of self-service displays and require that tobacco products be placed out of the reach of all consumers in a location accessible only to salespersons. Two of the cigarette petitioners ..., petitioner U.S. Smokeless Tobacco Company, and the cigar petitioners challenge the sales practices regulations on First Amendment grounds. The cigar petitioners additionally challenge a provision that prohibits sampling or promotional giveaways of cigars or little cigars. ...

. . .

... As we read the regulations, they basically require tobacco retailers to place tobacco products behind counters and require customers to have contact with a salesperson before they are able to handle a tobacco product.

The cigarette and smokeless tobacco petitioners contend that "the same First Amendment principles that require invalidation of the outdoor and indoor advertising restrictions require invalidation of the display regulations at issue in this case." The cigar petitioners contend that self-service displays for cigars cannot be prohibited because each brand of cigar is unique and customers traditionally have sought to handle and compare cigars at the time of purchase.

We reject these contentions. Assuming that petitioners have a cognizable speech interest in a particular means of displaying their products, ... these regulations withstand First Amendment scrutiny.

Massachusetts' sales practices provisions regulate conduct that may have a communicative component, but Massachusetts seeks to regulate the placement of tobacco products for reasons unrelated to the communication of ideas.... We conclude that the State has demonstrated a substantial interest in preventing access to tobacco products by minors and has adopted an appropriately narrow means of advancing that interest. ...

... Unattended displays of tobacco products present an opportunity for access without the proper age verification required by law. Thus, the State prohibits self-service and other displays that would allow an individual to obtain tobacco products without direct contact with a salesperson. It is clear that the regulations leave open ample channels of communication. The regulations do not significantly impede adult access to tobacco products. Moreover, retailers have other means of exercising any cognizable speech interest in the presentation of their products. We presume that vendors may place empty tobacco packaging on open display, and display actual tobacco products so long as that display is only accessible to sales personnel. As for cigars, there is no indication in the regulations that a customer is unable to examine a cigar prior to purchase, so long as that examination takes place through a salesperson.

. . .

We conclude that the sales practices regulations withstand First Amendment scrutiny. The means chosen by the State are narrowly tailored to prevent access to tobacco products by minors, are unrelated to expression, and leave open alternative avenues for vendors to convey information about products and for would-be customers to inspect products before purchase.

IV

. . .

To the extent that federal law and the First Amendment do not prohibit state action, States and localities remain free to combat the problem of underage tobacco use by appropriate means. ...

Justice Kennedy, with whom Justice Scalia joins, concurring in part and concurring in the judgment.

The obvious overbreadth of the outdoor advertising restrictions suffices to invalidate them under the fourth part of the test in *Central Hudson* ... As a result, in my view, there is no need to consider whether the restrictions satisfy the third part of the test, a proposition about which there is considerable doubt. Neither are we required to consider whether Central Hudson should be retained in the face of the substantial objections that can be made to it. My continuing concerns that the test gives insufficient protection to truthful, nonmisleading commercial speech require me to refrain from expressing agreement with the Court's application of the third part of *Central Hudson*. ... With the exception of Part III–B–1, then, I join the opinion of the Court.

Justice Thomas, concurring in part and concurring in the judgment.

I join the opinion of the Court (with the exception of Part III–B–1) because ... I would subject all of the advertising restrictions to strict scrutiny and would hold that they violate the First Amendment.

I

. . .

... In my view, an asserted government interest in keeping people ignorant by suppressing expression "is per se illegitimate and can no more justify regulation of 'commercial' speech than it can justify regulation of 'noncommercial' speech." ... That is essentially the interest asserted here, and, adhering to the views I expressed in *44 Liquormart*, I would subject the Massachusetts regulations to strict scrutiny.

B

Even if one accepts the premise that commercial speech generally is entitled to a lower level of constitutional protection than are other forms of speech, it does not follow that the regulations here deserve anything less than strict scrutiny. ... Even when speech falls into a category of reduced constitutional protection, the government may not engage in content discrimination for reasons unrelated to those characteristics of the speech that place it within the category. ...

. . .

C

. . .

Viewed as an effort to proscribe solicitation to unlawful conduct, these regulations clearly fail the *Brandenburg* test. A State may not "forbid or proscribe advocacy of the use of force or of law violation except where such advocacy is directed to inciting or producing imminent lawless action and is likely to incite or produce such action." ... Even if Massachusetts could prohibit advertisements reading, "Hey kids, buy cigarettes here," these regulations sweep much more broadly than that. They cover "any ... statement or representation ... the purpose or effect of which is to promote the use or sale" of tobacco products, whether or not the statement is directly or indirectly addressed to minors. ... On respondents' theory, all tobacco advertising may be limited because some of its viewers may not legally act on it.

. . .

At bottom, respondents' theory rests on the premise that an indirect solicitation is enough to empower the State to regulate speech, and that, as petitioners put it, even an advertisement directed at adults "will give any children who may happen to see it the wrong idea and therefore must be suppressed from public view." ...

... Even if Massachusetts has a valid interest in regulating speech directed at children—who, it argues, may be more easily misled, and to whom the sale of tobacco products is unlawful—it may not pursue that interest at the expense of the free speech rights of adults.

. . .

We have held consistently that speech "cannot be suppressed solely to protect the young from ideas or images that a legislative body thinks unsuitable for them." ... To be sure, in FCC v. Pacifica Foundation, 438 U.S. 726 (1978), we upheld the Federal Communications Commission's power to regulate indecent but nonobscene radio broadcasts. But *Pacifica* relied heavily on what it considered to be the "special justifications for regulation of the broadcast media that are not applicable to other speakers." ...

Outside of the broadcasting context, we have adhered to the view that "the governmental interest in protecting children from harmful materials" does not "justify an unnecessarily broad suppression of speech addressed to adults." ...

II

Under strict scrutiny, the advertising ban may be saved only if it is narrowly tailored to promote a compelling government interest. ... If that interest could be served by an alternative that is less restrictive of speech, then the State must use that alternative instead. ... Applying this standard, the regulations here must fail.

A

Massachusetts asserts a compelling interest in reducing tobacco use among minors. Applied to adults, an interest in manipulating market choices by keeping people ignorant would not be legitimate, let alone compelling. But assuming that there is a compelling interest in reducing underage smoking, and that the ban on outdoor advertising promotes this interest, I doubt that the same is true of the ban on point-of-sale advertising below five feet. ... Far from serving a compelling interest, the ban on displays below five feet seems to lack even a minimally rational relationship to any conceivable interest.

There is also considerable reason to doubt that the restrictions on cigar and smokeless tobacco outdoor advertising promote any state interest. Outdoor advertising for cigars, after all, is virtually nonexistent. Cigar makers use no billboards in Massachusetts, and in fact their nationwide outdoor advertising budget is only about $50,000 per year. To the extent outdoor advertising exists, there is no evidence that it is targeted at youth or has a significant effect on youth. . . .

Much the same is true of smokeless tobacco. Here respondents place primary reliance on evidence that, in the late 1960's, the U.S. Smokeless Tobacco Company increased its sales through advertising targeted at young males. But this does nothing to show that advertising affecting minors is a problem today. . . .

B

In any case, even assuming that the regulations advance a compelling state interest, they must be struck down because they are not narrowly tailored. The Court is correct, that the arbitrary 1,000–foot radius demonstrates a lack of narrow tailoring, but the problem goes deeper than that. A prohibited zone defined solely by circles drawn around schools and playgrounds is necessarily overinclusive, regardless of the radii of the circles. Consider, for example, a billboard located within 1,000 feet of a school but visible only from an elevated freeway that runs nearby. Such a billboard would not threaten any of the interests respondents assert, but it would be banned anyway, because the regulations take no account of whether the advertisement could even be seen by children. The prohibited zone is even more suspect where, as here, it includes all but 10 percent of the area in the three largest cities in the State.

The loose tailoring of the advertising ban is displayed not only in its geographic scope but also in the nature of the advertisements it affects. The regulations define "advertisement" very broadly; the term includes any "written . . . statement or representation, made by" a person who sells tobacco products, "the purpose or effect of which is to promote the use or sale of the product." . . . Almost everything a business does has the purpose of promoting the sale of its products, so this definition would cover anything a tobacco retailer might say. Some of the prohibited speech would not even be commercial. If a store displayed a sign promoting a candidate for Attorney General who had promised to repeal the tobacco regulations if elected, it probably would be doing so with the long-term purpose of promoting sales, and the display of such a sign would be illegal.

Even if the definition of "advertisement" were read more narrowly so as to require a specific reference to tobacco products, it still would have Draconian effects. It would, for example, prohibit a tobacconist from displaying a sign reading "Joe's Cigar Shop." . . . Respondents assert no interest in cigar retailer anonymity, and it is difficult to conceive of any other interest to which this rule could be said to be narrowly tailored.

The regulations fail the narrow tailoring inquiry for another, more fundamental reason. In addition to examining a narrower advertising ban, the State should have examined ways of advancing its interest that do not require limiting speech at all. Here, respondents had several alternatives. Most obviously, they could have directly regulated the conduct with which they were concerned. . . . Massachusetts already prohibits the sale of tobacco to minors, but it could take steps to enforce that prohibition more vigorously. It also could enact laws prohibiting the purchase, possession, or use of tobacco by minors. And, if its concern is that tobacco advertising communicates a message with which it disagrees, it could seek to counteract that message with "more speech, not enforced silence," Whitney v. California, 274 U.S. 357, 377 (1927) (Brandeis, J., concurring).

III

Underlying many of the arguments of respondents and their amici is the idea that tobacco is in some sense sui generis—that it is so special, so unlike any other object of regulation, that application of normal First Amendment principles should be suspended. ... [T]o uphold the Massachusetts tobacco regulations would be to accept a line of reasoning that would permit restrictions on advertising for a host of other products.

. . .

Respondents have identified no principle of law or logic that would preclude the imposition of restrictions on fast food and alcohol advertising similar to those they seek to impose on tobacco advertising. In effect, they seek a "vice" exception to the First Amendment. No such exception exists. ... If it did, it would have almost no limit. . . .

No legislature has ever sought to restrict speech about an activity it regarded as harmless and inoffensive. ... It is therefore no answer for the State to say that the makers of cigarettes are doing harm: perhaps they are. But in that respect they are no different from the purveyors of other harmful products, or the advocates of harmful ideas. When the State seeks to silence them, they are all entitled to the protection of the First Amendment.

Justice Stevens, with whom Justice Ginsburg and Justice Breyer join, and with whom Justice Souter joins as to Part I, concurring in part, concurring in the judgment in part, and dissenting in part.

Because I strongly disagree with the Court's conclusion that the Federal Cigarette Labeling and Advertising Act of 1965 (FCLAA or Act) ... precludes States and localities from regulating the location of cigarette advertising, I dissent from Parts II–A and II–B of the Court's opinion. On the First Amendment questions, I agree with the Court both that the outdoor advertising restrictions imposed by Massachusetts serve legitimate and important state interests and that the record does not indicate that the measures were properly tailored to serve those interests. Because the present record does not enable us to adjudicate the merits of those claims on summary judgment, I would vacate the decision upholding those restrictions and remand for trial on the constitutionality of the outdoor advertising regulations. Finally, because I do not believe that either the point-of-sale advertising restrictions or the sales practice restrictions implicate significant First Amendment concerns, I would uphold them in their entirety.

. . .

II

On the First Amendment issues raised by petitioners, my disagreements with the majority are less significant. I would, however, reach different dispositions as to the 1,000–foot rule and the height restrictions for indoor advertising, and my evaluation of the sales practice restrictions differs from the Court's.

The 1,000–Foot Rule

... [N]oble ends do not save a speech-restricting statute whose means are poorly tailored.

. . .

... I share the majority's concern as to whether the 1,000–foot rule unduly restricts the ability of cigarette manufacturers to convey lawful information to adult consumers. This, of course, is a question of line-drawing. ...

... Finding the appropriate balance is no easy matter. Though many factors plausibly enter the equation when calculating whether a child-directed location restriction goes too far in regulating adult speech, one crucial question is whether the regulatory scheme leaves available sufficient "alternative avenues of communication." ... Because I do not think the record contains sufficient information to enable us to answer that question, I would vacate the award of summary judgment upholding the 1,000–foot rule and remand for trial on that issue. ...

... The dearth of reliable statistical information as to the scope of the ban is problematic.

... More importantly, the Court lacks sufficient qualitative information as to the areas where cigarette advertising is prohibited and those where it is permitted....

Finally, the Court lacks information as to other avenues of communication available to cigarette manufacturers and retailers. ...

... While the ultimate question before us is one of law, the answer to that question turns on complicated factual questions relating to the practical effects of the regulations. As the record does not reveal the answer to these disputed questions of fact, the court should have denied summary judgment to both parties and allowed the parties to present further evidence.

. . .

The Sales Practice and Indoor Advertising Restrictions

... I ... write separately on this issue to make two brief points.

First, ... the sales practice restrictions are best analyzed as regulating conduct, not speech. See 218 F. 3d, at 53. While the decision how to display one's products no doubt serves a marginal communicative function, the same can be said of virtually any human activity performed with the hope or intention of evoking the interest of others. This Court has long recognized the need to differentiate between legislation that targets expression and legislation that targets conduct for legitimate non-speech-related reasons but imposes an incidental burden on expression. See, e.g., United States v. O'Brien, 391 U.S. 367 (1968). However difficult that line may be to draw, it seems clear to me that laws requiring that stores maintain items behind counters and prohibiting self-service displays fall squarely on the conduct side of the line. Restrictions as to the accessibility of dangerous or legally-restricted products are a common feature of the regulatory regime governing American retail stores. I see nothing the least bit constitutionally problematic in requiring individuals to ask for the assistance of a salesclerk in order to examine or purchase a handgun, a bottle of penicillin, or a package of cigarettes.

Second, though I admit the question is closer, I would, for similar reasons, uphold the regulation limiting tobacco advertising in certain retail establishments to the space five feet or more above the floor. When viewed in isolation, this provision appears to target speech. ... Nonetheless, I am ultimately persuaded that the provision is unobjectionable because it is little more than an adjunct to the other sales practice restrictions. As the Commonwealth of Massachusetts can properly legislate the placement of products and the nature of displays in its convenience stores, I would not draw a distinction between such restrictions and height restrictions on related product advertising. I would accord the Commonwealth some latitude in imposing restrictions that can have only the slightest impact on the ability of adults to purchase a poisonous product and may save some children from taking the first step on the road to addiction.

Thompson v. Western States Medical Center

535 U.S. 357, 122 S.Ct. 1497, 152 L.Ed.2d 563 (2002).

Justice O'Connor delivered the opinion of the Court.

Section 503A of the Food and Drug Administration Modernization Act of 1997 (FDAMA or Act), 111 Stat. 2328, 21 U.S.C. § 353a, exempts "compounded drugs" from the Food and Drug Administration's standard drug approval requirements as long as the providers of those drugs abide by several restrictions, including that they refrain from advertising or promoting particular compounded drugs. Respondents, a group of licensed pharmacies that specialize in compounding drugs, sought to enjoin enforcement of the subsections of the Act dealing with advertising and solicitation, arguing that those provisions violate the First Amendment's free speech guarantee. The District Court agreed with respondents and granted their motion for summary judgment ...

The Court of Appeals for the Ninth Circuit affirmed ... We conclude, as did the courts below, that § 503A's provisions regarding advertisement and promotion amount to unconstitutional restrictions on commercial speech, and we therefore affirm.

I

Drug compounding is a process by which a pharmacist or doctor combines, mixes, or alters ingredients to create a medication tailored to the needs of an individual patient. Compounding is typically used to prepare medications that are not commercially available, such as medication for a patient who is allergic to an ingredient in a mass-produced product. It is a traditional component of the practice of pharmacy ... Pharmacists may provide compounded drugs to patients only upon receipt of a valid prescription from a doctor or other medical practitioner licensed to prescribe medication. ...

. . .

For approximately the first 50 years . . . the FDA generally left regulation of compounding to the States. . . . The FDA eventually became concerned, however, that some pharmacists were manufacturing and selling drugs under the guise of compounding, thereby avoiding the FDCA's new drug requirements. In 1992, in response to this concern, the FDA issued a Compliance Policy Guide. . . . It stated that the "FDA believes that an increasing number of establishments with retail pharmacy licenses are engaged in manufacturing, distributing, and promoting unapproved new drugs for human use in a manner that is clearly outside the bounds of traditional pharmacy practice and that constitute violations of the [FDCA]." . . .

. . . [T]he Guide announced that it was FDA policy to permit pharmacists to compound drugs after receipt of a valid prescription for an individual patient or to compound drugs in "very limited quantities" before receipt of a valid prescription if they could document a history of receiving valid prescriptions "generated solely within an established professional practitioner-patient-pharmacy relationship" . . .

Congress turned portions of this policy into law when it enacted the FDAMA in 1997. The FDAMA . . . exempts compounded drugs from the FDCA's "new drug" requirements and other requirements provided the drugs satisfy a number of restrictions. . . .[M]ost relevant for this litigation, the prescription must be "unsolicited," § 353a(a), and the pharmacy, licensed pharmacist, or licensed physician compounding the drug may "not advertise or promote the compounding of any particular drug, class of drug, or type of drug." § 353a(c). The pharmacy, licensed pharmacist, or licensed physician may, however, "advertise and promote the compounding service." *Ibid.*

Respondents are a group of licensed pharmacies that specialize in drug compounding. They have prepared promotional materials that they distribute by mail and at medical conferences to inform patients and physicians of the use and effectiveness of specific compounded drugs. . . .

. . .

II

The parties agree that the advertising and soliciting prohibited by the FDAMA constitute commercial speech. . . .

. . .

Neither party has challenged the appropriateness of applying the *Central Hudson* framework to the speech-related provisions at issue here. . . .

III

The Government does not attempt to defend the FDAMA's speech-related provisions under the first prong of the *Central Hudson* test; *i.e.,* it does not argue that the prohibited advertisements would be about unlawful activity or would be misleading. Instead, the Government argues that the FDAMA satisfies the remaining three prongs of the *Central Hudson* test.

The Government asserts that three substantial interests underlie the FDAMA. The first is an interest in "preserv[ing] the effectiveness and integrity of the FDCA's new drug approval process and the protection of the public health that it provides." The second is an interest in "preserv[ing] the availability of compounded drugs for those individual patients who, for particularized medical reasons, cannot use commercially available products that have been approved by the FDA." Finally, the Government argues that "[a]chieving the proper balance between those two independently compelling but competing interests is itself a substantial governmental interest."

Explaining these interests, the Government argues that the FDCA's new drug approval requirements are critical to the public health and safety. . . .

. . . [T]he Government also acknowledges that "because obtaining FDA approval for a new drug is a costly process, requiring FDA approval of all drug products compounded by pharmacies for the particular needs of an individual patient would, as a practical matter, eliminate the practice of compounding, and [that this] would be undesirable because compounding is sometimes critical to the care of patients with drug allergies, patients who cannot tolerate particular drug delivery systems, and patients requiring special drug dosages."

. . . [T]he Government needs to be able to draw a line between small-scale compounding and large-scale drug manufacturing. That line must distinguish compounded drugs produced on such a small scale that they could not undergo safety and efficacy testing from drugs produced and sold on a large enough scale that they could undergo such testing and therefore must do so.

The Government argues that the FDAMA's speech-related provisions provide just such a line, *i.e.*, that, in the terms of *Central Hudson,* they "directly advanc[e] the governmental interest[s] asserted." . . . The Government argues that advertising . . . is "a fair proxy for actual or intended large-scale manufacturing," . . .

. . . [T]he Government has failed to demonstrate that the speech restrictions are "not more extensive than is necessary to serve [those] interest[s]."
. . .

Several non-speech-related means of drawing a line between compounding and large-scale manufacturing might be possible here. First, it seems that the Government could use the very factors the FDA relied on to distinguish compounding from manufacturing in its 1992 Compliance Policy Guide. For example, the Government could ban the use of "commercial scale manufacturing or testing equipment for compounding drug products." It could prohibit pharmacists from compounding more drugs in anticipation of receiving prescriptions than in response to prescriptions already received. It could prohibit pharmacists from "[o]ffering compounded drugs at wholesale to other state licensed persons or commercial entities for resale." Alternately, it could limit the amount of compounded drugs, either by volume or by numbers of prescriptions, that a given pharmacist or pharmacy sells out of State. Another possibility not suggested by the Compliance Policy Guide would be capping the amount of any particular compounded drug, either by drug volume, number of prescriptions, gross revenue, or profit that a pharmacist or pharmacy may make or sell in a given period of time. It might even be sufficient to rely solely on the non-speech-related provisions of the FDAMA, such as the requirement that compounding only be conducted in response to a prescription or a history of receiving a prescription, . . . and the limitation on the percentage of a pharmacy's total sales that out-of-state sales of compounded drugs may represent . . .

... Nowhere in the legislative history of the FDAMA or petitioners' briefs is there any explanation of why the Government believed forbidding advertising was a necessary as opposed to merely convenient means of achieving its interests. ... If the First Amendment means anything, it means that regulating speech must be a last—not first—resort. Yet here it seems to have been the first strategy the Government thought to try.

... The dissent describes another governmental interest—an interest in prohibiting the sale of compounded drugs to "patients who may not clearly need them," ... Nowhere in its briefs, however, does the Government argue that this interest motivated the advertising ban. Although, for the reasons given by the dissent, Congress conceivably could have enacted the advertising ban to advance this interest, we have generally only sustained statutes on the basis of hypothesized justifications when reviewing statutes merely to determine whether they are rational. ... The *Central Hudson* test is significantly stricter than the rational basis test, however, requiring the Government not only to identify specifically "a substantial interest to be achieved by [the] restrictio[n] on commercial speech," ... but also to prove that the regulation "directly advances" that interest and is "not more extensive than is necessary to serve that interest," ...

Even if the Government had argued that the FDAMA's speech-related restrictions were motivated by a fear that advertising compounded drugs would put people who do not need such drugs at risk by causing them to convince their doctors to prescribe the drugs anyway, that fear would fail to justify the restrictions. Aside from the fact that this concern rests on the questionable assumption that doctors would prescribe unnecessary medications (an assumption the dissent is willing to make based on one magazine article and one survey, neither of which was relied upon by the Government), this concern amounts to a fear that people would make bad decisions if given truthful information about compounded drugs. We have previously rejected the notion that the Government has an interest in preventing the dissemination of truthful commercial information in order to prevent members of the public from making bad decisions with the information. ...

Even if the Government had asserted an interest in preventing people who do not need compounded drugs from obtaining those drugs, the statute does not directly advance that interest. ... Although the advertising ban may reduce the demand for compounded drugs from those who do not need the drugs, it does nothing to prevent such individuals from obtaining compounded drugs other than requiring prescriptions. But if it is appropriate for the statute to rely on doctors to refrain from prescribing compounded drugs to patients who do not need them, it is not clear why it would not also be appropriate to rely on doctors to refrain from prescribing compounded drugs to patients who do not need them in a world where advertising was permitted.

. . . .

If the Government's failure to justify its decision to regulate speech were not enough to convince us that the FDAMA's advertising provisions were unconstitutional, the amount of beneficial speech prohibited by the FDAMA would be. ... It would prevent pharmacists with no interest in mass-producing medications, but who serve clienteles with special medical needs, from telling the doctors treating those clients about the alternative drugs available through compounding. For example, a pharmacist serving a children's hospital where many patients are unable to swallow pills would be prevented from telling the children's doctors about a new development in compounding that allowed a drug that was previously available only in pill form to be administered another way. ... The fact that the FDAMA would prohibit such seemingly useful speech even though doing so does not appear to directly further any asserted governmental objective confirms our belief that the prohibition is unconstitutional.

. . .

Justice Thomas, concurring.

I concur because I agree with the Court's application of the test set forth in *Central Hudson* ... I continue, however, to adhere to my view that cases such as this should not be analyzed under the *Central Hudson* test. . . .

Justice Breyer, with whom The Chief Justice, Justice Stevens, and Justice Ginsburg join, dissenting.

. . .

... I believe that the Court seriously undervalues the importance of the Government's interest in protecting the health and safety of the American public.

I

In my view, the advertising restriction "directly advances" the statute's important safety objective ... to confine the sale of untested, compounded, drugs to where they are medically needed. But to do so the statute must exclude from the area of permitted drug sales *both* (1) those drugs that traditional drug manufacturers might supply after testing—typically drugs capable of being produced in large amounts, *and* (2) those compounded drugs sought by patients who may not clearly need them—including compounded drugs produced in small amounts.

The ... statute, in seeking to confine distribution of untested tailored drugs, must look both at the amount supplied (to help decide whether ordinary manufacturers might provide a tested alternative) and at the nature of demand (to help separate genuine need from simple convenience). . . .

This second intermediate objective is logically related to Congress' primary end—the minimizing of safety risks. The statute's basic exemption from testing requirements inherently creates risks simply by placing untested drugs in the hands of the consumer. Where an individual has a specific medical need for a specially tailored drug those risks are likely offset. But where an untested drug is a convenience, not a necessity, that offset is unlikely to be present.

That presumably is why neither the Food and Drug Administration (FDA) nor Congress anywhere suggests that all that matters is the total *amount* of a particular drug's sales. ... That is why the statute itself, as well as the FDA policy that the statute reflects, lists several distinguishing factors, of which advertising is one. . . .

. . .

And that, in part, is why federal and state authorities have long permitted pharmacists to advertise the fact that they compound drugs, while forbidding the advertisement of individual compounds. . . .

These policies and statutory provisions reflect the view that individualized consideration is more likely present, and convenience alone is more likely absent, when demand for a compounding prescription originates with a doctor, not an advertisement. The restrictions try to assure that demand is generated doctor-to-patient-to-pharmacist, not pharmacist-to-advertisement-to-patient-to-doctor. And they do so in order to diminish the likelihood that those who do not genuinely need untested compounded drugs will not receive them.

There is considerable evidence that the relevant means—the advertising restrictions—directly advance this statutory objective. . . .

. . . [C]ompounded drugs carry with them special risks. After all, compounding is not necessarily a matter of changing a drug's flavor, but rather it is a matter of combining different ingredients in new, untested ways, say, adding a pain medication to an antihistamine to counteract allergies or increasing the ratio of approved ingredients in a salve to help the body absorb it at a faster rate. And the risks associated with the untested combination of ingredients or the quicker absorption rate or the working conditions necessary to change an old drug into its new form can, for some patients, mean infection, serious side effects, or even death. . . .

There is considerable evidence that consumer oriented advertising will create strong consumer-driven demand for a particular drug. . . .

And there is strong evidence that doctors will often respond affirmatively to a patient's request for a specific drug that the patient has seen advertised. . . .

In these circumstances, Congress could reasonably conclude that doctors will respond affirmatively to a patient's request for a compounded drug even if the doctor would not normally prescribe it. When a parent learns that a child's pill can be administered in liquid form, when a patient learns that a compounded skin cream has an enhanced penetration rate, or when an allergy sufferer learns that a compounded anti-inflammatory allergy medication can alleviate a sinus headache without the sedative effects of antihistamines, that parent or patient may well ask for the desired prescription. And the doctor may well write the prescription even in the absence of special need—at least if any risk likely to arise from lack of testing is so small that only *scientific testing,* not anecdote or experience, would reveal it. . . .

Of course, the added risks in any such individual case may be small. But those individual risks added together can significantly affect the public health. At least, the FDA and Congress could reasonably reach that conclusion. And that fact, along with the absence of any significant evidence that the advertising restrictions have prevented doctors from learning about, or obtaining, compounded drugs, means that the FDA and Congress could also conclude that the advertising restrictions "directly advance" the statute's safety goal. . . . There is no reason for this Court, as a matter of constitutional law, to reach a different conclusion.

II

I do not believe that Congress could have achieved its safety objectives in significantly less restrictive ways. Consider the several alternatives the Court suggests. . . .

. . .

The Court adds that "[t]he Government has not offered any reason why these possibilities, alone or in combination, would be insufficient." The Government's failure to do so may reflect the fact that only the Court, not any of the respondents, has here suggested that these "alternatives," alone or in combination, would prove sufficient. In fact, the FDA's Compliance Policy Guide, from which the Court draws its first four alternatives, specifically warned that these alternatives alone were insufficient to successfully distinguish traditional compounding from unacceptable manufacturing. . . .

III

The Court responds to the claim that advertising compounded drugs causes people to obtain drugs that do not promote their health, by finding it implausible given the need for a prescription and by suggesting that it is not relevant. The First Amendment, it says, does not permit the Government to control the content of advertising, where doing so flows from "fear" that "people would make bad decisions if given truthful information about compounded drugs." This response . . . fails to take account of considerations that make the claim more than plausible (if properly stated); and it is inconsistent with this Court's interpretation of the Constitution.

It is an oversimplification to say that the Government "fear[s]" that doctors or patients "would make bad decisions if given truthful information." Rather, the Government fears the safety consequences of multiple compound-drug prescription decisions initiated not by doctors but by pharmacist-to-patient advertising. Those consequences flow from the adverse cumulative effects of multiple individual decisions each of which may seem perfectly reasonable considered on its own. The Government fears that, taken together, these apparently rational individual decisions will undermine the safety testing system, thereby producing overall a net balance of harm . . . Consequently, the Government leaves pharmacists free to explain through advertisements what compounding is, to advertise that they engage in compounding, and to advise patients to discuss the matter with their physicians. And it forbids advertising the specific drug in question, not because it fears the "information" the advertisement provides, but because it fears the systematic effect . . . of advertisements that will not fully explain the complicated risks at issue. And this latter fear is more than plausible.

I do not deny that the statute restricts the circulation of some truthful information. . . . Nonetheless, this Court has not previously held that commercial advertising restrictions automatically violate the First Amendment. Rather, the Court has applied a more flexible test. It has examined the restriction's proportionality, the relation between restriction and objective, the fit between ends and means. . . . It has done so because it has concluded that, from a constitutional perspective, commercial speech does not warrant application of the Court's strictest speech-protective tests. And it has reached this conclusion in part because restrictions on commercial speech do not often repress individual self-expression; they rarely interfere with the functioning of democratic political processes; and they often reflect a democratically determined governmental decision to regulate a commercial venture in order to protect, for example, the consumer, the public health, individual safety, or the environment. . . .

. . . The Court, in my view, gives insufficient weight to the Government's regulatory rationale, and too readily assumes the existence of practical alternatives. It thereby applies the commercial speech doctrine too strictly. . . .

. . . [A]n overly rigid "commercial speech" doctrine will transform what ought to be a legislative or regulatory decision about the best way to protect the health and safety of the American public into a constitutional decision prohibiting the legislature from enacting necessary protections. As history in respect to the Due Process Clause shows, any such transformation would involve a tragic constitutional misunderstanding. . . .

    . . .

CHAPTER 14

RESTRICTIONS ON TIME, PLACE, OR MANNER OF EXPRESSION

SECTION 3. SPEECH ON PRIVATE PREMISES

Page 1402. Replace City of Renton v. Playtime Theatres, Inc.:

City of Los Angeles v. Alameda Books, Inc.

535 U.S. 425, 122 S.Ct. 1728, 152 L.Ed.2d 670 (2002).

Justice O'Connor announced the judgment of the Court and delivered an opinion, in which The Chief Justice, Justice Scalia, and Justice Thomas join.

Los Angeles Municipal Code § 12.70(C) (1983), as amended, prohibits "the establishment or maintenance of more than one adult entertainment business in the same building, structure or portion thereof." Respondents, two adult establishments that each operated an adult bookstore and an adult video arcade in the same building, filed a suit ... alleging that § 12.70(C) violates the First Amendment and seeking declaratory and injunctive relief. The District Court granted summary judgment to respondents ... The Court of Appeals for the Ninth Circuit affirmed ... We reverse and remand. ...

I

In 1977, the city of Los Angeles conducted a comprehensive study of adult establishments and concluded that concentrations of adult businesses are associated with higher rates of prostitution, robbery, assaults, and thefts in surrounding communities. Accordingly, the city enacted an ordinance prohibiting the establishment, substantial enlargement, or transfer of ownership of an adult arcade, bookstore, cabaret, motel, theater, or massage parlor or a place for sexual encounters within 1,000 feet of another such enterprise or within 500 feet of any religious institution, school, or public park. See Los Angeles Municipal Code § 12.70(C) (1978).

There is evidence that the intent of the city council when enacting this prohibition was not only to disperse distinct adult establishments housed in separate buildings, but also to disperse distinct adult businesses operated under common ownership and housed in a single structure. The ordinance the city enacted, however, directed that "[t]he distance between any two adult entertainment businesses shall be measured in a straight line ... from the closest exterior structural wall of each business." ... Subsequent to enactment, the city realized that this method of calculating distances created a loophole permitting the concentration of multiple adult enterprises in a single structure.

Concerned that allowing an adult-oriented department store to replace a strip of adult establishments could defeat the goal of the original ordinance, the city council amended § 12.70(C) by adding a prohibition on "the establishment or maintenance of more than one adult entertainment business in the same building, structure or portion thereof." Los Angeles Municipal Code § 12.70(C) (1983). The amended ordinance defines an "Adult Entertainment Business" as an adult arcade, bookstore, cabaret, motel, theater, or massage parlor or a place for sexual encounters, and notes that each of these enterprises "shall constitute a separate adult entertainment business even if operated in conjunction with another adult entertainment business at the same establishment." . . .

. . . Although respondents are located in different buildings, each operates its retail sales and rental operations in the same commercial space in which its video booths are located. There are no physical distinctions between the different operations within each establishment and each establishment has only one entrance. . . .

. . .

II

In Renton v. Playtime Theatres, Inc., [475 U.S. 41 (1986)], this Court considered the validity of a municipal ordinance that prohibited any adult movie theater from locating within 1,000 feet of any residential zone, family dwelling, church, park, or school. Our analysis of the ordinance proceeded in three steps. First, we found that the ordinance did not ban adult theaters altogether, but merely required that they be distanced from certain sensitive locations. The ordinance was properly analyzed, therefore, as a time, place, and manner regulation. . . . We next considered whether the ordinance was content neutral or content based. If the regulation were content based, it would be considered presumptively invalid and subject to strict scrutiny. . . . We held, however, that the Renton ordinance was aimed not at the content of the films shown at adult theaters, but rather at the secondary effects of such theaters on the surrounding community, namely at crime rates, property values, and the quality of the city's neighborhoods. Therefore, the ordinance was deemed content neutral. . . . Finally, given this finding, we stated that the ordinance would be upheld so long as the city of Renton showed that its ordinance was designed to serve a substantial government interest and that reasonable alternative avenues of communication remained available. . . . We concluded that Renton had met this burden, and we upheld its ordinance. . . .

The Court of Appeals applied the same analysis to evaluate the Los Angeles ordinance challenged in this case. . . . It explained that, even if the Los Angeles ordinance were content neutral, the city had failed to demonstrate, as required by the third step of the *Renton* analysis, that its prohibition on multiple-use adult establishments was designed to serve its substantial interest in reducing crime. The Court of Appeals noted that the primary evidence relied upon by Los Angeles to demonstrate a link between combination adult businesses and harmful secondary effects was the 1977 study conducted by the city's planning department. The Court of Appeals found, however, that the city could not rely on that study because it did not "suppor[t] a reasonable belief that [the] combination [of] businesses ... produced harmful secondary effects of the type asserted.'' ...

. . .

The Court of Appeals found that the 1977 study did not reasonably support the inference that a concentration of adult operations within a single adult establishment produced greater levels of criminal activity because the study focused on the effect that a concentration of establishments—not a concentration of operations within a single establishment—had on crime rates. The Court of Appeals pointed out that the study treated combination adult bookstore/arcades as single establishments and did not study the effect of any separate-standing adult bookstore or arcade.

The Court of Appeals misunderstood the implications of the 1977 study. While the study reveals that areas with high concentrations of adult establishments are associated with high crime rates, areas with high concentrations of adult establishments are also areas with high concentrations of adult operations, albeit each in separate establishments. It ... is rational for the city to infer that reducing the concentration of adult operations in a neighborhood, whether within separate establishments or in one large establishment, will reduce crime rates.

. . .

The error that the Court of Appeals made is that it required the city to prove that its theory about a concentration of adult operations attracting crowds of customers, much like a minimall or department store does, is a necessary consequence of the 1977 study. ... The Court of Appeals simply replaced the city's theory—that having many different operations in close proximity attracts crowds—with its own—that the size of an operation attracts crowds. ... The Court of Appeals' analysis ... implicitly requires the city to prove that its theory is the only one that can plausibly explain the data because only in this manner can the city refute the Court of Appeals' logic.

. . .

In *Renton,* we specifically refused to set such a high bar for municipalities that want to address merely the secondary effects of protected speech. We held that a municipality may rely on any evidence that is ''reasonably believed to be relevant'' for demonstrating a connection between speech and a substantial, independent government interest. ... This is not to say that a municipality can get away with shoddy data or reasoning. The municipality's evidence must fairly support the municipality's rationale for its ordinance. If plaintiffs fail to cast direct doubt on this rationale, either by demonstrating that the municipality's evidence does not support its rationale or by furnishing evidence that disputes the municipality's factual findings, the municipality meets the standard set forth in *Renton.* If plaintiffs succeed in casting doubt on a municipality's rationale in either manner, the burden shifts back to the municipality to supplement the record with evidence renewing support for a theory that justifies its ordinance. ... This case is at a very early stage in this process. It arrives on a summary judgment motion by respondents defended only by complaints that the 1977 study fails to prove that the city's justification for its ordinance is necessarily correct. Therefore, we conclude that the city, at this stage of the litigation, has complied with the evidentiary requirement in *Renton*.

Justice Souter faults the city for relying on the 1977 study not because the study fails to support the city's theory that adult department stores, like adult minimalls, attract customers and thus crime, but because the city does not demonstrate that free-standing single-use adult establishments reduce crime. In effect, Justice Souter asks the city to demonstrate, not merely by appeal to common sense, but also with empirical data, that its ordinance will successfully lower crime. Our cases have never required that municipalities make such a showing, certainly not without actual and convincing evidence from plaintiffs to the contrary. ... A municipality considering an innovative solution may not have data that could demonstrate the efficacy of its proposal because the solution would, by definition, not have been implemented previously. The city's ordinance banning multiple-use adult establishments is such a solution. Respondents contend that there are no adult video arcades in Los Angeles County that operate independently of adult bookstores. But without such arcades, the city does not have a treatment group to compare with the control group of multiple-use adult establishments ...

Our deference to the evidence presented by the city of Los Angeles is the product of a careful balance between competing interests. ... We are also guided by the fact that *Renton* requires that municipal ordinances receive only intermediate scrutiny if they are content neutral. ... There is less reason to be concerned that municipalities will use these ordinances to discriminate against unpopular speech. ...

Justice Souter would have us rethink this balance, and indeed the entire *Renton* framework. In *Renton,* the Court distinguished the inquiry into whether a municipal ordinance is content neutral from the inquiry into whether it is "designed to serve a substantial government interest and do not unreasonably limit alternative avenues of communication." ... The former requires courts to verify that the "predominate concerns" motivating the ordinance "were with the secondary effects of adult [speech], and not with the content of adult [speech]." ... The latter inquiry goes one step further and asks whether the municipality can demonstrate a connection between the speech regulated by the ordinance and the secondary effects that motivated the adoption of the ordinance. Only at this stage did *Renton* contemplate that courts would examine evidence concerning regulated speech and secondary effects. ... Justice Souter would either merge these two inquiries or move the evidentiary analysis into the inquiry on content neutrality, and raise the evidentiary bar that a municipality must pass. ...

... Justice Souter does not clarify the sort of evidence upon which municipalities may rely to meet the evidentiary burden he would require. It is easy to say that courts must demand evidence when "common experiences" or "common assumptions" are incorrect, but it is difficult for courts to know ahead of time whether that condition is met. Municipalities will, in general, have greater experience with and understanding of the secondary effects that follow certain protected speech than will the courts. ... For this reason our cases require only that municipalities rely upon evidence that is "reasonably believed to be relevant" to the secondary effects that they seek to address.

III

. . .

... [R]espondents argue, as an alternative basis to sustain the Court of Appeals' judgment, that the Los Angeles ordinance is not a typical zoning regulation. Rather, respondents explain, the prohibition on multiuse adult establishments is effectively a ban on adult video arcades because no such business exists independently of an adult bookstore. Respondents request that the Court hold that the Los Angeles ordinance is not a time, place, and manner regulation, and that the Court subject the ordinance to strict scrutiny. This also appears to be the theme of Justice Kennedy's concurrence. ... We consider that ... as simply a reformulation of the requirement that an ordinance warrants intermediate scrutiny only if it is a time, place, and manner regulation and not a ban. The Court of Appeals held, however, that the city's prohibition on the combination of adult bookstores and arcades is not a ban and respondents did not petition for review of that determination.

. . .

Justice Scalia, concurring.

I join the plurality opinion because I think it represents a correct application of our jurisprudence concerning regulation of the "secondary effects" of pornographic speech. As I have said elsewhere, however, in a case such as this our First Amendment traditions make "secondary effects" analysis quite unnecessary. The Constitution does not prevent those communities that wish to do so from regulating, or indeed entirely suppressing, the business of pandering sex. ...

Justice Kennedy, concurring in the judgment.

Speech can produce tangible consequences. It can change minds. It can prompt actions. These primary effects signify the power and the necessity of free speech. Speech can also cause secondary effects, however, unrelated to the impact of the speech on its audience. A newspaper factory may cause pollution, and a billboard may obstruct a view. These secondary consequences are not always immune from regulation by zoning laws even though they are produced by speech.

Municipal governments know that high concentrations of adult businesses can damage the value and the integrity of a neighborhood. The damage is measurable; it is all too real. The law does not require a city to ignore these consequences if it uses its zoning power in a reasonable way to ameliorate them without suppressing speech. ...

... In my view our precedents may allow the city to impose its regulation in the exercise of the zoning authority. The city is not, at least, to be foreclosed by summary judgment, so I concur in the judgment.

This separate statement seems to me necessary, however, for two reasons. First, *Renton* ... described a similar ordinance as "content neutral," and I agree with the dissent that the designation is imprecise. Second, in my view, the plurality's application of *Renton* might constitute a subtle expansion, with which I do not concur.

I

In *Renton*, the Court determined that while the material inside adult bookstores and movie theaters is speech, the consequent sordidness outside is not. The challenge is to correct the latter while leaving the former, as far as possible, untouched. If a city can decrease the crime and blight associated with certain speech by the traditional exercise of its zoning power, and at the same time leave the quantity and accessibility of the speech substantially undiminished, there is no First Amendment objection. This is so even if the measure identifies the problem outside by reference to the speech inside—that is, even if the measure is in that sense content based.

On the other hand, a city may not regulate the secondary effects of speech by suppressing the speech itself. . . . Though the inference may be inexorable that a city could reduce secondary effects by reducing speech, this is not a permissible strategy. The purpose and effect of a zoning ordinance must be to reduce secondary effects and not to reduce speech.

A zoning measure can be consistent with the First Amendment if it is likely to cause a significant decrease in secondary effects and a trivial decrease in the quantity of speech. It is well documented that multiple adult businesses in close proximity may change the character of a neighborhood for the worse. Those same businesses spread across the city may not have the same deleterious effects. At least in theory, a dispersal ordinance causes these businesses to separate rather than to close, so negative externalities are diminished but speech is not.

The calculus is a familiar one to city planners, for many enterprises other than adult businesses also cause undesirable externalities. . . .

. . . If the validity of the legislative classification for zoning purposes be fairly debatable, the legislative judgment must be allowed to control.

True, the First Amendment protects speech and not slaughterhouses. But in both contexts, the inference of impermissible discrimination is not strong. An equally strong inference is that the ordinance is targeted not at the activity, but at its side effects. If a zoning ordinance is directed to the secondary effects of adult speech, the ordinance does not necessarily constitute impermissible content discrimination. A zoning law need not be blind to the secondary effects of adult speech, so long as the purpose of the law is not to suppress it.

The ordinance at issue in this case is not limited to expressive activities. It also extends, for example, to massage parlors, which the city has found to cause similar secondary effects. . . . This ordinance, moreover, is just one part of an elaborate web of land-use regulations in Los Angeles, all of which are intended to promote the social value of the land as a whole without suppressing some activities or favoring others. . . . All this further suggests that the ordinance is more in the nature of a typical land-use restriction and less in the nature of a law suppressing speech.

For these reasons, the ordinance is not so suspect that we must employ the usual rigorous analysis that content-based laws demand in other instances. The ordinance may be a covert attack on speech, but we should not presume it to be so. In the language of our First Amendment doctrine it calls for intermediate and not strict scrutiny, as we held in *Renton*.

II

In *Renton,* the Court began by noting that a zoning ordinance is a time, place, or manner restriction. The Court then proceeded to consider the question whether the ordinance was "content based." The ordinance "by its terms [was] designed to prevent crime, protect the city's retail trade, maintain property values, and generally protec[t] and preserv[e] the quality of [the city's] neighborhoods, commercial districts, and the quality of urban life, not to suppress the expression of unpopular views." On this premise, the Court designated the restriction "content neutral." . . .

The Court appeared to recognize, however, that the designation was something of a fiction, which, perhaps, is why it kept the phrase in quotes. After all, whether a statute is content neutral or content based is something that can be determined on the face of it; if the statute describes speech by content then it is content based. And the ordinance in *Renton* "treat[ed] theaters that specialize in adult films differently from other kinds of theaters." . . . The fiction that this sort of ordinance is content neutral—or "content neutral"—is perhaps more confusing than helpful . . . These ordinances are content based and we should call them so.

Nevertheless, for the reasons discussed above, the central holding of *Renton* is sound: A zoning restriction that is designed to decrease secondary effects and not speech should be subject to intermediate rather than strict scrutiny. . . . As a matter of common experience, these sorts of ordinances are more like a zoning restriction on slaughterhouses and less like a tax on unpopular newspapers. The zoning context provides a built-in legitimate rationale, which rebuts the usual presumption that content-based restrictions are unconstitutional. For this reason, we apply intermediate rather than strict scrutiny.

III

The narrow question presented in this case is whether the ordinance at issue is invalid "because the city did not study the negative effects of such combinations of adult businesses, but rather relied on judicially approved statutory precedent from other jurisdictions." This question is actually two questions. First, what proposition does a city need to advance in order to sustain a secondary-effects ordinance? Second, how much evidence is required to support the proposition? The plurality skips to the second question and gives the correct answer; but in my view more attention must be given to the first.

. . . [A] city must advance some basis to show that its regulation has the purpose and effect of suppressing secondary effects, while leaving the quantity and accessibility of speech substantially intact. . . . A city may not assert that it will reduce secondary effects by reducing speech in the same proportion. On this point, I agree with Justice Souter. The rationale of the ordinance must be that it will suppress secondary effects—and not by suppressing speech.

. . .

. . . [I]t does not suffice to say that inconvenience will reduce demand and fewer patrons will lead to fewer secondary effects. . . . It is no trick to reduce secondary effects by reducing speech or its audience; but a city may not attack secondary effects indirectly by attacking speech.

The analysis requires a few more steps. If two adult businesses are under the same roof, an ordinance requiring them to separate will have one of two results: One business will either move elsewhere or close. The city's premise cannot be the latter. . . .

. . . The claim, therefore, must be that this ordinance will cause two businesses to split rather than one to close, that the quantity of speech will be substantially undiminished, and that total secondary effects will be significantly reduced. This must be the rationale of a dispersal statute.

Only after identifying the proposition to be proved can we ask the second part of the question presented: is there sufficient evidence to support the proposition? As to this, we have consistently held that a city must have latitude to experiment, at least at the outset, and that very little evidence is required. . . . As a general matter, courts should not be in the business of second-guessing fact-bound empirical assessments of city planners. . . . The Los Angeles City Council knows the streets of Los Angeles better than we do. . . . It is entitled to rely on that knowledge; and if its inferences appear reasonable, we should not say there is no basis for its conclusion.

In this case the proposition to be shown is supported by a single study and common experience. The city's study shows a correlation between the concentration of adult establishments and crime. . . . This original ordinance is not challenged here, and we may assume that it is constitutional.

If we assume that the study supports the original ordinance, then most of the necessary analysis follows. We may posit that two adult stores next door to each other attract 100 patrons per day. The two businesses split apart might attract 49 patrons each. (Two patrons, perhaps, will be discouraged by the inconvenience of the separation—a relatively small cost to speech.) On the other hand, the reduction in secondary effects might be dramatic, because secondary effects may require a critical mass. Depending on the economics of vice, 100 potential customers/victims might attract a coterie of thieves, prostitutes, and other ne'er-do-wells; yet 49 might attract none at all. If so, a dispersal ordinance would cause a great reduction in secondary effects at very small cost to speech. Indeed, the very absence of secondary effects might increase the audience for the speech; perhaps for every two people who are discouraged by the inconvenience of two-stop shopping, another two are encouraged by hospitable surroundings. In that case, secondary effects might be eliminated at no cost to speech whatsoever, and both the city and the speaker will have their interests well served.

Only one small step remains to justify the ordinance at issue in this case. The city may next infer—from its study and from its own experience—that two adult businesses under the same roof are no better than two next door. The city could reach the reasonable conclusion that knocking down the wall between two adult businesses does not ameliorate any undesirable secondary effects of their proximity to one another. If the city's first ordinance was justified, therefore, then the second is too. Dispersing two adult businesses under one roof is reasonably likely to cause a substantial reduction in secondary effects while reducing speech very little.

IV

. . . [T]his ordinance . . . might not withstand intermediate scrutiny. The ordinance does, however, survive the summary judgment motion that the Court of Appeals ordered granted in this case.

Justice Souter, with whom Justice Stevens and Justice Ginsburg join, and with whom Justice Breyer joins as to Part II, dissenting.

. . . I assume that the ordinance was constitutional when adopted, . . . and assume for purposes of this case that the original ordinance remains valid today.

. . .

From a policy of dispersing adult establishments, the city has thus moved to a policy of dividing them in two. The justification claimed for this application of the new policy remains, however, the 1977 survey, . . . and the 1977 survey provides no support for the breakup policy. Its evidentiary insufficiency bears emphasis and is the principal reason that I respectfully dissent from the Court's judgment today.

I

This ordinance stands or falls on the results of what our cases speak of as intermediate scrutiny, generally contrasted with the demanding standard applied under the First Amendment to a content-based regulation of expression. . . .

. . . [S]trict scrutiny leaves few survivors.

The comparatively softer intermediate scrutiny is reserved for regulations justified by something other than content of the message, such as a straightforward restriction going only to the time, place, or manner of speech or other expression. . . .

Although this type of land-use restriction has even been called a variety of time, place, or manner regulation, . . . equating a secondary-effects zoning regulation with a mere regulation of time, place, or manner jumps over an important difference between them. A restriction on loudspeakers has no obvious relationship to the substance of what is broadcast, while a zoning regulation of businesses in adult expression just as obviously does. And while it may be true that an adult business is burdened only because of its secondary effects, it is clearly burdened only if its expressive products have adult content. Thus, the Court has recognized that this kind of regulation, though called content neutral, occupies a kind of limbo between full-blown, content-based restrictions and regulations that apply without any reference to the substance of what is said. . . .

It would in fact make sense to give this kind of zoning regulation a First Amendment label of its own, and if we called it content correlated, we would not only describe it for what it is, but keep alert to a risk of content-based regulation that it poses. The risk lies in the fact that when a law applies selectively only to speech of particular content, the more precisely the content is identified, the greater is the opportunity for government censorship. Adult speech refers not merely to sexually explicit content, but to speech reflecting a favorable view of being explicit about sex and a favorable view of the practices it depicts; a restriction on adult content is thus also a restriction turning on a particular viewpoint, of which the government may disapprove.

This risk of viewpoint discrimination is subject to a relatively simple safeguard, however. If combating secondary effects of property devaluation and crime is truly the reason for the regulation, it is possible to show by empirical evidence that the effects exist, that they are caused by the expressive activity subject to the zoning, and that the zoning can be expected either to ameliorate them or to enhance the capacity of the government to combat them (say, by concentrating them in one area), without suppressing the expressive activity itself. This capacity of zoning regulation to address the practical problems without eliminating the speech is, after all, the only possible excuse for speaking of secondary-effects zoning as akin to time, place, or manner regulations.

In examining claims that there are causal relationships between adult businesses and an increase in secondary effects (distinct from disagreement), and between zoning and the mitigation of the effects, stress needs to be placed on the empirical character of the demonstration available. . . . The weaker the demonstration of facts distinct from disapproval of the "adult" viewpoint, the greater the likelihood that nothing more than condemnation of the viewpoint drives the regulation.

Equal stress should be placed on the point that requiring empirical justification of claims about property value or crime is not demanding anything Herculean. Increased crime, like prostitution and muggings, and declining property values in areas surrounding adult businesses, are all readily observable, often to the untrained eye and certainly to the police officer and urban planner. These harms can be shown by police reports, crime statistics, and studies of market value, all of which are within a municipality's capacity or available from the distilled experiences of comparable communities. . . .

And precisely because this sort of evidence is readily available, reviewing courts need to be wary when the government appeals, not to evidence, but to an uncritical common sense in an effort to justify such a zoning restriction. It is not that common sense is always illegitimate in First Amendment demonstration. The need for independent proof varies with the point that has to be established, and zoning can be supported by common experience when there is no reason to question it. . . . It has become a commonplace, based on our own cases, that concentrating adult establishments drives down the value of neighboring property used for other purposes. . . . In fact, however, the city found that general assumption unjustified by its 1977 study.

. . . In this case, however, the government has not shown that bookstores containing viewing booths, isolated from other adult establishments, increase crime or produce other negative secondary effects in surrounding neighborhoods, and we are thus left without substantial justification for viewing the city's First Amendment restriction as content correlated but not simply content based. By the same token, the city has failed to show any causal relationship between the breakup policy and elimination or regulation of secondary effects.

II

. . .

. . . My concern is not with the assumption behind the [1983] amendment itself, that a conglomeration of adult businesses under one roof, as in a minimall or adult department store, will produce undesirable secondary effects comparable to what a cluster of separate adult establishments brings about. That may or may not be so. The assumption that is clearly unsupported, however, goes to the city's supposed interest in applying the amendment to the book and video stores in question, and in applying it to break them up. The city, of course, claims no interest in the proliferation of adult establishments, the ostensible consequence of splitting the sales and viewing activities so as to produce two stores where once there was one. Nor does the city assert any interest in limiting the sale of adult expressive material as such, or reducing the number of adult video booths in the city, for that would be clear content-based regulation, and the city was careful in its 1977 report to disclaim any such intent.

Rather, the city apparently assumes that a bookstore selling videos and providing viewing booths produces secondary effects of crime, and more crime than would result from having a single store without booths in one part of town and a video arcade in another. But the city neither says this in so many words nor proffers any evidence to support even the simple proposition that an otherwise lawfully located adult bookstore combined with video booths will produce any criminal effects. The Los Angeles study treats such combined stores as one, and draws no general conclusion that individual stores spread apart from other adult establishments (as under the basic Los Angeles ordinance) are associated with any degree of criminal activity above the general norm; nor has the city called the Court's attention to any other empirical study, or even anecdotal police evidence, that supports the city's assumption. In fact, if the Los Angeles study sheds any light whatever on the city's position, it is the light of skepticism, for we may fairly suspect that the study said nothing about the secondary effects of freestanding stores because no effects were observed. The reasonable supposition, then, is that splitting some of them up will have no consequence for secondary effects whatever.

. . . The bookstores involved here are not concentrations of traditionally separate adult businesses that have been studied and shown to have an association with secondary effects, and they exemplify no new form of concentration like a mall under one roof. They are combinations of selling and viewing activities that have commonly been combined, and . . . no study conducted by the city has reported that this type of traditional business, any more than any other adult business, has a correlation with secondary effects in the absence of concentration with other adult establishments in the neighborhood. . . .

. . . [In *Renton,* the] limitations on location required no further support than the factual basis tying location to secondary effects; the zoning approved . . . had no effect on the way the owners of the stores carried on their adult businesses beyond controlling location, and no heavier burden than the location limit was approved by this Court.

The Los Angeles ordinance, however, does impose a heavier burden, and one lacking any demonstrable connection to the interest in crime control. . . . [T]he government's freedom of experimentation cannot displace its burden under the intermediate scrutiny standard to show that the restriction on speech is no greater than essential to realizing an important objective, in this case policing crime. Since we cannot make even a best guess that the city's breakup policy will have any effect on crime or law enforcement, we are a very far cry from any assurance against covert content-based regulation.

And concern with content-based regulation targeting a viewpoint is right to the point here, as witness a fact that involves no guesswork. . . .[T]wo establishments in place of one will entail two business overheads in place of one: two monthly rents, two electricity bills, two payrolls. Every month business will be more expensive than it used to be, perhaps even twice as much. That sounds like a good strategy for driving out expressive adult businesses. It sounds, in other words, like a policy of content-based regulation.

I respectfully dissent.

SECTION 5. GOVERNMENT SUBSIDIES TO SPEECH

Page 1436. Add at end of chapter:

Legal Services Corporation v. Velazquez

531 U.S. 533, 121 S.Ct. 1043, 149 L.Ed.2d 63 (2001).

Justice Kennedy delivered the opinion of the Court.

In 1974, Congress enacted the Legal Services Corporation Act, . . . establish[ing] the Legal Services Corporation (LSC) as a District of Columbia nonprofit corporation. LSC's mission is to distribute funds appropriated by Congress to eligible local grantee organizations "for the purpose of providing financial support for legal assistance in noncriminal proceedings or matters to persons financially unable to afford legal assistance." . . .

. . . In many instances the grantees are funded by a combination of LSC funds and other public or private sources. The grantee organizations hire and supervise lawyers to provide free legal assistance to indigent clients. . . .

This suit requires us to decide whether one of the conditions imposed by Congress on the use of LSC funds violates the First Amendment rights of LSC grantees and their clients. . . . [T]he restriction . . . prohibits legal representation funded by recipients of LSC moneys if the representation involves an effort to amend or otherwise challenge existing welfare law. As interpreted by the LSC and by the Government, the restriction prevents an attorney from arguing to a court that a state statute conflicts with a federal statute or that either a state or federal statute by its terms or in its application is violative of the United States Constitution.

Lawyers employed by New York City LSC grantees, together with private LSC contributors, LSC indigent clients, and various state and local public officials whose governments contribute to LSC grantees, brought suit in the United States District Court for the Southern District of New York to declare the restriction . . . invalid. The United States Court of Appeals for the Second Circuit approved an injunction against enforcement of the provision as an impermissible viewpoint-based discrimination in violation of the First Amendment,. . . . We agree that the restriction violates the First Amendment, and we affirm the judgment of the Court of Appeals.

I

From the inception of the LSC, Congress has placed restrictions on its use of funds. For instance, the LSC Act prohibits recipients from making available LSC funds, program personnel, or equipment to any political party, to any political campaign, or for use in "advocating or opposing any ballot measures." . . . The Act further proscribes use of funds in most criminal proceedings and in litigation involving nontherapeutic abortions, secondary school desegregation, military desertion, or violations of the Selective Service statute. . . . Fund recipients are barred from bringing class-action suits unless express approval is obtained from LSC. . . .

The restrictions at issue were part of a compromise set of restrictions enacted in the Omnibus Consolidated Rescissions and Appropriations Act of 1996 . . . The relevant portion of § 504(a)(16) prohibits funding of any organization

> "that initiates legal representation or participates in any other way, in litigation, lobbying, or rulemaking, involving an effort to reform a Federal or State welfare system, except that this paragraph shall not be construed to preclude a recipient from representing an individual eligible client who is seeking specific relief from a welfare agency if such relief does not involve an effort to amend or otherwise challenge existing law in effect on the date of the initiation of the representation."

The prohibitions apply to all of the activities of an LSC grantee, including those paid for by non-LSC funds. . . . We are concerned with the statutory provision which excludes LSC representation in cases which "involve an effort to amend or otherwise challenge existing law in effect on the date of the initiation of the representation."

In 1997, LSC adopted final regulations clarifying § 504(a)(16). . . . LSC interpreted the statutory provision to allow indigent clients to challenge welfare agency determinations of benefit ineligibility under interpretations of existing law. For example, an LSC grantee could represent a welfare claimant who argued that an agency made an erroneous factual determination or that an agency misread or misapplied a term contained in an existing welfare statute. According to LSC, a grantee in that position could argue as well that an agency policy violated existing law. . . . Under LSC's interpretation, however, grantees could not accept representations designed to change welfare laws, much less argue against the constitutionality or statutory validity of those laws. Even in cases where constitutional or statutory challenges became apparent after representation was well under way, LSC advised that its attorneys must withdraw. . . .

. . .

II

The United States and LSC rely on Rust v. Sullivan, 500 U.S. 173 (1991), as support for the LSC program restrictions. In *Rust*, Congress established program clinics to provide subsidies for doctors to advise patients on a variety of family planning topics. Congress did not consider abortion to be within its family planning objectives, however, and it forbade doctors employed by the program from discussing abortion with their patients. . . .

We upheld the law, reasoning that Congress had not discriminated against viewpoints on abortion, but had "merely chosen to fund one activity to the exclusion of the other." . . . The restrictions were considered necessary "to ensure that the limits of the federal program [were] observed." . . . Title X did not single out a particular idea for suppression because it was dangerous or disfavored; rather, Congress prohibited Title X doctors from counseling that was outside the scope of the project. . . .

The Court in *Rust* did not place explicit reliance on the rationale that the counseling activities of the doctors under Title X amounted to governmental speech; when interpreting the holding in later cases, however, we have explained *Rust* on this understanding. We have said that viewpoint-based funding decisions can be sustained in instances in which the government is itself the speaker, . . . or instances, like *Rust*, in which the government "used private speakers to transmit information pertaining to its own program." . . . As we said in Rosenberger [v. Rector & Visitors of Univ. of Va., 515 U.S. 819 (1995)], "[w]hen the government disburses public funds to private entities to convey a governmental message, it may take legitimate and appropriate steps to ensure that its message is neither garbled nor distorted by the grantee." . . . The latitude which may exist for restrictions on speech where the government's own message is being delivered flows in part from our observation that, "[w]hen the government speaks, for instance to promote its own policies or to advance a particular idea, it is, in the end, accountable to the electorate and the political process for its advocacy. If the citizenry objects, newly elected officials later could espouse some different or contrary position." Board of Regents of Univ. of Wis. System v. Southworth, [529 U.S. 217 (2000)].

Neither the latitude for government speech nor its rationale applies to subsidies for private speech in every instance, however. As we have pointed out, "[i]t does not follow . . . that viewpoint-based restrictions are proper when the [government] does not itself speak or subsidize transmittal of a message it favors but instead expends funds to encourage a diversity of views from private speakers." *Rosenberger* . . .

Although the LSC program differs from the program at issue in *Rosenberger* in that its purpose is not to "encourage a diversity of views," the salient point is that, like the program in *Rosenberger*, the LSC program was designed to facilitate private speech, not to promote a governmental message. . . . In . . . suits for benefits, an LSC-funded attorney speaks on the behalf of the client in a claim against the government for welfare benefits. The lawyer is not the government's speaker. The attorney defending the decision to deny benefits will deliver the government's message in the litigation. The LSC lawyer, however, speaks on the behalf of his or her private, indigent client. . . .

. . . The advice from the attorney to the client and the advocacy by the attorney to the courts cannot be classified as governmental speech even under a generous understanding of the concept. In this vital respect this suit is distinguishable from *Rust*.

The private nature of the speech involved here, and the extent of LSC's regulation of private expression, are indicated further by the circumstance that the Government seeks to use an existing medium of expression and to control it, in a class of cases, in ways which distort its usual functioning. Where the government uses or attempts to regulate a particular medium, we have been informed by its accepted usage in determining whether a particular restriction on speech is necessary for the program's purposes and limitations. In FCC v. League of Women Voters of Cal., 468 U.S. 364 (1984), the Court was instructed by its understanding of the dynamics of the broadcast industry in holding that prohibitions against editorializing by public radio networks were an impermissible restriction, even though the Government enacted the restriction to control the use of public funds. The First Amendment forbade the Government from using the forum in an unconventional way to suppress speech inherent in the nature of the medium. ... In Arkansas Ed. Television Comm'n v. Forbes, 523 U.S. 666 (1998), the dynamics of the broadcasting system gave station programmers the right to use editorial judgment to exclude certain speech so that the broadcast message could be more effective. And in *Rosenberger*, the fact that student newspapers expressed many different points of view was an important foundation for the Court's decision to invalidate viewpoint-based restrictions. . . .

When the government creates a limited forum for speech, certain restrictions may be necessary to define the limits and purposes of the program. ... The same is true when the government establishes a subsidy for specified ends. ... As this suit involves a subsidy, limited forum cases ... may not be controlling in a strict sense, yet they do provide some instruction. Here the program presumes that private, nongovernmental speech is necessary, and a substantial restriction is placed upon that speech. ... [L]awyers funded in the Government program may not undertake representation in suits for benefits if they must advise clients respecting the questionable validity of a statute which defines benefit eligibility and the payment structure. The limitation forecloses advice or legal assistance to question the validity of statutes under the Constitution of the United States. It extends further, it must be noted, so that state statutes inconsistent with federal law under the Supremacy Clause may be neither challenged nor questioned.

... Restricting LSC attorneys in advising their clients and in presenting arguments and analyses to the courts distorts the legal system by altering the traditional role of the attorneys ... Just as government ... could not elect to use a broadcasting network or a college publication structure in a regime which prohibits speech necessary to the proper functioning of those systems, ... it may not design a subsidy to effect this serious and fundamental restriction on advocacy of attorneys and the functioning of the judiciary.

. . .

Interpretation of the law and the Constitution is the primary mission of the judiciary when it acts within the sphere of its authority to resolve a case or controversy. Marbury v. Madison, 1 Cranch 137 (1803) ("It is emphatically the province and the duty of the judicial department to say what the law is"). An informed, independent judiciary presumes an informed, independent bar. Under § 504(a)(16), however, cases would be presented by LSC attorneys who could not advise the courts of serious questions of statutory validity. The disability is inconsistent with the proposition that attorneys should present all the reasonable and well-grounded arguments necessary for proper resolution of the case. By seeking to prohibit the analysis of certain legal issues and to truncate presentation to the courts, the enactment under review prohibits speech and expression upon which courts must depend for the proper exercise of the judicial power. . . .

The restriction imposed by the statute here threatens severe impairment of the judicial function. Section 504(a)(16) sifts out cases presenting constitutional challenges in order to insulate the Government's laws from judicial inquiry. If the restriction on speech and legal advice were to stand, the result would be two tiers of cases. In cases where LSC counsel were attorneys of record, there would be lingering doubt whether the truncated representation had resulted in complete analysis of the case, full advice to the client, and proper presentation to the court. The courts and the public would come to question the adequacy and fairness of professional representations when the attorney, either consciously to comply with this statute or unconsciously to continue the representation despite the statute, avoided all reference to questions of statutory validity and constitutional authority. A scheme so inconsistent with accepted separation-of-powers principles is an insufficient basis to sustain or uphold the restriction on speech.

It is no answer to say the restriction on speech is harmless because, under LSC's interpretation of the Act, its attorneys can withdraw. This misses the point. The statute is an attempt to draw lines around the LSC program to exclude from litigation those arguments and theories Congress finds unacceptable but which by their nature are within the province of the courts to consider.

The restriction on speech is even more problematic because in cases where the attorney withdraws from a representation, the client is unlikely to find other counsel. . . . Thus, with respect to the litigation services Congress has funded, there is no alternative channel for expression of the advocacy Congress seeks to restrict. This is in stark contrast to *Rust*. There, a patient could receive the approved Title X family planning counseling funded by the Government and later could consult an affiliate or independent organization to receive abortion counseling. Unlike indigent clients who seek LSC representation, the patient in *Rust* was not required to forfeit the Government-funded advice when she also received abortion counseling through alternative channels. Because LSC attorneys must withdraw whenever a question of a welfare statute's validity arises, an individual could not obtain joint representation so that the constitutional challenge would be presented by a non-LSC attorney, and other, permitted, arguments advanced by LSC counsel.

Finally, LSC and the Government maintain that § 504(a)(16) is necessary to define the scope and contours of the federal program, a condition that ensures funds can be spent for those cases most immediate to congressional concern. In support of this contention, they suggest the challenged limitation takes into account the nature of the grantees' activities and provides limited congressional funds for the provision of simple suits for benefits. In petitioners' view, the restriction operates neither to maintain the current welfare system nor insulate it from attack; rather, it helps the current welfare system function in a more efficient and fair manner by removing from the program complex challenges to existing welfare laws.

The effect of the restriction, however, is to prohibit advice or argumentation that existing welfare laws are unconstitutional or unlawful. Congress cannot recast a condition on funding as a mere definition of its program in every case, lest the First Amendment be reduced to a simple semantic exercise. Here, notwithstanding Congress' purpose to confine and limit its program, the restriction operates to insulate current welfare laws from constitutional scrutiny and certain other legal challenges, a condition implicating central First Amendment concerns. In no lawsuit funded by the Government can the LSC attorney, speaking on behalf of a private client, challenge existing welfare laws. As a result, arguments by indigent clients that a welfare statute is unlawful or unconstitutional cannot be expressed in this Government-funded program for petitioning the courts, even though the program was created for litigation involving welfare benefits, and even though the ordinary course of litigation involves the expression of theories and postulates on both, or multiple, sides of an issue.

... There can be little doubt that the LSC Act funds constitutionally protected expression; and in the context of this statute there is no programmatic message of the kind recognized in *Rust* and which sufficed there to allow the Government to specify the advice deemed necessary for its legitimate objectives. This serves to distinguish § 504(a)(16) from any of the Title X program restrictions upheld in *Rust*, and to place it beyond any congressional funding condition approved in the past by this Court.

Congress was not required to fund an LSC attorney to represent indigent clients; and when it did so, it was not required to fund the whole range of legal representations or relationships. The LSC and the United States, however, in effect ask us to permit Congress to define the scope of the litigation it funds to exclude certain vital theories and ideas. The attempted restriction is designed to insulate the Government's interpretation of the Constitution from judicial challenge. The Constitution does not permit the Government to confine litigants and their attorneys in this manner. We must be vigilant when Congress imposes rules and conditions which in effect insulate its own laws from legitimate judicial challenge. Where private speech is involved, even Congress' antecedent funding decision cannot be aimed at the suppression of ideas thought inimical to the Government's own interest. ...

For the reasons we have set forth, the funding condition is invalid. ...

The judgment of the Court of Appeals is

Affirmed.

Justice Scalia, with whom the Chief Justice, Justice O'Connor, and Justice Thomas join, dissenting.

Section 504(a)(16) ... defines the scope of a federal spending program. It does not directly regulate speech, and it neither establishes a public forum nor discriminates on the basis of viewpoint. The Court agrees with all this, yet applies a novel and unsupportable interpretation of our public-forum precedents to declare § 504(a)(16) facially unconstitutional. This holding not only has no foundation in our jurisprudence; it is flatly contradicted by a recent decision that is on all fours with the present case. ...

I

. . .

... Section 504(a)(16) ... withholds LSC funds from every entity that "participates in any ... way ... in litigation, lobbying, or rulemaking ... involving an effort to reform a Federal or State welfare system." It thus bans LSC-funded entities from participating on either side of litigation involving such statutes, from participating in rulemaking relating to the implementation of such legislation, and from lobbying Congress itself regarding any proposed changes to such legislation. ...

The restrictions relating to rulemaking and lobbying ... duplicate general prohibitions on the use of LSC funds for those activities found elsewhere in the Appropriations Act. ... The restriction on litigation, however, is unique, and it contains a proviso specifying what the restriction does not cover. Funding recipients may "represen[t] an individual eligible client who is seeking specific relief from a welfare agency if such relief does not involve an effort to amend or otherwise challenge existing law in effect on the date of the initiation of the representation." The ... LSC can sponsor neither challenges to nor defenses of existing welfare reform law. The litigation ban is symmetrical: Litigants challenging the covered statutes or regulations do not receive LSC funding, and neither do litigants defending those laws against challenge.

If a suit for benefits raises a claim outside the scope of the LSC program, the LSC-funded lawyer may not participate in the suit. ...

II

The LSC Act is a federal subsidy program, not a federal regulatory program. ... Regulations directly restrict speech; subsidies do not. Subsidies, it is true, may indirectly abridge speech, but only if the funding scheme is " 'manipulated' to have a 'coercive effect' " on those who do not hold the subsidized position. ... Proving unconstitutional coercion is difficult enough when the spending program has universal coverage and excludes only certain speech—such as a tax exemption scheme excluding lobbying expenses. The Court has found such programs unconstitutional only when the exclusion was "aimed at the suppression of dangerous ideas." ... The Court has found such selective spending unconstitutionally coercive only once, when the government created a public forum with the spending program but then discriminated in distributing funding within the forum on the basis of viewpoint. See Rosenberger v. Rector and Visitors of Univ. of Va. ... When the limited spending program does not create a public forum, proving coercion is virtually impossible, because simply denying a subsidy "does not 'coerce' belief," ...

In Rust v. Sullivan, ... the Court applied these principles to a statutory scheme that is in all relevant respects indistinguishable from § 504(a)(16). ... We rejected a First Amendment free-speech challenge to the funding scheme, explaining that "[t]he Government can, without violating the Constitution, selectively fund a program to encourage certain activities it believes to be in the public interest, without at the same time funding an alternative program which seeks to deal with the problem another way." ... This was not, we said, the type of "discriminat[ion] on the basis of viewpoint" that triggers strict scrutiny, ... because the " 'decision not to subsidize the exercise of a fundamental right does not infringe the right,' " ...

The same is true here. The LSC Act, like the scheme in *Rust*, ... does not create a public forum. Far from encouraging a diversity of views, it has always, as the Court accurately states, "placed restrictions on its use of funds," ... Nor does § 504(a)(16) discriminate on the basis of viewpoint, since it funds neither challenges to nor defenses of existing welfare law. The provision simply declines to subsidize a certain class of litigation, and under *Rust* that decision "does not infringe the right" to bring such litigation. ... No litigant who, in the absence of LSC funding, would bring a suit challenging existing welfare law is deterred from doing so by § 504(a)(16). *Rust* thus controls these cases and compels the conclusion that § 504(a)(16) is constitutional.

The Court contends that *Rust* is different because the program at issue subsidized government speech, while the LSC funds private speech. ... If the private doctors' confidential advice to their patients at issue in *Rust* constituted "government speech," it is hard to imagine what subsidized speech would not be government speech. Moreover, the majority's contention that the subsidized speech in these cases is not government speech because the lawyers have a professional obligation to represent the interests of their clients founders on the reality that the doctors in *Rust* had a professional obligation to serve the interests of their patients ...

The Court further asserts that these cases are different from *Rust* because the welfare funding restriction "seeks to use an existing medium of expression and to control it ... in ways which distort its usual functioning." This is wrong on both the facts and the law. It is wrong on the law because there is utterly no precedent for the novel and facially implausible proposition that the First Amendment has anything to do with government funding that—though it does not actually abridge anyone's speech—"distorts an existing medium of expression." ...

The Court's "nondistortion" principle is also wrong on the facts, since there is no basis for believing that § 504(a)(16), ... will distort the operation of the courts. It may well be that the bar of § 504(a)(16) will cause LSC-funded attorneys to decline or to withdraw from cases that involve statutory validity. But that means at most that fewer statutory challenges to welfare laws will be presented to the courts because of the unavailability of free legal services for that purpose. So what? The same result would ensue from excluding LSC-funded lawyers from welfare litigation entirely. It is not the mandated, nondistortable function of the courts to inquire into all "serious questions of statutory validity" in all cases. Courts must consider only those questions of statutory validity that are presented by litigants, and if the Government chooses not to subsidize the presentation of some such questions, that in no way "distorts" the courts' role. ...

Nor will the judicial opinions produced by LSC cases systematically distort the interpretation of welfare laws. Judicial decisions do not stand as binding "precedent" for points that were not raised, not argued, and hence not analyzed. ... The statutory validity that courts assume in LSC cases will remain open for full determination in later cases.

Finally, the Court is troubled "because in cases where the attorney withdraws from a representation, the client is unlikely to find other counsel." That is surely irrelevant, since it leaves the welfare recipient in no worse condition than he would have been in had the LSC program never been enacted. Respondents properly concede that even if welfare claimants cannot obtain a lawyer anywhere else, the Government is not required to provide one.

. . .

The only conceivable argument that can be made for distinguishing *Rust* is that there even patients who wished to receive abortion counseling could receive the nonabortion services that the Government-funded clinic offered, whereas here some potential LSC clients who wish to receive representation on a benefits claim that does not challenge the statutes will be unable to do so because their cases raise a reform claim that an LSC lawyer may not present. This difference, of course, is required by the same ethical canons that the Court elsewhere does not wish to distort. Rather than sponsor "truncated representation," Congress chose to subsidize only those cases in which the attorneys it subsidized could work freely. . . . And it is impossible to see how this difference from *Rust* has any bearing upon the First Amendment question, which . . . is whether the funding scheme is " 'manipulated' to have a 'coercive effect' " . . . It could be claimed to have such an effect if the client in a case ineligible for LSC representation could eliminate the ineligibility by waiving the claim that the statute is invalid; but he cannot. No conceivable coercive effect exists.

This has been a very long discussion to make a point that is embarrassingly simple: The LSC subsidy neither prevents anyone from speaking nor coerces anyone to change speech, and is indistinguishable in all relevant respects from the subsidy upheld in Rust v. Sullivan. . . .

. . .

. . . The Court's decision displays not only an improper special solicitude for our own profession; it also displays, I think, the very fondness for "reform through the courts"—the making of innumerable social judgments through judge-pronounced constitutional imperatives—that prompted Congress to restrict publicly funded litigation of this sort. . . . I respectfully dissent.

United States v. American Library Association, Inc.

___ U.S. ___, 123 S.Ct. 2297, ___ L.Ed.2d ___ (2003).

Chief Justice Rehnquist announced the judgment of the Court and delivered an opinion, in which Justice O'Connor, Justice Scalia, and Justice Thomas joined.

. . . Under [the Children's Internet Protection Act (CIPA)], a public library may not receive federal assistance to provide Internet access unless it installs software to block images that constitute obscenity or child pornography, and to prevent minors from obtaining access to material that is harmful to them. The District Court held these provisions facially invalid on the ground that they induce public libraries to violate patrons' First Amendment rights. We now reverse.

To help public libraries provide their patrons with Internet access, Congress offers two forms of federal assistance. First, the E-rate program established by the Telecommunications Act of 1996 entitles qualifying libraries to buy Internet access at a discount.... In the year ending June 30, 2002, libraries received $58.5 million in such discounts.... Second, pursuant to the Library Services and Technology Act (LSTA), ... the Institute of Museum and Library Services makes grants to state library administrative agencies to "electronically lin[k] libraries with educational, social, or information services," "assis[t] libraries in accessing information through electronic networks," and "pa[y] costs for libraries to acquire or share computer systems and telecommunications technologies.".... In fiscal year 2002, Congress appropriated more than $149 million in LSTA grants. These programs have succeeded greatly in bringing Internet access to public libraries: By 2000, 95% of the Nation's libraries provided public Internet access. ...

By connecting to the Internet, public libraries provide patrons with a vast amount of valuable information. But there is also an enormous amount of pornography on the Internet, much of which is easily obtained. The accessibility of this material has created serious problems for libraries, which have found that patrons of all ages, including minors, regularly search for online pornography. Some patrons also expose others to pornographic images by leaving them displayed on Internet terminals or printed at library printers.

Upon discovering these problems, Congress became concerned that the E-rate and LSTA programs were facilitating access to illegal and harmful pornography. ... Congress learned that adults "us[e] library computers to access pornography that is then exposed to staff, passersby, and children," and that "minors acces[s] child and adult pornography in libraries."

But Congress also learned that filtering software that blocks access to pornographic Web sites could provide a reasonably effective way to prevent such uses of library resources. ... By 2000, before Congress enacted CIPA, almost 17% of public libraries used such software on at least some of their Internet terminals, and 7% had filters on all of them. ... A library can set such software to block categories of material, such as "Pornography" or "Violence." When a patron tries to view a site that falls within such a category, a screen appears indicating that the site is blocked. ... But a filter set to block pornography may sometimes block other sites that present neither obscene nor pornographic material, but that nevertheless trigger the filter. To minimize this problem, a library can set its software to prevent the blocking of material that falls into categories like "Education," "History," and "Medical." ... A library may also add or delete specific sites from a blocking category and anyone can ask companies that furnish filtering software to unblock particular sites ...

... CIPA ... provides that a library may not receive E-rate or LSTA assistance unless it has "a policy of Internet safety for minors that includes the operation of a technology protection measure ... that protects against access" by all persons to "visual depictions" that constitute "obscen[ity]" or "child pornography," and that protects against access by minors to "visual depictions" that are "harmful to minors." ... The statute defines a "[t]echnology protection measure" as "a specific technology that blocks or filters Internet access to material covered by" CIPA. ... CIPA also permits the library to "disable" the filter "to enable access for bona fide research or other lawful purposes." ... Under the E-rate program, disabling is permitted "during use by an adult." ... Under the LSTA program, disabling is permitted during use by any person.

Appellees are a group of libraries, library associations, library patrons, and Web site publishers, including the American Library Association (ALA) and the Multnomah County Public Library in Portland, Oregon ...

Congress has wide latitude to attach conditions to the receipt of federal assistance in order to further its policy objectives. South Dakota v. Dole, 483 U.S. 203, 206 (1987). But Congress may not "induce" the recipient "to engage in activities that would themselves be unconstitutional." ... To determine whether libraries would violate the First Amendment by employing the filtering software that CIPA requires, we must first examine the role of libraries in our society.

... To fulfill their traditional missions, public libraries must have broad discretion to decide what material to provide to their patrons. Although they seek to provide a wide array of information, their goal has never been to provide "universal coverage." ... Instead, public libraries seek to provide materials "that would be of the greatest direct benefit or interest to the community." ... To this end, libraries collect only those materials deemed to have "requisite and appropriate quality."

We have held in two analogous contexts that the government has broad discretion to make content-based judgments in deciding what private speech to make available to the public. In Arkansas Ed. Television Comm'n v. Forbes, 523 U.S. 666, 672–673 (1998), we held that public forum principles do not generally apply to a public television station's editorial judgments regarding the private speech it presents to its viewers. "[B]road rights of access for outside speakers would be antithetical, as a general rule, to the discretion that stations and their editorial staff must exercise to fulfill their journalistic purpose and statutory obligations." ...

Similarly, in National Endowment for Arts v. Finley, 524 U.S. 569 (1998), we upheld an art funding program that required the National Endowment for the Arts (NEA) to use content-based criteria in making funding decisions. We explained that "[a]ny content-based considerations that may be taken into account in the grant-making process are a consequence of the nature of arts funding." *Id.*, at 585. In particular, "[t]he very assumption of the NEA is that grants will be awarded according to the 'artistic worth of competing applicants,' and absolute neutrality is simply inconceivable." ...

The principles underlying *Forbes* and *Finley* also apply to a public library's exercise of judgment in selecting the material it provides to its patrons. Just as forum analysis and heightened judicial scrutiny are incompatible with the role of public television stations and the role of the NEA, they are also incompatible with the discretion that public libraries must have to fulfill their traditional missions. Public library staffs necessarily consider content in making collection decisions and enjoy broad discretion in making them.

... [P]ublic forum principles ... are out of place in the context of this case. Internet access in public libraries is neither a "traditional" nor a "designated" public forum. ... First, this resource—which did not exist until quite recently—has not "immemorially been held in trust for the use of the public and, time out of mind, ... been used for purposes of assembly, communication of thoughts between citizens, and discussing public questions.'' ... We have ''rejected the view that traditional public forum status extends beyond its historic confines.'' ... The doctrines surrounding traditional public forums may not be extended to situations where such history is lacking.

gov't must intentionally make a public forum

Nor does Internet access in a public library satisfy our definition of a ''designated public forum.'' To create such a forum, the government must make an affirmative choice to open up its property for use as a public forum. The government does not create a public forum by inaction or by permitting limited discourse, but only by intentionally opening a non-traditional forum for public discourse. ...

... A public library does not acquire Internet terminals in order to create a public forum for Web publishers to express themselves, any more than it collects books in order to provide a public forum for the authors of books to speak. It provides Internet access ... for the same reasons it offers other library resources: to facilitate research, learning, and recreational pursuits by furnishing materials of requisite and appropriate quality. ...

... A library's failure to make quality-based judgments about all the material it furnishes from the Web does not somehow taint the judgments it does make. ... Most libraries already exclude pornography from their print collections because they deem it inappropriate for inclusion. We do not subject these decisions to heightened scrutiny; it would make little sense to treat libraries' judgments to block online pornography any differently, when these judgments are made for just the same reason.

Moreover, because of the vast quantity of material on the Internet and the rapid pace at which it changes, libraries cannot possibly segregate, item by item, all the Internet material that is appropriate for inclusion from all that is not. While a library could limit its Internet collection to just those sites it found worthwhile, it could do so only at the cost of excluding an enormous amount of valuable information that it lacks the capacity to review. ...

... [T]he dissents fault the tendency of filtering software to ''overblock''— that is, to erroneously block access to constitutionally protected speech that falls outside the categories that software users intend to block. Due to the software's limitations, ''[m]any erroneously blocked [Web] pages contain content that is completely innocuous for both adults and minors, and that no rational person could conclude matches the filtering companies' category definitions, such as 'pornography' or 'sex.' '' Assuming that such erroneous blocking presents constitutional difficulties, any such concerns are dispelled by the ease with which patrons may have the filtering software disabled. When a patron encounters a blocked site, he need only ask a librarian to unblock it or (at least in the case of adults) disable the filter. As the District Court found, libraries have the capacity to permanently unblock any erroneously blocked site, and the Solicitor General stated at oral argument that a ''library may ... eliminate the filtering with respect to specific sites ... at the request of a patron.'' ... The Solicitor General confirmed that a ''librarian can, in response to a request from a patron, unblock the filtering mechanism altogether,'' and further explained that a patron would not ''have to explain ... why he was asking a site to be unblocked or the filtering to be disabled.'' ... [S]ome patrons may be too embarrassed to request them. But the Constitution does not guarantee the right to acquire information at a public library without any risk of embarrassment.

Appellees urge us to affirm the District Court's judgment on the alternative ground that CIPA imposes an unconstitutional condition on the receipt of federal assistance. Under this doctrine, "the government may not deny a benefit to a person on a basis that infringes his constitutionally protected . . . freedom of speech" even if he has no entitlement to that benefit. . . . Appellees argue that CIPA imposes an unconstitutional condition on libraries . . . by requiring them, as a condition on their receipt of federal funds, to surrender their First Amendment right to provide the public with access to constitutionally protected speech.

We need not decide this question because, even assuming that appellees may assert an "unconstitutional conditions" claim, this claim would fail on the merits. Within broad limits, "when the Government appropriates public funds to establish a program it is entitled to define the limits of that program." . . . In *Rust* [v. Sullivan, 500 U.S. 173 (1991)], Congress had appropriated federal funding for family planning services and forbidden the use of such funds in programs that provided abortion counseling. . . . Recipients of these funds challenged this restriction, arguing that it impermissibly conditioned the receipt of a benefit on the relinquishment of their constitutional right to engage in abortion counseling. . . . We rejected that claim, recognizing that "the Government [was] not denying a benefit to anyone, but [was] instead simply insisting that public funds be spent for the purposes for which they were authorized." . . .

The same is true here. The E-rate and LSTA programs were intended to help public libraries fulfill their traditional role of obtaining material of requisite and appropriate quality for educational and informational purposes. . . . Especially because public libraries have traditionally excluded pornographic material from their other collections, Congress could reasonably impose a parallel limitation on its Internet assistance programs. . . .

Justice Stevens asserts the premise that "[a] federal statute penalizing a library for failing to install filtering software on every one of its Internet-accessible computers would unquestionably violate [the First] Amendment." . . . But—assuming again that public libraries have First Amendment rights— CIPA does not "penalize" libraries that choose not to install such software, or deny them the right to provide their patrons with unfiltered Internet access. Rather, CIPA simply reflects Congress' decision not to subsidize their doing so.

. . .

Appellees mistakenly contend, in reliance on Legal Services Corporation v. Velazquez, 531 U.S. 533 (2001), that CIPA's filtering conditions "[d]istor[t] the [u]sual [f]unctioning of [p]ublic [l]ibraries." In *Velazquez*, the Court concluded that a Government program of furnishing legal aid to the indigent differed from the program in *Rust* "[i]n th [e] vital respect" that the role of lawyers who represent clients in welfare disputes is to advocate *against* the Government, and there was thus an assumption that counsel would be free of state control. . . . The Court concluded that the restriction on advocacy in such welfare disputes would distort the usual functioning of the legal profession and the federal and state courts before which the lawyers appeared. Public libraries, by contrast, have no comparable role that pits them against the Government, and there is no comparable assumption that they must be free of any conditions that their benefactors might attach to the use of donated funds or other assistance.

Because public libraries' use of Internet filtering software does not violate their patrons' First Amendment rights, CIPA does not induce libraries to violate the Constitution, and is a valid exercise of Congress' spending power. Nor does CIPA impose an unconstitutional condition on public libraries. Therefore, the judgment of the District Court for the Eastern District of Pennsylvania is

Reversed.

Justice Kennedy, concurring in the judgment.

If, on the request of an adult user, a librarian will unblock filtered material or disable the Internet software filter without significant delay, there is little to this case. The Government represents this is indeed the fact.

. . .

If some libraries do not have the capacity to unblock specific Web sites or to disable the filter or if it is shown that an adult user's election to view constitutionally protected Internet material is burdened in some other substantial way, that would be the subject for an as-applied challenge, not the facial challenge made in this case.

The interest in protecting young library users from material inappropriate for minors is legitimate, and even compelling, as all Members of the Court appear to agree. Given this interest, and the failure to show that the ability of adult library users to have access to the material is burdened in any significant degree, the statute is not unconstitutional on its face. For these reasons, I concur in the judgment of the Court.

Justice Breyer, concurring in the judgment.

. . . I reach the plurality's ultimate conclusion in a different way.

In ascertaining whether the statutory provisions are constitutional, I would apply a form of heightened scrutiny, examining the statutory requirements in question with special care. The Act directly restricts the public's receipt of information. . . . And it does so through limitations imposed by outside bodies (here Congress) upon two critically important sources of information—the Internet as accessed via public libraries. . . . [W]e should not examine the statute's constitutionality as if it raised no special First Amendment concern— as if, like tax or economic regulation, the First Amendment demanded only a "rational basis" for imposing a restriction. Nor should we accept the Government's suggestion that a presumption in favor of the statute's constitutionality applies.

At the same time, in my view, the First Amendment does not here demand application of the most limiting constitutional approach—that of "strict scrutiny." The statutory restriction in question is, in essence, a kind of "selection" restriction (a kind of editing). It affects the kinds and amount of materials that the library can present to its patrons. And libraries often properly engage in the selection of materials, either as a matter of necessity (*i.e.*, due to the scarcity of

resources) or by design (*i.e.,* in accordance with collection development policies).
... "[S]trict scrutiny" implies too limiting and rigid a test for me to believe
that the First Amendment requires it in this context.

Instead, I would examine the constitutionality of the Act's restrictions here
as the Court has examined speech-related restrictions in other contexts where
circumstances call for heightened, but not "strict," scrutiny—where, for example, complex, competing constitutional interests are potentially at issue or
speech-related harm is potentially justified by unusually strong governmental
interests. Typically the key question in such instances is one of proper fit. ...

In such cases the Court has asked whether the harm to speech-related
interests is disproportionate in light of both the justifications and the potential
alternatives. It has considered the legitimacy of the statute's objective, the
extent to which the statute will tend to achieve that objective, whether there
are other, less restrictive ways of achieving that objective, and ultimately
whether the statute works speech-related harm that, in relation to that
objective, is out of proportion. ... This approach does not substitute a form of
"balancing" for less flexible, though more speech-protective, forms of "strict
scrutiny." Rather, it *supplements* the latter with an approach that is more
flexible but nonetheless provides the legislature with less than ordinary leeway
in light of the fact that constitutionally protected expression is at issue. ...

The Act's restrictions satisfy these constitutional demands.... [T]he software filters both "overblock," screening out some perfectly legitimate material,
and "underblock," allowing some obscene material to escape detection by the
filter. But no one has presented any clearly superior or better fitting alternatives.

At the same time, the Act contains an important exception that limits the
speech-related harm that "overblocking" might cause ... [allowing] libraries to
permit any adult patron access to an "overblocked" Web site; the adult patron
need only ask a librarian to unblock the specific Web site or, alternatively, ask
the librarian, "Please disable the entire filter."

. . .

Given the comparatively small burden that the Act imposes upon the
library patron seeking legitimate Internet materials, I cannot say that any
speech-related harm that the Act may cause is disproportionate when considered in relation to the Act's legitimate objectives. I therefore agree with the
plurality that the statute does not violate the First Amendment, and I concur
in the judgment.

Justice Stevens, dissenting.

... I agree with the plurality that it is neither inappropriate nor unconstitutional for a local library to experiment with filtering software as a means of
curtailing children's access to Internet Web sites displaying sexually explicit
images. I also agree with the plurality that the 7% of public libraries that
decided to use such software on *all* of their Internet terminals in 2000 did not
act unlawfully. Whether it is constitutional for the Congress of the United
States to impose that requirement on the other 93%, however, raises a vastly
different question. Rather than allowing local decisionmakers to tailor their
responses to local problems, the Children's Internet Protection Act (CIPA)

operates as a blunt nationwide restraint on adult access to "an enormous amount of" . . . constitutionally protected speech. In my view, this restraint is unconstitutional.

I

The unchallenged findings of fact made by the District Court reveal fundamental defects in the filtering software that is now available or that will be available in the foreseeable future. Because the software relies on key words or phrases to block undesirable sites, it does not have the capacity to exclude a precisely defined category of images. . . .

The effect of the overblocking is the functional equivalent of a host of individual decisions excluding hundreds of thousands of individual constitutionally protected messages from Internet terminals located in public libraries throughout the Nation. . . .

. . .

. . . The plurality . . . relies on the Solicitor General's assurance that the statute permits individual librarians to disable filtering mechanisms whenever a patron so requests. In my judgment, that assurance does not cure the constitutional infirmity in the statute.

Until a blocked site or group of sites is unblocked, a patron is unlikely to know what is being hidden and therefore whether there is any point in asking for the filter to be removed. It is as though the statute required a significant part of every library's reading materials to be kept in unmarked, locked rooms or cabinets, which could be opened only in response to specific requests. Some curious readers would in time obtain access to the hidden materials, but many would not. Inevitably, the interest of the authors of those works in reaching the widest possible audience would be abridged.

II

The plurality incorrectly argues that the statute does not impose 'an unconstitutional condition on public libraries.' On the contrary, it impermissibly conditions the receipt of Government funding on the restriction of significant First Amendment rights.

. . .

. . . [W]e have always assumed that libraries have discretion when making decisions regarding what to include in, and exclude from, their collections. . . . Given our Nation's deep commitment 'to safeguarding academic freedom' and to the 'robust exchange of ideas,' . . . a library's exercise of judgment with respect to its collection is entitled to First Amendment protection.

A federal statute penalizing a library for failing to install filtering software on every one of its Internet-accessible computers would unquestionably violate that Amendment. . . . I think it equally clear that the First Amendment protects libraries from being denied funds for refusing to comply with an identical rule. An abridgment of speech by means of a threatened denial of benefits can be just as pernicious as an abridgment by means of a threatened penalty.

Our cases holding that government employment may not be conditioned on the surrender of rights protected by the First Amendment illustrate the point. . . .

The issue in this case does not involve governmental attempts to control the speech or views of its employees. It involves the use of its treasury to impose controls on an important medium of expression. In an analogous situation, we specifically held that when 'the Government seeks to use an existing medium of expression and to control it, in a class of cases, in ways which distort its usual functioning,' the distorting restriction must be struck down under the First Amendment. . . .

The plurality argues that the controversial decision in Rust v. Sullivan . . . requires rejection of appellees' unconstitutional conditions claim. But, as subsequent cases have explained, *Rust* only involved and only applies to instances of governmental speech—that is, situations in which the government seeks to communicate a specific message. . . . These programs thus are designed to provide access, particularly for individuals in low-income communities, . . . to a vast amount and wide variety of private speech. They are not designed to foster or transmit any particular governmental message.

. . .

The plurality's reliance on National Endowment for Arts v. Finley . . . is also misplaced. That case involved a challenge to a statute setting forth the criteria used by a federal panel of experts administering a federal grant program. Unlike this case, the Federal Government was not seeking to impose restrictions on the administration of a nonfederal program. . . . *Rust* would appear to permit restrictions on a federal program such as the NEA arts grant program at issue in *Finley*.

Further, like a library, the NEA experts in *Finley* had a great deal of discretion to make judgments as to what projects to fund. But unlike this case, *Finley* did not involve a challenge by the NEA to a governmental restriction on its ability to award grants. Instead, the respondents were performance artists who had applied for NEA grants but were denied funding. . . . If this were a case in which library patrons had challenged a library's decision to install and use filtering software, it would be in the same posture as *Finley*. Because it is not, *Finley* does not control this case.

Also unlike *Finley*, the Government does not merely seek to control a library's discretion with respect to computers purchased with Government funds or those computers with Government-discounted Internet access. . . . [I]f a library attempts to provide Internet service for even *one* computer through an E-rate discount, that library must put filtering software on *all* of its computers with Internet access, not just the one computer with E-rate discount.

This Court should not permit federal funds to be used to enforce this kind of broad restriction of First Amendment rights, particularly when such a restriction is unnecessary to accomplish Congress' stated goal. . . . The abridgment of speech is equally obnoxious whether a rule like this one is enforced by a threat of penalties or by a threat to withhold a benefit.

. . .

Justice Souter, with whom Justice Ginsburg joins, dissenting.

I agree in the main with Justice Stevens that the blocking requirements of the Children's Internet Protection Act ... impose an unconstitutional condition on the Government's subsidies to local libraries for providing access to the Internet. I also agree with the library appellees on a further reason to hold the blocking rule invalid in the exercise of the spending power under Article I, § 8: the rule mandates action by recipient libraries that would violate the First Amendment's guarantee of free speech if the libraries took that action entirely on their own. I respectfully dissent on this further ground.

I

Like the other Members of the Court, I have no doubt about the legitimacy of governmental efforts to put a barrier between child patrons of public libraries and the raw offerings on the Internet otherwise available to them there, and if the only First Amendment interests raised here were those of children, I would uphold application of the Act. ...

Nor would I dissent if I agreed with the majority of my colleagues, that an adult library patron could, consistently with the Act, obtain an unblocked terminal simply for the asking. I realize the Solicitor General represented this to be the Government's policy, and if that policy were communicated to every affected library as unequivocally as it was stated to us at argument, local librarians might be able to indulge the unblocking requests of adult patrons to the point of taking the curse off the statute for all practical purposes. But the Federal Communications Commission, in its order implementing the Act, pointedly declined to set a federal policy on when unblocking by local libraries would be appropriate under the statute. ...

In any event, we are here to review a statute, and the unblocking provisions simply cannot be construed, even for constitutional avoidance purposes, to say that a library must unblock upon adult request, no conditions imposed and no questions asked. ...

We therefore have to take the statute on the understanding that adults will be denied access to a substantial amount of nonobscene material harmful to children but lawful for adult examination, and a substantial quantity of text and pictures harmful to no one. ...

We likewise have to examine the statute on the understanding that the restrictions on adult Internet access have no justification in the object of protecting children. Children could be restricted to blocked terminals, leaving other unblocked terminals in areas restricted to adults and screened from casual glances. And of course the statute could simply have provided for unblocking at adult request, with no questions asked. ...

The question for me, then, is whether a local library could itself constitutionally impose these restrictions on the content otherwise available to an adult patron through an Internet connection, at a library terminal provided for public use. The answer is no. A library that chose to block an adult's Internet access to material harmful to children (and whatever else the undiscriminating filter might interrupt) would be imposing a content-based restriction on communication of material in the library's control that an adult could otherwise lawfully see. This would simply be censorship. ...

II

The Court's plurality does not treat blocking affecting adults as censorship, but chooses to describe a library's act in filtering content as simply an instance of the kind of selection from available material that every library ... must perform. ... But this position does not hold up.

A

Public libraries are indeed selective in what they acquire to place in their stacks, as they must be. There is only so much money and so much shelf space ... Selectivity is thus necessary and complex, and these two characteristics explain why review of a library's selection decisions must be limited ...

At every significant point, however, the Internet blocking here defies comparison to the process of acquisition. Whereas traditional scarcity of money and space require a library to make choices about what to acquire, and the choice to be made is whether or not to spend the money to acquire something, blocking is the subject of a choice made after the money for Internet access has been spent or committed. Since it makes no difference to the cost of Internet access whether an adult calls up material harmful for children or the Articles of Confederation, blocking (on facts like these) is not necessitated by scarcity of either money or space. In the instance of the Internet, what the library acquires is electronic access, and the choice to block is a choice to limit access that has already been acquired. Thus, deciding against buying a book means there is no book (unless a loan can be obtained), but blocking the Internet is merely blocking access purchased in its entirety and subject to unblocking if the librarian agrees. The proper analogy therefore is not to passing up a book that might have been bought; it is either to buying a book and then keeping it from adults lacking an acceptable "purpose," or to buying an encyclopedia and then cutting out pages with anything thought to be unsuitable for all adults.

B

... The plurality ... argues ... that the traditional responsibility of public libraries has called for denying adult access to certain books, or bowdlerizing the content of what the libraries let adults see. But, in fact, the plurality's conception of a public library's mission has been rejected by the libraries themselves. And no library that chose to block adult access in the way mandated by the Act could claim that the history of public library practice in this country furnished an implicit gloss on First Amendment standards, allowing for blocking out anything unsuitable for adults.

Institutional history of public libraries in America discloses an evolution toward a general rule, now firmly rooted, that any adult entitled to use the library has access to any of its holdings. To be sure, this freedom of choice was apparently not within the inspiration for the mid–19th century development of public libraries ... [There] was a growing understanding that a librarian's job was to guarantee that "all people had access to all ideas," ...

By the time McCarthyism began its assaults, appellee American Library Association had developed a Library Bill of Rights against censorship ... and an Intellectual Freedom Committee to maintain the position that beyond enforcing existing laws against obscenity, "there is no place in our society for extra-legal efforts to coerce the taste of others, to confine adults to the reading matter deemed suitable for adolescents, or to inhibit the efforts of writers to achieve artistic expression." ... So far as I have been able to tell, this statement expressed the prevailing ideal in public library administration after World War II, and it seems fair to say as a general rule that libraries by then had ceased to deny requesting adults access to any materials in their collections. ...

. . .

... [I]n 1973, the ALA adopted a policy opposing the practice ... of keeping certain books off the open shelves, available only on specific request. ... The statement conceded that "closed shelf," "locked case," "adults only," or "restricted shelf" collections were "common to many libraries in the United States." ... The ALA nonetheless came out against it, in these terms: "While the limitation differs from direct censorship activities, such as removal of library materials or refusal to purchase certain publications, it nonetheless constitutes censorship, albeit a subtle form." ...

Amidst these and other ALA statements from the latter half of the 20th century, however, one subject is missing. There is not a word about barring requesting adults from any materials in a library's collection ... The silence bespeaks an American public library that gives any adult patron any material at hand, and a history without support for the plurality's reading of the First Amendment as tolerating a public library's censorship of its collection against adult enquiry.

C

... Quite simply, we can smell a rat when a library blocks material already in its control, just as we do when a library removes books from its shelves for reasons having nothing to do with wear and tear, obsolescence, or lack of demand. Content-based blocking and removal tell us something that mere absence from the shelves does not.

. . .

After a library has acquired material ..., the variety of possible reasons that might legitimately support an initial rejection are no longer in play. Removal of books or selective blocking by controversial subject matter is not a function of limited resources and less likely than a selection decision to reflect an assessment of esthetic or scholarly merit. Removal (and blocking) decisions being so often obviously correlated with content, they tend to show up for just what they are, and because such decisions tend to be few, courts can examine them without facing a deluge. The difference between choices to keep out and choices to throw out is thus enormous, a perception that underlay the good sense of the plurality's conclusion in Board of Ed., Island Trees Union Free School Dist. No. 26 v. Pico, 457 U.S. 853 (1982), that removing classics from a school library in response to pressure from parents and school board members violates the Speech Clause.

. . .

CHAPTER 15

PROTECTION OF PENUMBRAL FIRST AMENDMENT RIGHTS

SECTION 3. FREEDOM OF ASSOCIATION

D. COMPULSORY ASSOCIATION MEMBERSHIP

Page 1465. Replace Glickman v. Wileman Brothers & Elliott, Inc.:

United States v. United Foods, Inc.

533 U.S. 405, 121 S.Ct. 2334, 150 L.Ed.2d 438 (2001).

Justice Kennedy delivered the opinion of the Court.

Four Terms ago, in Glickman v. Wileman Brothers & Elliott, Inc., 521 U.S. 457 (1997), the Court rejected a First Amendment challenge to the constitutionality of a series of agricultural marketing orders that, as part of a larger regulatory marketing scheme, required producers of certain California tree fruit to pay assessments for product advertising. In this case a federal statute mandates assessments on handlers of fresh mushrooms to fund advertising for the product. . . .

The statute in question, enacted by Congress in 1990, is the Mushroom Promotion, Research, and Consumer Information Act. . . . The Act authorizes the Secretary of Agriculture to establish a Mushroom Council to pursue the statute's goals. Mushroom producers and importers, as defined by the statute, submit nominations from among their group to the Secretary, who then designates the Council membership. . . . To fund its programs, the Act allows the Council to impose mandatory assessments upon handlers of fresh mushrooms in an amount not to exceed one cent per pound of mushrooms produced or imported. . . . The assessments can be used for "projects of mushroom promotion, research, consumer information, and industry information." . . . It is undisputed, though, that most monies raised by the assessments are spent for generic advertising to promote mushroom sales.

Respondent United Foods, Inc., is a large agricultural enterprise based in Tennessee. It grows and distributes many crops and products, including fresh mushrooms. In 1996 respondent refused to pay its mandatory assessments under the Act. The forced subsidy for generic advertising, it contended, is a violation of the First Amendment. . . . The United States filed an action in the United States District Court, . . . seeking an order compelling respondent to pay. . . .

After *Glickman* was decided, ... [t]he District Court, holding *Glickman* dispositive of the First Amendment challenge, granted the Government's motion for summary judgment. The Court of Appeals ... reversed ... We agree with the Court of Appeals and now affirm.

. . .

We have used standards for determining the validity of speech regulations which accord less protection to commercial speech than to other expression. ... That approach, in turn, has been subject to some criticism. ... We need not enter into the controversy, for even viewing commercial speech as entitled to lesser protection, we find no basis under either *Glickman* or our other precedents to sustain the compelled assessments sought in this case. It should be noted, moreover, that the Government itself does not rely upon *Central Hudson* to challenge the Court of Appeals decision, and we therefore do not consider whether the Governments interest could be considered substantial for purposes of the *Central Hudson* test. The question is whether the government may underwrite and sponsor speech with a certain viewpoint using special subsidies exacted from a designated class of persons, some of whom object to the idea being advanced.

... Our precedents concerning compelled contributions to speech provide the beginning point for our analysis. The fact that the speech is in aid of a commercial purpose does not deprive respondent of all First Amendment protection.... The subject matter of the speech may be of interest to but a small segment of the population; yet those whose business and livelihood depend in some way upon the product involved no doubt deem First Amendment protection to be just as important for them as it is for other discrete, little noticed groups in a society which values the freedom resulting from speech in all its diverse parts. First Amendment concerns apply here because of the requirement that producers subsidize speech with which they disagree.

... Here the disagreement could be seen as minor: Respondent wants to convey the message that its brand of mushrooms is superior to those grown by other producers. It objects to being charged for a message which seems to be favored by a majority of producers. The message is that mushrooms are worth consuming whether or not they are branded. First Amendment values are at serious risk if the government can compel a particular citizen, or a discrete group of citizens, to pay special subsidies for speech on the side that it favors; and there is no apparent principle which distinguishes out of hand minor debates about whether a branded mushroom is better than just any mushroom. As a consequence, the compelled funding for the advertising must pass First Amendment scrutiny.

In the Governments view the assessment in this case is permitted by *Glickman* because it is similar in important respects. It imposes no restraint on the freedom of an objecting party to communicate its own message; the program does not compel an objecting party (here a corporate entity) itself to express views it disfavors; and the mandated scheme does not compel the expression of political or ideological views. ... The program sustained in *Glickman* differs from the one under review in a most fundamental respect. In *Glickman* the mandated assessments for speech were ancillary to a more comprehensive program restricting marketing autonomy. Here, for all practical purposes, the advertising itself, far from being ancillary, is the principal object of the regulatory scheme.

. . . In deciding [*Glickman*] we emphasized "the importance of the statutory context in which it arises." . . . The California tree fruits were marketed "pursuant to detailed marketing orders that ha[d] displaced many aspects of independent business activity." . . . The producers of tree fruit who were compelled to contribute funds for use in cooperative advertising "d[id] so as a part of a broader collective enterprise in which their freedom to act independently [wa]s already constrained by the regulatory scheme." . . . [T]heir mandated participation in an advertising program with a particular message was the logical concomitant of a valid scheme of economic regulation.

The features of the marketing scheme found important in *Glickman* are not present in the case now before us. . . . [A]lmost all of the funds collected under the mandatory assessments are for one purpose: generic advertising. Beyond the collection and disbursement of advertising funds, there are no marketing orders that regulate how mushrooms may be produced and sold, no exemption from the antitrust laws, and nothing preventing individual producers from making their own marketing decisions. . . .

It is true that the party who protests the assessment here is required simply to support speech by others, not to utter the speech itself. We conclude, however, that the mandated support is contrary to the First Amendment principles set forth in cases involving expression by groups which include persons who object to the speech, but who, nevertheless, must remain members of the group by law or necessity. . . .

. . .

. . . [I]n *Glickman* . . ., the market for tree fruit was cooperative. . . . Though four Justices who join this opinion disagreed, the majority of the Court in *Glickman* found the compelled contributions were nothing more than additional economic regulation, which did not raise First Amendment concerns. . . .

The statutory mechanism as it relates to handlers of mushrooms is concededly different from the scheme in *Glickman*; here the statute does not require group action, save to generate the very speech to which some handlers object. . . . We have not upheld compelled subsidies for speech in the context of a program where the principal object is speech itself. . . . [T]he expression respondent is required to support is not germane to a purpose related to an association independent from the speech itself. . . . [T]he assessments are not permitted under the First Amendment.

. . .

The Government argues the advertising here is government speech, and so immune from the scrutiny we would otherwise apply. . . .

The Governments failure to raise its argument in the Court of Appeals deprived respondent of the ability to address significant matters that might have been difficult points for the Government. For example, although the Government asserts that advertising is subject to approval by the Secretary of Agriculture, respondent claims the approval is pro forma. . . .

... Although in some instances we have allowed a respondent to defend a judgment on grounds other than those pressed or passed upon below, ... it is quite a different matter to allow a petitioner to assert new substantive arguments attacking, rather than defending, the judgment when those arguments were not pressed in the court whose opinion we are reviewing, or at least passed upon by it.

... [T]he judgment of the Court of Appeals is

Affirmed.

Justice Stevens, concurring.

Justice Breyer has correctly noted that the program at issue in this case, like that in Glickman ... "does not compel speech itself; it compels the payment of money." ... It does not follow, however, that the First Amendment is not implicated when a person is forced to subsidize speech to which he objects. ... The incremental impact on the liberty of a person who has already surrendered far greater liberty to the collective entity (either voluntarily or as a result of permissible compulsion) does not, in my judgment, raise a significant constitutional issue if it is ancillary to the main purpose of the collective program.

This case, however, raises the open question whether such compulsion is constitutional when nothing more than commercial advertising is at stake. The naked imposition of such compulsion, like a naked restraint on speech itself, seems quite different to me. We need not decide whether other interests ... might justify a compelled subsidy like this, but surely the interest in making one entrepreneur finance advertising for the benefit of his competitors, including some who are not required to contribute, is insufficient.

Justice Thomas, concurring.

... I write separately ... to reiterate my views that ... [a]ny regulation that compels the funding of advertising must be subjected to the most stringent First Amendment scrutiny.

Justice Breyer, with whom Justice Ginsburg joins, and with whom Justice O'Connor joins as to Parts I and III, dissenting.

The Court, in my view, ... introduces into First Amendment law an unreasoned legal principle that may well pose an obstacle to the development of beneficial forms of economic regulation. I consequently dissent.

I

... [In *Glickman* we] ... gave the following reasons in support of our conclusion:

> "First, the marketing orders impose no restraint on the freedom of any producer to communicate any message to any audience. Second, they do not compel any person to engage in any actual or symbolic speech. Third, they do not compel the producers to endorse or to finance any political or ideological views." ...

This case, although it involves mushrooms rather than fruit, is identical in each of these three critical respects....

The Court sees an important difference in what it says is the fact that Wilemans fruit producers were subject to regulation....

... The Court in *Wileman* did not refer to the presence of price or output regulations. ...

... [I]t is difficult to understand why the presence or absence of price and output regulations could make a critical First Amendment difference. The Court says that collective fruit advertising (unlike mushroom advertising) was the "logical concomitant" of the more comprehensive "economic" regulatory "scheme." ... But it does not explain how that could be so. ...

... [T]he advertising here relates directly, not in an incidental or subsidiary manner, to the regulatory programs underlying goal of "maintain [ing] and expand[ing] existing markets and uses for mushrooms." ... As the Mushroom Acts economic goals indicate, collective promotion and research is a perfectly traditional form of government intervention in the marketplace. And compelled payment may be needed to produce those benefits where, otherwise, some producers would take a free ride on the expenditures of others. ...

Compared with traditional "command and control," price, or output regulation, this kind of regulation—which relies upon self-regulation through industry trade associations and upon the dissemination of information—is more consistent, not less consistent, with producer choice. It is difficult to see why a Constitution that seeks to protect individual freedom would consider the absence of "heavy regulation," to amount to a special, determinative reason for refusing to permit this less intrusive program. If the Court classifies the former, more comprehensive regulatory scheme as "economic regulation" for First Amendment purposes, it should similarly classify the latter, which does not differ significantly but for the comparatively greater degree of freedom that it allows.

. . . .

II

... Nearly every human action that the law affects, and virtually all governmental activity, involves speech....

That, I believe, is why it is important to understand that the regulatory program before us is a "species of economic regulation," ... which does not "warrant special First Amendment scrutiny," ... I would so characterize the program for three reasons.

First, the program does not significantly interfere with protected speech interests. It does not compel speech itself; it compels the payment of money. Money and speech are not identical.... Indeed, the contested requirement—that individual producers make a payment to help achieve a governmental objective—resembles a targeted tax. ...

Second, this program furthers, rather than hinders, the basic First Amendment "commercial speech" objective. The speech at issue amounts to ordinary product promotion within the commercial marketplace—an arena typically characterized both by the need for a degree of public supervision and the absence of a special democratic need to protect the channels of public debate, i.e., the communicative process itself. ... No one here claims that the mushroom producers are restrained from contributing to a public debate, moving public opinion, writing literature, creating art, invoking the processes of democratic self-government, or doing anything else more central to the First Amendments concern with democratic self-government.

. . . Unlike many of the commercial speech restrictions this Court has previously addressed, the program before us promotes the dissemination of truthful information to consumers. And to sustain the objecting producers constitutional claim will likely make less information, not more information, available. Perhaps that is why this Court has not previously applied "compelled speech" doctrine to strike down laws requiring provision of additional commercial speech.

Third, there is no special risk of other forms of speech-related harm. . . . [T]here is no risk of significant harm to an individuals conscience. The program does not censor producer views unrelated to its basic regulatory justification. And there is little risk of harming any "discrete, little noticed grou[p]." . . .

Taken together, these circumstances lead me to classify this common example of government intervention in the marketplace as involving a form of economic regulation, not "commercial speech," for purposes of applying First Amendment presumptions. . . .

. . .

The Courts decision converts "a question of economic policy for Congress and the Executive" into a "First Amendment issue," contrary to *Wileman*. For these reasons, I dissent.

SECTION 4.   APPLICATION OF THE FIRST AMENDMENT TO GOVERNMENT REGULATION OF ELECTIONS

A.   CHOOSING AND ELECTING CANDIDATES FOR PUBLIC OFFICE

Page 1476.   Add at beginning of subsection:

Republican Party of Minnesota v. White

536 U.S. 765, 122 S.Ct. 2528, 153 L.Ed.2d 694 (2002).

Justice Scalia delivered the opinion of the Court.

The question presented in this case is whether the First Amendment permits the Minnesota Supreme Court to prohibit candidates for judicial election in that State from announcing their views on disputed legal and political issues.

I

Since Minnesota's admission to the Union in 1858, the State's Constitution has provided for the selection of all state judges by popular election. . . . Since 1912, those elections have been nonpartisan. . . . Since 1974, they have been subject to a legal restriction which states that a "candidate for a judicial office, including an incumbent judge, 'shall not' announce his or her views on disputed legal or political issues." ... This prohibition, promulgated by the Minnesota Supreme Court and based on Canon 7(B) of the 1972 American Bar Association (ABA) Model Code of Judicial Conduct, is known as the "announce clause." Incumbent judges who violate it are subject to discipline, including removal, censure, civil penalties, and suspension without pay. ... Lawyers who run for judicial office also must comply with the announce clause. ... Those who violate it are subject to, *inter alia*, disbarment, suspension, and probation. ...

In 1996, one of the petitioners, Gregory Wersal, ran for associate justice of the Minnesota Supreme Court. In the course of the campaign, he distributed literature criticizing several Minnesota Supreme Court decisions on issues such as crime, welfare, and abortion. A complaint against Wersal challenging, among other things, the propriety of this literature was filed with the Office of Lawyers Professional Responsibility, the agency which, under the direction of the Minnesota Lawyers Professional Responsibility Board, investigates and prosecutes ethical violations of lawyer candidates for judicial office. The Lawyers Board dismissed the complaint; with regard to the charges that his campaign materials violated the announce clause, it expressed doubt whether the clause could constitutionally be enforced. Nonetheless, fearing that further ethical complaints would jeopardize his ability to practice law, Wersal withdrew from the election. In 1998, Wersal ran again for the same office. Early in that race, he sought an advisory opinion from the Lawyers Board with regard to whether it planned to enforce the announce clause. The Lawyers Board responded equivocally, stating that, although it had significant doubts about the constitutionality of the provision, it was unable to answer his question because he had not submitted a list of the announcements he wished to make.

Shortly thereafter, Wersal filed this lawsuit in Federal District Court against respondents, seeking, *inter alia*, a declaration that the announce clause violates the First Amendment and an injunction against its enforcement. Wersal alleged that he was forced to refrain from announcing his views on disputed issues during the 1998 campaign, to the point where he declined response to questions put to him by the press and public, out of concern that he might run afoul of the announce clause. Other plaintiffs in the suit, including the Minnesota Republican Party, alleged that, because the clause kept Wersal from announcing his views, they were unable to learn those views and support or oppose his candidacy accordingly. The ... District Court found in favor of respondents, holding that the announce clause did not violate the First Amendment. ...[T]he United States Court of Appeals for the Eighth Circuit affirmed. ...

II

Before considering the constitutionality of the announce clause, we must be clear about its meaning. Its text says that a candidate for judicial office shall not "announce his or her views on disputed legal or political issues." ...

We know that "announc[ing] ... views" on an issue covers much more than *promising* to decide an issue a particular way. The prohibition extends to the candidate's mere statement of his current position, even if he does not bind himself to maintain that position after election. ...

There are, however, some limitations that the Minnesota Supreme Court has placed upon the scope of the announce clause that are not (to put it politely) immediately apparent from its text. The statements that formed the basis of the complaint against Wersal in 1996 included criticism of past decisions of the Minnesota Supreme Court. . . . The Judicial Board issued an opinion stating that judicial candidates may criticize past decisions . . . The Eighth Circuit relied on the Judicial Board's opinion in upholding the announce clause, and the Minnesota Supreme Court recently embraced the Eighth Circuit's interpretation . . .

There are yet further limitations upon the apparent plain meaning of the announce clause: In light of the constitutional concerns, the District Court construed the clause to reach only disputed issues that are likely to come before the candidate if he is elected judge. . . . The Eighth Circuit accepted this limiting interpretation by the District Court, and in addition construed the clause to allow general discussions of case law and judicial philosophy. . . . The Supreme Court of Minnesota adopted these interpretations as well when it ordered enforcement of the announce clause in accordance with the Eighth Circuit's opinion. . . .

It seems to us, however, that—like the text of the announce clause itself— these limitations upon the text of the announce clause are not all that they appear to be. First, respondents acknowledged at oral argument that statements critical of past judicial decisions are *not* permissible if the candidate also states that he is against *stare decisis*. Thus, candidates must choose between stating their views critical of past decisions and stating their views in opposition to *stare decisis*. Or, to look at it more concretely, they may state their view that prior decisions were erroneous only if they do not assert that they, if elected, have any power to eliminate erroneous decisions. Second, limiting the scope of the clause to issues likely to come before a court is not much of a limitation at all. . . .[T]he "disputed legal or political issues" raised in the course of a state judicial election . . . will be those legal or political disputes that are the proper (or by past decisions have been made the improper) business of the state courts. And within that relevant category, "[t]here is almost no legal or political issue that is unlikely to come before a judge of an American court, state or federal, of general jurisdiction." . . . Third, construing the clause to allow "general" discussions of case law and judicial philosophy turns out to be of little help in an election campaign. . . .

In any event, it is clear that the announce clause prohibits a judicial candidate from stating his views on any specific nonfanciful legal question within the province of the court for which he is running, except in the context of discussing past decisions—and in the latter context as well, if he expresses the view that he is not bound by *stare decisis*.

Respondents contend that this still leaves plenty of topics for discussion on the campaign trail. These include a candidate's "character," "education," "work habits," and "how [he] would handle administrative duties if elected." Indeed, the Judicial Board has printed a list of preapproved questions which judicial candidates are allowed to answer. These include how the candidate feels about cameras in the courtroom, how he would go about reducing the caseload, how the costs of judicial administration can be reduced, and how he proposes to ensure that minorities and women are treated more fairly by the court system.

Whether this list of preapproved subjects, and other topics not prohibited by the announce clause, adequately fulfill the First Amendment's guarantee of freedom of speech is the question to which we now turn.

III

As the Court of Appeals recognized, the announce clause both prohibits speech on the basis of its content and burdens a category of speech that is "at the core of our First Amendment freedoms"—speech about the qualifications of candidates for public office. . . .

The Court of Appeals concluded that respondents had established two interests as sufficiently compelling to justify the announce clause: preserving the impartiality of the state judiciary and preserving the appearance of the impartiality of the state judiciary. Respondents reassert these two interests before us, arguing that the first is compelling because it protects the due process rights of litigants, and that the second is compelling because it preserves public confidence in the judiciary. Respondents are rather vague, however, about what they mean by "impartiality." . . . Clarity on this point is essential before we can decide whether impartiality is indeed a compelling state interest, and, if so, whether the announce clause is narrowly tailored to achieve it.

A

One meaning of "impartiality" in the judicial context—and of course its root meaning—is the lack of bias for or against either *party* to the proceeding. . . . This is the traditional sense in which the term is used. . . .

We think it plain that the announce clause is not narrowly tailored to serve impartiality (or the appearance of impartiality) in this sense. Indeed, the clause is barely tailored to serve that interest *at all*, inasmuch as it does not restrict speech for or against particular *parties*, but rather speech for or against particular *issues*. . . .

B

It is perhaps possible to use the term "impartiality" in the judicial context (though this is certainly not a common usage) to mean lack of preconception in favor of or against a particular *legal view*. . . . A judge's lack of predisposition regarding the relevant legal issues in a case has never been thought a necessary component of equal justice, and with good reason. For one thing, it is virtually impossible to find a judge who does not have preconceptions about the law. . . . Indeed, even if it were possible to select judges who did not have preconceived views on legal issues, it would hardly be desirable to do so. . . . And since avoiding judicial preconceptions on legal issues is neither possible nor desirable, pretending otherwise by attempting to preserve the "appearance" of that type of impartiality can hardly be a compelling state interest either.

C

A third possible meaning of "impartiality" (again not a common one) might be described as open-mindedness. This quality in a judge demands, not that he have no preconceptions on legal issues, but that he be willing to consider views that oppose his preconceptions, and remain open to persuasion, when the issues arise in a pending case. . . .

Respondents argue that the announce clause serves the interest in open-mindedness, or at least in the appearance of open-mindedness, because it relieves a judge from pressure to rule a certain way in order to maintain consistency with statements the judge has previously made. The problem is, however, that statements in election campaigns are such an infinitesimal portion of the public commitments to legal positions that judges (or judges-to-be) undertake, that this object of the prohibition is implausible. Before they arrive on the bench (whether by election or otherwise) judges have often committed themselves on legal issues that they must later rule upon. . . .

. . . In Minnesota, a candidate for judicial office may not say "I think it is constitutional for the legislature to prohibit same-sex marriages." He may say the very same thing, however, up until the very day before he declares himself a candidate, and may say it repeatedly (until litigation is pending) after he is elected. As a means of pursuing the objective of open-mindedness that respondents now articulate, the announce clause is so woefully underinclusive as to render belief in that purpose a challenge to the credulous. . . .

. . .

Moreover, the notion that the special context of electioneering justifies an *abridgment* of the right to speak out on disputed issues sets our First Amendment jurisprudence on its head. "[D]ebate on the qualifications of candidates" is "at the core of our electoral process and of the First Amendment freedoms," not at the edges. . . . We have never allowed the government to prohibit candidates from communicating relevant information to voters during an election.

. . .

. . . Justice Ginsburg greatly exaggerates the difference between judicial and legislative elections. . . . [C]omplete separation of the judiciary from the enterprise of "representative government" might have some truth in those countries where judges neither make law themselves nor set aside the laws enacted by the legislature. It is not a true picture of the American system. . . .

IV

To sustain the announce clause, the Eighth Circuit relied heavily on the fact that a pervasive practice of prohibiting judicial candidates from discussing disputed legal and political issues developed during the last half of the 20th century. It is true that a "universal and long-established" tradition of prohibiting certain conduct creates "a strong presumption" that the prohibition is constitutional: "Principles of liberty fundamental enough to have been embodied within constitutional guarantees are not readily erased from the Nation's consciousness." *McIntyre v. Ohio Elections Comm'n,* 514 U.S. 334, 375–377 (1995) (Scalia, J., dissenting). The practice of prohibiting speech by judicial candidates on disputed issues, however, is neither long nor universal.

. . . We know of no restrictions upon statements that could be made by judicial candidates (including judges) throughout the 19th and the first quarter of the 20th century. Indeed, judicial elections were generally partisan during this period, the movement toward nonpartisan judicial elections not even beginning until the 1870's. . . . Thus, not only were judicial candidates (including judges) discussing disputed legal and political issues on the campaign trail, but they were touting party affiliations and angling for party nominations all the while.

    . . .

                                    * * *

There is an obvious tension between the article of Minnesota's popularly approved Constitution which provides that judges shall be elected, and the Minnesota Supreme Court's announce clause which places most subjects of interest to the voters off limits. . . . If the State chooses to tap the energy and the legitimizing power of the democratic process, it must accord the participants in that process . . . the First Amendment rights that attach to their roles. . . .

The Minnesota Supreme Court's canon of judicial conduct prohibiting candidates for judicial election from announcing their views on disputed legal and political issues violates the First Amendment. Accordingly, we reverse the grant of summary judgment to respondents and remand the case for proceedings consistent with this opinion.

It is so ordered.

Justice O'Connor, concurring.

I join the opinion of the Court but write separately to express my concerns about judicial elections generally. . . .

We of course want judges to be impartial, in the sense of being free from any personal stake in the outcome of the cases to which they are assigned. But if judges are subject to regular elections they are likely to feel that they have at least some personal stake in the outcome of every publicized case. Elected judges cannot help being aware that if the public is not satisfied with the outcome of a particular case, it could hurt their reelection prospects. . . . Even if judges were able to suppress their awareness of the potential electoral consequences of their decisions and refrain from acting on it, the public's confidence in the judiciary could be undermined simply by the possibility that judges would be unable to do so.

Moreover, contested elections generally entail campaigning. And campaigning for a judicial post today can require substantial funds. . . . Even if judges were able to refrain from favoring donors, the mere possibility that judges' decisions may be motivated by the desire to repay campaign contributors is likely to undermine the public's confidence in the judiciary. . . .

    . . .

Minnesota has chosen to select its judges through contested popular elections instead of through an appointment system or a combined appointment and retention election system along the lines of the Missouri Plan. In doing so the State has voluntarily taken on the risks to judicial bias described above. As a result, the State's claim that it needs to significantly restrict judges' speech in order to protect judicial impartiality is particularly troubling. If the State has a problem with judicial impartiality, it is largely one the State brought upon itself by continuing the practice of popularly electing judges.

Justice Kennedy, concurring.

I agree with the Court that Minnesota's prohibition on judicial candidates' announcing their legal views is an unconstitutional abridgment of the freedom of speech. There is authority for the Court to apply strict scrutiny analysis to resolve some First Amendment cases, . . . and the Court explains in clear and forceful terms why the Minnesota regulatory scheme fails that test. So I join its opinion.

I adhere to my view, however, that content-based speech restrictions that do not fall within any traditional exception should be invalidated without inquiry into narrow tailoring or compelling government interests. The speech at issue here does not come within any of the exceptions to the First Amendment recognized by the Court. . . . The political speech of candidates is at the heart of the First Amendment, and direct restrictions on the content of candidate speech are simply beyond the power of government to impose.

. . .

Minnesota may choose to have an elected judiciary. It may strive to define those characteristics that exemplify judicial excellence. It may enshrine its definitions in a code of judicial conduct. It may adopt recusal standards more rigorous than due process requires, and censure judges who violate these standards. What Minnesota may not do, however, is censor what the people hear as they undertake to decide for themselves which candidate is most likely to be an exemplary judicial officer. . . .

. . .

If Minnesota believes that certain sorts of candidate speech disclose flaws in the candidate's credentials, democracy and free speech are their own correctives. . . .

. . .

. . . This case does not present the question whether a State may restrict the speech of judges because they are judges—for example, as part of a code of judicial conduct; the law at issue here regulates judges only when and because they are candidates. Whether the rationale of *Pickering v. Board of Ed. of Township High School Dist. 205, Will Cty.,* 391 U.S. 563, 568 (1968), and *Connick v. Myers,* 461 U.S. 138 (1983), could be extended to allow a general speech restriction on sitting judges—regardless of whether they are campaigning—in order to promote the efficient administration of justice, is not an issue raised here.

Petitioner Gregory Wersal was not a sitting judge but a challenger; he had not voluntarily entered into an employment relationship with the State or surrendered any First Amendment rights. His speech may not be controlled or abridged in this manner. Even the undoubted interest of the State in the excellence of its judiciary does not allow it to restrain candidate speech by reason of its content. Minnesota's attempt to regulate campaign speech is impermissible.

Justice Stevens, with Whom Justice Souter, Justice Ginsburg, and Justice Breyer join, dissenting.

... I ... join [Justice Ginsburg's] opinion without reservation. I add these comments to emphasize the force of her arguments and to explain why I find the Court's reasoning even more troubling than its holding. The limits of the Court's holding are evident: Even if the Minnesota Lawyers Professional Responsibility Board (Board) may not sanction a judicial candidate for announcing his views on issues likely to come before him, it may surely advise the electorate that such announcements demonstrate the speaker's unfitness for judicial office. If the solution to harmful speech must be more speech, so be it. The Court's reasoning, however, will unfortunately endure beyond the next election cycle. By obscuring the fundamental distinction between campaigns for the judiciary and the political branches, and by failing to recognize the difference between statements made in articles or opinions and those made on the campaign trail, the Court defies any sensible notion of the judicial office and the importance of impartiality in that context.

. . .

The disposition of this case on the flawed premise that the criteria for the election to judicial office should mirror the rules applicable to political elections is profoundly misguided. I therefore respectfully dissent.

Justice Ginsburg, with Whom Justice Stevens, Justice Souter, and Justice Breyer join, dissenting.

... Unlike their counterparts in the political branches, judges are expected to refrain from catering to particular constituencies or committing themselves on controversial issues in advance of adversarial presentation. ...

. . .

The ability of the judiciary to discharge its unique role rests to a large degree on the manner in which judges are selected....

The question this case presents is whether the First Amendment stops Minnesota from furthering its interest in judicial integrity through this precisely targeted speech restriction.

I

. . .

... I would differentiate elections for political offices, in which the First Amendment holds full sway, from elections designed to select those whose office it is to administer justice without respect to persons. ...

Legislative and executive officials serve in representative capacities. ...

Judges, however, are not political actors. They do not sit as representatives of particular persons, communities, or parties; they serve no faction or constituency. ... They must strive to do what is legally right, all the more so when the result is not the one "the home crowd" wants. ...

Thus, the rationale underlying unconstrained speech in elections for political office—that representative government depends on the public's ability to choose agents who will act at its behest—does not carry over to campaigns for the bench. ...

. . .

... The balance the State sought to achieve—allowing the people to elect judges, but safeguarding the process so that the integrity of the judiciary would not be compromised—should encounter no First Amendment shoal.

. . . .

This Court has recognized in the past, as Justice O'Connor does today, a "fundamental tension between the ideal character of the judicial office and the real world of electoral politics." ... We have no warrant to resolve that tension, however, by forcing States to choose one pole or the other. Judges are not politicians, and the First Amendment does not require that they be treated as politicians simply because they are chosen by popular vote. Nor does the First Amendment command States who wish to promote the integrity of their judges in fact and appearance to abandon systems of judicial selection that the people, in the exercise of their sovereign prerogatives, have devised.

For more than three-quarters of a century, States like Minnesota have endeavored, through experiment tested by experience, to balance the constitutional interests in judicial integrity and free expression within the unique setting of an elected judiciary. ... I would uphold it as an essential component in Minnesota's accommodation of the complex and competing concerns in this sensitive area. ...

B.   POLITICAL FUNDRAISING AND EXPENDITURES

Page 1496.   Replace Federal Election Commission v. National Right to Work Committee:

Federal Election Commission v. Beaumont

___ U.S. ___, 123 S.Ct. ___, ___ L.Ed.2d ___ (2003).

Justice Souter delivered the opinion of the Court.

Since 1907, federal law has barred corporations from contributing directly to candidates for federal office. We hold that applying the prohibition to nonprofit advocacy corporations is consistent with the First Amendment.

I

The current statute makes it "unlawful ... for any corporation whatever ... to make a contribution or expenditure in connection with" certain federal elections, ... 2 U.S.C. § 441b(a) ... The prohibition does not, however, forbid "the establishment, administration, and solicitation of contributions to a separate segregated fund to be utilized for political purposes." ... Such a PAC ... may be wholly controlled by the sponsoring corporation, whose employees and stockholders or members generally may be solicited for contributions. ...

Respondents are a corporation known as North Carolina Right to Life, Inc., three of its officers, and a North Carolina voter (here, together, NCRL) ... NCRL challenges the constitutionality of § 441b and the FEC's regulations implementing that section ... The corporation ... provide[s] counseling to pregnant women and ... urge[s] alternatives to abortion, and as a nonprofit advocacy corporation it is exempted from federal taxation ... It has no shareholders and, although it receives some donations from traditional business corporations, it is "overwhelmingly funded by private contributions from individuals." . . .

The District Court granted summary judgment to NCRL and held § 441b unconstitutional as applied to the corporation . . . A divided Court of Appeals for the Fourth Circuit affirmed, relying primarily on *Massachusetts Citizens for Life,* [479 U.S. 238 (1986),] in which this Court held it unconstitutional to apply the statute to independent expenditures by Massachusetts Citizens for Life, Inc., a nonprofit advocacy corporation in some respects like NCRL. . . .

. . .

We now reverse.

II

A

Any attack on the federal prohibition of direct corporate political contributions goes against the current of a century of congressional efforts to curb corporations' potentially "deleterious influences on federal elections," which we have canvassed a number of times before. . . . The current law grew out of a "popular feeling" in the late 19th century "that aggregated capital unduly influenced politics, an influence not stopping short of corruption." . . . A demand for congressional action gathered force in the campaign of 1904, which made a national issue of the political leverage exerted through corporate contributions, and after the election and new revelations of corporate political overreaching, President Theodore Roosevelt made banning corporate political contributions a legislative priority. . . .

Since 1907, there has been continual congressional attention to corporate political activity, sometimes resulting in refinement of the law, sometimes in overhaul. One feature, however, has stayed intact . . . and much of the periodic amendment was meant to strengthen the original, core prohibition on direct corporate contributions. . . .

Today, as in 1907, the law focuses on the "special characteristics of the corporate structure" that threaten the integrity of the political process. . . .

Hence, the public interest in "restrict[ing] the influence of political war chests funneled through the corporate form." . . .

. . . [N]ot only has the original ban on direct corporate contributions endured, but so have the original rationales for the law. . . .

Quite aside from war-chest corruption and the interests of contributors and owners, however, another reason for regulating corporate electoral involvement has emerged with restrictions on individual contributions, and recent cases have recognized that restricting contributions by various organizations hedges against their use as conduits for "circumvention of [valid] contribution limits." . . . To the degree that a corporation could contribute to political candidates, the individuals "who created it, who own it, or whom it employs," . . . could exceed the bounds imposed on their own contributions by diverting money through the corporation . . .

In sum, our cases on campaign finance regulation represent respect for the "legislative judgment that the special characteristics of the corporate structure require particularly careful regulation." . . .

B

That historical prologue would discourage any broadside attack on corporate campaign finance regulation or regulation of corporate contributions, and NCRL accordingly questions § 441b only to the extent the law places nonprofit advocacy corporations like itself under the general ban on direct contributions. But not even this more focused challenge can claim a blank slate, for . . . our explanation in [Federal Election Comm'n v.] *National Right to Work* [Comm'n, 459 U.S. 197 (1982),] all but decided the issue against NCRL's position.

National Right to Work addressed the provision of § 441b restricting a nonstock corporation to its membership when soliciting contributions to its PAC, and we considered whether a nonprofit advocacy corporation without members of the usual sort could be held to violate the law by soliciting a donation to its PAC from any individual who had at one time contributed to the corporation. . . . We sustained the FEC's position that a fund drive as broad as this went beyond the solicitation of "members" permitted by § 441b, . . . holding that the statutory restriction was no infringement on those First Amendment associational rights closely akin to speech. . . . We concluded that the congressional judgment to regulate corporate political involvement "warrants considerable deference" and "reflects a permissible assessment of the dangers posed by [corporations] to the electoral process." . . .

. . .

But *National Right to Work* does not stand alone in its bearing on the issue here, and equal significance must be accorded to *Massachusetts Citizens for Life*, the very case upon which NCRL and the Court of Appeals have placed principal reliance. There, we held the prohibition on independent expenditures under § 441b unconstitutional as applied to a nonprofit advocacy corporation. . . . [T]he majority . . . distinguished *National Right to Work* on the ground of its addressing regulation of contributions, not expenditures. . . .

C

The upshot is that, although we have never squarely held against NCRL's position here, we could not hold for it without recasting our understanding of the risks of harm posed by corporate political contributions, of the expressive significance of contributions, and of the consequent deference owed to legislative judgments on what to do about them. NCRL's efforts, however, fail to unsettle existing law on any of these points.

. . .

. . . [R]ecognition that degree of scrutiny turns on the nature of the activity regulated is the only practical way to square two leading cases: *National Right to Work* approved strict solicitation limits on a PAC organized to make contributions, . . . whereas *Massachusetts Citizens for Life* applied a compelling interest test to invalidate the ban on an advocacy corporation's expenditures in light of PAC regulatory burdens. . . . Each case involved § 441b, after all, and the same "ban" on the same corporate "sources" of political activity applied in both cases.

It is not that the difference between a ban and a limit is to be ignored; it is just that the time to consider it is when applying scrutiny at the level selected, not in selecting the standard of review itself. But even when NCRL urges precisely that, and asserts that § 441b is not sufficiently "closely drawn," the claim still rests on a false premise, for NCRL is simply wrong in characterizing § 441b as a complete ban. ... The PAC option allows corporate political participation without the temptation to use corporate funds for political influence, quite possibly at odds with the sentiments of some shareholders or members, and it lets the government regulate campaign activity through registration and disclosure ... without jeopardizing the associational rights of advocacy organizations' members ...

... [A] unanimous Court in *National Right to Work* did not think the regulatory burdens on PACs, including restrictions on their ability to solicit funds, rendered a PAC unconstitutional as an advocacy corporation's sole avenue for making political contributions. ... There is no reason to think the burden on advocacy corporations is any greater today, or to reach a different conclusion here.

. . .

Justice Kennedy, concurring in the judgment.

My position, expressed in dissenting opinions in previous cases, has been that the Court erred in sustaining certain state and federal restrictions on political speech in the campaign finance context and misapprehended basic First Amendment principles in doing so. ... I adhere to this view, and so can give no weight to those authorities in the instant case.

That said, it must be acknowledged that *Federal Election Comm'n v. Massachusetts Citizens for Life, Inc.,* 479 U.S. 238 (1986) (MCFL), contains language supporting the Court's holding here that corporate contributions can be regulated more closely than corporate expenditures. ...

Were we presented with a case in which the distinction between contributions and expenditures under the whole scheme of campaign finance regulation were under review, I might join Justice Thomas' opinion. The Court does not undertake that comprehensive examination here, however. And since there is language in *MCFL* that supports today's holding, I concur in the judgment.

Justice Thomas, with whom Justice Scalia joins, dissenting.

I continue to believe that campaign finance laws are subject to strict scrutiny. Accordingly, I would affirm the judgment of the Court of Appeals and respectfully dissent from the Court's contrary disposition.

Page 1504. Delete Colorado Republican Federal Campaign Committee v. Federal Election Commission:

Page 1504. Add after Nixon v. Shrink Missouri Government PAC:

Federal Election Commission v. Colorado Republican Federal Campaign Committee

533 U.S. 431, 121 S.Ct. 2351, 150 L.Ed.2d 461 (2001).

Justice Souter delivered the opinion of the Court.

In Colorado Republican Federal Campaign Comm. v. Federal Election Comm'n, 518 U.S. 604 (1996) (*Colorado I*), we held that spending limits set by the Federal Election Campaign Act were unconstitutional as applied to the Colorado Republican Party's independent expenditures in connection with a senatorial campaign. We remanded for consideration of the party's claim that all limits on expenditures by a political party in connection with congressional campaigns are facially unconstitutional and thus unenforceable even as to spending coordinated with a candidate. Today we reject that facial challenge to the limits on parties' coordinated expenditures.

I

... [I]n Buckley v. Valeo, ... we held that the Act's limitations on contributions to a candidate's election campaign were generally constitutional, but that limitations on election expenditures were not. . . .

The simplicity of the distinction is qualified, however, by the Act's provision for a functional, not formal, definition of "contribution," which includes "expenditures made by any person in cooperation, consultation, or concert, with, or at the request or suggestion of, a candidate, his authorized political committees, or their agents," ... Expenditures coordinated with a candidate, that is, are contributions under the Act.

The Federal Election Commission originally took the position that any expenditure by a political party in connection with a particular election for federal office was presumed to be coordinated with the party's candidate. ... The Commission thus operated on the assumption that all expenditure limits imposed on political parties were, in essence, contribution limits and therefore constitutional. . . . Such limits include 2 U.S.C. § 441a(d)(3), which provides that in elections for the United States Senate, each national or state party committee is limited to spending the greater of $20,000 (adjusted for inflation . . .) or two cents multiplied by the voting age population of the State in which the election is held. . . .

Colorado I was an as-applied challenge to § 441a(d)(3) (which we spoke of as the Party Expenditure Provision), occasioned by the Commission's enforcement action against the Colorado Republican Federal Campaign Committee (Party) for exceeding the campaign spending limit through its payments for radio advertisements attacking Democratic Congressman and senatorial candidate Timothy Wirth. ... The Party defended in part with the claim that the party expenditure limitations violated the First Amendment, and the principal opinion in *Colorado I* agreed that the limitations were unconstitutional as applied to the advertising expenditures at issue. Unlike the Commission, the Members of the Court who joined the principal opinion thought the payments were "independent expenditures" as that term had been used in our prior cases, owing to the facts that the Party spent the money before selecting its own senatorial candidate and without any arrangement with potential nominees. . . .

The Party's broader claim remained: that although prior decisions of this Court had upheld the constitutionality of limits on coordinated expenditures by political speakers other than parties, the congressional campaign expenditure limitations on parties themselves are facially unconstitutional, and so are incapable of reaching party spending even when coordinated with a candidate. ... On remand the District Court held for the Party, ... and a divided panel of the Court of Appeals ... affirmed. We ... reverse.

II

Spending for political ends and contributing to political candidates both fall within the First Amendment's protection of speech and political association. ... But ... limits on political expenditures deserve closer scrutiny than restrictions on political contributions. ... Restraints on expenditures generally curb more expressive and associational activity than limits on contributions do. ... A further reason for the distinction is that limits on contributions are more clearly justified by a link to political corruption than limits on other kinds of unlimited political spending are.... At least this is so where the spending is not coordinated with a candidate or his campaign. ...

Given these differences, we have routinely struck down limitations on independent expenditures by candidates, other individuals, and groups, ... while repeatedly upholding contribution limits....

The First Amendment line between spending and donating is easy to draw when it falls between independent expenditures by individuals or political action committees (PACs) without any candidate's approval (or wink or nod), and contributions in the form of cash gifts to candidates. ... But facts speak less clearly once the independence of the spending cannot be taken for granted, and money spent by an individual or PAC according to an arrangement with a candidate is therefore harder to classify. ...

Colorado I addressed the FEC's effort to stretch the functional treatment of coordinated expenditures further than the plain application of the statutory definition. ... FEC argued that parties and candidates are coupled so closely that all of a party's expenditures on an election campaign are coordinated with its candidate; ... *Colorado I* held otherwise, however, the principal opinion's view being that some party expenditures could be seen as "independent" for constitutional purposes. ... The principal opinion found no reason to see these expenditures as more likely to serve or be seen as instruments of corruption than independent expenditures by anyone else. So there was no justification for subjecting party election spending across the board to the kinds of limits previously invalidated when applied to individuals and nonparty groups. The principal opinion observed that "[t]he independent expression of a political party's views is 'core' First Amendment activity no less than is the independent expression of individuals, candidates, or other political committees." Since the FEC did not advance any other convincing reason for refusing to draw the independent-coordinated line accepted since *Buckley*, ... that was the end of the case so far as it concerned independent spending. ...

But that still left the question whether the First Amendment allows coordinated election expenditures by parties to be treated functionally as contributions, the way coordinated expenditures by other entities are treated. *Colorado I* found no justification for placing parties at a disadvantage when spending independently; but was there a case for leaving them entirely free to coordinate unlimited spending with candidates when others could not? The principal opinion in *Colorado I* noted that coordinated expenditures "share some of the constitutionally relevant features of independent expenditures." ... But it also observed that "many [party coordinated expenditures] are ... virtually indistinguishable from simple contributions." ... Coordinated spending by a party, in other words, covers a spectrum of activity, as does coordinated spending by other political actors. The issue in this case is, accordingly, whether a party is otherwise in a different position from other political speakers, giving it a claim to demand a generally higher standard of scrutiny before its coordinated spending can be limited. The issue is posed by two questions: does limiting coordinated spending impose a unique burden on parties, and is there reason to think that coordinated spending by a party would raise the risk of corruption posed when others spend in coordination with a candidate? The issue is best viewed through the positions developed by the Party and the Government in this case.

III

The Party's argument that its coordinated spending, like its independent spending, should be left free from restriction under the *Buckley* line of cases boils down to this: because a party's most important speech is aimed at electing candidates and is itself expressed through those candidates, any limit on party support for a candidate imposes a unique First Amendment burden. The point of organizing a party, the argument goes, is to run a successful candidate who shares the party's policy goals. Therefore, while a campaign contribution is only one of several ways that individuals and nonparty groups speak and associate politically, ... financial support of candidates is essential to the nature of political parties as we know them. And coordination with a candidate is a party's natural way of operating, not merely an option that can easily be avoided. Limitation of any party expenditure coordinated with a candidate, the Party contends, is therefore a serious, rather than incidental, imposition on the party's speech and associative purpose, and that justifies a stricter level of scrutiny than we have applied to analogous limits on individuals and nonparty groups. But whatever level of scrutiny is applied, the Party goes on to argue, the burden on a party reflects a fatal mismatch between the effects of limiting coordinated party expenditures and the prevention of corruption or the appearance of it.

The Government's argument for treating coordinated spending like contributions goes back to *Buckley*. There, the rationale for endorsing Congress's equation of coordinated expenditures and contributions was that the equation "prevent[s] attempts to circumvent the Act through prearranged or coordinated expenditures amounting to disguised contributions." ... The idea was that coordinated expenditures are as useful to the candidate as cash, and that such "disguised contributions" might be given "as a quid pro quo for improper commitments from the candidate" (in contrast to independent expenditures, which are poor sources of leverage for a spender because they might be duplicative or counterproductive from a candidate's point of view). ... In effect, therefore, *Buckley* subjected limits on coordinated expenditures by individuals and nonparty groups to the same scrutiny it applied to limits on their cash contributions. The standard of scrutiny requires the limit to be " 'closely drawn' to match a 'sufficiently important interest,' ... though the dollar amount of the limit need not be 'fine tun[ed],' " ...

The Government develops this rationale a step further in applying it here. Coordinated spending by a party should be limited not only because it is like a party contribution, but for a further reason. A party's right to make unlimited expenditures coordinated with a candidate would induce individual and other nonparty contributors to give to the party in order to finance coordinated spending for a favored candidate beyond the contribution limits binding on them. The Government points out that a degree of circumvention is occurring under present law (which allows unlimited independent spending and some coordinated spending). Individuals and nonparty groups who have reached the limit of direct contributions to a candidate give to a party with the understanding that the contribution to the party will produce increased party spending for the candidate's benefit. The Government argues that if coordinated spending were unlimited, circumvention would increase: because coordinated spending is as effective as direct contributions in supporting a candidate, an increased opportunity for coordinated spending would aggravate the use of a party to funnel money to a candidate from individuals and nonparty groups, who would thus bypass the contribution limits that Buckley upheld.

IV

Each of the competing positions is plausible at first blush. Our evaluation of the arguments, however, leads us to reject the Party's claim to suffer a burden unique in any way that should make a categorical difference under the First Amendment. On the other side, the Government's contentions are ultimately borne out by evidence, entitling it to prevail in its characterization of party coordinated spending as the functional equivalent of contributions.

A

In assessing the Party's argument, we start with a word about what the Party is not saying. First, we do not understand the Party to be arguing that the line between independent and coordinated expenditures is conceptually unsound when applied to a political party instead of an individual or other association. . . .

Second, we do not understand the Party to be arguing that associations in general or political parties in particular may claim a variety of First Amendment protection that is different in kind from the speech and associational rights of their members. The Party's point, rather, is best understood as a factual one: coordinated spending is essential to parties because "a party and its candidate are joined at the hip," owing to the very conception of the party as an organization formed to elect candidates. Parties, thus formed, have an especially strong working relationship with their candidates, and the speech this special relationship facilitates is much more effective than independent speech.

There are two basic arguments here. The first turns on the relationship of a party to a candidate: a coordinated relationship between them so defines a party that it cannot function as such without coordinated spending, the object of which is a candidate's election. We think political history and political reality belie this argument. The second argument turns on the nature of a party as uniquely able to spend in ways that promote candidate success. We think that this argument is a double-edged sword, and one hardly limited to political parties.

1

The assertion that the party is so joined at the hip to candidates that most of its spending must necessarily be coordinated spending is a statement at odds with the history of nearly 30 years under the Act. It is well to remember that ever since the Act was amended in 1974, coordinated spending by a party committee in a given race has been limited by the provision challenged here. . . . It was not until 1996 and the decision in *Colorado I* that any spending was allowed above that amount, and since then only independent spending has been unlimited. As a consequence, the Party's claim that coordinated spending beyond the limit imposed by the Act is essential to its very function as a party amounts implicitly to saying that for almost three decades political parties have not been functional or have been functioning in systematic violation of the law. The Party, of course, does not in terms make either statement, and we cannot accept either implication. . . . [T]he political scientists who have weighed in on this litigation observe that "there is little evidence to suggest that coordinated party spending limits adopted by Congress have frustrated the ability of political parties to exercise their First Amendment rights to support their candidates," . . .

2

There is a different weakness in the seemingly unexceptionable premise that parties are organized for the purpose of electing candidates, so that imposing on the way parties serve that function is uniquely burdensome. The fault here is not so much metaphysics as myopia, a refusal to see how the power of money actually works in the political structure.

When we look directly at a party's function in getting and spending money, it would ignore reality to think that the party role is adequately described by speaking generally of electing particular candidates. The money parties spend comes from contributors with their own personal interests. . . . In fact, many PACs naturally express their narrow interests by contributing to both parties during the same electoral cycle, and sometimes even directly to two competing candidates in the same election. . . . Parties are thus necessarily the instruments of some contributors whose object is not to support the party's message or to elect party candidates across the board, but rather to support a specific candidate for the sake of a position on one, narrow issue, or even to support any candidate who will be obliged to the contributors.

Parties thus perform functions more complex than simply electing candidates; whether they like it or not, they act as agents for spending on behalf of those who seek to produce obligated officeholders. It is this party role, which functionally unites parties with other self-interested political actors, that the Party Expenditure Provision targets. This party role, accordingly, provides good reason to view limits on coordinated spending by parties through the same lens applied to such spending by donors, like PACs, that can use parties as conduits for contributions meant to place candidates under obligation.

3

Insofar as the Party suggests that its strong working relationship with candidates and its unique ability to speak in coordination with them should be taken into account in the First Amendment analysis, we agree. . . . [T]he party is efficient in generating large sums to spend and in pinpointing effective ways to spend them. . . .

It does not, however, follow from a party's efficiency in getting large sums and spending intelligently that limits on a party's coordinated spending should be scrutinized under an unusually high standard, and in fact any argument from sophistication and power would cut both ways. On the one hand, one can seek the benefit of stricter scrutiny of a law capping party coordinated spending by emphasizing the heavy burden imposed by limiting the most effective mechanism of sophisticated spending. And yet it is exactly this efficiency culminating in coordinated spending that (on the Government's view) places a party in a position to be used to circumvent contribution limits that apply to individuals and PACs, and thereby to exacerbate the threat of corruption and apparent corruption that those contribution limits are aimed at reducing. ...

4

The preceding question assumes that parties enjoy a power and experience that sets them apart from other political spenders. But in fact the assumption is too crude. While parties command bigger spending budgets than most individuals, some individuals could easily rival party committees in spending. ...

Just as rich donors, media executives, and PACs have the means to speak as loudly as parties do, they would also have the capacity to work effectively in tandem with a candidate, just as a party can do. ... Yet all of them are subject to coordinated spending limits upheld in *Buckley*. ... A party, indeed, is now like some of these political actors in yet another way: in its right under *Colorado I* to spend money in support of a candidate without legal limit so long as it spends independently. A party may spend independently every cent it can raise wherever it thinks its candidate will shine, on every subject and any viewpoint.

A party is not, therefore, in a unique position. ...

5

The Party's arguments for being treated differently from other political actors subject to limitation on political spending under the Act do not pan out. ... Indeed, parties' capacity to concentrate power to elect is the very capacity that apparently opens them to exploitation as channels for circumventing contribution and coordinated spending limits binding on other political players. And some of these players could marshal the same power and sophistication for the same electoral objectives as political parties themselves.

We accordingly apply to a party's coordinated spending limitation the same scrutiny we have applied to the other political actors, that is, scrutiny appropriate for a contribution limit, enquiring whether the restriction is "closely drawn" to match what we have recognized as the "sufficiently important" government interest in combating political corruption. ... [T]he issue remains whether adequate evidentiary grounds exist to sustain the limit under that standard, on the theory that unlimited coordinated spending by a party raises the risk of corruption (and its appearance) through circumvention of valid contribution limits. ...

B

Since there is no recent experience with unlimited coordinated spending, the question is whether experience under the present law confirms a serious threat of abuse from the unlimited coordinated party spending as the Government contends. ... It clearly does. Despite years of enforcement of the challenged limits, substantial evidence demonstrates how candidates, donors, and parties test the limits of the current law, and it shows beyond serious doubt how contribution limits would be eroded if inducement to circumvent them were enhanced by declaring parties' coordinated spending wide open. ...

Under the Act, a donor is limited to $2,000 in contributions to one candidate in a given election cycle. The same donor may give as much as another $20,000 each year to a national party committee supporting the candidate. What a realist would expect to occur has occurred. Donors give to the party with the tacit understanding that the favored candidate will benefit. ...

Although the understanding between donor and party may involve no definite commitment and may be tacit on the donor's part, the frequency of the practice and the volume of money involved has required some manner of informal bookkeeping by the recipient. In the Democratic Party, at least, the method is known as "tallying," a system that helps to connect donors to candidates through the accommodation of a party. ...

Such is the state of affairs under the current law, which requires most party spending on a candidate's behalf to be done independently, and thus less desirably from the point of view of a donor and his favored candidate. If suddenly every dollar of spending could be coordinated with the candidate, the inducement to circumvent would almost certainly intensify. Indeed, if a candidate could be assured that donations through a party could result in funds passed through to him for spending on virtually identical items as his own campaign funds, a candidate enjoying the patronage of affluent contributors would have a strong incentive not merely to direct donors to his party, but to promote circumvention as a step toward reducing the number of donors requiring time-consuming cultivation. ...

V

While this evidence rules out denying the potential for corruption by circumvention, the Party does try to minimize the threat. It says that most contributions to parties are small, with negligible corrupting momentum to be carried through the party conduit. But some contributions are not small; they can go up to $20,000, ... and the record shows that even under present law substantial donations turn the parties into matchmakers whose special meetings and receptions give the donors the chance to get their points across to the candidates. The Party again discounts the threat of outflanking contribution limits on individuals and nonparty groups by stressing that incumbent candidates give more excess campaign funds to parties than parties spend on coordinated expenditures. But the fact that parties may do well for themselves off incumbents does not defuse concern over circumvention; if contributions to a party were not used as a funnel from donors to candidates, there would be no reason for using the tallying system the way the witnesses have described it.

Finally, the Party falls back to claiming that, even if there is a threat of circumvention, the First Amendment demands a response better tailored to that threat than a limitation on spending, even coordinated spending. The Party has two suggestions.

First, it says that better crafted safeguards are in place already, in particular the earmarking rule of § 441a(a)(8), which provides that contributions that "are in any way earmarked or otherwise directed through an intermediary or conduit to [a] candidate" are treated as contributions to the candidate. The Party says that this provision either suffices to address any risk of circumvention or would suffice if clarified to cover practices like tallying. This position, however, ignores the practical difficulty of identifying and directly combating circumvention under actual political conditions. Donations are made to a party by contributors who favor the party's candidates in races that affect them; donors are (of course) permitted to express their views and preferences to party officials; and the party is permitted (as we have held it must be) to spend money in its own right. When this is the environment for contributions going into a general party treasury, and candidate-fundraisers are rewarded with something less obvious than dollar-for-dollar pass-throughs (distributed through contributions and party spending), circumvention is obviously very hard to trace. The earmarking provision, even if it dealt directly with tallying, would reach only the most clumsy attempts to pass contributions through to candidates. To treat the earmarking provision as the outer limit of acceptable tailoring would disarm any serious effort to limit the corrosive effects of . . . "understandings" regarding what donors give what amounts to the party. . . .

The Party's second preferred prescription for the threat of an end run calls for replacing limits on coordinated expenditures by parties with limits on contributions to parties, the latter supposedly imposing a lesser First Amendment burden. The Party thus invokes the general rule that contribution limits take a lesser First Amendment toll, expenditure limits a greater one. That was one strand of the reasoning in *Buckley*. . . . It was also one strand of the logic of the *Colorado I* principal opinion. . . .

In each of those cases, however, the Court's reasoning contained another strand. The analysis ultimately turned on the understanding that the expenditures at issue were not potential alter egos for contributions, but were independent and therefore functionally true expenditures, qualifying for the most demanding First Amendment scrutiny employed in *Buckley*. . . .

Here, however, just the opposite is true. There is no significant functional difference between a party's coordinated expenditure and a direct party contribution to the candidate, and there is good reason to expect that a party's right of unlimited coordinated spending would attract increased contributions to parties to finance exactly that kind of spending. Coordinated expenditures of money donated to a party are tailor-made to undermine contribution limits. Therefore the choice here is not, as in *Buckley* and *Colorado I*, between a limit on pure contributions and pure expenditures. The choice is between limiting contributions and limiting expenditures whose special value as expenditures is also the source of their power to corrupt. Congress is entitled to its choice.

* * *

We hold that a party's coordinated expenditures, unlike expenditures truly independent, may be restricted to minimize circumvention of contribution limits. We therefore reject the Party's facial challenge and, accordingly, reverse the judgment of the United States Court of Appeals for the Tenth Circuit.

It is so ordered.

Justice Thomas, with whom Justice Scalia and Justice Kennedy join, and with whom The Chief Justice joins as to Part II, dissenting.

... Because this provision sweeps too broadly, interferes with the party-candidate relationship, and has not been proved necessary to combat corruption, I respectfully dissent.

I

As an initial matter, I continue to believe that Buckley v. Valeo ... should be overruled. ... I remain baffled that this Court has extended the most generous First Amendment safeguards to filing lawsuits, wearing profane jackets, and exhibiting drive-in movies with nudity, but has offered only tepid protection to the core speech and associational rights that our Founders sought to defend.

In this case, the Government does not attempt to argue that the Party Expenditure Provision satisfies strict scrutiny ... Nor could it. ...

II

We need not, however, overrule *Buckley* and apply strict scrutiny in order to hold the Party Expenditure Provision unconstitutional. Even under *Buckley* ... the regulation cannot pass constitutional muster. ... The rationale for [the] distinction between contributions and independent expenditures has been that, whereas ceilings on contributions by individuals and political committees "entai[l] only a marginal restriction" on First Amendment interests ...

A

... [A]t least implicitly, the Court draws two conclusions: coordinated expenditures are no different from contributions, and political parties are no different from individuals and political committees. Both conclusions are flawed.

1

... The Court considers a coordinated expenditure to be an " 'expenditur[e] made by any person in cooperation, consultation, or concert, with, or at the request or suggestion of, a candidate, his authorized political committees, or their agents.' " ... By restricting such speech, the Party Expenditure Provision undermines parties' "freedom to discuss candidates and issues," ibid., and cannot be reconciled with our campaign finance jurisprudence.

2

Even if I were to ignore the breadth of the statutory text, and to assume that all coordinated expenditures are functionally equivalent to contributions, I still would strike down the Party Expenditure Provision. ... Restricting contributions by individuals and political committees may ... entail only a "marginal restriction," . . . but the same cannot be said about limitations on political parties.

Political parties and their candidates are "inextricably intertwined" in the conduct of an election. . . . A party nominates its candidate; a candidate often is identified by party affiliation throughout the election and on the ballot; and a party's public image is largely defined by what its candidates say and do. . . . Because of this unity of interest, it is natural for a party and its candidate to work together and consult with one another during the course of the election. . . .

As the District Court explained, to break this link between the party and its candidates would impose "additional costs and burdens to promote the party message." This observation finds full support in the record. . . . Thus, far from being a mere "marginal" restraint on speech, . . . the Party Expenditure Provision has restricted the party's most natural form of communication; has precluded parties "from effectively amplifying the voice of their adherents," . . . and has had a "stifling effect on the ability of the party to do what it exists to do." . . .

The Court nevertheless concludes that these concerns of inhibiting party speech are rendered "implausible" by the nearly 30 years of history in which coordinated spending has been statutorily limited. I am unpersuaded. . . . First, the Court does not examine the record or the findings of the District Court, but instead relies wholly on the "observ[ations]" of the "political scientists" who happen to have written an amicus brief in support of the petitioner. I find more convincing, and more relevant, the record evidence that the parties have developed. . . . Second, we have never before upheld a limitation on speech simply because speakers have coped with the limitation for 30 years. . . . And finally, if the passage of time were relevant to the constitutional inquiry, I would wonder why the Court adopted a "30–year" rule rather than the possible countervailing "200–year" rule. For nearly 200 years, this country had congressional elections without limitations on coordinated expenditures by political parties. Nowhere does the Court suggest that these elections were not "functional," ante, at 14, or that they were marred by corruption.

According to the Court, "[p]arties are . . . the instruments of some contributors whose object is not to support the party's message or to elect party candidates across the board." There are two flaws in the Court's analysis. First, no one argues that a party's role is merely to get particular candidates elected. Surely, among other reasons, parties also exist to develop and promote a platform. The point is simply that parties and candidates have shared interests, that it is natural for them to work together, and that breaking the connection between parties and their candidates inhibits the promotion of the party's message. Second, the mere fact that some donors contribute to both parties and their candidates does not necessarily imply that the donors control the parties or their candidates. . . .

B

But even if I were to view parties' coordinated expenditures as akin to contributions by individuals and political committees, I still would hold the Party Expenditure Provision constitutionally invalid. . . . The question is whether the Government has demonstrated both that coordinated expenditures by parties give rise to corruption and that the restriction is "closely drawn" to curb this corruption. I believe it has not.

1

. . .

Considering that we have never upheld an expenditure limitation against political parties, I would posit that substantial evidence is necessary to justify the infringement of parties' First Amendment interests. But we need not accept this high evidentiary standard to strike down the Party Expenditure Provision for want of evidence. Under the least demanding evidentiary requirement, the Government has failed to carry its burden, for it has presented no evidence at all of corruption or the perception of corruption. The Government does not, and indeed cannot, point to any congressional findings suggesting that the Party Expenditure Provision is necessary, or even helpful, in reducing corruption or the perception of corruption. . . .

. . .

The dearth of evidence is unsurprising in light of the unique relationship between a political party and its candidates: "The very aim of a political party is to influence its candidate's stance on issues and, if the candidate takes office or is reelected, his votes." . . .

. . . [T]he Court relies upon an alternative theory of corruption. According to the Court, the Party Expenditure Provision helps combat circumvention of the limits on individual donors' contributions, which limits are necessary to reduce corruption by those donors. The primary problem with this contention, however, is that it too is plainly contradicted by the findings of the District Court and the overwhelming evidence in the record. And this contention is particularly surprising in light of *Colorado I*, in which we discussed the same opportunity for corruption through circumvention, and, far from finding it dispositive, concluded that any opportunity for corruption was "at best, attenuated." . . .

. . . The best evidence the Court can come up with . . . is the Democratic Senatorial Campaign Committee's (DSCC) use of the "tally system," which "connect[s] donors to candidates through the accommodation of a party." The tally system is not evidence of corruption-by-circumvention. In actuality, the DSCC is not acting as a mere conduit, allowing donors to contribute money in excess of the legal limits. The DSCC instead has allocated money based on a number of factors, including "the financial strength of the campaign," "what [the candidate's] poll numbers looked like," and "who had the best chance of winning or who needed the money most." . . . As the District Court found, "the primary consideration in allocating funds is which races are marginal—that is which races are ones where party money could be the difference between winning and losing." . . .

. . .

Finally, even if the tally system were evidence of corruption-through-circumvention, it is only evidence of what is occurring under the current system, not of additional "corruption" that would arise in the absence of the Party Expenditure Provision. The Court speculates that, if we invalidated the

Party Expenditure Provision, "the inducement to circumvent would almost certainly intensify." But that is nothing more than supposition....

2

Even if the Government had presented evidence that the Party Expenditure Provision affects corruption, the statute still would be unconstitutional, because there are better tailored alternatives for addressing the corruption. In addition to bribery laws and disclosure laws, ... the Government has two options that would not entail the restriction of political parties' First Amendment rights.

First, the Government could enforce the earmarking rule of 2 U.S.C. § 441a(a)(8), under which contributions that "are in any way earmarked or otherwise directed through an intermediary or conduit to [a] candidate" are treated as contributions to the candidate. ...

According to the Court, reliance on this earmarking provision "ignores the practical difficulty of identifying and directly combating circumvention" ... The Court, however, does not cite any evidence to support this assertion. Nor does it articulate what failed steps the Government already has taken. ...

In any event, there is a second, well-tailored option for combating corruption that does not entail the reduction of parties' First Amendment freedoms. ...If indeed $20,000 is enough to corrupt a candidate (an assumption that seems implausible on its face and is, in any event, unsupported by any evidence), the proper response is to lower the cap. That way, the speech restriction is directed at the source of the alleged corruption—the individual donor—and not the party. ...

In my view, it makes no sense to contravene a political party's core First Amendment rights because of what a third party might unlawfully try to do.
...

CHAPTER 16

FREEDOM OF THE PRESS

SECTION 6. SPECIAL PROBLEMS OF THE ELECTRONIC MEDIA

Page 1582. Add after Turner Broadcasting System v. Federal Communications Commission:

ELDRED v. ASHCROFT, 537 U.S. 186 (2003). This was an action challenging provisions of the 1998 Copyright Term Extension Act extending the copyright term of existing copyrights. Petitioners' major argument—that the enlargement of the term for existing works violated the Copyright Clause's "limited times" restriction—was rejected by the Court. (See p. 6, supra.) It also was claimed that the enlarged terms violated the First Amendment rights of those who wished to reproduce works that would otherwise have passed into the public domain. The Court rejected the argument that "strict scrutiny" review was appropriate. Petitioners' reliance on *Turner Broadcasting* was misplaced—the statute challenged there involved "must carry" regulations that went to the heart of the First Amendment in compelling expression of others' speech. Here, no one is obliged to reproduce another's speech. The Copyright Clause and the First Amendment were adopted close in time, indicating the Framers' view that limited copyright monopolies were consistent with free speech principles. Copyright law contains built-in provisions accommodating freedom of expression—copyright extends only to "expression," not "ideas," and is subject to a fair use defense.

Page 1583. Add at end of chapter:

Ashcroft v. ACLU

535 U.S. 564, 122 S.Ct. 1700, 152 L.Ed.2d 771 (2002).

[The report in this case appears supra p. 177.]

CHAPTER 17

RELIGION AND THE CONSTITUTION

SECTION 1.   THE ESTABLISHMENT CLAUSE

B.   GOVERNMENT RELIGIOUS EXERCISES, CEREMONIES, DISPLAYS AND PRACTICES

2.   RELIGIOUS SPEECH AND DISPLAYS ON PUBLIC PROPERTY

Page 1627.   Add at end of subsection:

Good News Club v. Milford Central School

533 U.S. 98, 121 S.Ct. 2093, 150 L.Ed.2d 151 (2001).

Justice Thomas delivered the opinion of the Court.

This case presents two questions. The first question is whether Milford Central School violated the free speech rights of the Good News Club when it excluded the Club from meeting after hours at the school. The second question is whether any such violation is justified by Milford's concern that permitting the Club's activities would violate the Establishment Clause. We conclude that Milford's restriction violates the Club's free speech rights and that no Establishment Clause concern justifies that violation.

I

... In 1992, respondent Milford Central School (Milford) enacted a community use policy adopting seven ... purposes for which its building could be used after school. Two of the stated purposes are relevant here. First, district residents may use the school for "instruction in any branch of education, learning or the arts." Second, the school is available for "social, civic and recreational meetings and entertainment events, and other uses pertaining to the welfare of the community, provided that such uses shall be nonexclusive and shall be opened to the general public."

Stephen and Darleen Fournier reside within Milford's district and therefore are eligible to use the school's facilities as long as their proposed use is approved by the school. Together they are sponsors of the local Good News Club, a private Christian organization for children ages 6 to 12. Pursuant to Milford's policy, ... the Fourniers submitted a request to Dr. Robert McGruder, interim superintendent of the district, in which they sought permission to hold the Club's weekly afterschool meetings in the school cafeteria. ... McGruder formally denied the Fourniers' request on the ground that the proposed use—to have "a fun time of singing songs, hearing a Bible lesson and memorizing scripture," was "the equivalent of religious worship." According to McGruder, the community use policy, which prohibits use "by any individual or organization for religious purposes," foreclosed the Club's activities.

. . . Milford's attorney requested information to clarify the nature of the Club's activities. The Club sent a set of materials used or distributed at the meetings and the following description of its meeting:

> "The Club opens its session with Ms. Fournier taking attendance. As she calls a child's name, if the child recites a Bible verse the child receives a treat. After attendance, the Club sings songs. Next Club members engage in games that involve, inter alia, learning Bible verses. Ms. Fournier then relates a Bible story and explains how it applies to Club members' lives. The Club closes with prayer. Finally, Ms. Fournier distributes treats and the Bible verses for memorization."

McGruder and Milford's attorney reviewed the materials and concluded that "the kinds of activities proposed to be engaged in by the Good News Club were not a discussion of secular subjects such as child rearing, development of character and development of morals from a religious perspective, but were in fact the equivalent of religious instruction itself." . . . [T]he Milford Board of Education adopted a resolution rejecting the Club's request to use Milford's facilities "for the purpose of conducting religious instruction and Bible study."

. . . [P]etitioners, the Good News Club, Ms. Fournier, and her daughter Andrea Fournier (collectively, the Club), filed an action under 42 U.S.C. § 1983 against Milford in the United States District Court for the Northern District of New York. . . .

. . . .

. . . [T]he District Court . . . granted Milford's motion for summary judgment. . . .

. . . [A] divided panel of the United States Court of Appeals for the Second Circuit affirmed. . . .

There is a conflict among the Courts of Appeals on the question whether speech can be excluded from a limited public forum on the basis of the religious nature of the speech. . . . We granted certiorari to resolve this conflict.

II

The standards that we apply to determine whether a State has unconstitutionally excluded a private speaker from use of a public forum depend on the nature of the forum. . . . We have previously declined to decide whether a school district's opening of its facilities . . . creates a limited or a traditional public forum. . . . Because the parties have agreed that Milford created a limited public forum when it opened its facilities in 1992, we need not resolve the issue here. Instead, we simply will assume that Milford operates a limited public forum.

When the State establishes a limited public forum, the State is not required to and does not allow persons to engage in every type of speech. The State may be justified "in reserving [its forum] for certain groups or for the discussion of certain topics." . . . The State's power to restrict speech, however, is not without limits. The restriction must not discriminate against speech on the basis of viewpoint, ... and the restriction must be "reasonable in light of the purpose served by the forum," ...

III

Applying this test, we first address whether the exclusion constituted viewpoint discrimination. We are guided in our analysis by two of our prior opinions, *Lamb's Chapel* [v. Center Moriches Union Free School Dist., 508 U.S. 384 (1993)] and *Rosenberger* [v. Rector and Visitors of Univ. of Va., 515 U.S. 819 (1995)]. In *Lamb's Chapel*, we held that a school district violated the Free Speech Clause of the First Amendment when it excluded a private group from presenting films at the school based solely on the films' discussions of family values from a religious perspective. Likewise, in *Rosenberger*, we held that a university's refusal to fund a student publication because the publication addressed issues from a religious perspective violated the Free Speech Clause. Concluding that Milford's exclusion of the Good News Club based on its religious nature is indistinguishable from the exclusions in these cases, we hold that the exclusion constitutes viewpoint discrimination. Because the restriction is viewpoint discriminatory, we need not decide whether it is unreasonable in light of the purposes served by the forum.

Milford has opened its limited public forum to activities that serve a variety of purposes, including events "pertaining to the welfare of the community." ... In short, any group that "promote[s] the moral and character development of children" is eligible to use the school building.

Just as there is no question that teaching morals and character development to children is a permissible purpose under Milford's policy, it is clear that the Club teaches morals and character development to children. For example, no one disputes that the Club instructs children to overcome feelings of jealousy, to treat others well regardless of how they treat the children, and to be obedient, even if it does so in a nonsecular way. Nonetheless, because Milford found the Club's activities to be religious in nature—"the equivalent of religious instruction itself," it excluded the Club from use of its facilities.

Applying *Lamb's Chapel*, we find it quite clear that Milford engaged in viewpoint discrimination when it excluded the Club from the afterschool forum. In *Lamb's Chapel*, the local New York school district similarly had adopted ... "social, civic or recreational use" ... as a permitted use in its limited public forum. The district also prohibited use "by any group for religious purposes." ... Citing this prohibition, the school district excluded a church that wanted to present films teaching family values from a Christian perspective. We held that, because the films "no doubt dealt with a subject otherwise permissible" under the rule, the teaching of family values, the district's exclusion of the church was unconstitutional viewpoint discrimination. ...

Like the church in *Lamb's Chapel*, the Club seeks to address a subject otherwise permitted under the rule, the teaching of morals and character, from a religious standpoint. ... The only apparent difference between the activity of Lamb's Chapel and the activities of the Good News Club is that the Club chooses to teach moral lessons from a Christian perspective through live storytelling and prayer, whereas Lamb's Chapel taught lessons through films. This distinction is inconsequential. Both modes of speech use a religious viewpoint. Thus, the exclusion of the Good News Club's activities, like the exclusion of Lamb's Chapel's films, constitutes unconstitutional viewpoint discrimination.

Our opinion in *Rosenberger* also is dispositive. In *Rosenberger*, a student organization at the University of Virginia was denied funding for printing expenses because its publication, Wide Awake, offered a Christian viewpoint. Just as the Club emphasizes the role of Christianity in students' morals and character, Wide Awake "challenge[d] Christians to live, in word and deed, according to the faith they proclaim and ... encourage[d] students to consider what a personal relationship with Jesus Christ means." ... Because the university "select[ed] for disfavored treatment those student journalistic efforts with religious editorial viewpoints," we held that the denial of funding was unconstitutional. ... Although in *Rosenberger* there was no prohibition on religion as a subject matter, our holding did not rely on this factor. Instead, we concluded simply that the university's denial of funding to print Wide Awake was viewpoint discrimination, just as the school district's refusal to allow Lamb's Chapel to show its films was viewpoint discrimination. Given the obvious religious content of Wide Awake, we cannot say that the Club's activities are any more "religious" or deserve any less First Amendment protection than did the publication of Wide Awake in *Rosenberger*.

Despite our holdings in *Lamb's Chapel* and *Rosenberger*, the Court of Appeals, like Milford, believed that its characterization of the Club's activities as religious in nature warranted treating the Club's activities as different in kind from the other activities permitted by the school. ...

We disagree that something that is "quintessentially religious" or "decidedly religious in nature" cannot also be characterized properly as the teaching of morals and character development from a particular viewpoint. ... What matters for purposes of the Free Speech Clause is that we can see no logical difference in kind between the invocation of Christianity by the Club and the invocation of teamwork, loyalty, or patriotism by other associations to provide a foundation for their lessons. ... [W]e reaffirm our holdings in *Lamb's Chapel* and *Rosenberger* that speech discussing otherwise permissible subjects cannot be excluded from a limited public forum on the ground that the subject is discussed from a religious viewpoint. Thus, we conclude that Milford's exclusion of the Club from use of the school, pursuant to its community use policy, constitutes impermissible viewpoint discrimination.

IV

Milford argues that, even if its restriction constitutes viewpoint discrimination, its interest in not violating the Establishment Clause outweighs the Club's interest in gaining equal access to the school's facilities. ... We disagree.

We have said that a state interest in avoiding an Establishment Clause violation "may be characterized as compelling," and therefore may justify content-based discrimination. ... However, it is not clear whether a State's interest in avoiding an Establishment Clause violation would justify viewpoint discrimination. ... We need not, however, confront the issue in this case, because we conclude that the school has no valid Establishment Clause interest.

We rejected Establishment Clause defenses similar to Milford's in ... *Lamb's Chapel* ... [W]e explained that "[t]he showing of th[e] film series would not have been during school hours, would not have been sponsored by the school, and would have been open to the public, not just to church members." ...

...

Milford attempts to distinguish *Lamb's Chapel* ... by emphasizing that Milford's policy involves elementary school children. According to Milford, children will perceive that the school is endorsing the Club and will feel coercive pressure to participate, because the Club's activities take place on school grounds, even though they occur during nonschool hours. This argument is unpersuasive.

First, we have held that "a significant factor in upholding governmental programs in the face of Establishment Clause attack is their neutrality towards religion." *Rosenberger*, ... Milford's implication that granting access to the Club would do damage to the neutrality principle defies logic. For the "guarantee of neutrality is respected, not offended, when the government, following neutral criteria and evenhanded policies, extends benefits to recipients whose ideologies and viewpoints, including religious ones, are broad and diverse." *Rosenberger* ... The Good News Club seeks nothing more than to be treated neutrally and given access to speak about the same topics as are other groups. Because allowing the Club to speak on school grounds would ensure neutrality, not threaten it, Milford faces an uphill battle in arguing that the Establishment Clause compels it to exclude the Good News Club.

Second, to the extent we consider whether the community would feel coercive pressure to engage in the Club's activities, ... the relevant community would be the parents, not the elementary school children. It is the parents who choose whether their children will attend the Good News Club meetings. Because the children cannot attend without their parents' permission, they cannot be coerced into engaging in the Good News Club's religious activities. Milford does not suggest that the parents of elementary school children would be confused about whether the school was endorsing religion. Nor do we believe that such an argument could be reasonably advanced.

Third, whatever significance we may have assigned in the Establishment Clause context to the suggestion that elementary school children are more impressionable than adults, ... we have never extended our Establishment Clause jurisprudence to foreclose private religious conduct during nonschool hours merely because it takes place on school premises where elementary school children may be present.

None of the cases discussed by Milford persuades us that our Establishment Clause jurisprudence has gone this far. For example, Milford cites Lee v. Weisman [505 U.S. 577 (1992)] for the proposition that "there are heightened concerns with protecting freedom of conscience from subtle coercive pressure in the elementary and secondary public schools," ... In *Lee*, however, we concluded that attendance at the graduation exercise was obligatory. ... We did not place independent significance on the fact that the graduation exercise might take place on school premises.... Here, where the school facilities are being used for a nonschool function and there is no government sponsorship of the Club's activities, *Lee* is inapposite.

Equally unsupportive is Edwards v. Aguillard, 482 U.S. 578 (1987), in which we held that a Louisiana law that proscribed the teaching of evolution as part of the public school curriculum, unless accompanied by a lesson on creationism, violated the Establishment Clause. In *Edwards*, we mentioned that students are susceptible to pressure in the classroom, particularly given their possible reliance on teachers as role models. But we did not discuss this concern in our application of the law to the facts. Moreover, we did note that mandatory attendance requirements meant that State advancement of religion in a school would be particularly harshly felt by impressionable students. But we did not suggest that, when the school was not actually advancing religion, the impressionability of students would be relevant to the Establishment Clause issue. Even if *Edwards* had articulated the principle Milford believes it did, the facts in *Edwards* are simply too remote from those here to give the principle any weight. *Edwards* involved the content of the curriculum taught by state teachers during the schoolday to children required to attend. Obviously, when individuals who are not schoolteachers are giving lessons after school to children permitted to attend only with parental consent, the concerns expressed in Edwards are not present.

Fourth, even if we were to consider the possible misperceptions by schoolchildren in deciding whether Milford's permitting the Club's activities would violate the Establishment Clause, the facts of this case simply do not support Milford's conclusion. There is no evidence that young children are permitted to loiter outside classrooms after the schoolday has ended. Surely even young children are aware of events for which their parents must sign permission forms. The meetings were held in a combined high school resource room and middle school special education room, not in an elementary school classroom. The instructors are not schoolteachers. And the children in the group are not all the same age as in the normal classroom setting; their ages range from 6 to 12. In sum, these circumstances simply do not support the theory that small children would perceive endorsement here.

Finally, even if we were to inquire into the minds of schoolchildren in this case, we cannot say the danger that children would misperceive the endorsement of religion is any greater than the danger that they would perceive a hostility toward the religious viewpoint if the Club were excluded from the public forum. . . .

. . . We cannot operate . . . under the assumption that any risk that small children would perceive endorsement should counsel in favor of excluding the Club's religious activity. We decline to employ Establishment Clause jurisprudence using a modified heckler's veto, in which a group's religious activity can be proscribed on the basis of what the youngest members of the audience might misperceive. . . .

. . .

V

When Milford denied the Good News Club access to the school's limited public forum on the ground that the Club was religious in nature, it discriminated against the Club because of its religious viewpoint in violation of the Free Speech Clause of the First Amendment. Because Milford has not raised a valid

Establishment Clause claim, we do not address the question whether such a claim could excuse Milford's viewpoint discrimination.

. . .

Justice Scalia, concurring.

I join the Court's opinion but write separately to explain further my views on two issues.

I

First, I join Part IV of the Court's opinion, regarding the Establishment Clause issue, with the understanding that its consideration of coercive pressure, and perceptions of endorsement, "to the extent" that the law makes such factors relevant, is consistent with the belief (which I hold) that in this case that extent is zero. ... Physical coercion is not at issue here; and so-called "peer pressure," if it can even been considered coercion, is, when it arises from private activities, one of the attendant consequences of a freedom of association that is constitutionally protected ... What is at play here is not coercion, but the compulsion of ideas—and the private right to exert and receive that compulsion (or to have one's children receive it) is protected by the Free Speech and Free Exercise Clauses, ... not banned by the Establishment Clause. A priest has as much liberty to proselytize as a patriot.

As to endorsement, I have previously written that "[r]eligious expression cannot violate the Establishment Clause where it (1) is purely private and (2) occurs in a traditional or designated public forum, publicly announced and open to all on equal terms." ...

II

Second, since we have rejected the only reason that respondent gave for excluding the Club's speech from a forum that clearly included it (the forum was opened to any "us[e] pertaining to the welfare of the community . . .") I do not suppose it matters whether the exclusion is characterized as viewpoint or subject-matter discrimination. ...

As I understand it, the point of disagreement between the Court and the dissenters ... with regard to petitioner's Free Speech Clause claim is not whether the Good News Club must be permitted to present religious viewpoints on morals and character in respondent's forum. . . .

The disagreement, rather, regards the portions of the Club's meetings that are not "purely" "discussions" of morality and character from a religious viewpoint. The Club, for example, urges children "who already believe in the Lord Jesus as their Savior" to "[s]top and ask God for the strength and the 'want' . . . to obey Him,". . . . The dissenters ... say that the presence of such additional speech, because it is purely religious, transforms the Club's meetings into something different in kind from other, nonreligious activities that teach moral and character development. . . . I disagree.

. . .

From no other group does respondent require the sterility of speech that it demands of petitioners. ... The Club may not ... independently discuss the religious premise on which its views are based—that God exists and His assistance is necessary to morality. It may not defend the premise, and it absolutely must not seek to persuade the children that the premise is true. The children must, so to say, take it on faith. This is blatant viewpoint discrimination.

. . .

The dissenters emphasize that the religious speech used by the Club as the foundation for its views on morals and character is not just any type of religious speech.... In Justice Stevens' view, it is speech "aimed principally at proselytizing or inculcating belief in a particular religious faith." This does not ... distinguish the Club's activities from those of the other groups using respondent's forum—which have not, as Justice Stevens suggests, been restricted to roundtable "discussions" of moral issues. ...

Justice Souter, while agreeing that the Club's religious speech "may be characterized as proselytizing," thinks that it is even more clearly excludable from respondent's forum because it is essentially "an evangelical service of worship." But we have previously rejected the attempt to distinguish worship from other religious speech ... If the distinction did have content, it would be beyond the courts' competence to administer. ...

. . .

Justice Breyer, concurring in part.

I agree with the Court's conclusion and join its opinion to the extent that they are consistent with the following three observations. First, the government's "neutrality" in respect to religion is one, but only one, of the considerations relevant to deciding whether a public school's policy violates the Establishment Clause. ...

Second, the critical Establishment Clause question here may well prove to be whether a child, participating in the Good News Club's activities, could reasonably perceive the school's permission for the club to use its facilities as an endorsement of religion. ...

Third, the Court cannot fully answer the Establishment Clause question this case raises, given its procedural posture. ...

To deny one party's motion for summary judgment ... is not to grant summary judgment for the other side. There may be disputed "genuine issue[s]" of "material fact," ... particularly about how a reasonable child participant would understand the school's role.... The Court's invocation of what is missing from the record and its assumptions about what is present in the record only confirm that both parties, if they so desire, should have a fair opportunity to fill the evidentiary gap in light of today's opinion. ...

Justice Stevens, dissenting.

The Milford Central School has invited the public to use its facilities for educational and recreational purposes, but not for "religious purposes." Speech for "religious purposes" may reasonably be understood to encompass three different categories. First, there is religious speech that is simply speech about a particular topic from a religious point of view. ... Second, there is religious speech that amounts to worship, or its equivalent. ... Third, there is an intermediate category that is aimed principally at proselytizing or inculcating belief in a particular religious faith.

A public entity may not generally exclude even religious worship from an open public forum. . . . Similarly, a public entity that creates a limited public forum for the discussion of certain specified topics may not exclude a speaker simply because she approaches those topics from a religious point of view. . . .

. . . The novel question that this case presents concerns the constitutionality of a public school's attempt to limit the scope of a public forum it has created. More specifically, the question is whether a school can, consistently with the First Amendment, create a limited public forum that admits the first type of religious speech without allowing the other two.

. . . If a school decides to authorize after school discussions of current events in its classrooms, it may not exclude people from expressing their views simply because it dislikes their particular political opinions. But must it therefore allow organized political groups—for example, the Democratic Party, the Libertarian Party, or the Ku Klux Klan—to hold meetings, the principal purpose of which is not to discuss the current-events topic from their own unique point of view but rather to recruit others to join their respective groups? I think not. . . .

School officials may reasonably believe that evangelical meetings designed to convert children to a particular religious faith pose the same risk. And, just as a school may allow meetings to discuss current events from a political perspective without also allowing organized political recruitment, so too can a school allow discussion of topics such as moral development from a religious (or nonreligious) perspective without thereby opening its forum to religious proselytizing or worship. . . .

. . .

This case is undoubtedly close. Nonetheless, regardless of whether the Good News Club's activities amount to "worship," it does seem clear, based on the facts in the record, that the school district correctly classified those activities as falling within the third category of religious speech and therefore beyond the scope of the school's limited public forum. . . .

. . .

Justice Souter, with whom Justice Ginsburg joins, dissenting.

. . .

I

. . .

This case, like *Lamb's Chapel*, properly raises no issue about the reasonableness of Milford's criteria for restricting the scope of its designated public forum. . . .

The sole question before the District Court was, therefore, whether, in refusing to allow Good News's intended use, Milford was misapplying its unchallenged restriction in a way that amounted to imposing a viewpoint-based restriction on what could be said or done by a group entitled to use the forum for an educational, civic, or other permitted purpose. . . .

. . .

. . . [T]he . . . undisputed facts in this case differ from those in *Lamb's Chapel*, as night from day. . . .

. . .

It is beyond question that Good News intends to use the public school premises not for the mere discussion of a subject from a particular, Christian point of view, but for an evangelical service of worship calling children to commit themselves in an act of Christian conversion. The majority avoids this reality only by resorting to the bland and general characterization of Good News's activity as "teaching of morals and character, from a religious standpoint." If the majority's statement ignores reality, as it surely does, then today's holding may be understood only in equally generic terms. Otherwise, indeed, this case would stand for the remarkable proposition that any public school opened for civic meetings must be opened for use as a church, synagogue, or mosque.

II

I also respectfully dissent from the majority's refusal to remand on all other issues, insisting instead on acting as a court of first instance in reviewing Milford's claim that it would violate the Establishment Clause to grant Good News's application. . . .

. . .

What we know about this case looks very little like . . . *Lamb's Chapel*. The cohort addressed by Good News is not university students with relative maturity, or even high school pupils, but elementary school children as young as six. The Establishment Clause cases have consistently recognized the particular impressionability of schoolchildren, . . . and the special protection required for those in the elementary grades in the school forum. . . .

Nor is Milford's limited forum anything like the sites for wide-ranging intellectual exchange that were home to the challenged activities in . . . *Lamb's Chapel*. See also *Rosenberger* . . . .

The timing and format of Good News's gatherings . . . may well affirmatively suggest the imprimatur of officialdom in the minds of the young children. The club is open solely to elementary students (not the entire community, as in Lamb's Chapel), only four outside groups have been identified as meeting in the school, and Good News is, seemingly, the only one whose instruction follows immediately on the conclusion of the official school day. . . . In fact, the temporal and physical continuity of Good News's meetings with the regular school routine seems to be the whole point of using the school. When meetings were held in a community church, 8 or 10 children attended; after the school became the site, the number went up three-fold.

. . .

C.   FINANCIAL AID TO CHURCH-RELATED SCHOOLS AND CHURCH-RELATED INSTRUCTION

1.   ELEMENTARY AND SECONDARY SCHOOLS

Page 1643.   Add at end of subsection:

Zelman v. Simmons–Harris

536 U.S. 639, 122 S.Ct. 2460, 153 L.Ed.2d 604 (2002).

Chief Justice Rehnquist delivered the opinion of the Court.

The State of Ohio has established a pilot program designed to provide educational choices to families with children who reside in the Cleveland City School District. The question presented is whether this program offends the Establishment Clause of the United States Constitution. We hold that it does not.

There are more than 75,000 children enrolled in the Cleveland City School District. The majority of these children are from low-income and minority families. Few of these families enjoy the means to send their children to any school other than an inner-city public school. For more than a generation, however, Cleveland's public schools have been among the worst performing public schools in the Nation. In 1995, a Federal District Court ... placed the entire Cleveland school district under state control. ... The district had failed to meet any of the 18 state standards for minimal acceptable performance. Only 1 in 10 ninth graders could pass a basic proficiency examination, and students at all levels performed at a dismal rate compared with students in other Ohio public schools. More than two-thirds of high school students either dropped or failed out before graduation. Of those students who managed to reach their senior year, one of every four still failed to graduate. Of those students who did graduate, few could read, write, or compute at levels comparable to their counterparts in other cities.

It is against this backdrop that Ohio enacted, among other initiatives, its Pilot Project Scholarship Program ... The program provides financial assistance to families in any Ohio school district that is or has been "under federal court order requiring supervision and operational management of the district by the state superintendent." .... Cleveland is the only Ohio school district to fall within that category.

The program provides two basic kinds of assistance to parents of children in a covered district. First, the program provides tuition aid for students in kindergarten through third grade, expanding each year through eighth grade, to attend a participating public or private school of their parent's choosing. ... Second, the program provides tutorial aid for students who choose to remain enrolled in public school. ...

The tuition aid portion of the program is designed to provide educational choices to parents who reside in a covered district. Any private school, whether religious or nonreligious, may participate in the program and accept program students so long as the school is located within the boundaries of a covered district and meets statewide educational standards. ... Participating private schools must agree not to discriminate on the basis of race, religion, or ethnic background, or to "advocate or foster unlawful behavior or teach hatred of any person or group on the basis of race, ethnicity, national origin, or religion.". . . . Any public school located in a school district adjacent to the covered district may also participate in the program. . . . Adjacent public schools are eligible to receive a $2,250 tuition grant for each program student accepted in addition to the full amount of per-pupil state funding attributable to each additional student. . . . All participating schools, whether public or private, are required to accept students in accordance with rules and procedures established by the state superintendent. . . .

Tuition aid is distributed to parents according to financial need. Families with incomes below 200% of the poverty line are given priority and are eligible to receive 90% of private school tuition up to $2,250. . . . For these lowest-income families, participating private schools may not charge a parental co-payment greater than $250. . . . For all other families, the program pays 75% of tuition costs, up to $1,875, with no co-payment cap. . . . These families receive tuition aid only if the number of available scholarships exceeds the number of low-income children who choose to participate. . . . Where tuition aid is spent depends solely upon where parents who receive tuition aid choose to enroll their child. If parents choose a private school, checks are made payable to the parents who then endorse the checks over to the chosen school. . . .

The tutorial aid portion of the program provides tutorial assistance through grants to any student in a covered district who chooses to remain in public school. Parents arrange for registered tutors to provide assistance to their children and then submit bills for those services to the State for payment. . . . Students from low-income families receive 90% of the amount charged for such assistance up to $360. All other students receive 75% of that amount. . . . The number of tutorial assistance grants offered to students in a covered district must equal the number of tuition aid scholarships provided to students enrolled at participating private or adjacent public schools. . . .

The program has been in operation within the Cleveland City School District since the 1996–1997 school year. In the 1999–2000 school year, 56 private schools participated in the program, 46 (or 82%) of which had a religious affiliation. None of the public schools in districts adjacent to Cleveland have elected to participate. More than 3,700 students participated in the scholarship program, most of whom (96%) enrolled in religiously affiliated schools. Sixty percent of these students were from families at or below the poverty line. In the 1998–1999 school year, approximately 1,400 Cleveland public school students received tutorial aid. This number was expected to double during the 1999–2000 school year.

. . .

In July 1999, respondents filed this action in United States District Court, seeking to enjoin the reenacted program on the ground that it violated the Establishment Clause of the United States Constitution. . . . In December 1999, the District Court granted summary judgment for respondents. In December 2000, a divided panel of the Court of Appeals affirmed the judgment of the District Court . . . We . . . now reverse the Court of Appeals.

The Establishment Clause of the First Amendment, applied to the States through the Fourteenth Amendment, prevents a State from enacting laws that have the "purpose" or "effect" of advancing or inhibiting religion. *Agostini v. Felton*, 521 U.S. 203, 222–223 (1997) ... There is no dispute that the program challenged here was enacted for the valid secular purpose of providing educational assistance to poor children in a demonstrably failing public school system. Thus, the question presented is whether the Ohio program nonetheless has the forbidden "effect" of advancing or inhibiting religion.

To answer that question, our decisions have drawn a consistent distinction between government programs that provide aid directly to religious schools ... and programs of true private choice, in which government aid reaches religious schools only as a result of the genuine and independent choices of private individuals ... While our jurisprudence with respect to the constitutionality of direct aid programs has "changed significantly" over the past two decades, ... our jurisprudence with respect to true private choice programs has remained consistent and unbroken. Three times we have confronted Establishment Clause challenges to neutral government programs that provide aid directly to a broad class of individuals, who, in turn, direct the aid to religious schools or institutions of their own choosing. Three times we have rejected such challenges.

In Mueller [v. Allen, 463 U.S. 388 (1983)], we rejected an Establishment Clause challenge to a Minnesota program authorizing tax deductions for various educational expenses, including private school tuition costs, even though the great majority of the program's beneficiaries (96%) were parents of children in religious schools. ... We ... found it irrelevant to the constitutional inquiry that the vast majority of beneficiaries were parents of children in religious schools ... That the program was one of true private choice, with no evidence that the State deliberately skewed incentives toward religious schools, was sufficient for the program to survive scrutiny under the Establishment Clause.

In Witters [v. Washington Dept. of Servs. for Blind, 474 U.S. 481 (1986)], we used identical reasoning to reject an Establishment Clause challenge to a vocational scholarship program that provided tuition aid to a student studying at a religious institution to become a pastor. ...

Five Members of the Court, in separate opinions, emphasized the general rule from *Mueller* that the amount of government aid channeled to religious institutions by individual aid recipients was not relevant to the constitutional inquiry. ... Our holding thus rested not on whether few or many recipients chose to expend government aid at a religious school but, rather, on whether recipients generally were empowered to direct the aid to schools or institutions of their own choosing.

Finally, in Zobrest [v. Catalina Foothills School Dist., 509 U.S. 1 (1993)], we applied *Mueller* and *Witters* to reject an Establishment Clause challenge to a federal program that permitted sign-language interpreters to assist deaf children enrolled in religious schools. Reviewing our earlier decisions, we stated that "government programs that neutrally provide benefits to a broad class of citizens defined without reference to religion are not readily subject to an Establishment Clause challenge." . . .

. . .

true private choice

Mueller, *Witters*, and *Zobrest* thus make clear that where a government aid program is neutral with respect to religion, and provides assistance directly to a broad class of citizens who, in turn, direct government aid to religious schools wholly as a result of their own genuine and independent private choice, the program is not readily subject to challenge under the Establishment Clause. A program that shares these features permits government aid to reach religious institutions only by way of the deliberate choices of numerous individual recipients. The incidental advancement of a religious mission, or the perceived endorsement of a religious message, is reasonably attributable to the individual recipient, not to the government, whose role ends with the disbursement of benefits. . . . [W]e have never found a program of true private choice to offend the Establishment Clause.

We believe that the program challenged here is a program of true private choice, consistent with *Mueller*, *Witters*, and *Zobrest*, and thus constitutional. As was true in those cases, the Ohio program is neutral in all respects toward religion. It is part of a general and multifaceted undertaking by the State of Ohio to provide educational opportunities to the children of a failed school district. It confers educational assistance directly to a broad class of individuals defined without reference to religion, *i.e.*, any parent of a school-age child who resides in the Cleveland City School District. The program permits the participation of *all* schools within the district, religious or nonreligious. Adjacent public schools also may participate and have a financial incentive to do so. Program benefits are available to participating families on neutral terms, with no reference to religion. The only preference stated anywhere in the program is a preference for low-income families, who receive greater assistance and are given priority for admission at participating schools.

There are no "financial incentive[s]" that "ske[w]" the program toward religious schools. *Witters*, *supra*, at 487–488. Such incentives "[are] not present . . . where the aid is allocated on the basis of neutral, secular criteria that neither favor nor disfavor religion, and is made available to both religious and secular beneficiaries on a nondiscriminatory basis." *Agostini*, *supra*, at 231. . . .

Respondents suggest that even without a financial incentive for parents to choose a religious school, the program creates a "public perception that the State is endorsing religious practices and beliefs." . . . But we have repeatedly recognized that no reasonable observer would think a neutral program of private choice, where state aid reaches religious schools solely as a result of the numerous independent decisions of private individuals, carries with it the *imprimatur* of government endorsement. . . . The argument is particularly misplaced here since "the reasonable observer in the endorsement inquiry must be deemed aware" of the "history and context" underlying a challenged program. . . . Any objective observer familiar with the full history and context of the Ohio program would reasonably view it as one aspect of a broader undertaking to assist poor children in failed schools, not as an endorsement of religious schooling in general.

There also is no evidence that the program fails to provide genuine opportunities for Cleveland parents to select secular educational options for their school-age children. Cleveland schoolchildren enjoy a range of educational choices: They may remain in public school as before, remain in public school with publicly funded tutoring aid, obtain a scholarship and choose a religious school, obtain a scholarship and choose a nonreligious private school, enroll in a community school, or enroll in a magnet school. That 46 of the 56 private schools now participating in the program are religious schools does not condemn it as a violation of the Establishment Clause. The Establishment Clause question is whether Ohio is coercing parents into sending their children to religious schools, and that question must be answered by evaluating *all* options Ohio provides Cleveland schoolchildren, only one of which is to obtain a program scholarship and then choose a religious school.

... It is true that 82% of Cleveland's participating private schools are religious schools, but it is also true that 81% of private schools in Ohio are religious schools. To attribute constitutional significance to this figure, moreover, would lead to the absurd result that a neutral school-choice program might be permissible in some parts of Ohio, such as Columbus, where a lower percentage of private schools are religious schools, but not in inner-city Cleveland, where Ohio has deemed such programs most sorely needed, but where the preponderance of religious schools happens to be greater. Likewise, an identical private choice program might be constitutional in some States, such as Maine or Utah, where less than 45% of private schools are religious schools, but not in other States, such as Nebraska or Kansas, where over 90% of private schools are religious schools.

... The constitutionality of a neutral educational aid program simply does not turn on whether and why, in a particular area, at a particular time, most private schools are run by religious organizations, or most recipients choose to use the aid at a religious school. ...

. . .

Respondents finally claim that we should look to Committee for Public Ed. & Religious Liberty v. Nyquist, 413 U.S. 756 (1973), to decide these cases. We disagree for two reasons. First, the program in *Nyquist* was quite different from the program challenged here. *Nyquist* involved a New York program that gave a package of benefits exclusively to private schools and the parents of private school enrollees. Although the program was enacted for ostensibly secular purposes, ... we found that its "function" was "*unmistakably* to provide desired financial support for nonpublic, sectarian institutions," ... Its genesis, we said, was that private religious schools faced "increasingly grave fiscal problems." ... The program thus provided direct money grants to religious schools. ... It provided tax benefits "unrelated to the amount of money actually expended by any parent on tuition," ensuring a windfall to parents of children in religious schools. ... It similarly provided tuition reimbursements designed explicitly to "offe[r] ... an incentive to parents to send their children to sectarian schools." ... Indeed, the program flatly prohibited the participation of any public school, or parent of any public school enrollee. ... Ohio's program shares none of these features.

Second, were there any doubt that the program challenged in *Nyquist* is far removed from the program challenged here, we expressly reserved judgment with respect to "a case involving some form of public assistance (*e.g.*, scholarships) made available generally without regard to the sectarian-nonsectarian, or public-nonpublic nature of the institution benefited." . . . [W]e now hold that *Nyquist* does not govern neutral educational assistance programs that, like the program here, offer aid directly to a broad class of individual recipients defined without regard to religion.

In sum, the Ohio program is entirely neutral with respect to religion. It provides benefits directly to a wide spectrum of individuals, defined only by financial need and residence in a particular school district. It permits such individuals to exercise genuine choice among options public and private, secular and religious. The program is therefore a program of true private choice. In keeping with an unbroken line of decisions rejecting challenges to similar programs, we hold that the program does not offend the Establishment Clause.

. . .

Justice O'Connor, concurring.

. . . While I join the Court's opinion, I write separately for two reasons. First, although the Court takes an important step, I do not believe that today's decision, when considered in light of other longstanding government programs that impact religious organizations and our prior Establishment Clause jurisprudence, marks a dramatic break from the past. Second, given the emphasis the Court places on verifying that parents of voucher students in religious schools have exercised "true private choice," I think it is worth elaborating on the Court's conclusion that this inquiry should consider all reasonable educational alternatives to religious schools that are available to parents. To do otherwise is to ignore how the educational system in Cleveland actually functions.

I

These cases are different from prior indirect aid cases in part because a significant portion of the funds appropriated for the voucher program reach religious schools without restrictions on the use of these funds. The share of public resources that reach religious schools is not, however, as significant as respondents suggest. . . .

. . . Even if one assumes that all voucher students came from low-income families and that each voucher student used up the entire $2,250 voucher, at most $8.2 million of public funds flowed to religious schools under the voucher program in 1999–2000. . . .

Although $8.2 million is no small sum, it pales in comparison to the amount of funds that federal, state, and local governments already provide religious institutions. Religious organizations may qualify for exemptions from the federal corporate income tax, . . . and property taxes in all 50 States, . . . clergy qualify for a federal tax break on income used for housing expenses . . . In addition, the Federal Government provides individuals, corporations, trusts, and estates a tax deduction for charitable contributions to qualified religious groups . . . Finally, the Federal Government and certain state governments provide tax credits for educational expenses, many of which are spent on education at religious schools. . . .

. . .

. . . Federal dollars also reach religiously affiliated organizations through public health programs such as Medicare, . . . and Medicaid, . . ., through educational programs such as the Pell Grant program, . . . and the G. I. Bill of Rights, . . . and through child care programs such as the Child Care and Development Block Grant Program . . .

. . .

Against this background, the support that the Cleveland voucher program provides religious institutions is neither substantial nor atypical of existing government programs. . . .

II

Nor does today's decision signal a major departure from this Court's prior Establishment Clause jurisprudence. A central tool in our analysis of cases in this area has been the *Lemon* test. . . .

The Court's opinion in these cases focuses on a narrow question related to the *Lemon* test: how to apply the primary effects prong in indirect aid cases? . . . Courts are instructed to consider two factors: first, whether the program administers aid in a neutral fashion, without differentiation based on the religious status of beneficiaries or providers of services; second, and more importantly, whether beneficiaries of indirect aid have a genuine choice among religious and nonreligious organizations when determining the organization to which they will direct that aid. If the answer to either query is "no," the program should be struck down under the Establishment Clause.

Justice Souter portrays this inquiry as a departure from *Everson*. A fair reading of the holding in that case suggests quite the opposite. . . . How else could the Court have upheld a state program to provide students transportation to public and religious schools alike? What the Court clarifies in these cases is that the Establishment Clause also requires that state aid flowing to religious organizations through the hands of beneficiaries must do so only at the direction of those beneficiaries. Such a refinement of the *Lemon* test surely does not betray *Everson*.

III

There is little question in my mind that the Cleveland voucher program is neutral as between religious schools and nonreligious schools. . . .

I do not agree that the nonreligious schools have failed to provide Cleveland parents reasonable alternatives to religious schools in the voucher program. . . .

. . .

In my view the more significant finding in these cases is that Cleveland parents who use vouchers to send their children to religious private schools do so as a result of true private choice. . . .

I find the Court's answer to the question whether parents of students eligible for vouchers have a genuine choice between religious and nonreligious schools persuasive. . . .

. . .

Based on the reasoning in the Court's opinion, which is consistent with the realities of the Cleveland educational system, I am persuaded that the Cleveland voucher program affords parents of eligible children genuine nonreligious options and is consistent with the Establishment Clause.

Justice Thomas, concurring.

. . .

. . . Today's decision properly upholds the program as constitutional, and I join it in full.

I

. . . I agree with the Court that Ohio's program easily passes muster under our stringent test, but, as a matter of first principles, I question whether this test should be applied to the States.

. . .

. . . When rights are incorporated against the States through the Fourteenth Amendment they should advance, not constrain, individual liberty.

. . . Thus, while the Federal Government may "make no law respecting an establishment of religion," the States may pass laws that include or touch on religious matters so long as these laws do not impede free exercise rights or any other individual religious liberty interest. By considering the particular religious liberty right alleged to be invaded by a State, federal courts can strike a proper balance between the demands of the Fourteenth Amendment on the one hand and the federalism prerogatives of States on the other.

. . . I can accept that the Fourteenth Amendment protects religious liberty rights. But I cannot accept its use to oppose neutral programs of school choice through the incorporation of the Establishment Clause. There would be a tragic irony in converting the Fourteenth Amendment's guarantee of individual liberty into a prohibition on the exercise of educational choice.

II

. . .

While the romanticized ideal of universal public education resonates with the cognoscenti who oppose vouchers, poor urban families just want the best education for their children, who will certainly need it to function in our high-tech and advanced society. . . . If society cannot end racial discrimination, at least it can arm minorities with the education to defend themselves from some of discrimination's effects.

. . . [S]chool choice programs that involve religious schools appear unconstitutional only to those who would twist the Fourteenth Amendment against itself by expansively incorporating the Establishment Clause. Converting the

Fourteenth Amendment from a guarantee of opportunity to an obstacle against education reform distorts our constitutional values and disserves those in the greatest need.

.   .   .

Justice Stevens, dissenting.

Is a law that authorizes the use of public funds to pay for the indoctrination of thousands of grammar school children in particular religious faiths a "law respecting an establishment of religion" within the meaning of the First Amendment? In answering that question, I think we should ignore three factual matters that are discussed at length by my colleagues.

First, the severe educational crisis that confronted the Cleveland City School District when Ohio enacted its voucher program is not a matter that should affect our appraisal of its constitutionality. . . .

Second, the wide range of choices that have been made available to students *within the public school system* has no bearing on the question whether the State may pay the tuition for students who wish to reject public education entirely and attend private schools that will provide them with a sectarian education. . . .

Third, the voluntary character of the private choice to prefer a parochial education over an education in the public school system seems to me quite irrelevant to the question whether the government's choice to pay for religious indoctrination is constitutionally permissible. Today, however, the Court seems to have decided that the mere fact that a family that cannot afford a private education wants its children educated in a parochial school is a sufficient justification for this use of public funds.

Justice Souter, with whom Justice Stevens, Justice Ginsburg, and Justice Breyer join, dissenting.

. . . If there were an excuse for giving short shrift to the Establishment Clause, it would probably apply here. But there is no excuse. Constitutional limitations are placed on government to preserve constitutional values in hard cases, like these. . . . I therefore respectfully dissent.

The applicability of the Establishment Clause to public funding of benefits to religious schools was settled in *Everson* . . ., which inaugurated the modern era of establishment doctrine. The Court stated the principle in words from which there was no dissent:

"No tax in any amount, large or small, can be levied to support any religious activities or institutions, whatever they may be called, or whatever form they may adopt to teach or practice religion." . . .

The Court has never in so many words repudiated this statement, let alone, in so many words, overruled *Everson*.

Today, however, the majority holds that the Establishment Clause is not offended by Ohio's Pilot Project Scholarship Program. . . . The money will thus pay for eligible students' instruction not only in secular subjects but in religion as well, in schools that can fairly be characterized as founded to teach religious doctrine and to imbue teaching in all subjects with a religious dimension . . .

How can a Court consistently leave *Everson* on the books and approve the Ohio vouchers? The answer is that it cannot. It is only by ignoring *Everson* that the majority can claim to rest on traditional law in its invocation of neutral aid provisions and private choice to sanction the Ohio law. It is, moreover, only by ignoring the meaning of neutrality and private choice themselves that the majority can even pretend to rest today's decision on those criteria.

I

The majority's statements of Establishment Clause doctrine cannot be appreciated without some historical perspective on the Court's announced limitations on government aid to religious education, and its repeated repudiation of limits previously set. . . . [D]octrinal bankruptcy has been reached today.

Viewed with the necessary generality, the cases can be categorized in three groups. In the period from 1947 to 1968, the basic principle of no aid to religion through school benefits was unquestioned. Thereafter for some 15 years, the Court termed its efforts as attempts to draw a line against aid that would be divertible to support the religious, as distinct from the secular, activity of an institutional beneficiary. Then, starting in 1983, concern with divertibility was gradually lost in favor of approving aid in amounts unlikely to afford substantial benefits to religious schools, when offered evenhandedly without regard to a recipient's religious character, and when channeled to a religious institution only by the genuinely free choice of some private individual. Now, the three stages are succeeded by a fourth, in which the substantial character of government aid is held to have no constitutional significance, and the espoused criteria of neutrality in offering aid, and private choice in directing it, are shown to be nothing but examples of verbal formalism.

. . .

. . . [i]t was not until today that substantiality of aid has clearly been rejected as irrelevant by a majority of this Court, just as it has not been until today that a majority, not a plurality, has held purely formal criteria to suffice for scrutinizing aid that ends up in the coffers of religious schools. Today's cases are notable for their stark illustration of the inadequacy of the majority's chosen formal analysis.

II

Although it has taken half a century since *Everson* to reach the majority's twin standards of neutrality and free choice, the facts show that, in the majority's hands, even these criteria cannot convincingly legitimize the Ohio scheme.

A

Consider first the criterion of neutrality. . . .[I]n its limited significance, formal neutrality seemed to serve some purpose. Today, however, the majority employs the neutrality criterion in a way that renders it impossible to understand.

Neutrality in this sense refers, of course, to evenhandedness in setting eligibility as between potential religious and secular recipients of public money. . . . Thus, for example, the aid scheme in *Witters* provided an eligible recipient with a scholarship to be used at any institution within a practically unlimited universe of schools, ...; it did not tend to provide more or less aid depending on which one the scholarship recipient chose, and there was no indication that the maximum scholarship amount would be insufficient at secular schools. ...

In order to apply the neutrality test, then, it makes sense to ... ask whether the voucher provisions ... were written in a way that skewed the scheme toward benefitting religious schools.

This, however, is not what the majority asks. The majority looks not to the provisions for tuition vouchers, ... but to every provision for educational opportunity....

The illogic is patent. If regular, public schools (which can get no voucher payments) "participate" in a voucher scheme with schools that can, and public expenditure is still predominantly on public schools, then the majority's reasoning would find neutrality in a scheme of vouchers available for private tuition in districts with no secular private schools at all. "Neutrality" as the majority employs the term is, literally, verbal and nothing more. ...

Why the majority does not simply accept the fact that the challenge here is to the more generous voucher scheme and judge its neutrality in relation to religious use of voucher money seems very odd. It seems odd, that is, until one recognizes that comparable schools for applying the criterion of neutrality are also the comparable schools for applying the other majority criterion, whether the immediate recipients of voucher aid have a genuinely free choice of religious and secular schools to receive the voucher money. And in applying this second criterion, the consideration of "*all* schools" is ostensibly helpful to the majority position.

B

The majority addresses the issue of choice the same way it addresses neutrality, by asking whether recipients or potential recipients of voucher aid have a choice of public schools among secular alternatives to religious schools. Again, however, the majority asks the wrong question and misapplies the criterion. The majority has confused choice in spending scholarships with choice from the entire menu of possible educational placements, most of them open to anyone willing to attend a public school.... When the choice test is transformed from where to spend the money to where to go to school, it is cut loose from its very purpose.

Defining choice as choice in spending the money or channeling the aid is, moreover, necessary if the choice criterion is to function as a limiting principle at all. ...

. . .

... [L]eaving the selection of alternatives for choice wide open, as the majority would, virtually guarantees the availability of a "choice" that will satisfy the criterion, limiting the choices to spending choices will not guarantee a negative result in every case. There may, after all, be cases in which a voucher recipient will have a real choice, with enough secular private school desks in relation to the number of religious ones, and a voucher amount high enough to meet secular private school tuition levels. ...

It is not, of course, that I think even a genuine choice criterion is up to the task of the Establishment Clause when substantial state funds go to religious teaching; the discussion in Part III, *infra*, shows that it is not. The point is simply that if the majority wishes to claim that choice is a criterion, it must define choice in a way that can function as a criterion with a practical capacity to screen something out.

. . .

III

I do not dissent merely because the majority has misapplied its own law, for even if I assumed *arguendo* that the majority's formal criteria were satisfied on the facts, today's conclusion would be profoundly at odds with the Constitution. Proof of this is clear on two levels. The first is circumstantial, in the now discarded symptom of violation, the substantial dimension of the aid. The second is direct, in the defiance of every objective supposed to be served by the bar against establishment.

A

The scale of the aid to religious schools approved today is unprecedented, both in the number of dollars and in the proportion of systemic school expenditure supported. Each measure has received attention in previous cases. On one hand, the sheer quantity of aid, when delivered to a class of religious primary and secondary schools, was suspect on the theory that the greater the aid, the greater its proportion to a religious school's existing expenditures, and the greater the likelihood that public money was supporting religious as well as secular instruction. . . .

On the other hand, the Court has found the gross amount unhelpful for Establishment Clause analysis when the aid afforded a benefit solely to one individual, however substantial as to him, but only an incidental benefit to the religious school at which the individual chose to spend the State's money. . . . The majority's reliance on the observations of five Members of the Court in *Witters* as to the irrelevance of substantiality of aid in that case is therefore beside the point in the matter before us, which involves considerable sums of public funds systematically distributed through thousands of students attending religious elementary and middle schools in the city of Cleveland.

. . .

B

It is virtually superfluous to point out that every objective underlying the prohibition of religious establishment is betrayed by this scheme, but something has to be said about the enormity of the violation. . . .

. . .

When government aid goes up, so does reliance on it; the only thing likely to go down is independence. If Justice Douglas in *Allen* was concerned with state agencies, influenced by powerful religious groups, choosing the textbooks that parochial schools would use, 392 U.S., at 265 (dissenting opinion), how much more is there reason to wonder when dependence will become great enough to give the State of Ohio an effective veto over basic decisions on the content of curriculums? A day will come when religious schools will learn what political leverage can do, just as Ohio's politicians are now getting a lesson in the leverage exercised by religion.

. . .

... *Everson*'s statement is still the touchstone of sound law, even though the reality is that in the matter of educational aid the Establishment Clause has largely been read away. True, the majority has not approved vouchers for religious schools alone, or aid earmarked for religious instruction. But no scheme so clumsy will ever get before us, and in the cases that we may see, like these, the Establishment Clause is largely silenced. I do not have the option to leave it silent, and I hope that a future Court will reconsider today's dramatic departure from basic Establishment Clause principle.

Justice Breyer, with whom Justice Stevens and Justice Souter join, dissenting.

I join Justice Souter's opinion, and I agree substantially with Justice Stevens. I write separately, however, to emphasize the risk that publicly financed voucher programs pose in terms of religiously based social conflict. I do so because I believe that the Establishment Clause concern for protecting the Nation's social fabric from religious conflict poses an overriding obstacle to the implementation of this well-intentioned school voucher program. And by explaining the nature of the concern, I hope to demonstrate why, in my view, "parental choice" cannot significantly alleviate the constitutional problem.

I

... The Clauses reflect the Framers' vision of an American Nation free of the religious strife that had long plagued the nations of Europe. ...

In part for this reason, the Court's 20th century Establishment Clause cases—both those limiting the practice of religion in public schools and those limiting the public funding of private religious education—focused directly upon social conflict, potentially created when government becomes involved in religious education. ...

. . .

The upshot is the development of constitutional doctrine that reads the Establishment Clause as avoiding religious strife, *not* by providing every religion with an *equal opportunity* (say, to secure state funding or to pray in the public schools), but by drawing fairly clear lines of *separation* between church and state—at least where the heartland of religious belief, such as primary religious education, is at issue.

II

. . .

Consider the voucher program here at issue. That program insists that the religious school accept students of all religions. Does that criterion treat fairly groups whose religion forbids them to do so? The program also insists that no participating school "advocate or foster unlawful behavior or teach hatred of

any person or group on the basis of race, ethnicity, national origin, or religion."
. . .

How are state officials to adjudicate claims that one religion or another is advocating, for example, civil disobedience in response to unjust laws, the use of illegal drugs in a religious ceremony, or resort to force to call attention to what it views as an immoral social practice? What kind of public hearing will there be in response to claims that one religion or another is continuing to teach a view of history that casts members of other religions in the worst possible light? How will the public react to government funding for schools that take controversial religious positions on topics that are of current popular interest—say, the conflict in the Middle East or the war on terrorism? . . .

. . . .

III

. . . [V]oucher programs differ . . . in both *kind* and *degree* from aid programs upheld in the past. They differ in kind because they direct financing to a core function of the church: the teaching of religious truths to young children.

. . . History suggests, not that . . . private school teaching of religion is undesirable, but that *government funding* of this kind of religious endeavor is far more contentious than providing funding for secular textbooks, computers, vocational training, or even funding for adults who wish to obtain a college education at a religious university. . . .

Vouchers also differ in *degree*. The aid programs recently upheld by the Court involved limited amounts of aid to religion. But the majority's analysis here appears to permit a considerable shift of taxpayer dollars from public secular schools to private religious schools. . . .[T]he secular aid upheld in *Mitchell* differs dramatically from the present case. Although it was conceivable that minor amounts of money could have, contrary to the statute, found their way to the religious activities of the recipients, . . . that case is at worst the camel's nose, while the litigation before us is the camel itself.

IV

I do not believe that the "parental choice" aspect of the voucher program sufficiently offsets the concerns I have mentioned. Parental choice cannot help the taxpayer who does not want to finance the religious education of children. It will not always help the parent who may see little real choice between inadequate nonsectarian public education and adequate education at a school whose religious teachings are contrary to his own. It will not satisfy religious minorities unable to participate because they are too few in number to support the creation of their own private schools. It will not satisfy groups whose religious beliefs preclude them from participating in a government-sponsored program, and who may well feel ignored as government funds primarily support the education of children in the doctrines of the dominant religions. And it does little to ameliorate the entanglement problems or the related problems of social division . . . Consequently, the fact that the parent may choose which school can cash the government's voucher check does not alleviate the Establishment Clause concerns associated with voucher programs.

V

The Court, in effect, turns the clock back. It adopts, under the name of "neutrality," an interpretation of the Establishment Clause that this Court rejected more than half a century ago. ... In a society composed of many different religious creeds, I fear that this present departure from the Court's earlier understanding risks creating a form of religiously based conflict potentially harmful to the Nation's social fabric. Because I believe the Establishment Clause was written in part to avoid this kind of conflict, ... I respectfully dissent.

†